Comté du Périgord vers 1750. 1 Fi Dordogne 9, Archives Départementales de la Dordogne.

Justice in the Sarladais
1770–1790

Justice in the
Sarladais
1770–1790

Steven G. Reinhardt

LOUISIANA STATE UNIVERSITY PRESS
Baton Rouge and London

Designer: Rebecca Lloyd Lemna
Typeface: Sabon
Typesetter: G & S Typesetters, Inc.
Printer and binder: Thomson-Shore, Inc.

Portions of Chapter III originally appeared in the *Journal of Interdisciplinary History,* XIII
(1983), 437–60, and are included with the permission of the editors of the *Journal of Interdisciplinary History* and the MIT Press, Cambridge, Massachusetts. © 1983 by The Massachusetts Institute of Technology and the editors of the *Journal of Interdisciplinary History.* Portions of Chapters IV and IX first appeared in "The Selective Prosecution of Crime in Ancien
Régime France: Theft in the Sénéchaussée of Sarlat," *European History Quarterly,* XVI (January, 1986), 3–24.

Library of Congress Cataloging-in-Publication Data

Reinhardt, Steven G., 1949–
    Justice in the Sarladais, 1770–1790 / Steven G. Reinhardt.
      p.   cm.
    Includes bibliographical references and index.
    ISBN 0-8071-1587-8 (cloth). — ISBN 0-8071-1658-0 (paper)
      1. Justice, Administration of—France—Sarlat Region—History.
    2. Judicial statistics—France—Sarlat Region.   I. Title.
    KJW9600.S373R45   1991
    347.44'72—dc20   90-28831
                                                       CIP

In memory of Milton G. Reinhardt

Contents

Illustrations

Tables

Preface

MANY HISTORIANS of crime and criminality in the Old Regime have argued that the development of capitalist economic and social relations in some regions of France, most notably Normandy, entailed a concomitant "modernization" of criminal activity, wherein theft replaced violence as the characteristic crime of the epoch.[1] Other authors have subsequently challenged these findings, pointing out that in regions farther removed from the currents of change affecting northern and northeastern France, a more traditional profile persisted, in which reported crime remained predominantly violent in character. They argue that this traditional pattern of crime endured well beyond the Revolution of 1789 at least in part because the rural worlds of these areas remained virtually intact. Moreover, they assert that alterations in patterns of reported and prosecuted crime are more likely to reflect a transformation in repressive mentalities on the part of the authorities than any change in criminality.[2]

In the course of the eighteenth century, the justice of the French Crown continued to supplement and, to a certain extent, supplant other means of redress available to the populace. Although this process had been going on for centuries, it was as yet incomplete. Delinquent

1. Bernadette Boutelet, "Etude par sondage de la criminalité du bailliage de Pont-de-l'Arche (XVIIe–XVIIIe siècles): De la violence au vol: En marche vers l'escroquerie," *Annales de Normandie,* XII (1962), 235–62; Jean-Claude Gégot, "Etude par sondage de la criminalité dans le bailliage de Falaise (XVIIe–XVIIIe siècles): Criminalité diffuse ou société criminelle?" *Annales de Normandie,* XVI (1966), 103–64; Marie-Madeleine Champin, "Un Cas typique de justice bailliagère: La Criminalité dans le bailliage d'Alençon de 1715 à 1745," *Annales de Normandie,* XXII (1972), 47–84; Alain Margot, "La Criminalité dans le bailliage de Mamers (1695–1750)," *Annales de Normandie,* XXII (1972), 185–224.

2. V. A. C. Gatrell, Bruce Lenman, and Geoffrey Parker (eds.), *Crime and the Law: The Social History of Crime in Western Europe Since 1500* (London, 1980), 8–9; Philippe Henry, *Crime, justice et société dans la principauté de Neuchâtel au XVIIIe siècle (1707–1806)* (Neuchâtel, 1984), 654–55; Julius R. Ruff, *Crime, Justice and Public Order in Old Regime France: The Sénéchaussées of Libourne and Bazas, 1696–1789* (London, 1984), 183.

behavior and social tensions were still often resolved infrajudicially by informal arbitration and private vengeance, allowing only a few minor conflicts and serious crimes to surface before the royal courts.[3] Additionally, seigneurial tribunals handled a surprisingly large number of cases until the end of the Old Regime. Historians have discovered that, although the relatively restricted sphere of activity of the royal courts undoubtedly differed from region to region, popular justice in general better maintained its viability in the more isolated areas of France. But it would be misleading to attribute the persistence of informal judicial activity only to the weakness of officialdom. The populace's reluctance to have recourse to royal justice and its loyalty to informal methods both stemmed directly from and, in turn, safeguarded the cohesion of the traditional community, enabling it to ignore or resist the encroachments of the modern state.[4]

In this study I explore the relationship between royal, or official, justice and the alternative forms of redress available between 1770 and 1790 in the Sarladais, a relatively backward *pays* in a comparatively isolated French region, the Périgord. The internal unity and stability of judicial and repressive institutions within the jurisdiction of the Sénéchaussée of Sarlat—combined with its long tradition of peasant unrest—make it a good choice for a monograph.[5] The Crown's longstanding yet only partially successful drive to monopolize the legal power it still shared with unofficial popular agents as well as seigneurial authorities in the Sarladais had resulted in a relationship that can be characterized as a temporary stalemate. During this period, each of the rival systems at work in this region specialized in different forms of redress and appealed to distinctive yet at times overlapping clienteles. Popular justice and seigneurial tribunals filtered out petty disputes and misdemeanors, generally allowing only the more serious cases to reach the royal court. In turn, a lower royal court such as that

3. For an excellent summary of this process, see Pieter Spierenburg, *The Spectacle of Suffering: Executions and the Evolution of Repression: From a Preindustrial Metropolis to the European Experience* (Cambridge, Eng., 1984), 10–12.

4. P. Henry, *Crime, justice et société*, 705.

5. For a history of the disorders that occurred in 1637 in the Périgord, see Roland Mousnier, *Peasant Uprisings in Seventeenth-Century France, Russia, and China*, trans. Brian Pearce (New York, 1970), 77–86, and Yves-Marie Bercé, *Histoire des croquants: Etude des soulèvements populaires au XVIIe siècle dans le sud-ouest de la France* (2 vols.; Geneva, 1974).

of the Sénéchaussée of Sarlat often acted as a court of appeal for affairs that involved persons from outside the traditional village community and for serious crimes such as murder that either could not easily be settled informally by arbitration or had created a situation too volatile to be left to private resolution. The seigneurial tribunals of the *pays*, although closely regulated and restricted by royal ordinances to handling petty criminal affairs, often worked closely with popular agents of adjudication and played an important role in the daily lives of the peasantry. In short, no single system was capable of meeting the demands for redress that arose from a diverse population. Together, however, they provided an adequate system for the inhabitants of the Sarladais.[6]

I further argue that the concept of formal versus informal adjudication and dispute settlement is intimately intertwined with the distinction between popular and elite culture. France in the late eighteenth century included many small *pays* such as the Sarladais that continued to possess a degree of independence and cultural autonomy because of their relative isolation from the main currents of change affecting other regions of France. In such areas, the traditional distinction between popular and elite culture, although somewhat effaced, remained intact. In this context *popular culture* can be defined as the systematic attempt to understand the world—and act upon that understanding—that was still shared by the majority of the population of eighteenth-century France. In other words, popular culture consisted of an internally coherent vision of the world as well as the collective behavior that translated that world view into action. Between 1500 and 1800, popular culture gradually receded before the advancing official culture embraced by many educated members of society's elite. This certainly does not imply that cultural unity prevailed in 1800 or even before 1500, for cultural as well as social stratification existed within each community from a very early date. But in the rural world of eighteenth-century France, only members of the elite minority could read and write the official language, French; they nonetheless continued to speak the local dialect, or patois, used to transmit the predominantly oral culture and

6. Alfred Soman was the first to use the concept of symbiosis to characterize the relationship between the various judicial systems, in a paper presented at the Economic History Congress in Edinburgh in 1978. See his article "Deviance and Criminal Justice in Western Europe, 1300–1800: An Essay in Structure," *Criminal Justice History*, I (1980), 3–28.

thereby spanned both cultures, unlike the illiterate majority of peasants and craftsmen rooted exclusively in popular culture. Nobles and educated persons were therefore often bicultural, just as they were bilingual.[7]

Because a cultural system represents an adaptation to an environment, the social, economic, and political evolution of France from 1770 to 1790 logically entailed concomitant cultural changes whose intensity varied geographically and socially, depending on a region's or a group's participation in that evolution. Those individuals who allied themselves with elite culture and its representatives sought to attain greater control through the enforcement of religious orthodoxy, the centralization of political power in the hands of the Crown, and the advancement of capitalist economic relations. The imposition of the King's Law by royal representatives and its acceptance as the sole guide to social and economic relations were essential to this process of centralization. In theory, at least, the objective norms of official justice would guarantee the security of all, and clear the field of traditional restraints on the free play of individual initiative. Whereas curés saw their drive to civilize the masses as the introduction of discipline and God's truth into darkness and superstition, legal theorists promoting the concept of the King's Law contended that they were introducing law and order into a wilderness of chaotic custom. The existence of seigneurial justice had always represented a challenge to royal authority. Royal judicial authorities also refused to recognize either the coherence of popular culture or the legitimacy of its informal judicial functions. In regions such as the Sarladais, magistrates were nevertheless only too conscious of the financial, administrative, and attitudinal limitations within which royal justice operated and therefore begrudgingly recognized the de facto jurisdiction of both seigneurial and popular justice.[8]

Traditional culture was in the main transmitted orally; it left few written records apart from those created by agents of repression. Criminal court records are therefore extremely valuable, not only because they offer a picture of crime in all its variety and a realistic portrait of

7. See Robert Muchembled, *Culture populaire et culture des élites (XVe–XVIIIe siècles)* (Paris, 1978), 10–11; Peter Burke, *Popular Culture in Early Modern Europe* (New York, 1978), 28, 271–72, 276–77; Michel de Certeau, Dominique Julia, and Jacques Revel, "Une Ethnographie de la langue: L'Enquête de Grégoire sur les patois," *Annales: Economies, sociétés, civilisations,* XXX (1975), 3.

8. For a comparison of the Sarladais with the principality of Neuchâtel, see P. Henry, *Crime, justice et société,* 217–19, 337–39, 343, 347–48.

how royal justice worked, but also because they allow ordinary people from the past to speak directly to us again. Even more important, they document what are essentially crimes against royal laws but not necessarily violations of social custom; hence, they reveal the delicate and dissimulated workings of group justice—rarely perceptible manifestations of the toleration and solidarities that came into play vis-à-vis certain kinds of transgressions. Because custom and law did not always coincide, royal agents frequently encountered both active and passive resistance in their efforts to investigate crimes and enforce court orders. By isolating the instances in which official law conflicted or coincided with popular custom and identifying the individuals involved, one can discern the de facto jurisdiction and clientele of the rival systems.

Although the repression of popular culture in its various aspects entailed the repression of group justice, this process cannot be viewed as exclusively the work of outside agents of church and state. Just as individuals in each community had earlier abandoned a magical vision of the universe and rejected sorcery as a viable means of manipulating the material world, instead joining with judges and curés in the prosecution of witches, individuals in the eighteenth century similarly abandoned their conception of a static, balanced community and in some cases rejected informal adjudication, instead turning to the royal courts for redress. The repression of witchcraft in seventeenth-century France stemmed from a crisis in the relations between the relatively static rural world and the changing exterior world. The equilibrium that both popular culture and sorcery had long sought to maintain fell victim to the royal judges, curés, and members of the community who in greater numbers perceived the bonds that tied them to their fellows as a form of bondage. In similar fashion, the halting advance of royal justice can only be understood in light of the gradual erosion of popular justice that came about through the steady pressure of royal authorities and the growing rejection of private vengeance, arbitration, and informal collective sanctions by members of the community anxious to free themselves from the moral economy of the popular classes.[9]

9. See Burke, *Popular Culture*, 240–41; Yves Castan, *Honnêteté et rélations sociales en Languedoc au XVIIIe siècle* (Paris, 1974), 56, 184, 213; Muchembled, *Culture populaire*, 50–51, 227–28; Jean Boutier, "Jacqueries en pays croquant: Les Révoltes paysannes en Aquitaine (décembre 1789–mars 1790)," *Annales: Economies, sociétés, civilisations*, XXXIV (1979), 769; Edward P. Thompson, "The Moral Economy of the English Crowd in the Eighteenth Century," *Past and Present*, L (1971), 78.

In the Sarladais on the eve of the French Revolution, the three systems of popular, royal, and seigneurial justice remained simultaneously complementary and competitive, offering different forms of redress and holding special appeal for different segments of the population. The goal of popular justice was the restoration of social equilibrium through arbitration and measured, often ritualized violence. In the farthest reaches of the sénéchaussée, peasant proprietors, sharecroppers, and woodsmen chose to settle petty disputes, misdemeanors, and even certain felonies, notably theft, infrajudicially in order to minimize expenses as well as the damage done to personal and family honor. In contrast to informal justice, royal criminal justice had the goal, at least in theory, of rigorous and even ostentatious enforcement of the King's Law. Members of some social groups, particularly urban and rural bourgeois living in Sarlat and its environs, found such punitive justice to be not only more convenient but also more congenial to their needs and distinctly preferable to the alternatives. Seigneurial tribunals, which handled only minor offenses and disputes over the rights and duties owed the seigneur, were privately owned and sometimes crudely manipulated by seigneurs anxious to defend their prerogatives. People who wished to challenge the social hierarchy therefore often looked elsewhere for judicial redress. Although the relationship between the three rival systems remained virtually static in the Sarladais during the twenty years under examination, the seeds of eventual change, albeit dormant, are nonetheless perceptible in this isolated rural corner of France during the last two decades of the Old Regime.

Acknowledgments

WHEN A BOOK is this long in the making, an author accumulates a considerable number of debts, intellectual and otherwise. Present at the very beginning of this project was William H. Beik, formerly of Northern Illinois University, now of Emory University, who first directed me toward the subject and helped me settle upon a suitable archival collection. Without his careful guidance, astute criticism, and supportive friendship this study would never have been completed. Samuel Kinser likewise contributed significantly to this work by initiating me into the history of *mentalités* during my graduate studies at Northern Illinois University. There I also received my introduction to criminological studies under the capable direction of Theodore N. Ferdinand, currently of Northeastern University in Boston, who helped me add a more rigorous, interdisciplinary dimension to my historical approach. An assistantship from the Department of History at Northern Illinois University and a generous grant from the Social Science Research Council made my research for this work possible.

The gracious reception and sound advice I received from the staff of the Archives Départementales de la Dordogne, in Périgueux, exceeded my expectations. The aid of Noël Becquart, who was then conservateur-en-chef, and especially the day-to-day technical assistance and kindness of Jacqueline Faure made my year of archival research much more productive and enjoyable than I could have imagined. I would also like to thank Janine, Claude, and Jacques Chastanet for the warm hospitality they showed me and my wife. Equally kind were Jeannine and Guy Rousset, who not only shared their knowledge of the region but also provided us with a surrogate family while far from home. Both families introduced us to a Périgord and to Périgourdins we would not otherwise have encountered and therefore deserve our sincere thanks.

I am grateful to Jean Valette, conservateur-en-chef of the Archives Départementales de la Gironde, in Bordeaux, for granting me permission to examine the then-unclassified records of the Tournelle de Sarlat. I also cannot overlook the intellectual and personal debt I owe to Bernard Fournioux, the late Jacques Crouzy, and Guy Mandon.

Yves-Marie Bercé, of the Université de Rheims, and Nicole Castan, of the Université de Toulouse, were gracious enough to meet with me in Limoges and Toulouse in the early, painfully tentative stages of my research. Their advice and encouragement on those occasions as well as the more general inspiration provided by their seminal work immeasurably influenced the questions I asked and the research I undertook. In Paris, Alfred Soman played a similar role as he persuaded me of the need to concentrate on infrajudicial methods of dispute settlement. Robert Muchembled, whom I have never had the pleasure to meet, also deserves recognition for the abundant influence his work has exercised on my own.

Julius R. Ruff, of Marquette University, merits special recognition for his friendship, support, and intellectual influence during the preparation of this volume. I believe that my work stands as a natural complement to his own on the nearby sénéchaussées of Libourne and Bazas. I am grateful to Albert N. Hamscher, of Kansas State University, for clarifying some of the intricacies of criminal jurisprudence, as well as of the funding of the royal judicial system. Jonathan Dewald, of the University of California at Irvine, kindly gave early drafts of the manuscript his keen scrutiny, and this work has profited from his comments. I am likewise grateful to Ralph Gibson, of the University of Lancaster, whose readiness to review drafts and willingness to share his expertise have greatly improved my foray into Périgourdin social and economic history.

Edward F. Haas, of Wright State University, and Stephen Webre, of Louisiana Tech University, deserve thanks for their unflagging personal support, which kept my hope and dedication alive during our years of service at the Louisiana Historical Center of the Louisiana State Museum in New Orleans. The sound advice and friendship of John T. O'Connor, of the University of New Orleans, also boosted my sagging spirits on a number of occasions. I would also like to thank Michael J. Sartisky, of the Louisiana Endowment for the Humanities, who provided personal encouragement as well as considerable logistical support during my employment as assistant director. My gratitude goes as well to Kenneth Philp, chair of the Department of History at the University of Texas at Arlington, for his continued assistance. I must also thank Margaret Fisher Dalrymple and Catherine Landry of Louisiana State University Press, whose expertise helped make this book a reality.

My wife, Joan Wesselmann Reinhardt, shared with me her own considerable knowledge of eighteenth-century France and showed remarkable tolerance and forbearance through seemingly endless years of research and writing. To her I acknowledge my greatest debt.

Justice in the Sarladais
1770–1790

I

The Sarladais in the
Late Eighteenth Century

*There are, I believe, more associations common to the
inhabitants of a rude and wild, than of a well-culti-
vated and fertile country; their ancestors have more
seldom changed their place of residence; their mutual
recollection of remarkable objects is more accurate;
the high and the low are more interested in each
other's welfare; the feelings of kindred and relationship are more widely extended, and, in a word, the
bonds of patriotic affection, always honourable even
when a little too exclusively strained, have more influence on men's feelings and actions.*

—Sir Walter Scott, *The Heart of Mid-Lothian*

The Sarladais on the eve of the French Revolution
was a poor, traditional region that moved mostly to its own rhythms.
Yet in some select ways it was attuned to the outer world. Within this
predominantly rural society, conflicts and criminal activity arose from
a variety of sources: economic deprivation, challenges to personal and
familial honor, infringements on age-old collective rights, and conflicting economic interests between peasants and seigneurs, sharecroppers
and masters, parishioners and curés. But the halting advance of agrarian individualism, the stirrings of a bourgeoisie dominated by the liberal professions, and a nascent sense of egalitarianism also generated
new tensions and therefore influenced the pattern of criminality. In
short, the Sarladais was not altogether immune to the forces at work in
the rest of France. Although more closely linked to the past than to the
future, the region nevertheless bore the marks of inceptive economic,
social, and cultural change.

Contemporary travelers and government officials agreed that the Périgord in general, and the Sarladais in particular—although not as isolated as the Auvergne or perhaps as backward as the Limousin—was quite poor. The few industries in the Sarladais languished, its agriculture was hopelessly handicapped by the infertility of the soil and encumbered by traditionalism, its commerce was negligible, its customs were too well preserved, and its isolated scholars and *notables* were either preoccupied with their own narrow interests or anxious to escape to Paris. The 1765 edition of Diderot's *Encyclopédie* briefly describes Sarlat as a town in the Périgord, one and one-half leagues from the right bank of the Dordogne River, containing a royal présidial/sénéchaussée tribunal and a bishopric of modest revenues. "Its inhabitants," the author writes, "are very poor, and engage in no other commerce except that of walnut oil." He did not comment on another, less visible characteristic: the growing imbalance between the region's resources and the number of its inhabitants.[1]

Moreover, the situation of the Périgord as a whole had not improved significantly during the eighteenth century. The author of a 1743 memoir to the intendant of Guyenne wrote that, in general, the subdelegation of Sarlat was believed to be one of the poorest in the kingdom because of its lack of commerce. Its poverty was evident in the limited diet of its inhabitants—who relied too heavily on maize and chestnuts—and in their manner of dress. He reported that in winter they were barely covered with clothing, which was so patched together that the people appeared to be beggars. His assessment was confirmed by a report prepared in 1770 by a doctor from Montignac, Pierre de La Servolle, who wrote that in no other area of the kingdom could be found children with abdomens so swollen from malnutrition.[2] Even if one allows for some exaggeration in the reports of administrators anxious to garner royal revenues for their districts, the picture that emerges of the Périgord in general and of the Sarladais in particular remains grim.

The soil of the eighteenth-century Périgord was the central cause of

1. Denis Diderot (ed.), *Encyclopédie, ou dictionnaire raisonné des sciences, des arts et des métiers* (17 vols.; Paris, 1751–65), XIV, 660; Anne-Marie Cocula, "Vivre et survivre en Périgord au XVIIIe siècle," in Arlette Higounet-Nadal (ed.), *Histoire du Périgord* (Toulouse, 1983), 210. Translations are mine throughout.

2. Mémoire de la subdélégation de Sarlat pour Monseigneur Tourny, intendant de Guyenne, August 5, 1743, C 1317, Archives Départementales de la Gironde, Bordeaux, hereinafter cited as ADG; Lettre de M. Servolle, docteur en médecin, à M. Duchesne, premier sécrétaire de l'intendant, February 12, 1770, C 475, ADG.

its poverty. Because the region is essentially a transitional zone between the flatlands of the Aquitaine and the mountains of the Massif Central, between the plateau of Quercy and the gently rolling countryside of the Charentais, its topography is highly diverse. In the northeastern highlands of the Nontronnais, where infertile topsoils cover granite bedrock, the rocky surface is predominantly gray in color, and vegetation is sparse. In the eighteenth century, junipers, gorse, and scrub oaks covered the moors, chestnut trees grew in scattered clumps, and rye, oats, and buckwheat were the only cereals that thrived in the area's relatively cool climate. Cultivation was necessarily confined to the limited space along the river and stream valleys, where some wheat was grown. Population density in the area was understandably low. In contrast, the western section of the Périgord gradually descends to the sea, with rolling hills, wide plains, and a milder maritime climate.[3]

The Sarladais itself consists in the main of chalky limestone hills and plateaus at an altitude of 300 to 350 meters, littered with sinkholes and caves, and drained by deep valleys bordered by sharp bluffs with grottos cut into the soluble bedrock. In the eighteenth century, maize thrived in the broad river valleys, as did wheat, fruit trees, and walnut trees. Most of the region was blanketed with an iron-rich flinty rubble and sandy soil, which supported large expanses of chestnuts, pines, and oaks that darkened the landscape, giving rise to the area's designation as the "Périgord Noir." To the east and southeast of Sarlat, the green hills of the Sarladais gradually yielded to the barren, gray plateaus surrounding Martel, in Quercy. The limestone plateau of the Sarladais that extends directly to the south, beyond the Dordogne River valley, was covered in the eighteenth century with a forest of chestnut trees that effectively isolated the region. To the southwest, along the valley of the Dropt River between Monpazier and Eymet, lay the more indistinct frontier between the Périgord and the Aquitaine. The mild climate, broad, fertile floodplain, and gentle slopes of the left bank of the Dordogne River near Bergerac announced the gradual transition into the Libournais. The roughly parallel drainage systems of the Dronne, Isle,

3. Although the Périgord had an overall average of 30 to 40 inhabitants per square kilometer, some areas had as few as 10 per square kilometer, others as many as 70 per square kilometer. See Guy Mandon, "Les Curés en Périgord au dix-huitième siècle: Contribution à l'étude du clergé paroissial sous l'ancien régime" (Thèse de 3ème cycle, Université de Bordeaux, 1979), 27. Also see Guy Florenty, "L'Evolution démographique de Saint-Cyprien et de son canton au XVIIIe siècle," *mémoire* for the D.E.S. (Université de Bordeaux, 1974), 13.

Vézère, and Dordogne rivers effectively linked the five distinct *pays* of the Périgord (Bergeracois, Sarladais, Riberacois, Nontronnais, and Central Périgord), which were further bonded by the Périgord's natural geographic isolation from surrounding regions.[4]

The climate of the Périgord varies, much like its topography. During the relatively mild winter, the region comes under the maritime influence of the Atlantic and is buffeted by rains, especially in the northeastern highlands nearest the Limousin, where frosts are also more frequent. Although the climate is generally mild, temperatures vary considerably between the northeastern highlands and the southwestern plains, with harvests near Mussidan as much as twenty days earlier than those near Nontron and Thiviers, less than forty kilometers away. During the summer months, when the Mediterranean influence prevails, droughts can set in—punctuated only by violent hailstorms that often ruin crops. Nicolas Desmarest, a representative of the Académie des Sciences who toured the region between 1761 and 1764, estimated that because of the frequent hailstorms the agricultural revenues of one out of every five years were assumed to be lost.[5]

On May 21, 1770, a thunderstorm dropped hail on Sarlat and the surrounding countryside, causing extensive damage to crops. Moreover, the considerable rainfall that accompanied the hailstorm flooded the valley in which Sarlat is located. Quickly overflowing the canals and conduits, the floodwaters poured into the streets. Since Sarlat's medieval walls were intact and its gates were closed, the city began to fill with water. The city fathers were finally compelled to breach the walls to let

---

4. Léon Michel, *Le Périgord: Le Pays et les hommes* (Périgueux, 1969), 27–28; François-de-Paule Latapie, "L'Industrie et le commerce en Guienne sous le regne de Louis XVI: Journal de Tournée," *Archives historiques du Département de la Gironde,* XXXVIII (1903), 394–97; Gérard Fayolle, *La Vie quotidienne en Périgord au temps de Jacquou le Croquant* (Paris, 1977), 30–32.

5. André de Fayolle, *Topographie agricole du département de la Dordogne en Fructidor an IX* (Périgueux, 1939), 38, 76; Remarques de M. Desmarest (de l'Académie des Sciences) sur la géographie physique, les productions et les manufactures de la généralité de Bordeaux, lors de ses tournées depuis 1761 jusqu'en 1764, MS 26, Archives Départementales de la Dordogne, Périgueux, hereinafter cited as ADD. In its *cahier de doléances*, the parish of Saint-André-de-Double complained, "This *pays* cannot go three years without being ill-treated by frost or beaten by hail." The correspondence between the subdelegate of Sarlat and the intendant in Bordeaux contains frequent appeals for aid from curés whose parishes were devastated by hailstorms and freezes. See G. Livet, "La Vie paysanne avant la Révolution dans la Double du Périgord," *Bulletin de la Société Historique et Archéologique du Périgord,* LXIX (1942), 127.

MAP 1

Regions of Old Regime France

FLANDRE
ARTOIS   HAINAUT

Picardie

Normandie   *Champagne*   *Lorraine*

Ile-de-France

PERCHE   BEAUCE   BRIE   BARROIS

Bretagne   *Maine*   *Alsace*

Orléanais

SOLOGNE   *Bourgogne*   *Franche-Comté*

Anjou   TOURAINE   NIVERNAIS

VENDÉE   *Poitou*   BERRY

MARCHE   *Bourbonnais*

ANGOUMOIS   FOREZ

SAINTONGE   *Limousin*   *Savoie*

Médoc   PÉRIGORD   *Auvergne*

Bordelais   *Guyenne*   Sarladais   *Dauphiné*

Bazadois   GÉVAUDAN   COMTAT

Landes   Agenais   Quercy

Provence

PAYS BASQUE   *Gascogne*   *Languedoc*

BÉARN   BIGORRE

FOIX

Roussillon

the floodwaters escape.[6] The hailstorm also severely damaged the roof of the hôtel de ville, occupied in its entirety by the présidial/séné-chaussée of Sarlat, forcing the tribunal to suspend its sessions until repairs were completed.[7]

The cumulative effect of the poor climatic conditions from 1772 to

6. Mémoire des officiers municipaux de Sarlat, à M. l'Intendant, September 10, 1770, C 475, ADG. Also see Jean-Joseph Escande, *Histoire de Sarlat* (1903; rpr. Marseilles, 1976), 431–33.

7. The royal domain agreed to share the cost of repairs with the municipality of Sarlat. See Lettre à M. l'Intendant de Meyrignac, subdélégué de Sarlat, February 16, 1771, Lettre de l'Intendant à Meyrignac, February 23, 1771, both in C 476, ADG.

1775 was extremely serious for many rural parishes, where the ruin or near ruin of crops resulted in severe shortages. Erratic weather in the autumn of 1773 not only reduced chestnuts in number and size but also damaged the harvest of maize, especially near Villefranche, Monpazier, and Biron. The next spring, the curé of Villefranche-en-Périgord appealed to the intendant in Bordeaux, explaining that the failure of these two staple crops had reduced his flock to a state of poverty so dire that entire families were forced to consume their seed grain and beg for their bread. The subdelegate confirmed that approximately two-thirds of the inhabitants of thirteen parishes found themselves in the same situation.[8]

Marginal notations made by curés in the parish registers of Cénac, near Domme, reveal the anxieties and hardships that erratic weather often brought. One curé noted that the hard freeze of January, 1766, was as severe as that of 1709 and caused the Dordogne River to freeze over in several spots. His parishioners ignored his warnings and amused themselves by building a fire on the ice, cooking omelettes, and dancing. The river finally thawed in February, when warm weather and rain caused the premature sprouting of the winter wheat—which was lost entirely when winter returned unexpectedly. A hailstorm moved through the parish on May 23, stripping the grapevines of their leaves and fruit, ruining the rye, and heavily damaging the wheat. Despite these localized disasters, the curé hoped for a respectable harvest that year. But the following year the parish was not as fortunate. A late freeze on Easter Day, April 19, ruined the rye planted in the lowlands, and a second freeze on May 11 destroyed the newly emerged buds on the grapevines; as a result, the parish produced only 3 *barriques* of wine instead of the normal 150. "The harm done in this department by storms would be difficult to describe, and the number of families ruined by the devastation they wrought is very great," Guillaume Delfau concluded in 1804.[9]

8. Lettre à M. l'Intendant, du curé Jean-Pierre Breu, curé de Villefranche-en-Périgord, February 20, 1774, Lettre de Meyrignac, subdélégué de Sarlat, à M. l'Intendant, April 4, 1774, both in C 479, ADG; Anne-Marie Cocula, *Les Gens de la rivière de Dordogne de 1750 à 1850* (Lille, 1979), 580–81.

9. Louis Carvès, "Le Froid et la misère en Sarladais au XVIIIe siècle," *Bulletin de la Société Historique et Archéologique du Périgord*, XII (1886), 504–506; Guillaume Delfau, *Annuaire statistique du département de la Dordogne pour l'an XII de la République* (Périgueux, 1804), 65.

In the opinion of Inspecteur des Manufactures François-de-Paule Latapie, the chestnut tree was the most useful resource of the Périgord. It yielded not only *feuillard* (thin, pliable sticks used as cask hoops), barrel staves, and rot-resistant *échalas* (vineyard props) but also the chestnuts so essential for the subsistence of man and beast alike. Upon his arrival in Sarlat on his first tour of inspection, Latapie remarked that *taillis* (chestnut coppices) extended as far as the eye could see in all directions. But at least one other contemporary observer questioned the long-term effect of overreliance on the chestnut. In 1761 Desmarest remarked: "As long as the Périgourdin will live with his pigs and find his food at the foot of the chestnut tree, he will not extend his vision beyond his parish. I do not propose, though, that his chestnut trees be cut down as long as he has no other source of food. But new needs must be stimulated in him if he is to devote himself to agriculture and produce an export." [10]

The resources of the forest constituted an essential element in the diet of the populace, supplying chestnuts, walnuts, and acorns for humans and pigs—not to mention truffles, mushrooms, and an assortment of game animals taken in widespread poaching. Because chestnuts were especially important as a dietary staple during the winter months, the occurrence of damaging freezes, disease, or hail raised wheat prices almost automatically and brought distress to the inhabitants of the countryside. Latapie confirmed as much during his second tour of inspection in 1782, when he remarked, in the vicinity of Domme, that although the slopes around the larger bourgs were covered with vineyards, the rest of the countryside was blanketed by chestnut trees, with walnut trees in the valleys. He added, "Chestnuts were lacking the previous year, which drove up the cost of wheat noticeably in this *pays*." [11]

Despite the overwhelming importance of the Périgourdin forest, the inhabitants of the region systematically exploited and even squandered its resources. The winter freeze of 1709 that killed nearly all wal-

10. Latapie, "L'Industrie et le commerce en Guienne," 414, 422; Remarques de Desmarest.

11. Lettre de Meyrignac, subdélégué de Sarlat, à l'Intendant, November 19, 1770, C 475, ADG; Meyrignac à l'Intendant, October 25, 1773, C 478 ADG; François-de-Paule Latapie, "Tournée de 1782," *Archives historiques du Département de la Gironde,* LIV (1921–22), 145.

MAP 2

*The Périgord in the
Eighteenth Century*

Sénéchaussée of Sarlat   — + — + —

nuts and most chestnuts had not been followed by methodical replanting; as a result, by 1743 walnuts had recovered by only one-third, chestnuts by three-quarters. Not until 1763 was recovery from the freeze complete. Frequent cuttings, overgrazing, and fires, as well as the careless clearing, exhaustion, and subsequent abandonment of marginal lands, had deteriorated the forest cover and created wastelands where none had previously existed. When traveling from Terrasson to Périgueux in 1778, Latapie skirted the once-formidable Forêt Barade and reported that "today it is much cleared and reduced to moors over a large extent." [12]

In contrast to these sterile moors and wooded uplands were the oases of fertility and population that existed along the valleys of the Dronne River in the Riberacois and the Dordogne River in the Sarladais and Bergeracois. In effect, three types of regions existed within the Périgord: the hills and barren plateaus, removed from major lines of communication and commerce; the river valleys, with their fertile fields and diversified population; and the navigable rivers themselves, which linked the Périgord to the Bordelais and the Atlantic. The Dordogne River and its tributaries were lifelines of communication connecting the haut-pays of Quercy, Limousin, and the Périgord to the port of Libourne and, beyond it, to Bordeaux itself. Wood, chestnuts, juniper berries, and, from time to time, grain and the intermittent products of the iron forges all moved downstream—but seldom in sufficient quantities to counterbalance the essential products moving upstream: salt from the Charentais and colonial goods. Wine alone might possibly have balanced the trade, but restrictions imposed by downstream rivals on the movement of wines effectively delayed their arrival in Libourne until after Saint Martin's Day (November 11) and in Bordeaux until after Christmas. [13]

On the southern bank of the Dordogne exist fewer and smaller tributaries. Parishes even five kilometers from the river consequently

12. Mémoires, August 5, 1743, *ca.* 1763, both in C 1317, ADG; Cocula, "Vivre et survivre en Périgord," in Higounet-Nadal (ed.), *Histoire du Périgord*, 215. Although woodlands and moors covered more than half of the department of the Dordogne (nearly the equivalent of the Périgord), reported André de Fayolle in 1802, the major portion of the forests had already been cut over (*Topographie agricole*, 48). Also see Remarques de Desmarest; Guillaume Delfau, *Annuaire du département de la Dordogne pour l'année sextile XI, de l'ère français* (Périgueux, 1803), 86 ff.; Latapie, "L'Industrie et le commerce en Guienne," 440.

13. Cocula, *Les Gens de la rivière de Dordogne,* 138; Paul Butel and Philippe Roudié, "La Production et commercialisation des vins du Libournais au début du XIXe siècle," *Annales du Midi,* LXXXI (1969), 379–408; Roger Dion, "L'Ancien Privilège de Bordeaux," *Revue géographique des Pyrenées et du Sud-Ouest,* XXVI (1955), 223–36; G. Martin, "Les Intendants de Guyenne au XVIIIe siècle et les privilèges des vins bordelais," *Revue historique de Bordeaux et du Département de la Gironde,* I (1908), 461–70.

displayed many of the characteristics of economic autarky: The artisan class was small and showed little diversity, for example, and the profession of *négociant* (wholesale merchant) was often entirely absent. On the opposite bank, at a distance of ten kilometers from the river port of Vitrac, Sarlat shared much the same fate. The intendant of Guyenne, Bazin de Bezons, wrote in 1698: "Sarlat is a town that is very poorly located. There is a bishopric, présidial, and an election; it is in a basin completely surrounded by mountains; there is no river, and it is one and one-half leagues from the Dordogne; the inhabitants are very clean, but their *pays* is poor, with many mountains." The absence of the river was, in Bezons' mind, synonymous with stagnation. Latapie also noted the unfavorable and unhealthful location of Sarlat, situated in a valley at the bottom of which flowed "a dirty little stream" that could swell into a torrent. Because of its poor location and the anarchy of its narrow, winding streets, Sarlat was commonly known not only for its lack of commerce but also, in the opinion of Desmarest, for its "humidity and dreadful filthiness."[14]

Libourne, at the confluence of the Dordogne and Isle rivers, could be reached year-round by ocean-going vessels and therefore played the dominant role in river traffic. Beyond Castillon, where the incoming tide ceased to aid upstream navigation, the strength of the current necessitated towing. Here began the towpaths that paralleled the courses of the Dordogne and Vézère rivers through the Sarladais.[15] Bergerac also enjoyed frequent and regular commercial exchanges, but it was often an obligatory terminus, the last stop for much upriver traffic. Although the Dordogne was easily navigable to that point, just upriver from the city lay the rocky shallows of the Gratusse, near Lalinde, and the Pesqueyroux, near Saint-Cyprien, where sailors and haulers were needed to assist barges through the rapids. Upriver to the town of Souillac, the shallowness of the Dordogne prohibited navigation except from November through March, when winter rains raised the water level. Geographic factors therefore combined with the commercial privileges of

14. Bazin de Bezons, quoted in Cocula, *Les Gens de la rivière de Dordogne,* 120; Latapie, "L'Industrie et le commerce en Guienne," 424; Remarques de Desmarest. Bezons exaggerated the size of the hills surrounding Sarlat.

15. Royal ordinances required owners of property bordering the river to leave on one side a twenty-four-foot frontage free of encumbrances for the towpath, as well as ten feet on the opposite bank (Cocula, *Les Gens de la rivière de Dordogne,* 230).

downstream rivals to relegate upriver ports like Domme to the role of way stations, where downriver loads were moved from flatboats to heavier barges that could then proceed to Libourne or Bordeaux.[16]

The Vézère River had once been navigable all the way to Terrasson, but in the eighteenth century, boats could advance only as far as Montignac, and then only at high water. Moustier and Saint-Léon-sur-Vézère served as ports of assembly for local products shipped downriver during the months of navigation. Because the Isle River was navigable only as far as Saint-Médard or, during high water, Mussidan, the central Périgord also remained relatively isolated and commercially stagnant. Even the creation of the Bordeaux-Limoges route at mid-century, during the intendancy of Louis, marquis de Tourny, could not transform Périgueux into a center of exchange: On the eve of the Revolution it remained stagnant and little changed since the end of the sixteenth century.[17]

Where they existed, the roads did little to relieve the relative isolation that stifled the Périgord. Alone of all contemporary travelers through the region, Latapie tempered his remarks on the roads, distinguishing between the "superb" ones in the river valleys and the "detestable" ones across the uplands. The comments of other observers more closely resemble those of Pierre Vergniaud, a future member of the National Convention, who stated, "I do not believe the roads of hell could be any worse than those of the Périgord." A more detailed assessment is provided by Delfau, who in the Year XI wrote: "There are few departments where the roads have been more neglected than in that of the Dordogne. In general, the roads, or, to be more specific, the portions of roads existing in this department, are a disgrace to the art; they stand in testimony to the profound ignorance of the engineers who laid them out." Even before the Revolution, when years of neglect further deteri-

---

16. De Fayolle, *Topographie agricole*, 120. Arthur Young describes Souillac in 1787 as "a little town in a thriving state, having some rich merchants. They receive staves from the mountains of Auvergne by their river Dordogne, which is navigable eight months in the year; these they export to Bordeaux and Libourne; also wine, corn, and cattle, and import salt in great quantities" (*Travels in France During the Years 1787, 1788, and 1789,* ed. Constantia Maxwell [Cambridge, Eng., 1929], 23). The city of Domme is situated atop a high bluff, while its port lies below, nearer Cénac (Cocula, *Les Gens de la rivière de Dordogne,* 121, 505, 686).

17. Cocula, "Vivre et survivre en Périgord," in Higounet-Nadal (ed.), *Histoire du Périgord,* 218, 229–30.

orated the roads, Latapie found that it was often easier to travel cross-country than to use the wretched roads near Monpazier.[18]

Oxcarts and mules nonetheless moved considerable goods within the Périgord. Since the network of rivers is essentially east-west in its orientation, overland routes guaranteed north-south links between the river valleys. In effect, the network of roads served as a complementary communications system that extended into the interior of the region and enabled its inhabitants to transport local products to assembly points on the nearest navigable river. The small port of Moustier on the Vézère River, for example, served as a depot for wood products, wines, chestnuts, and juniper berries gathered in a radius of twenty kilometers, as well as for the iron products manufactured at the Forge d'Ans and the Forge de Plazac. All were carried or carted along bad roads to the river port, where sailing barges arrived to transport the products downstream to Bordeaux. Good-quality wines from Domme moved overland to the Auvergne; similarly, merchants from the lower Limousin arrived almost annually in the Montignac-Terrasson area to purchase wine and transport it home by horse carts.[19]

Overland transport in the second half of the century, although undeniably archaic and prohibitively expensive for many goods, did provide most areas of the Aquitaine with at least tenuous ties to the wider commercial currents of the Bordelais. If, at the end of the century, a new appreciation of the benefits of trade sparked more numerous petitions for the improvement of roads, it was in most cases less a question of breaking down isolation than of further developing the degree of commerce that already existed.[20] Tributaries and primitive roads linked the

18. P. Vergniaud, quoted in Cocula, *Les Gens de la rivière de Dordogne*, 121; Delfau, *Annuaire . . . l'année sextile XI*, 252; Latapie, "Tournée de 1782," 143. Arthur Young, who skirted the eastern edge of the Sarladais, reported that the road between Uzerche and Brive was "the finest road in the world, everywhere formed in the most perfect manner, and kept in the highest preservation" (*Travels*, 22).

19. Jean-Pierre Poussou, "Sur le rôle des transports terrestres dans l'économie du Sud-Ouest au XVIIIe siècle," *Annales du Midi*, XC (1978), 410–11; Marcel Secondat, "Evolution économique d'une communauté rurale: Plazac depuis le XVIIIe siècle," *Bulletin de la Société Historique et Archéologique du Périgord*, CII (1975), 3, 177; Mémoire du Sr. Pomarel, July 30, 1761, C 1317, ADG; Guy Duboscq, "Le Cahier des doléances du Tiers Etat d'Auriac-en-Périgord, 8 mars 1789," *Bulletin de la Société Historique et Archéologique du Périgord*, LXIII (1936), 64.

20. Poussou suggests that the Périgord possessed so few good roads because the transportation requirements of its exports were adequately met by the river system ("Sur le rôle des transports terrestres," 404). Also see Emmanuel Le Roy Ladurie, "De la Crise

various *pays* in the Périgord to the Dordogne River valley for at least part of the year. But the poor condition of local roads meant that the major paths of commerce and communication led primarily in the direction of Bergerac, Libourne, and Bordeaux. Overall, the Périgord suffered from being relatively near yet still too far from the great commercial currents of the Bordelais and the Atlantic, of which the Dordogne River valley was really the northernmost axis.

With a few notable exceptions, the state of agriculture in the Périgord was much the same in 1802 as in 1770, reported André de Fayolle. Nonetheless, some agricultural progress had been achieved in the course of the eighteenth century. Physiocratic reforms had little impact on the region, except for the gradual introduction by a few landowners of arboricultural techniques for the planting and care of chestnut and walnut trees. The most significant advancement was the slow revolution accomplished by the cultivation of maize (known locally as *bled d'espagne*). At the time of the Fronde, maize was not unknown in the region, but not until 1693 did it first appear at the Périgueux market. By the mid-eighteenth century, it was commercialized in the valley of the Dordogne and had become the primary cereal on which the peasantry depended for their subsistence, because of its high yield (as much as 40 : 1 in comparison to the norm of 3 : 1 or 4 : 1 for other grains) and its ability to thrive both in upland hollows and on alluvial plains.[21]

Maize was often alternated with wheat in a biennial rotation without fallow; if cut before maturation it also served as excellent fodder for cattle. The success of maize combined with the availability of chestnuts allowed the peasantry to use their wheat as a cash crop for sale on local and regional markets. Another, more dubious indicator of progress was the clearing of new fields to produce additional grain and

---

ultime à la vraie croissance," in Le Roy Ladurie (ed.), *L'Age classique des paysans, 1340–1789* (Paris, 1975), 404–406, Vol. II of Georges Duby and Armand Wallon (eds.), *Histoire de la France rurale*, 4 vols.; Guy Mandon, "Progrès agricoles et défrichements en Périgord au XVIIIe siècle," *Bulletin de la Société Historique et Archéologique du Périgord*, CVII (1980), 182–83.

21. De Fayolle, *Topographie agricole*, 47; Cocula, "Vivre et survivre en Périgord," in Higounet-Nadal (ed.), *Histoire du Périgord*, 214. The figures for yields are from Delfau, *Annuaire . . . l'année sextile XI*, and are quoted in Mandon, "Progrès agricoles," 179. The Sieur Pomarel, lawyer, road commissioner, and author of a *mémoire* on the parish of Pazayac (near Terrasson), credited maize with saving the region from famine (Mémoire du Sr. Pomarel, July 30, 1761, C 1317, ADG).

wine; unfortunately, soil exhaustion and erosion were too often the by-products of extending the arable onto marginal lands.[22]

De Fayolle cataloged the endemic woes that plagued the region's agriculture: wasteful methods of sowing and cultivation; archaic agricultural implements; the poor quality of the soil, exacerbated by erosion and continuous cultivation; the lack of pasturage, livestock, and manure; the prevalence of sharecropping; the extreme fragmentation of ownership, as well as the parcellation of fields; and the peasantry's stubborn resistance to innovation. The salient feature of Périgourdin economic life was the region's subsistence polyculture, which generally condemned its populace to chronic undernourishment rather than periodic, outright starvation. De Fayolle remarked that although in good years the department of the Dordogne, roughly coextensive with the Périgord, was able to produce enough to feed itself, only one of every three years did not necessitate the importation of grain.[23]

In the Jurassic highlands of the northeast, only hardy cereals such as rye, barley, oats, and buckwheat could survive in the relatively sandy soil and cool climate; little maize was planted, and wheat (*froment*) prospered only in the valleys, where soils were somewhat better. In contrast, the fertile rolling hills of the western Périgord made the Riberacois one of the few areas to produce a grain surplus. Merchants purchased good-quality grain at local markets for shipment downriver to Bordeaux, where much of it was milled into flour for export to the Antilles. In the equally fertile floodplain of the Dordogne River, both maize and wheat thrived, while viticulture produced a quantity of good wines in the vicinity of Domme and Bergerac. In 1756 the subdelegate reported that the bottomland parishes normally produced three times as much grain as they needed for subsistence, whereas the upland parishes (almost the entire subdelegation) rarely produced enough to meet their needs. In the vicinity of Saint-Cyprien and Trémolat, where the alluvial plain was relatively broad and contained some of the area's richest land, population density was high (seventy inhabitants per square kilometer) and exploitation of the soil intensive. Peasants devoted their fields principally to the cultivation of wheat, which they

22. Remarques de Desmarest; Mandon, "Progrès agricoles," 180–83. Also see Boutier, "Jacqueries en pays croquant," 779.
23. De Fayolle, *Topographie agricole*, 98.

then sold to pay their taxes, retaining maize, barley, and chestnuts for their own consumption.[24]

In the department of the Dordogne as a whole, 57 percent of the surface area in 1804 was comprised of woods and wasteland, 30 percent of arable land, 7 percent of vineyards, and 4 percent of meadows. If the entire surface area had been arable, Delfau speculated, the populace could have fed itself; but since more than half was in moors and chestnut trees or was "absolutely sterile," the department had to be judged "fort pauvre."[25]

The dearth of pasturage and, subsequently, of hooved livestock deprived Périgourdin cultivators of the manure needed to render their mediocre fields more productive. Once or twice annually the peasants collected the manure and straw litter that accumulated in the fetid, windowless stables typical of the region. They then usually piled the manure in their courtyards—where rains leached its beneficial content—before mixing it with dried leaves, heather, or gorse and spreading it on the fields. Although cows were normally kept only for plowing and producing calves, their milk was used to make butter in several parishes near Terrasson. Moreover, oxen often were purchased as calves from the Limousin and fattened for reexportation; according to Delfau, exported oxen exceeded in value the department's third most valuable commodity, wine.[26] Pigs were the single most important object of commerce in the Périgord. They by far brought the best return on a minimal investment, for they did not require pasturage or meadows and could be fattened on maize, chestnuts, acorns, buckwheat, barley, oats, and potatoes.

Given the importance of livestock raising to the populace, the suspension in spring, 1775, of fairs of horned beasts to halt the spread of

24. Remarques de Desmarest; Richard Beaudry, "Subsistances et population en Périgord au XVIIIe siècle, 1740–1789," *mémoire* for the D.E.S. (Université de Bordeaux, 1970), 37; Description de la subdélégation de Sarlat, 1756, 2 C26, ADD; Observations générales sur différentes mémoires, *ca.* 1763, C 1317, ADG. G. Florenty, "Saint-Cyprien," 13; Mémoire de la subdélégation de Sarlat pour Monseigneur de Tourny, Intendant de Guyenne, August 5, 1743, C 1317, ADG.

25. He estimates population density for the department at 868 inhabitants per square league (54.25 inhabitants per square kilometer). See Delfau, *Annuaire statistique . . . l'an XII,* 171.

26. De Fayolle, *Topographie agricole,* 101, 111; Delfau, *Annuaire statistique . . . l'an XII,* 279 ff.

an epizootic rampant in Quercy naturally evoked numerous protests. On March 30, 1775, the leading citizens of Montignac petitioned the intendant to lift the ban on all fairs and markets of oxen and cattle, pointing out that the disease had not yet appeared in the Sarladais and that the commerce in animals was the only means by which the populace obtained the cash needed to pay royal taxes and purchase necessities. A deputy from Sarlat argued that the suspension of fairs had caused "the direst poverty" in the countryside because many peasants had in the course of the winter already sold their oxen and were subsequently prevented from purchasing new ones to begin their spring plowing. When the intendant on March 16, 1776, forbade the raising of pigs within the limits of cities in the Périgord, his ordinance likewise provoked a storm of protest, particularly from the mayor and *jurade* of Monpazier, who contended that since their city was situated on a hilltop, it enjoyed salubrious air and therefore was not exposed to risk. The mayor proposed the creation of a police regulation limiting the number of pigs each person could raise and forbidding pigs in the streets unless conducted by an appointed public swineherd.[27]

Another obstacle to livestock raising was the relative scarcity of common lands in the Périgord. De Fayolle remarked that rights of *vaine pâture* and passage were not well established and that the few common lands that did exist were of limited extent. The royal edict of 1766, which offered subsidies and tax incentives to encourage individuals to enclose commons, failed to accomplish that goal in the Périgord precisely because the region—unlike the rest of Guyenne—had little communal agriculture and few commons to impede the spread of agricultural individualism. The overwhelming majority of the land cleared as a result of the edict consisted of moors and scrub growth that were then converted into vineyards. In only one instance did Desmarest refer to commons in the province: moors belonging to the small town of Isle that were subsequently planted in grapevines. According to the intendant, the commons near Besse, on the southern margin of the Périgord, near Villefranche, were the only commons worth mentioning in the entire subdelegation of Sarlat.[28]

27. Plainte du 30 mars 1775 des principaux habitants de la ville et comté de Montignac, Lettre de Cejayol, deputé de la ville de Sarlat, à M. l'Intendant, April 17, 1775, and Lettre de Meyrignac à l'Intendant, March 13, 1775, all in C 481, ADG; Lettre de Meyrignac à M. l'Intendant, August 5, 1776, C 482, ADG.

28. De Fayolle, *Topographie agricole,* 49; Mandon, "Progrès agricoles," 169,

The malaise of Périgourdin agriculture in the eighteenth century derived not only from the location of the region, the mediocrity of its soil, and its poor transportation network but also from its extreme fragmentation of holdings. Although the Périgord has characteristically been regarded as *la terre classique du métayage,* the diversity of the region thwarts generalization.[29] Any analysis that considers the extent of holdings but not their quality can be deceptive, for large holdings normally consisted of woods and moors, whereas arable lands tended to be divided among smallholders. The concentration of ownership in the early nineteenth century was not extreme: In the Dordogne, 6.2 percent of all proprietors held half the land in units of more than 20 hectares; in contrast, 1.1 percent of the landowners in the Loir-et-Cher, for example, possessed half the land in units of more than 100 hectares. Under the July Monarchy, the Dordogne was therefore not a department particularly dominated by large landholders.[30] A few hundred large landowners, perhaps, played a primary role in the Dordogne, but alongside them existed a number of well-to-do peasants and rural bourgeois who lived off their lands. Finally, there existed a large class of small landowners who lived modestly by their own labor—sometimes independent but most often obliged to work part of the time for others.[31]

Southwest France at the end of the Old Regime was both a haven of small and moderate peasant proprietors and the classic land of share-

174, 177, 181–82. According to the intendant, the people of the surrounding parishes used this 8,000-arpent expanse of moors to graze their livestock and gather heather for fertilizer. Significantly, the intendant asked the subdelegate to verify their claim, for he wished either to clear the land or to reforest it (Lettre de l'Intendant à Meyrignac, July 10, 1780, C 488, ADG).

29. René Pijassou states flatly that the predominant mode of *faire valoir* from the seventeenth century to the mid-nineteenth century was sharecropping (*Regards sur la révolution agricole en Périgord* [Périgueux, 1967], 10). Beaudry notes that although the number of peasant smallholders was often large, their holdings were relatively insignificant in size ("Subsistances et population en Périgord," 23–28). The phrase *la terre classique du métayage* originated with Armand Audiganne, in "Le Métayage et la culture dans le Périgord," *Revue des deux mondes,* June 1, 1867, 614.

30. Georges Dupeux agrees that *la grande propriété* was most typical of the Northeast (Normandy, Picardy, Île-de-France, the *pays* of the Loire) and of Languedoc and Nivernais. He does contend, however, that large holdings were more likely to be lands of high quality located in rich plains and valleys or the loam soils of the Paris Basin (*La Société française, 1789–1970* [Paris, 1972], 112–13).

31. Ralph Gibson, "Les Notables et l'Eglise dans le diocèse de Périgueux, 1821–1905" (Thèse de IIIème cycle, Université de Lyon, 1979), 12–18.

cropping. North of the Garonne River, rare were the peasants who did not possess some land: 15 to 20 percent in Rouergue, fewer in Limousin and the Périgord. Overall, the peasantry possessed the majority of the soil—50 percent in Bas-Quercy, 55 percent in Limousin—but in innumerable small plots. Even as late as 1851, small proprietors composed the majority of the agricultural population in almost half the communes of the department of the Dordogne. Whereas sharecroppers constituted a majority in the Nontronnais, small landowners dominated almost exclusively in the valley of the Dordogne River, near Bergerac and Sarlat. In comparison with those in the rest of France, sharecroppers in the Dordogne did indeed constitute a larger percentage of the agricultural population (24.5 percent, as opposed to 6.9 percent nationwide), but so, too, did small landowners (48 percent in the department, as opposed to 35 percent nationwide). Rare in the Dordogne were *journaliers,* or day laborers, who found that they were unable to support themselves in a region of polyculture and therefore emigrated.[32]

If one assumes a holding of five hectares to be the minimum necessary for self-sufficiency and commercial exploitation, then one can conclude that approximately half the small landowners in the Sarladais never produced an agricultural surplus from their holdings and seldom produced enough to survive. They managed to subsist by relying on the auxiliary resources (especially chestnuts and poached game) and employment furnished by the forests of the *pays*. Depending on the season, they found work as woodcutters, charcoal burners, *feuillardiers,* or forge workers. These poor but precariously independent small landowners, whose economic situation was hardly better and sometimes worse than that of sharecroppers, made up the majority of the Dordogne's population. This class engaging in subsistence polyculture would increase in size during the nineteenth century, as sharecroppers either abandoned the land and migrated to the cities or struggled to accumulate capital and purchase their own land.[33]

The Revolution and the sale of *biens nationaux* did little to alter the distribution of landed wealth in the department. In the districts of Sarlat and Belvès, peasants represented the majority submitting bids,

32. Boutier, "Jacqueries en pays croquant," 779; Gibson, "Les Notables et l'Eglise," 27.

33. Gibson, "Les Notables et l'Eglise," 34–37, 43, 67–68.

but only for the cheapest lots. In addition, only in a small number of the communes did the directors of the sale dispose of considerable properties. In the cantons of Monpazier and Villefranche, where the properties of curés were virtually all that was offered for sale, many of these small plots were purchased by peasants or even by the curés themselves, who repurchased the property attached to the presbytère. Moreover, most of the department's *grands seigneurs* did not emigrate during the Revolution and managed to preserve their holdings from confiscation. Some families that did lose land later repurchased the confiscated property, using either their own name or that of a surrogate. In the Sarladais at least, traditional noble property for the most part survived the revolutionary turmoil intact. It is therefore not surprising to find the nobility of the department as a whole still in possession of an important part of the landed wealth at the beginning of the nineteenth century.[34] Even in areas of the Périgord where land ownership was concentrated in the hands of a few proprietors, the actual cultivation of the land was necessarily carried out in small units. Whether the land belonged to a single individual or to several people, it was always parceled and in the hands of peasants or sharecroppers, who were able to apply their energies only to relatively modest plots.[35]

An examination of the agriculture practiced in the triangular region between Hautefort, Montignac, and Saint-Pierre-de-Chignac reveals the various methods used in the Périgord in the eighteenth century. This area contains the diverse topographical elements found in the Périgord as a whole: limestone bluffs and plateaus eroded by an occasional stream, the valley of the Auvézère River, and the wooded expanse of the Forêt Barade. In this area of fragmented holdings, tenant farming was most common. Small parcels of land, vineyards, woods, and meadows were leased either to sharecroppers or to small land-

34. Jacques Crouzy, "La Terre et l'homme en Sarladais" (Thèse de IIIème cycle, Université de Bordeaux, 1969), 148–51; Noël Becquart, "La Vente des biens nationaux de 1ère origine dans le district de Belvès," *Bulletin de la Société Historique et Archéologique du Périgord*, CIV (1977), 295–96. In contrast, René Pijassou argues that the sale of biens nationaux constituted a "vast movement of landed transfers and of noble dispossession" that profited not only the bourgeoisie but also many modest buyers ("La Crise révolutionnaire," in Higounet-Nadal [ed.], *Histoire du Périgord*, 265–67). See also De Fayolle, *Topographie agricole*, 49; Gibson, "Les Notables et l'Eglise," 47.

35. Although he favored small properties, Arthur Young criticized the extreme fragmentation that characterized the system in France: "In all modes of occupying the land, the great evil is the smallness of farms" (*Travels*, 297, 298, 299–300).

owners whose own holdings were insufficient for subsistence. Among the 250 leases found and analyzed, money leases equaled sharecropping arrangements, which were usually at half shares. Large proprietors (noble and non-noble) seem to have preferred to lease their property to *fermiers,* who, in turn, often sublet to sharecroppers. In contrast, bourgeois officeholders, merchants, and, more rarely, artisans or peasants who owned property preferred to let their land at half shares directly to sharecroppers.[36]

An evaluation of the in-kind revenues in sharecropping leases and the annual return from money leases proves the modesty of these tenant farms—even allowing for a notorious tendency to underestimate their value. Half of the holdings yielded rents valued at no more than 100 livres; rare were those with rents above 200 livres. Truly exceptional were those at half shares whose in-kind payments attained a value of 200 livres. The most frequent duration of rental and half-share leases was five years (40 percent of the leases); next were leases of nine years and seven years. Three half-share leases of twenty-nine years were for *métairies* whose revenue derived primarily from vineyards and chestnut trees. The average value of the livestock entrusted to each sharecropper was 250 livres—the equivalent of a pair of oxen (150 to 180 livres), one or two calves, a few pigs, and a varying number of sheep or goats. The seed grain provided by the owner generally consisted of wheat, maize, barley, oats, and rye; he also supplied beans, peas, and lentils. The proprietor generally retained use of the woods for himself, allowing each sharecropper only firewood, acorns for his pigs, and forest litter for the livestock. He most often divided the harvest of walnuts and chestnuts with the sharecroppers; in only a minority of the leases did the owner allow sharecroppers to retain the entire harvest of nuts, provided that they maintained and replanted the trees.[37]

The plight of the sharecropper who lived on the isolated farmstead of his métairie was not necessarily worse than that of the small landowner, whose dwelling was more likely to be located in a village. The size of the average métairie in the department was 10 to 20 hectares (25 to 50 acres) in the early nineteenth century. Even if a sharecropper kept only half the produce from a plot that size, he still retained more than the total production of a large number of small landowners. To over-

36. Cocula, "Vivre et survivre en Périgord," in Higounet-Nadal (ed.), *Histoire du Périgord,* 219–20.
37. *Ibid.*

come the potential insecurity of their circumstances, many sharecroppers created an associated network of nuclear and extended family members. According to De Fayolle, cultivation of the average métairie required two or three men, two women, and several children (who tended the livestock)—assuming that the sharecropper wished to avoid the expense of hiring workers to tend the animals.[38]

Many sharecroppers sought a further hedge against insecurity in loyalty to their land and master. A high number of the 250 leases analyzed for the late eighteenth century were simply renewed upon expiration, suggesting that a majority of these sharecroppers were relatively immobile and experienced longevity of tenure. But longevity of tenure does not necessarily denote fidelity to the land or one's master. Marcel Secondat discovered that in the rural parish of Plazac, near Montignac, sharecroppers generally found themselves short of grain soon after the division of the harvest and relied heavily on advances from their masters. As a result of these successive loans, when leases expired sharecroppers often owed their proprietor the entire harvest, as well as their share of the sale of any livestock. Additional debts accrued where masters advanced taille payments. Proprietors were not reluctant to seize furniture and meager possessions if a sharecropper attempted to leave without clearing his debt; thus, menaced with legal action and the seizure of his goods, many a sharecropper effectively found himself tied to the land in a kind of debt peonage. In the final resort, however, decamping was the sharecropper's only real bargaining weapon.[39]

Sharecroppers necessarily lived on the isolated métairies they farmed, in low, poorly ventilated dwellings made of stone and covered with clay tiles, slate, or flat stones (*lauzes*). Dwellings normally consisted of two rooms, or perhaps only one room serving as both bedroom and kitchen, with a hayloft above. An open door and, sometimes, a small shuttered window—both closed during inclement weather— were the only avenues other than the chimney by which light and ventilation penetrated the smoke-blackened interior. At night, earthenware lamps that burned walnut oil provided illumination. Inventories conducted upon seizures reveal that furnishings ordinarily consisted of crudely fashioned, hand-hewn furniture: a large bed in which the entire family slept, a table and two benches, an armoire or cabinet, and a

38. Gibson, "Les Notables et l'Eglise," 37; De Fayolle, *Topographie agricole,* 54.
39. Secondat, "Evolution économique d'une communauté rurale," *Bulletin de la Société Historique et Archéologique du Périgord,* CII (1975), 326–27.

bread bin. Near the door there was generally a ladder leading to the hayloft and, beneath the ladder, a supply of firewood. In a corner might be found a sack of grain resting on a plank to protect it from the humidity of the beaten-earth floor. In another corner was a sink, which drained directly to the outside through a hole in the wall. From the beams ears of corn and skeins of wool often were suspended. Possessions included cast-iron pots and cauldrons, as well as earthenware storage jars for water and walnut oil. Alongside the cottage usually stood a low barn, a pigsty, and a sheep pen—all windowless. Cultivators employed the same kinds of tools used for centuries: a wooden plow with a cast-iron plowshare, mattocks, long-handled hoes with two tines, billhooks, sickles (for grains), scythes (for hay), and wooden pitchforks.[40]

Inventories after death reveal that a relatively prosperous peasant ordinarily possessed a house of one or two rooms, a hayloft, and a cellar, plus perhaps a barn or stable. His house was more often composed of two rooms: a bedroom with one or two beds and a kitchen with a sideboard, table, and assorted utensils—usually in copper, seldom in iron. The household dishes were most often of pewter, supplemented perhaps by a couple of pieces of faience. The beds were large and high, with a canopy closed by curtains. Bedding was normally composed of a straw-filled mattress below with a down-filled mattress above, wool blankets, and a bolster or pillows, also of feather.[41]

The line dividing sharecroppers from small proprietors was often indistinct. De Fayolle remarked that many small proprietors did not own sufficient land to support their families or to keep their livestock; they therefore rented métairies, hired themselves out to tend cattle or to work as journaliers, or often emigrated to the Gironde on a seasonal basis to work in the grape harvest. Those peasant proprietors who owned more land, plus a pair of oxen or cows to plow their fields, enjoyed greater security. In Plazac, for example, great domains were absent, and the largest landowners possessed only four or five métairies each. The number of small proprietors who lived on their own land and farmed it with their families, without subletting to sharecroppers or tenants, was appreciable. These small independent landowners—not

40. *Ibid.*, 332–34; De Fayolle, *Topographie agricole*, 55, 60–61; Eugène Le Roy, *Jacquou le Croquant* (1900; rpr. Paris, 1976), 21–22.

41. F. Florenty, "Etude démographique d'une paroisse sarladaise: Domme, 1770–1820," *mémoire* for the D.E.S. (Université de Bordeaux, 1972), 28.

counting carpenters, joiners, blacksmiths, weavers, and *praticiens,* who owned land in addition to practicing a trade—paid 10 to 40 livres in taxes and constituted 28 percent of those subject to the taille in 1783. Nonetheless, sharecropping was still the most common way of working the land in the parish, Secondat concluded.[42]

In general, only isolated, small plots in Plazac were leased at fixed prices, payable in money. Most proprietors, fearing the instability of prices and the depreciation of the currency, prudently required in-kind payment of half the profits. At the bottom of the economic scale were *bordiers, domestiques,* and *métiviers.* A proprietor often disposed of a field or cottage on the border of his domain by renting it to an individual unable to cultivate a standard métairie. This bordier, in turn, usually cultivated several scattered parcels—a vineyard here, a field there— which he leased at half shares. For these small plots, the owner usually did not supply livestock, only seed grain and tools. Large landowners reserved for their own use a few fields, vineyards, and meadows located nearest the town or their own dwellings. They kept oxen for plowing and employed domestiques or *valets de ferme* to sleep in the barn alongside the mangers and care for the livestock. These large landholders confided the plowing, sowing, and harvesting of their lands to métiviers, who worked under the direction of the proprietor and were paid in kind for their work, but not provided lodging. Only if the proprietor could not find a métivier to work a field in exchange for a portion of the harvest would he hire journaliers, usually at five sous per day or for a fixed price per job, plus bread and a *chopine* of wine. Landowners who hired domestiques to care for their livestock generally employed them on an annual basis, at approximately sixty livres per year in 1788–89 (plus a bonus when the oxen were sold).[43]

Contemporary observers concurred that sharecropping had a pernicious effect on the rural economy of the Périgord. De Fayolle insists that sharecroppers lived in the direst poverty, were treated nearly the same as domestiques, and were dismissed at will. Although a number of them enjoyed longevity of tenure and were better off than many small

42. De Fayolle, *Topographie agricole,* 49–50; Secondat, "Evolution économique d'une communauté rurale," *Bulletin de la Société Historique et Archéologique du Périgord,* CII (1975), 179–80.

43. Secondat, "Evolution économique d'une communauté rurale," *Bulletin de la Société Historique et Archéologique du Périgord,* CII (1975), 191–95. Also see De Fayolle, *Topographie agricole,* 58–59.

landowners, the possibility of dismissal or nonrenewal was very real for them and not only deterred serious efforts at improving the land but also encouraged the short-term exploitation of its resources. Desmarest complained in 1761 that sharecroppers often cut chestnut trees and failed to replant them for future use. "The status of the sharecropper," he wrote, "is such that he has no regard whatsoever for the property entrusted to him for cultivation and is wary of even considering any form of improvements."[44]

Absentee owners and large proprietors with far-flung holdings often entrusted them to fermiers, who leased large tracts in exchange for money rents and then subdivided and sublet them to individual sharecroppers. De Fayolle considered this system even worse than sharecropping, for the fermier was likewise interested only in making the land pay as much as possible during his tenure: "There is an incontestable fact in this department, and that is that a property, if not located on excellent ground, when it has had the misfortune to experience three or four consecutive leases of nine years each, is a ruined property, especially if it passed from one fermier to another with each lease."[45] Contemporary observers concluded that as long as sharecropping continued to be a dominant method of cultivation in the region, the Périgord would be incapable of progress.

In retrospect, however, sharecropping appears to have been less a cause of agricultural stagnation than a symptom. The malaise derived less from the method of payment than from the intrinsically weak productivity of an agricultural regime plagued by poor soils, relative isolation from markets, autoconsumption, and overpopulation resulting in fragmentation of ownership and parcellation of fields. Apart from their willing acceptance of maize, Périgourdin peasants generally ignored agricultural innovation because they could not afford the luxury of experimentation and had little choice but to exploit their small holdings to the utmost. Sharecroppers had no way of learning or applying new methods, and large landowners had little incentive to practice them. In fact, proprietors compensated for the modest return of each métairie by extending the area and multiplying the number of such units of exploi-

44. De Fayolle, *Topographie agricole*, 56–58; Remarques de Desmarest. Also see Young, *Travels*, 296–98.
45. De Fayolle, *Topographie agricole*, 59.

tation. The sharecropper, like the small peasant landowner, simply struggled to survive as best he could in these circumstances.[46]

In 1756, the subdelegate Baudot de Jully enumerated five areas of commerce in the subdelegation of Sarlat. The first centered on the river port below the city of Domme, which not only served as a point where loads were transferred to heavier river craft but also was an assembly point for the area's viticultural products. The great majority of the subregion's wine was sent to Libourne and Bordeaux and then shipped to Brittany, England (during peacetime), Holland, and, in smaller amounts, the Baltic market. When abundant harvests permitted, maize and chestnuts also joined the flow of goods downriver, along with a certain amount of stavewood destined for the wine barrels of the Bordelais. The commerce in wine was carefully organized: Domme merchants had agents in Bordeaux and in turn regulated the principal commodity of upriver traffic, salt. Because Domme was an important stop on the north-south overland route between Limoges and Cahors, it served as an important regional center for the distribution of salt toward the Sarladais and Quercy. For the same reason, it shipped a minor portion of its wines north to the Limousin.[47]

The second area of commerce within the subdelegation was the "low country" in the vicinity of Bergerac, which produced the white wines especially valued by the Dutch but also in demand on the markets of northern Europe and England. The Dutch had entered the Bordeaux market in the mid-seventeenth century, and through them, Bordelais traders had subsequently penetrated the Baltic market. Périgourdin trade in wine with Holland and the North was normally conducted through intermediaries in Bordeaux, Libourne, and Bergerac; only occasionally were local merchants in Quercy, the Agenais, or the upper Dordogne River valley in direct correspondence with the wider European market. The products moving upriver in exchange for wine were

46. Michel Morineau, "Y a-t-il eu une révolution agricole en France au XVIIIe siècle?" *Revue historique*, CCXXXIX (1968), 299–326; Cocula, "Vivre et survivre en Périgord," in Higounet-Nadal (ed.), *Histoire du Périgord*, 221; De Fayolle, *Topographie agricole*, 129–30. Little agricultural progress was made elsewhere in France, either, at this time.

47. Description de la subdélégation de Sarlat; F. Florenty, "Etude démographique," 13–16; De Fayolle, *Topographie agricole*, 84, 119.

not Dutch goods but colonial products (sugar and coffee) from the Antilles, fish and salt from the French Atlantic seaboard, and sometimes grain from Brittany or the Vendée in times of shortage.

The Dutch share of the Bordeaux market as a whole diminished in the eighteenth century as the share of Bremen and Hamburg increased. Although the trade in wines with northern Europe expanded along with the colonial trade in the second half of the century, Baltic merchants preferred Bordeaux wines over the *vins primeurs* of Bergerac. The decline in the Dordogne wine trade created real hardship in the fifty parishes in the vicinity of Bergerac. Beginning in about 1730 they had expanded their vineyards to meet the growing demand of the Dutch market, even converting arable land from grain to wine production. When the slump began around midcentury, the parishes were therefore extremely vulnerable and had neither maize nor chestnuts to balance their highly specialized agricultural regime. By 1763 their revenues had been reduced by approximately half. Increasingly hard pressed to pay their taxes, the parishes petitioned for lower taille assessments. In 1766, the traders of Bergerac estimated that in the previous thirty years their commerce with Holland had declined by three-fourths.[48]

The low country near Bergerac also produced a surplus of grain—nearly three times as much as it needed for subsistence, according to Jully. This surplus was exported to Libourne and Bordeaux. "In contrast," Jully remarked, "the upper country that constitutes nearly all of the subdelegation hardly harvests more than it needs for its subsistence unless the year is very abundant." But unlike the commerce in products such as wine and wood, the downriver traffic in grain was intermittent; in fact, in times of shortages, grains were shipped upriver. During agricultural crises such as that of 1770–73, grain from Languedoc moved down the Garonne River and then up the Dordogne to bring relief to the Périgord and Limousin (via Souillac). In the spring of 1773, local unrest ignited disturbances all along the Dordogne. Troops sent to the region only provoked rather than calmed the populace. Disturbances in Bergerac came to an end only when grain boats that had

48. Paul Butel, *Les Négociants bordelais: L'Europe et les Iles* (Paris, 1974), 52–57, 60, 96; Cocula, *Les Gens de la rivière de Dordogne*, 511, 516. Also see Mémoire contenante les raisons qui exigent une nouvelle refonte de l'élection de Sarlat, *ca.* 1763, C 1317, ADG.

halted upstream for fear of pillaging finally arrived in Bergerac on May 28 and 29.[49]

Much to the perplexity and consternation of the local populace, grain often moved simultaneously upriver and downriver. Bordeaux merchants and their agents in the hinterland cities generally purchased from the Périgord, the Agenais, and Quercy good-quality grains destined for Bordeaux itself or for milling into flour for shipment to the Antilles. Local subdelegates often warned that the shipment of grains and the subsequent rise of prices within their jurisdictions would lead to popular unrest. But the adoption and spread of maize cultivation actually released more local grain for export to the flour mills.[50] Moreover, the production of lesser-quality grain in Brittany and the Vendée indirectly supported the shipment of Périgourdin grains to the colonies. In 1746 a Bordeaux trader admitted that the inhabitants of his metropolis—able to eat good bread at a reasonable price—were relatively privileged compared with the inhabitants of other parts of the Aquitaine. "Whereas the grains from Brittany are consumed by the *menu peuple*," he wrote, "the fine grains of the Périgord and Haut-Pays will be reserved for the bakeries of Bordeaux."[51]

In contrast to the seasonal, nonreciprocal contacts between Dordogne merchants and the Dutch market, commercial exchanges with neighboring regions of France were constant and reciprocal. Ships from Brittany brought grain (wheat and rye), beans, fish, and cattle from Quiberon. Many arrived in Libourne with ballast or stopped off on islands in the Charente (Ré and Oléron) for salt, which they then exchanged for a cargo of wine for the return voyage. Trading ties between the lower Dordogne, Aunis, Saintonge, and Poitou were equally complementary and centered on salt, which the barks of Libourne transported back home after carrying wines, tiles, and timbers to La Rochelle, Oléron, Ré, and Rochefort. Commerce with the upper Dordogne,

49. Description de la subdélégation de Sarlat. Additional relief materialized on May 31 and June 4 in the form of grain sent upriver via Bordeaux. See Cocula, *Les Gens de la rivière de Dordogne,* 513–15; Iain Cameron, *Crime and Repression in the Auvergne and the Guyenne, 1720–1790* (Cambridge, Eng., 1981), 63–69, 234–41.

50. Lettre de Meyrignac à l'Intendant, May 17, 1773, Lettre de Meyrignac à l'Intendant, June 2, 1773, both in C 478, ADG. Also see Delfau, *Annuaire statistique . . . l'an XII,* 280ff.

51. Quoted in Butel, *Les Négociants bordelais,* 86 (also see 75, 91, 95); Cocula, *Les Gens de la rivière de Dordogne,* 512–13; De Fayolle, *Topographie agricole,* 119.

though seasonal because of low water, was also relatively direct and reciprocal, with Libourne acting only as a stopping point between the valley and the littoral.[52]

The third area of Sarladais commerce designated by Jully centered on the parishes along the Dordogne River and particularly the Vézère River, which sent an assortment of cereals, maize, chestnuts, juniper berries, and especially stavewood to Bordeaux and wines to Limoges. The account books of two bourgeois families in Plazac reveal the nature and scope of commercial activities along the Vézère. The Tibeyrant and Dalbavie, the only large proprietors of the parish, possessed holdings that greatly surpassed in number and extent the domains of local seigneurs. They therefore filled their storehouses and cellars with grain and wine and engaged in commerce far beyond the limits of the parish. They were, of course, the principal "grain bankers" of Plazac, lending seed corn and grain to all who fell short before harvest. Moreover, they were associates of merchants in Bergerac and Bordeaux, for whom they purchased all available grain in the vicinity of Montignac and of Thenon. Grain from the Thenon area they sent overland to Limoges; grain from Montignac and its environs they gathered at Saint-Léon-sur-Vézère and sent downriver to Bergerac or Libourne, where it was loaded onto larger vessels destined for Bordeaux. Whereas the commerce in grain was intermittent, that in wine was not only continual but also far ranging. Very little wine was sold locally; although cabaret owners occasionally bought some to supplement their supplies, everyone else either had his own vineyard or was too poor to purchase wine.[53]

Bernard Dalbavie also purchased sacks of green chestnuts, which he sold at Moustier and Saint-Léon to boatmasters. The nuts were then transported to Bordeaux, whence they were shipped to Holland. In similar fashion, Dalbavie bought sacks of juniper berries from peasants who painstakingly collected them from hillsides in the surrounding parishes. They were also exported to Holland. Although these hardly constituted significant exports, they nonetheless integrated otherwise unproductive lands into a network of commercial exchanges and provided local inhabitants with at least labor-intensive employment

52. Cocula, *Les Gens de la rivière de Dordogne,* 511–13.
53. Secondat, "Evolution économique d'une communauté rurale," *Bulletin de la Société Historique et Archéologique du Périgord,* CIII (1976), 34–37.

and limited income in a region where opportunities to acquire either were rare.[54]

But the commerce in wood products played the greatest part in sustaining the modest commercial importance of Plazac in the eighteenth century. Once again, Antoine Tibeyrant and Bernard Dalbavie controlled this trade. Acting in partnership or separately, they were responsible for the exploitation of the local forests. To avoid the delays and uncertainties incurred in contracting with individual charcoal burners, Tibeyrant and Dalbavie formed a partnership to purchase entire forests and produce charcoal for the iron forges of the Périgord. They reserved the tallest trees for naval masts and sawed the thickest trees into planks. Oaks produced *merrain:* staves and bottoms for the wine barrels of the Bordelais. Young chestnuts yielded rot-resistant vine props and pliant hoop wood (*feuillard*) for barrel hoops and fish baskets, as well as lathing for roofs. Young oaks of twenty-five to thirty years were cut into cordwood for the production of charcoal by a small army of journaliers and sharecroppers who spent their winters as woodsmen and charcoal burners. Tibeyrant and Dalbavie developed their commerce in charcoal on a relatively large scale, associating with merchants in Lalinde, Bergerac, Domme, and Terrasson. They transported the remainder of their wood products overland to Moustier, where boatmen loaded them onto smacks for transportation to Bergerac, Libourne, and Bordeaux.[55]

Because after 1742 the methodical exploitation of local wood yielded less and less, the traders of Plazac increasingly purchased nearly all of their forests in the Limousin and sent their woodsmen upstream to work them. Merrain produced in the vicinity of Uzerche was thrown into the Vézère River—usually beginning at Easter, by which time the river had crested—and floated downstream to Saint-Léon. Tibeyrant directed teams of men on foot or horseback, who, along the banks or in boats, guided the wood past snags, shallows, and mills, prevented theft, and constructed barriers at Saint-Léon to collect the wood as it arrived. There, the woodsmen worked quickly to retrieve the wood and carefully stack it on the shore. If too much accumulated or heavy rains swelled the river, the barrier could break, scattering wood downstream

54. *Ibid.,* 41–42; Cocula, *Les Gens de la rivière de Dordogne,* 390.
55. Secondat, "Evolution économique d'une communaute rurale," *Bulletin de la Société Historique et Archéologique du Périgord,* CIII (1976), 42–44.

all the way to Le Bugue. A certain amount was always lost, spoiled, or stolen. In the float of 1760, when the last of the merrain had arrived at Saint-Léon, approximately 10,000 pieces were missing. The royal sergeants called on by Tibeyrant and Dalbavie to track the wood discovered much of it in a few villages in the parish of Thonac, just upstream from Saint-Léon. The owners prosecuted the thieves before the seigneurial tribunal of Losse. But in the late 1760s, Tibeyrant and Dalbavie apparently began to abandon the system of floats. By 1782 and 1783, wood was more commonly transported overland in carts or downriver in the smacks that had brought salt, tallow, and butter (from Holland) upriver.[56]

Another important item of commerce for the merchants of Plazac was the ironware produced at the Forge du Vimont, two kilometers upstream from Plazac, and at the Forge d'Ans, on the Auvézère River. Delfau estimated that for the department of the Dordogne in 1804, iron and ironware constituted the fourth most valuable export after pigs, oxen, and wine. At least nine forges and workshops existed in the vicinity of Sarlat. Although the forges of the arrondissement of Sarlat generally were not as large or as active as those in the arrondissements of Périgueux and Nontron, the forge at Vimont, north of Plazac, was among the most important in the Périgord in the early eighteenth century. During the six months of smelting each year, the forge and its dependencies formed in effect a large village, whose inhabitants worked night and day to feed the furnaces iron ore from the surrounding parishes and charcoal sometimes brought from a great distance. The forge produced cast-iron cannonballs and cannons for the navy and cauldrons for the sugar refineries of the Antilles, but most often cast-iron pots of all shapes and sizes, chimney plaques, and wrought iron. Iron products from Vimont as well as from neighboring forges were transported overland to ports on the Vézère and loaded onto smacks destined for Libourne. There cannons and cannonballs were transferred onto royal vessels that took them to the arsenals of La Rochelle and Rochefort; cauldrons and kettles were delivered to the merchants of Bordeaux for shipment to the colonies. Assorted ironware produced at Vimont, as well as at Tayac, Les Eyzies, and Le Bugue, was also sold locally at various downriver stops.[57]

56. *Ibid.*, 45–55.
57. Delfau, *Annuaire statistique . . . l'an XII*, 279 ff, and *Annuaire . . . l'année sextile XI*, 92–93. De Fayolle notes that forty-nine forges and twenty-nine furnaces

The forges of the Sarladais, the area around Thiviers, and the Nontronnais were true industries in regard to the number of workers employed, the importance of the forgemasters, and the size of their orders from the outside world. Desmarest noted that "iron is almost the only important branch of commerce presently in the province." The forges were nonetheless still rural in character: Apart from a few mining specialists, their workers were peasants who alternated mining and smelting with agricultural work. The wars of Louis XV, which often lost control of the high seas for France, slowed the exportation of Vimont's sugar cauldrons; as a result, smeltings became more infrequent in the course of the eighteenth century. The Revolution at first stimulated production, but the persistence of the wars and the impossibility of exporting cauldrons to the colonies or even Spain finally proved fatal to the forge at Vimont, as well as the other small-scale ironworks in the Sarladais. As for the large forgemasters of the Nontronnais, they were often reluctant to risk their revenues on further expansion and preferred to retire as local *notables*. Therefore, at the end of the eighteenth century, forges throughout the Périgord were in decline, owing perhaps as much to the timidity of their owners as to the economic difficulties of the time.[58]

The fourth area of commerce identified by Jully was the trade in livestock prevalent in those parts of the subdelegation removed from the rivers. The commerce in oxen, sheep, and especially pigs fattened on maize and chestnuts was distributed across the *pays* in the numerous fairs and markets of the interior. According to Jully, it constituted the principal commercial activity of the jurisdiction and generated the income needed by the peasantry to pay its taxes. Delfau agreed that the sale of pigs was the single most important and most lucrative branch of commerce in the region.[59]

The trade in walnuts and walnut oil was the fifth and final area of commercial activity in the subdelegation that Jully noted. By 1756 pro-

---

existed in the department, most of them located in the Nontronnais (*Topographie agricole*, 115–16). Also see Secondat, "Evolution économique d'une communauté rurale," *Bulletin de la Société Historique et Archéologique du Périgord*, CIII (1976), 58–59; Cocula, *Les Gens de la rivière de Dordogne*, 146.

58. Secondat, "Evolution économique d'une communauté rurale," *Bulletin de la Société Historique et Archéologique du Périgord*, CIII (1976), 60–62; Cocula, "Vivre et survivre en Périgord," in Higounet-Nadal (ed.), *Histoire du Périgord*, 216–17.

59. Description de la subdélégation de Sarlat; Delfau, *Annuaire statistique . . . l'an XII*, 279 ff.

duction levels equaled those prior to the damaging freeze of 1709. Although freezes in 1790 and 1795 caused some losses, in 1804 walnut oil was the sixth most valuable export after pigs, oxen, wine, ironware, and grain. Delfau observed that many more walnuts and chestnuts would have been available for export if not for the scarcity of grain in the upland parishes, which forced the populace to consume the nuts. Walnut oil, extracted by ordinary presses, not only was used locally as a substitute for butter and for illumination in clay lamps but also was exported to Languedoc, Bordeaux, and, in smaller quantities, Corrèze and Cantal.[60]

Aside from iron production, industrial activity in the Périgord was either nonexistent, primarily artisanal in nature, or strictly local in scope. Blessed with neither abundant sources of fossil fuels nor other raw materials, and deprived of market outlets and individual capital, the traditional industries of the region could not convert from artisanal production to true industrial production and consequently suffered from a profound malaise at the end of the eighteenth century. The faience works at Bergerac, Thiviers, and Le Bugue were languishing, and the Périgourdin glassworks that had existed since the Middle Ages were also in decline by the eighteenth century. The paper mills of the region around Couze could not compete with those of Angoulême. With the exception of the ironworks, industries of the Périgord rarely employed more than ten workers each.[61]

Sluggishness likewise characterized the textile industry, much to the dismay of both Desmarest and Latapie. With few exceptions, the production of coarse linens and woolens prevailed, denoting the modesty of a clientele forced by poverty to rely almost exclusively on its own labor or that of the parish weaver working seasonally. When Latapie toured the Périgord in 1778, he carefully cataloged examples of local industry, paying special attention to the handful of ill-fated government efforts to promote textile production. But these establishments were more akin to *ateliers de charité* than to true industrial enterprises: Their revenues seldom if ever equaled their expenses, and their survival

    60. Delfau, *Annuaire . . . l'année sextile XI,* 92–93; Remarques de Desmarest; G. Florenty, "Saint-Cyprien," 18; F. Florenty, "Etude démographique," 11–12.
    61. Beaudry, "Subsistances et population en Périgord," 68, 72. Latapie notes that a forge near Sainte-Croix employed more than forty full-time workers ("L'Industrie et le commerce en Guienne," 400).

depended heavily on the largesse of benefactors as well as support from the Crown.[62]

More important centers of textile production existed at Bergerac and Bourdeilles. In 1778 Bergerac contained workshops that produced woolen *bonnets* (caps), and numbered among its populace forty stocking makers, four master sergemakers, thirty weavers, and five fullers. Latapie considered the workshops of Bourdeilles, which also produced *bonnets* and cotton stockings, the most notable of the Généralité de Bordeaux after those of Agen. But the maritime wars of the late eighteenth century apparently slowed or halted the supply of cotton to such enterprises, and the Revolution further interrupted trade. As a result, by the turn of the century the workshops of Bergerac had closed, and those of Bourdeilles were in serious decline. De Fayolle reported that the Revolution even halted all production of woolen and cotton cloth at the hospital in Périgueux.[63]

Much more typical of the Périgord was the situation Latapie discovered in 1782 in Belvès, where a dozen master sergemakers and ten master weavers worked. "These men told me," Latapie recounted, "that there is hardly a parish in the vicinity of Belvès that does not have its sergemakers and weavers. But all of them, both those in town as well as those around it, work almost entirely for local use and transport very little to the fairs of the principal cities."[64] Such was also the case at Le Bugue, where eight sergemakers and a few linen weavers worked only by commission for merchants who supplied them with raw materials and then generally sold the finished cloth locally, sometimes at Bordeaux. With few exceptions, small-scale, local production and autoconsumption therefore characterized both agricultural and industrial production in the Périgord.

A factor contributing to the malaise that gripped the Périgord in the second half of the century was the chronic imbalance between the re-

---

62. De Fayolle, *Topographie agricole,* 118; Cocula, "Vivre et survivre en Périgord," in Higounet-Nadal (ed.), *Histoire du Périgord,* 217; F. Florenty, "Etude démographique," 10; Remarques de Desmarest; Latapie, "L'Industrie et le commerce en Guienne," 453, 456–58; Procès-verbal de la Maison de Charité, April 6, 1780, C 488, ADG.

63. Latapie, "L'Industrie et le commerce en Guienne," 453, 456–58; De Fayolle, *Topographie agricole,* 24, 117–18.

64. Latapie, "Tournée de 1782," 144.

gion's resources and the number of its inhabitants. The first censuses of the Revolution and the Empire reveal that the population of the department of the Dordogne was approximately 400,000, with less than 5 percent of the inhabitants living in towns. The entire department in 1804 contained only a dozen *villes* or bourgs with more than 2,000 inhabitants each: Four of them counted more than 3,000 persons, and only three of those four claimed more than 5,000 citizens. Bergerac was by far the largest city of the region, with 8,544 inhabitants, whereas Périgueux numbered 5,581 inhabitants—fewer than at the beginning of the fourteenth century. The Sénéchaussée of Sarlat comprised 205 parishes with approximately 116,000 inhabitants in the late eighteenth century. Six urban centers existed within the jurisdiction: Sarlat, with 5,250 inhabitants; Montignac, with 3,053; Terrasson, with 2,961; Domme/Cénac, with 2,747; Belvès, with 2,075; and Saint-Cyprien, with 2,055. Population density in the region varied from 70 inhabitants per square kilometer in the valley of the Dordogne to 30 to 40 inhabitants per square kilometer in the wooded upland parishes.[65]

Two specific signs betray the troubles of the region: the persistence of demographic crises, and the growing exodus of its inhabitants. The characteristic demographic traits of the Old Regime persisted in the Périgord (as in all of the Aquitaine) at a time when they were disappearing elsewhere. Even though the demographic crises were not pronounced enough to stem overall population growth, they did make its advance irregular. Moreover, the crises evidently became more numerous (but less severe and perhaps more localized) in the second half of the century. Although these years of food shortages and relatively high mortality may not have constituted true subsistence crises, they nonetheless left the populace in a continual state of malnutrition.[66]

Demographic crises occurred in Saint-Cyprien and surrounding parishes intermittently in the 150 years from the reign of Louis XIV to the coronation of Napoleon. Unlike the more general crises of the preceding century, the crisis of 1748–51 was localized along the valley of

65. Cocula, "Vivre et survivre en Périgord," in Higounet-Nadal (ed.), *Histoire du Périgord,* 210, 264; De Fayolle, *Topographie agricole,* 16; Delfau, *Annuaire statistique . . . l'an XII,* 55; Recensement général de la population, 1806, 6 M10, ADD; G. Florenty, "Saint-Cyprien," 13. If the total population of France in 1789 was 26 million, the nation had a population density of 48 people per square kilometer.

66. Cocula, "Vivre et survivre en Périgord," in Higounet-Nadal (ed.), *Histoire du Périgord,* 211; Richard Beaudry, "Alimentation et population rurale en Périgord au XVIIIe siècle," *Annales de démographie historique* (1976), 50–51.

the Dordogne. The crises of 1759–60 and 1765–68 stemmed from abnormal amounts of rain and early frosts, which first impeded plowing and then damaged harvests. Much more serious in its repercussions was the extended crisis of 1770–76, which was really a chain of crises with three peaks of short duration, in 1770, 1772–73, and 1774–75. The cumulative effects of this long series of poor harvests and unfavorable climatic conditions struck the elderly and children at the end of the summer and in early autumn, when fevers commonly plagued the populace of southwest France. The crisis of 1788 was minor in comparison, but was followed from 1790 to 1794 by a series of regular peaks in mortality that began in the spring and attained their maximum in the course of the summer. Only in the final years of the century did the rhythm of pronounced annual variations and violent crises slacken; the few crises that followed no longer presented a periodic character, and mortality seldom equaled natality.[67]

During the first half of the eighteenth century, the number of demographic crises provoked exclusively by agricultural failures progressively lessened. Although the populace and local authorities remained preoccupied with shortages and grain prices, the risk of famine per se seems to have diminished because of the spread of maize cultivation and the freer movement of grains. Epidemics, however, continued to occur frequently and constituted the principal cause of death, striking a populace weakened by chronic malnutrition and living in deplorable hygienic conditions. Seasonal mortality showed little variation from the pattern characteristic of the Southwest. Typhoid was endemic here as elsewhere in France until the 1860s. Dysentery, diarrhea, and malaria contributed to the highest mortality levels of the year, occurring from August through November, when newborns and young children made up the largest group of victims.[68]

Poor hygiene contributed significantly to the persistence of high mortality. When an epidemic struck the bourg of Allas-de-Berbiguières in the summer of 1746, the inspecting doctor blamed the insalubrity of the manure-filled narrow streets, the poor diet, and especially the con-

67. G. Florenty, "Saint-Cyprien," 54–61.
68. Ibid., 41–42, 61–62, 76; F. Florenty, "Etude démographique," 17–18, 33, 46–47, 59–60. For comparison with the Limousin, see Alain Corbin, Archaïsme et modernité en Limousin au XIXe siècle, 1845–1880 (Paris, 1975), 108–10; Jean-Pierre Peter, "Une Enquête de la Société Royale de Médecine: Malades et maladies à la fin du XVIIIe siècle," Annales: Economies, sociétés, civilisations, XXII (1967), 746.

taminated drinking water drawn from "a fountain resembling a lake into which a stream filled with refuse disgorged its contents, and in which the inhabitants did their laundry and washed their livestock." These factors combined not only to spawn the disease but also to perpetuate and even spread it, he reasoned.[69] Desmarest, writing in the 1760s, also deplored the filthiness that resulted from holding livestock markets in the center of town: "The pigs and the fowl leave a manure that corrupts the air and renders it unhealthy. This evil is widespread throughout the Périgord, and it would be most desirable if someone would correct this problem by moving the markets, especially those for livestock, far from all dwellings." He described the narrow medieval streets and densely packed houses of Sarlat as "humid and frightfully dirty." In Périgueux, the commissioner of the Quartier du Plantier reported that because none of the neighborhood's four hundred inhabitants possessed latrines, they threw their waste out of their windows or deposited it at the base of the city walls, where it emitted an unbearable stench and bred countless diseases.[70]

Although population growth in the region was relatively slow and halting, the Périgord had long been overpopulated in relation to its resources and the work it offered its inhabitants. The only outlet was emigration, and in the second half of the century Périgourdins surpassed all their Aquitaine neighbors in immigration to Bordeaux. The mortuary records of the Hôpital Saint-André in Bordeaux disclose that the number of Périgourdin immigrants to that city tripled between 1740 and 1780, with greater numbers coming from more prosperous, densely settled eastern areas such as the Riberacois and the north bank of the Double River. Emigration normally began with seasonal work in the vineyards, followed by longer-term employment. Some emigrants eventually returned home with their earnings; others made their way even to the Antilles. An additional indicator of pressure on the resource base of the Périgord was its reputation in the seventeenth and eighteenth centuries as a great provider of soldiers.[71]

---

69. He recommended that the manure be removed, the fountain kept clean, and the air purified by burning aromatic plants at frequent intervals (Rapport de Grézin, docteur en médecine, à M. de Jully, subdélégué à Sarlat, de l'intendant de Guyenne, July 19, 1746, C 2664, ADG).

70. Remarques de Desmarest; Jean-Joseph Escande, *Histoire du Périgord* (1934; rpr. Marseilles, 1980), 498.

71. Beaudry, "Subsistances et population en Périgord," 168; Jean-Pierre Poussou,

The Sarladais not only contributed its share of vagabonds, beggars, and migrant workers to the westward flow but also served as a transit zone for migrants lured to the Bordelais from the Auvergne and the Limousin. During troubled years of shortage such as the early 1770s, the region was filled with native and "foreign" beggars and vagabonds searching for food and employment. In January, 1774, the lieutenant of the maréchaussée, Gigounoux de Verdon, stated in his report on the Sarladais: "The roads are flooded with a quantity of Auvergnats and Limogeans who have brought with them their wives and children. I questioned them and threatened to arrest them. They replied to me that they had no food in their home districts and had come here to beg for bread. They further stated that they were not at all afraid to go to a *dépôt* or to prison because at least there they would be assured of getting bread." Verdon went on to warn the intendant that if he wished to avoid "tragic accidents," he should send grain quickly.[72]

Although famine was no longer a primary cause of death in the Périgord, malnutrition continued to claim lives. Chestnuts gathered in October—removed from their prickly husks and carefully dried over a fire to prevent sprouting and molding—assured the subsistence of many families during the winter months. The preparation of chestnuts was extremely simple: One removed their skins, threw them into a covered kettle with boiling water and a pinch of salt, and steamed them until tender. They were then eaten at mealtime or throughout the day. Although they did not readily lend themselves to the practice, chestnuts were ground and mixed with flour to make bread, according to Emmanuel Le Roy Ladurie and others.[73] In bread or alone, they were the primary staple of the peasant's diet during the autumn and winter months.

Maize, which was equally indispensable to the peasantry, was prepared in diverse ways. Although ground maize tended to ferment

---

Bordeaux et le Sud-Ouest au XVIIIe siècle: Croissance économique et attraction urbaine (Paris, 1983), 134–35. Also see Cocula, "Vivre et survivre en Périgord," in Higounet-Nadal (ed.), *Histoire du Périgord*, 212–13.

72. Lettre de Gigounoux de Verdon, lieutenant de la maréchaussée, à Monseigneur l'Intendant, à Terrasson, January 7, 1774, C 479, ADG.

73. Emmanuel Le Roy Ladurie, *The Peasants of Languedoc*, trans. John Day (Urbana, 1974), 68. Richard Beaudry contends that chestnuts were not actually used to make bread. The confusion on this point is undoubtedly aggravated by the tendency of sources to use the term *pain* in a generic sense to refer to all sorts of food ("Alimentation et population rurale," 45).

quickly, it constituted up to two-thirds of the loaf of bread eaten by the poor. It was also pressed into compact dumplings cooked in soup or was simply sprinkled into soups as a thickener. In addition, the inhabitants of the Périgord fricasseed ground maize in a skillet or shaped it into pancakes to be baked under the coals. Peasants also consumed a great many turnips (boiled, roasted, or baked), as well as beans, peas, lentils, cabbages, and greens, which they usually made into soups seasoned with salt and walnut oil. Bread, the mainstay of the peasant's diet elsewhere in France, was eaten in moderation in the Périgord. Composed of a mixture of rye, barley, buckwheat, millet, maize, and perhaps chestnuts—rarely of wheat—Périgourdin bread was typically dark, hard, and coarse. Meat consumption, although not unknown, was exceptional for the mass of the populace. Chickens, ducks, and geese raised by the peasantry were commonly reserved for sale at market, as was the game poached in the forests, but some meat did find its way to the peasant's table, especially at Christmas and Mardi Gras. When the family pig was butchered in February, all portions were used or carefully preserved in salt for later consumption. These were the months for social gatherings, especially celebrations of marriages and betrothals. At *veillées* held in the autumn and winter months, the first chestnuts and walnuts were washed down with new wine, or piquette.[74]

Vitamin and mineral deficiencies were unavoidable in a populace whose diet relied too heavily on carbohydrates and nearly omitted lipides and proteins. Milk products were virtually nonexistent in the diet of the Périgourdin peasant, leading to deficiencies in calcium and Vitamin D. Because cereal proteins, especially those found in maize, do not assure growth, it is not surprising that contemporaries commented on the province's small and misshapen inhabitants.[75] Moreover, a diet

---

74. Peter, "Une Enquête," 747; Beaudry, "Alimentation et population rurale," 45–46, 48; Cocula, "Vivre et survivre en Périgord," in Higounet-Nadal (ed.), *Histoire du Périgord*, 221–22; Fayolle, *La Vie quotidienne en Périgord*, 128–30; De Fayolle, *Topographie agricole*, 50–51; R. J. Bernard, "Peasant Diet in Eighteenth-Century Gévaudan," in Elborg Forster and Robert Forster (eds.), *European Diet from Pre-Industrial to Modern Times* (New York, 1975), 37–39. The veillée, one of the essential elements of peasant social life, was practiced until a late date. In the Limousin, as in the Périgord, it survived in a modified fashion until the end of World War II. See Corbin, *Archaïsme et modernité en Limousin*, 299–301.

75. Beaudry, "Alimentation et population rurale," 48–49; Cocula, "Vivre et survivre en Périgord," in Higounet-Nadal (ed.), *Histoire du Périgord*, 223. Also see Bernard, "Peasant Diet," 37–39; Mémoire de la subdélégation de Sarlat pour M. de Tourny, In-

too rich in carbohydrates can contribute to pulmonary illnesses. The extremely low consumption of milk products and fats also resulted in skin lesions and scrofula, which one observer held to be endemic in the region. The loss of teeth undoubtedly stemmed from the lack of Vitamin C, which was destroyed by overcooking vegetables in soups. Swollen bellies and deformed bones, symptoms of rickets, resulted from insufficient Vitamin D, absent from maize and chestnuts.[76]

Diet in the Périgord, as elsewhere, was an infallible indicator of socioeconomic status. On the basis of diet, Pierre de La Servolle, a doctor and correspondent of the Royal Society of Medicine who wrote a meticulous memoir on the nursing of infants and the care of children, distinguished between three types of poor among the women of the countryside near Montignac. The first group consisted of the wives of landowners who worked their own land. These women worked primarily at home, did not perform hard labor in the fields, and twice daily ate soup made with salt pork and vegetables. They normally ate bread composed of two-thirds wheat flour and one-third cornmeal, and consumed chestnuts, eggs, and fruit. They often drank wine with their meals. The second group consisted of the wives of poorer peasants who owned smaller plots or were sharecroppers. These women worked in the fields with their husbands and were therefore exposed to the rigors of the weather. They ate coarser food than women in the first group, but they, too, drank wine or water-diluted wine with their meals. Their soup, ordinarily made with *herbes* (peas, lentils, green vegetables), walnut oil, garlic, onions, and salt, was eaten with bread made almost entirely of maize. Women in the third category were the wives of journaliers, domestiques, and beggars, none of whom possessed fields or a house of their own. These wives labored alongside their husbands on the land of others, sometimes traveling quite far to their daily work. They took their infants to the fields with them, placing them in the shel-

---

tendant de Guyenne, August 5, 1743, C 1317, ADG. Périgourdins were, nonetheless, taller than the inhabitants of the Limousin. Army recruits from the departments of Corrèze and Haute-Vienne, where the inhabitants relied heavily on chestnuts, were among the shortest in France (Corbin, *Archaïsme et modernité en Limousin*, 103).

76. Bernard, "Peasant Diet," 39. The most significant disorder that resulted from heavy reliance on maize was pellagra, which was noted in 1767 at Périgueux, in 1776 at Brantôme, and in 1773 at Saint-Perdoux-de-Marceuil, where it reportedly left some inhabitants insane (Beaudry, "Alimentation et population rurale," 53–54; also see Abel Poitrineau, *La Vie rurale en Basse-Auvergne au XVIIIe siècle* [Paris, 1965], 106–108).

ter of a tree and nursing them when they cried. "The nourishment of these unfortunate mothers," La Servolle wrote, "is scarcely different from that of animals."[77]

In the predominantly agricultural society of the Périgord, where commerce and industry were of limited importance, socioprofessional structure was relatively simple. Apart from the few bona fide ports, most parishes along the Dordogne and Vézère rivers were not noticeably affected by their proximity to lines of communication, and their socioprofessional structure was therefore scarcely distinguishable from that of land-locked parishes. In contrast, truly riverine parishes were characterized by a more complex structure of occupations. Cut off from upland forests and deprived of large expanses of arable, the inhabitants of such communities had little choice but to rely on the river for their livelihood.[78]

Within the parish of Domme, situated on the bluff overlooking the Dordogne and highly involved in river trade, marriage acts for the years between 1800 and 1820 reveal that approximately 61 percent of married men were involved in agricultural work as journaliers, *travailleurs,* sharecroppers, and *cultivateurs* or *laboureurs* (small proprietors). During roughly the same period (1802–15), only 49 percent of grooms in the parish of Saint-Cyprien, another river port, were engaged in agricultural trades. In contrast, the same category represented 70 percent of occupations in the rural, highland parishes of Audrix and Marnac. Only 29 percent of grooms in the parish of Domme were artisans, as were 27 percent in the seventeen parishes in the canton of Saint-Cyprien, where they were employed (in descending order of importance) in textiles (as carders, weavers, and tailors), woodworking (as coopers, *feuillardiers,* charcoal burners, and boat carpenters), building (as masons and joiners), ironwork, the food trades, and tanning.[79]

77. Mémoire . . . de M. La Servolle, February, 1770, C 475, ADG.

78. Cocula, *Les Gens de la rivière de Dordogne,* 565–66, 568–71.

79. Within Saint-Cyprien itself, greater variety existed among the artisanry. Whereas villages in the rest of the canton possessed only millers and tavern keepers, Saint-Cyprien had bakers, butchers, and distillers—not to mention glassworkers, two spurriers, three master wigmakers, two gunsmiths, and one pewterer (G. Florenty, "Saint-Cyprien," 104; F. Florenty, "Etude démographique," 26). It should be noted that in the Southwest many persons classified as *laboureurs* were, in fact, sharecroppers. Georges Bussière states that a man who worked a specific piece of land was commonly referred to

Among the *notables* of both Saint-Cyprien and Domme were a relatively small number of merchants—1 to 2 percent of the active population. The bourg of Saint-Cyprien, considered apart from its canton, counted 2.4 percent of its population as merchants. Much more numerous were members of the judicial and administrative professions (clerks, notaries, *praticiens*, attorneys) and the medical profession (doctors, surgeons, veterinaries), as well as bourgeois and nobles, who constituted 9.4 percent of the active population of Saint-Cyprien and 6.8 percent of that of Domme at the end of the century. As much was true in Périgueux, where members of the liberal professions, especially *hommes de loi*—judges, bailiffs, clerks, attorneys, and notaries—were responsible for as much as 16 to 17 percent of the *capitation* (royal head tax) assessments. In short, although the Périgord at the end of the eighteenth century was overwhelmingly rural in character and backward in commercial development, it counted among its populace a relatively large number of individuals from the liberal professions.[80]

In the early nineteenth century, the proportion of the total population that paid 200 francs in taxes and therefore qualified to vote under the July Monarchy (1830–48) was disproportionately smaller in the Dordogne (5.5 percent) than in France as a whole (6.8 percent), or even in neighboring departments that were equally agricultural in character. Only 4.3 percent of the total population in the arrondissement of Sarlat qualified as electors. More significantly, a disproportionately high percentage (approximately 20 percent) of the electors from the Dordogne were *hommes de loi*—especially notaries—who considered their professional status to be equal or secondary in importance to their status as landowners. In comparison with other areas in the Dordogne and elsewhere in France, the arrondissement of Sarlat contained a striking percentage of electors from the liberal professions: 21.9 percent, as opposed to 15.4 percent for Bergerac, 9.6 percent for Toulouse,

---

in the Périgord as a *laboureur* (Boutier, "Jacqueries en pays croquant," 771–72; Bussière, *Etudes historiques sur la Révolution en Périgord* [3 vols.; Bordeaux, 1877–1903], III, 238).

80. The term *marchand* was applied to individuals of widely divergent profession and fortune, from *marchands-colporteurs* (peddlers) to négociants. In the predominantly rural canton of Saint-Cyprien considered as a whole, professionals and *notables* constituted only 4.7 percent of the active population (F. Florenty, "Etude démographique," 89; G. Florenty, "Saint-Cyprien," 104–105, 561; Cocula, "Vivre et survivre en Périgord," in Higounet-Nadal [ed.], *Histoire du Périgord,* 230–31).

12.8 percent for Albi, 10.8 percent for Castres, and 9.3 percent for Moissac. This unusually high percentage derived not only from Sarlat's status as an administrative and judicial center but also from the relative weakness of its commercial sector. Whereas 37.1 percent of electors in the arrondissement of Toulouse, 27.3 percent of those from Castres, and 19.4 percent of those from Albi (all administrative and judicial centers) were listed as industrialists, merchants, or bankers, only 10.8 percent of electors from Sarlat were involved in commerce. In other words, the distinctive socioprofessional profile of Sarlat's electors derives as much from its relative isolation from commercial currents as from its position as the center of an *élection*, a subdelegation, and a sénéchaussée.[81]

Further examination of Périgourdin *notables* in the early nineteenth century confirms the view that the area was not dominated by wealthy, large landowners. Although cadastral studies reveal a disparity of landed wealth, the Dordogne does not appear to be extreme in this respect in comparison with other regions in France. Alongside the few hundred large proprietors existed a sizable proportion of well-off peasants (*coqs de village*), an influential rural bourgeoisie, and a large group of independent and semi-independent small landowners. Many of the wealthiest landowners apparently resided on their land, especially in the south of the department, near Bergerac, and all along the Dordogne River valley. In the canton of Sarlat, almost all the large landowners lived either in the same commune as their holdings or in the neighboring commune. A picture of the Sarladais *notables* therefore emerges in which bourgeois and noble proprietors of moderate wealth remained intimately involved in working their lands, whether they exploited their holdings directly by employing domestiques or indirectly by confiding them to sharecroppers.[82]

Within the *élection* of Périgueux, the nobility was most solidly entrenched in the north, in the valleys of the Isle and Auvézère rivers. The picture is quite different in the southern part of the *élection*, between

81. Gibson, "Les Notables et l'Eglise," 73–75, 77. For a comparison with areas in the nearby Limousin, see Corbin, *Archaïsme et modernité en Limousin,* 226–29.

82. Crouzy, "La Terre et l'homme en Sarladais," 152–54; Gibson, "Les Notables et l'Eglise," 83–86, 89–90, 95, 100–102, 124; P. Robert, *L'Agriculture en Dordogne* (Bordeaux, 1958), 109. For a comparison with the *notables* of Limousin, see Corbin, *Archaïsme et modernité en Limousin,* 261–62.

the Isle and the Dordogne rivers, where noble holdings were often heavily forested and produced modest revenues. Fraud and concealment alone cannot explain the modesty of the declared income of many Périgourdin nobles, who lived in need, if not poverty. According to the *dixième* rôles of 1711 and 1712, less than 15 percent of nobles admitted or declared more than 1,000 livres in annual income; most had incomes below 200 livres, the equivalent of the return from leasing out a few farms or from one métairie. To avoid derogation, some nobles managed family enterprises such as forges, or somewhat clandestinely engaged in commerce.[83]

At the pinnacle of the aristocracy were approximately 40 Périgourdin nobles who counted annual revenues in excess of 25,000 livres each. These were heads of the old titled families that held parishes in virtual fiefdom and lived in their ancestral châteaus. But Latapie reported few such patriarchs during his travels. The comte de Saint-Exupéry, who, according to Latapie, "spent his life caring for the poor and mediating the disputes of his neighbors," possessed an annual income of only 10,000 livres. Even if the patriarchs themselves resided on their lands, their sons left home to seek their fortunes at court or in the army; their daughters often remained unmarried for lack of an appropriate dowry or a suitable partner.[84]

In other Sarladais parishes, great nobles were altogether absent. There were no large domains in Plazac, for example, where two nobles possessed only four or five métairies or mills each. Among the 320 persons who paid the taille in 1783 were 90 small proprietors who paid between 10 and 40 livres each, 30 who held 1 or 2 métairies each, and 4 who possessed 3 to 5 métairies each. Approximately half as many (58) of the *taillables* were either sharecroppers or bordiers, and another 25 were designated as journaliers. An additional 68 persons of unknown profession who paid 1 to 10 livres each were undoubtedly mostly sharecroppers and journaliers. The only large proprietors of the parish were the Tibeyrant and the Dalbavie, bourgeois who had

---

83. An inquest of 1725 revealed that 30 percent of 400 noble families in the Basse-Auvergne had annual incomes of less than 500 livres each (Poitrineau, *La Vie rurale en Basse-Auvergne*, 631–32; Cocula, "Vivre et survivre en Périgord," in Higounet-Nadal [ed.], *Histoire du Périgord*, 226).

84. Latapie, "L'Industrie et le commerce en Guienne," 432–33; Cocula, "Vivre et survivre en Périgord," in Higounet-Nadal (ed.), *Histoire du Périgord*, 227.

rounded out their holdings in the course of the century at the expense of their neighbors, many of them *hobereaux*—poor country nobles who periodically sold a métairie to liquidate debts. The holdings of these two dominant families greatly surpassed in number, value, and extent the domains of the few local seigneurs.[85]

Large landholdings by privileged persons were relatively uncommon and generally confined to parishes in which only a small proportion of the land was arable. In the parish of Urval—situated on the steep bluff above the Dordogne River, crisscrossed with ravines, and containing poor soil—land belonging to three privileged persons (two of them nobles) generated half the parish revenue in 1761 and 1762. A comparable situation existed in the interior parish of Saint-Pompon, the majority of which lay in briars and heather, where land belonging to three noblemen generated 35 percent of parish revenues. In contrast, the parish of Marnac contained some of the best alluvial soils in the *élection*. Competition for the fertile land was intense, and innumerable small peasant and bourgeois proprietors predominated. Here privileged holdings generated only 9.4 percent of the estimated parish revenue.[86] Nearer Bergerac the picture is complicated by the higher revenue produced by intensive viticulture and the greater proportion of land held by privileged bourgeois. Within the Sarladais as a whole, the contrast between parishes was striking: Lowland parishes generally were richer, smaller in surface area, and dominated by fragmented holdings; wooded upland parishes were poorer, larger in extent, and more likely to contain a higher proportion of large, privileged holdings. Overall, the surface area of the department that was in noble hands in the first half of the nineteenth century was almost exactly 10 percent.[87]

85. Secondat, "Evolution économique d'une communauté rurale," *Bulletin de la Société Historique et Archéologique du Périgord*, CII (1975), 179.

86. Mémoires pour la refonte générale de l'élection de Sarlat pour connaître le revenu de toutes les paroisses, *ca.* 1762, C 1317, ADG.

87. The proportion of noble holdings in the Auvergne tended to be smaller in the mountainous areas, rarely 20 percent, and generally about 30 percent (and up to 50 percent) in the plains (Poitrineau, *La Vie rurale en Basse-Auvergne*, 148–55). For the proportions in France as a whole, see Ernest Labrousse *et al., Des derniers temps de l'âge seigneurial aux préludes de l'âge industriel (1660–1789)* (Paris, 1970), 475–77, Vol. II of Fernand Braudel and Ernest Labrousse (eds.), *Histoire économique et sociale de la France,* 4 vols.; Ralph Gibson, "The French Nobility in the Nineteenth Century—Particularly in the Dordogne," in Jolyon Howorth and Philip G. Cerny (eds.), *Elites in France: Origins, Reproduction and Power* (London, 1981), 15.

The Sarladais has traditionally been known as "a feudal *pays* par excellence, a *pays* of cottages and châteaus." In reality, however, nobles in the Sarladais were no more numerous than elsewhere. Yet, as already mentioned, they did reside on their lands and had the reputation of being involved not only in the cultivation of their holdings but also in day-to-day parish affairs—perhaps as a direct corollary of their relative impoverishment. In contrast, Desmarest in the early 1760s describes a local noble in the vicinity of Bourdeilles who neglected his property and lived in idleness:

> Early each morning [he] hurries to swell the ranks of the idlers who put on airs and promenade in the marketplace. There he discusses in his Gascon patois whatever news may have come his way, talking about affairs of state while he neglects his own. This swarm of idlers successively besieges all of the shops. I have no idea what people think of this sort of life, but I believe it is dangerous for public morality to have idlers such as these make spectacles of themselves. Moreover, this sort of spectacle is very common in the small towns of the Périgord.[88]

In the Sarladais, however, nobles were reputed to be quite traditional in their mentality and behavior, struggling to sustain the reciprocal ties that formerly had bound them to their vassals.

Although mutual hostility and suspicion had come more and more to characterize relations between vassals and seigneurs, glimmerings of their former solidarity against outsiders (especially representatives of the royal government) still appeared occasionally. River parishes often united to protect their *bateliers* (boatmen) from the navy commissioners who came to claim them for naval duty. Boat owners, vineyard proprietors, and merchants all depended on the services of the boatmen and therefore conspired to shelter them from royal agents. Bateliers could also rely on the protection offered by the local nobility, which possessed its own privileged network of clients outside the control of the local administration and royal government. A commissioner for the navy discovered as much in 1781, when he visited the Sarladais to recruit sailors. He reported that in Sarlat: "I was received rather coldly. Here the nobility controls the people, and it does not appear to be favorably disposed toward my work." Despite or perhaps because of the nobility's relative poverty, traditional mentality, close involvement

---

88. Bussière, *Etudes historiques*, III, 234; Remarques de Desmarest.

in parish affairs, and pretensions toward paternalism, both the peasantry and bourgeoisie reputedly resented the nobles of the Sarladais.[89]

Seigneurialism in the Périgord remained important and profitable. In general, proprietors were not "capitalists" in that they did not seek to consolidate their holdings and to maximize their profits by exploiting salaried labor. Their essential goal was rather the simple reproduction of rent, ideally seigneurial rent, which required little or no investment. The tensions spawned by the seigneurial system were not peculiar to the last years of the Old Regime; they had always existed between peasants who wished to extract themselves from seigneurial dependence and seigneurs who wished to keep and expand their rights. But during the three decades prior to the Revolution, seigneurs in the Southwest apparently did intensify their pressure on the peasantry by reviving lapsed dues, revising *terriers* (estate registers), and, in general, managing their estates more efficiently. The result was increased popular resentment of seigneurialism and the privileged order that reinforced it. Moreover, bourgeois involvement in the seigneurial regime was pronounced in the Sarladais. Because rural bourgeois often acted as attorneys, notaries, fiscal agents, and judges for seigneurs, they found themselves targets of peasant hostility in 30 percent of the incidents occurring during the winter of 1789–90. What was truly unusual about the Revolutionary crisis of those years, however, was the conjuncture of an economic crisis with the collapse of the powers that governed the countryside.[90]

At the summit of the Périgourdin Third Estate existed a bourgeoisie that was primarily professional and only secondarily commercial in character. Although many of its members practiced a profession and lived in town, it remained firmly rooted in the countryside. It was composed almost entirely of *rentiers du sol,* landed proprietors who often regarded their profession of notary, attorney, doctor, or legal practitioner as an ancillary activity that facilitated the achievement of their main goals: economic stability, social respectability, and political influence. One sector of this bourgeoisie, the *hommes de loi,* apparently became wealthier and more influential within the liberal professions as

89. Cocula, *Les Gens de la rivière de Dordogne,* 177; Gibson, "Les Notables et l'Eglise," 239–43.

90. Harvest dues in the Southwest were among the highest in the kingdom. See Peter M. Jones, *The Peasantry in the French Revolution* (Cambridge, Eng., 1988), 44, 48–49, 54–57. Also see Boutier, "Jacqueries en pays croquant," 766–67, 771, 778–79.

the eighteenth century progressed. As late as the July Monarchy, twice as many members of the liberal professions (especially *hommes de loi*) qualified as electors in the canton of Sarlat as did bankers, merchants, and manufacturers.[91]

Members of this rural bourgeoisie generally dwelled in villages and remained close to the land. In effect, they were the dominant force in the countryside. It was they who most often held the debts of the peasantry, which accumulated alarmingly in the early nineteenth century. Moreover, families such as the Tibeyrant and Dalbavie of Plazac possessed a virtual monopoly on the collection and farming out of the tithe and *rentes* (seigneurial dues) of the parish. They lent seed and grain to all whose harvest fell short, sold to all who could pay, and profited from the bankruptcy of local landowners.[92]

Below them existed a minority of *laboureurs* and *cultivateurs* who had patiently accumulated their holdings at the expense of the poorest peasants and most indebted nobles. Aspiring toward bourgeois status, they were anxious to safeguard and conceal their wealth, which they knew was vulnerable to the taille assessor, a subsistence crisis, or a personal tragedy. Such a tragedy could suddenly destroy the family unit and transform their children into orphans, who were usually placed as shepherds and domestiques on neighboring farms. Although these better-off peasants are often difficult to detect in records of the period, they can be distinguished from the uniformly poor journaliers, who ordinarily declared only a few sheets and pieces of furniture among their assets valued at approximately 300 livres. In contrast, the marriage portion of *cultivateurs* in the parish of Domme averaged more than 900 livres and ranged as high as 3,720 livres.[93]

Clerics constituted perhaps 2 or 3 percent of the population in the

91. In the recruitment of priests within the diocese of Périgueux, the liberal professions sponsored one-third of all vocations throughout the century. Before 1750 doctors and notaries predominated; during the latter half of the century *hommes de loi* and royal officials did (Mandon, "Les Curés en Périgord," 24–27).

92. Secondat, "Evolution économique d'une communauté rurale," *Bulletin de la Société Historique et Archéologique du Périgord,* CIII (1976), 34–35; Gibson, "Les Notables et l'Eglise," 103–107; Gibson, "The French Nobility in the Nineteenth Century," 33–35.

93. Cocula, "Vivre et survivre en Périgord," in Higounet-Nadal (ed.), *Histoire du Périgord,* 223–24; G. Florenty, "Saint-Cyprien," 103. One can identify small proprietors in the register of bidders for the sale of biens nationaux of the clergy in 1791 in the district of Belvès (Becquart, "La Vente des biens nationaux," 292–96).

diocese of Périgueux, with approximately 1 curé per 550 inhabitants in the eighteenth century. Given the entrenched traditions and isolation of many parishes, curés had difficulty making inroads into popular indifference to official religion. Since the diocese experienced the effects of the Counter-Reformation relatively late—and then only briefly—it began to undergo dechristianization after 1772 before it was even properly christianized. As a result, anguished curés often complained that the religious mentality of the Périgourdin population in the late eighteenth and early nineteenth centuries was characterized by a profound ignorance of Church doctrines and by polytheistic or even animistic beliefs, coupled with a lively interest in the secular affairs and affective life of the parish.[94] The nadir of formal religious practice in the region was probably reached during the July Monarchy. When curés were asked in 1838 to describe the status of Christian worship in their parishes, they lamented that the populace was generally superstitious and apathetic if not irreligious.[95]

Périgourdin curés, mindful of popular resistance to religious instruction and perhaps overwhelmed by the magnitude of their task, used all available methods to lure their parishioners into church. During the shortages of the winter and spring of 1768–69, for example, the curé of Sarlat decided to assemble different groups of poor on Sundays and feast days to explain that they must bear their poverty with patience, to warn them not to desert or abandon the cultivation of their lands, and to instruct them in the spirit of religion, which, he believed, most of them did not practice for lack of being acquainted with it. To attract them to religious instruction, he decided to meet their temporal needs at least for the day in question and therefore distributed bread after religious services. He had the consolation of seeing more than eight hundred poor people—fathers, mothers, and children; journaliers and sharecroppers—eagerly come to the designated churches in the hope

94. Mandon, "Les Curés en Périgord," 79. Calvinism was almost entirely confined to the Bergeracois and a few enclaves, such as Le Bugue (Anne-Marie Cocula, "L'Apprentissage de l'ordre," in Higounet-Nadal [ed.], *Histoire du Périgord*, 203–205; Gibson, "Les Notables et l'Eglise," 46–48).

95. See especially the responses of the curés of Agonac, Notre-Dame-de-Sanilhac, Savignac-les-Eglises, and Saint-Sulpice-d'Excideuil (Notices sur les paroisses du diocèse, 1838, 3 V5 38, ADD). In 1864 the curé of the parish of Ars remarked, "Leave a parish without a priest for twenty years and the people will worship animals" (Gibson, "Les Notables et l'Eglise," 55).

that after having attended mass or catechism they would receive enough bread for the day.[96]

Curés of the Périgord theoretically were drawn from any family (noble or non-noble) able to guarantee the candidate an annual income of 100 livres or pledge property equivalent to at least 2,000 livres. In reality, however, all members of the agricultural professions were excluded, as were 90 percent of those of other professions. Whereas in other dioceses recruitment from rural milieux seems to have become more comon in the eighteenth century, in the dioceses of Périgueux and Bordeaux this was not the case. Although the required income of 100 livres per year was no longer the obstacle it had been in the seventeenth century, annual room and board in the seminaries was 200 livres, with few scholarships available. Counter-Reformation prelates, believing that the priest had to be a scholar to carry out his functions and wishing to dissuade those with purely mercenary motives from entering the seminary, required that candidates for the priesthood undergo twelve years of training. Consequently, only quite wealthy families could afford to support a seminarian.[97]

Issued from the wealthier milieux of society, Périgourdin curés possessed revenues in the middle range of incomes in the region and generally enjoyed a standard of living superior to that of the poor nobility. On the eve of the Revolution, they received an average *bénéfice* (revenue) of between 1,667 and 1,870 livres: 40 percent possessed revenues of more than 2,000 livres, and 33 percent had incomes between 1,000 and 2,000 livres. Moreover, the value of the average bénéfice—even after adjustment for inflation—had risen approximately 25 percent over the previous sixty years. The typical income of a curé in the diocese of Périgueux was nonetheless comparable with that of priests in the rest of France. The curé was in many respects a rentier du sol; he derived income not only from the tithe but also from seigneurial rents and the direct cultivation or lease of lands in his possession. Because of

96. Mémoire du curé de Sarlat, January, 1769, Lettre de Meyrignac, subdélégué de Sarlat, à M. l'Intendant, January 3, 1769, both in C 3650, ADG; Mémoire du curé de Sarlat à Monseigneur de Farges, Intendant, 1769, C 467, ADG.

97. Mandon, "Les Curés en Périgord," 26–31, 35–36, 109, 117. Timothy Tackett discovered that 98 percent of curés in the diocese of Gap were commoners (*Priest and Parish in Eighteenth-Century France: A Social and Political Study of the Curés in a Diocese of Dauphiné, 1750–1791* [Princeton, 1977], 174).

the tithe, the curé found himself in possession of a sizable surplus of cereals, which he, in turn, sold on the market. In times of shortage or famine, the actual value of his portion was, of course, even higher.[98]

The tithe contributed the essential part of the curé's income, which rose significantly faster than the cost of living. The actual growth in the product of the tithe occurred especially in the last twenty years of the Old Regime, influenced by some changes in the agricultural regime. Maize, when first introduced to the Périgord, was grown only in small amounts, and curés therefore did not always bother to collect on it, or did so at a lower rate. But curés were generally quite attentive to agricultural conditions in their parishes, and as the crop became more widespread—owing in part to its exemption from the tithe—they began to take legal recourse to obtain payment or a higher rate of payment on maize. As a result, in some parishes it was even subject to the *grosse dîme* and was included in almost all of the declarations of revenue made in 1791. Thanks to the tithe, about 8 percent of the total parish harvest (before taxes) ended up in the curé's barn, providing him with a security quite unknown to the great majority of his parishioners. Because most curés of the diocese measured their revenues in thousands, their status was on the order of *une très honnête aisance*—that of a well-off bourgeois or of a nobleman able to maintain himself at a level appropriate to his position without derogation.[99]

The typical presbytère was a two-story dwelling, with the kitchen and other common rooms below and at least three rooms above used as a study and bedrooms. Near the building were a barn, stable, poultry yard, and commons large enough to provide wood and pasture. Given his wealth, the curé was an important employer in the parish, hiring *valets de ferme,* domestiques, spinners, and artisans, not to mention field hands during the harvest season. He often made in-kind loans to his parishioners and therefore was in an excellent position to profit

98. The tithe in the diocese of Périgueux was, on the average, one-twelfth, which was high when compared with rates in the diocese of Bordeaux, but modest when compared with those in lower Languedoc or the Pyrenées (one-tenth), not to mention those in Brittany (one-seventh to one-eighth) (Mandon, "Les Curés en Périgord," 247, 258–59, 268, 276–79). Tackett found that more than 90 percent of the curés in Gap had ecclesiastic incomes of less than 1,000 livres each, with the average income being between 500 and 750 livres. But compared with curés in the rest of France, the clergy of the Dauphiné was relatively disfavored economically (*Priest and Parish,* 118–19, 144–46).

99. Mandon, "Les Curés en Périgord," 292–94, 376–77.

from the rise in agricultural prices that occurred in the course of the eighteenth century.[100]

As collector of the tithe and supervisor of his parishioners' morality, the curé often met with resentment and friction in his relations with his flock. A significant cause of conflict apparently was the rural population's adherence to sub-Christian if not pre-Christian religious practices. If one is to believe the anguished complaints of the curés, Christian worship in the Périgord was characterized by a profound ignorance of the tenets of the faith, recourse to syncretistic practices, and an inclination to regard the curé as a kind of wizard with magical powers. Bishops often attempted to enlist the aid of the curés in their campaign against popular ignorance of official liturgy, against celebrations that too often degenerated into scenes of debauchery and license, and against cabarets that remained open during holy services.

In 1760 the archpriest of the diocese of Périgueux complained to the intendant about disorderly feast-day gatherings in the parish of Audrix, on the plateau above Saint-Cyprien, which attracted inhabitants from a dozen surrounding parishes. He noted that the feast itself was suspect because it revered "Saint Valery," who was not even recognized as a saint in the diocese. Furthermore, the so-called devotions were purely secular in nature: The feast was a fair at which merchants set up stalls in the cemetery alongside the church. The curé complained: "There one sees several cabarets filled with people into the night. Drunkenness, swearing, blasphemy, arguments, obscene songs, quarrels, and battles are the consequences of this so-called fête. Here is the meeting place for all intrigues and the scene of the most scandalous activity." He further lamented that he had been forced to tolerate this situation for seven or eight years. Because his own efforts to intervene had proved not only futile but dangerous, he asked the intendant to forbid the inhabitants of the surrounding parishes to attend the fête, and to send mounted constables of the maréchaussée to curb these public excesses.[101]

---

100. *Ibid.*, 432; Labrousse *et al.*, *Des derniers temps de l'âge seigneurial*, 396.

101. Correspondance, 1760, C 473, ADG; Mandon, "Les Curés en Périgord," 510–11, 506–507. Tackett notes, "Objections by curés to their parishioners' profane celebrations of religious holidays were a prevailing theme throughout the eighteenth century in the diocese of Gap" (*Priest and Parish*, 213). For other examples of clerical attempts to limit or abolish acts of popular impiety, see 204–208. Examples from the nine-

In contrast, many other curés acted as intermediaries between the bishop and their parishioners. For fear of losing the confidence or gaining the animosity of their flocks, they often tacitly indulged popular credulity by ringing church bells to ward off hailstorms and by organizing processions to appeal for good weather. Far from acting as iconoclasts, some Périgourdin curés seem to have modified their pastoral activity to conform to the expectations of traditional popular piety. In these instances, the curé himself often contributed to the resultant synthesis of popular and official worship. Abundant evidence nonetheless testifies to the confrontation of two religious cultures, official and popular.[102]

Additional sources of serious conflict between curés and their parishioners were questions concerning collection of the tithe and honorific rights. Lawsuits readily arose over disagreements on the rate of the tithe and its application to various crops. Whereas some cases were rapidly resolved before a notary at minimal cost to both parties, others dragged on for years, sometimes even decades. In the eighteenth century, the Sénéchaussée of Périgueux considered fifty-six lawsuits involving curés and lay parishioners in disputes over the tithe, half of them contesting its application to maize. One-third of the cases were heard between 1770 and 1789. Curés additionally quarreled with parish nobles over the right to possess a pew or a tomb in the parish church. Such conflicts concerning honorific rights occurred more frequently toward the end of the century, as curés were importuned by a growing number of parishioners desirous of signaling their social ascension and more capable of paying for honorific rights. Moreover, many curés personally objected to noble pretensions precisely because they manifested to the assembled parish the supremacy of the château over the presbytère. When curés were prosecuted for verbal or physical violence, the

---

teenth-century Limousin are found in Corbin, *Archaïsme et modernité en Limousin*, 661–77. On the persistence of popular festivals, consult Cocula, "Trois Siècles de carnaval à Sarlat," *Annales du Midi*, XCIII (1981), 5–16.

102. Mandon, "Les Curés en Périgord," 545, 573; Cocula, "L'Apprentissage de l'ordre," in Higounet-Nadal (ed.), *Histoire du Périgord*, 207–208. Also consult Georges Rocal, *Les Vieilles Coutumes dévotieuses et magiques du Périgord* (1922; rpr. Périgueux, 1971). For a comparison of popular piety in the Périgord with that in other regions, see Gérard Bouchard, *Le Village immobile: Sennely-en-Sologne au XVIIIe siècle* (Paris, 1972), 289–93, 339–41; Eugen Weber, *Peasants into Frenchmen: The Modernization of Rural France, 1870–1914* (Stanford, 1976), 343–45, 369–70; Tackett, *Priest and Parish*, 209–15, 220.

plaintiffs were usually nobles or *notables* aspiring to nobility. Because many curés were also nobles, the majority of these conflicts must be seen as essentially squabbles between rivals for power in the parish. In contrast, curés and bourgeois most often clashed over the tithe and questions surrounding the curé's privileged status.[103]

In addition to the tithe, the theme of morality dominated curé-parishioner relations. Even in cases concerning the moral misconduct of curés, charges of abuse in the collection of the tithe were without fail introduced by the plaintiffs. Conversely, although a variety of other issues may have been at the origin of a lawsuit, the moral conduct of the curé was invariably challenged. In many respects, the curé had become a *notable* whose wealth and way of life set him off from his parishioners and made him more imposing—and simultaneously alienated him from his flock. The fact that resentment and bitterness sometimes characterized relations with the curé, who acted both as a representative of secular authority and as a living symbol of Christian morality, is therefore hardly surprising.[104]

Contemporary observers and historians concur that the Sarladais in the late eighteenth century was mired in the stagnant backwaters of France. Limited in its outside contacts to a nonreciprocal trade in agricultural products handled almost exclusively through intermediaries in Bergerac, Libourne, and Bordeaux, the Périgord in general was effectively excluded from the prosperity enjoyed elsewhere in the Aquitaine Basin. Poor soils, rugged topography, and isolation from major markets condemned the region to subsistence polyculture with extremely fragmented units of cultivation. Seen in this light, sharecropping was less a cause of agricultural stagnation than a symptom. Small proprietors and sharecroppers compensated for low productivity by extending the arable or multiplying the number of units under cultivation and by for-

---

103. Mandon, "Les Curés en Périgord," 168–82; Cocula, "L'Apprentissage de l'ordre," in Higounet-Nadal (ed.), *Histoire du Périgord*, 207. Also see Jean-Louis Audebert, "La Criminalité des moeurs dans la Sénéchaussée de Périgueux, 1740–1789," *mémoire* for the D.E.S. (Université de Bordeaux, 1971). Tackett discovered that in lawsuits with laymen, the curé's antagonist was, in more than half the cases, a member of the local elite. Although the single most common subject of litigation was the tithe, honorific rights were also a sore point in the diocese of Gap (*Priest and Parish*, 171–76, 186–89, 192).

104. Mandon, "Les Curés en Périgord," 550–58, 579–82, 588–89, 603, 673; Boutier, "Jacqueries en pays croquant," 769–70.

aging, poaching, and taking seasonal employment in either the vineyards of the Bordelais or the forges and forests of the Périgord. Day
laborers (at one end of the social scale) and large landowners (at the
other) were both disproportionately few in number in the Sarladais,
where the division of land among small proprietors was especially pronounced. One of the few signs of progress on the horizon was the
steady advance of maize cultivation, which permitted even poor cultivators to sell their wheat and thereby pay their taxes and participate,
albeit marginally, in the local market economy.

The cultivation of maize and the freer movement of grain combined
to alleviate the chronic demographic pressure experienced by the inhabitants of the region. The demographic traits of the Old Regime persisted, but in the second half of the century crises were invariably less
severe and more localized, although more numerous. Consequently, although the Périgord remained overpopulated in relation to its resources
and the work it offered its inhabitants, the region nevertheless experienced slow population growth. Overreliance on chestnuts and maize,
however, led to chronic malnutrition, deformities, and disorders stemming from vitamin deficiencies.

With nearly three-quarters of all males engaged principally in agricultural work, the socioprofessional structure of the rural world of the
Périgord was understandably simple. The nobles of the Sarladais were
known for their involvement in local affairs, perhaps as a direct corollary of their relative impoverishment and their residence on ancestral
lands. Traditional in their beliefs and behavior, they demanded deference and apparently often received it. But undercurrents of tension persisted and occasionally surfaced in violence between peasants and seigneurs, who were overzealous in the enforcement of their feudal rights
or ostentatious in observing their honorific privileges. Although old
habits of protection and deference may have survived, they were clearly
eroding under new pressures.

The bourgeoisie of the region was dominated by members of the
liberal professions, especially *hommes de loi,* for whom the management of their landed property was often more important than the exercise of their profession. A few influential merchants such as Dalbavie
and Tibeyrant of Plazac acted as grain bankers and money lenders and
therefore occasionally became the object of individual rancor and retaliation. But as a class, the bourgeoisie successfully deflected popular
animosity and directed it toward the privileged nobility, which pro-

vided a much more visible and therefore convenient target for peasant resentment and bourgeois jealousy. Overall, however, popular culture dominated day-to-day life from the backstreets and marketplace of Sarlat itself to the more isolated reaches of the Sarladais. Members of the educated, French-speaking elite not only understood and spoke patois dialects but also shared many of the assumptions of the *menu peuple,* and much the same world view.

In similar fashion, the curés of the Périgord, although recruited primarily from the ranks of the provincial nobility and bourgeoisie, reflected the influence of popular culture. Indeed, they had little choice but to acknowledge and frequently even condone popular behavior and beliefs that were basically inimical to their proselytizing mission. As recipients of the tithe and possessors of private holdings, they were often the prime beneficiaries of a parish's agricultural wealth as well as its major employers. The collection of the tithe was a source of continual strain if not open conflict between curés and their parishioners. In fact, the peasantry readily accepted maize cultivation in part because this new cereal initially was exempt from the tithe—an oversight that curés attempted to correct via litigation. As a result of the tension generated by the confrontation of two religious cultures, popular and official, many curés found themselves estranged from their parishioners. Within this predominantly rural, traditional setting, old and new sources of disagreement sparked conflicts and provoked forms of criminality that were at least superficially quite familiar, yet increasingly distinctive.

II

Official Justice in the Sarladais

*We must not forget, however, that while the letter of
the law may seem brutally oppressive, sentences in
practice were usually light. The laws were meant to be
deterrent rather than to make people suffer. Though
the authorities committed arbitrary, even violent acts,
this was simply a matter of habit or indifference; at
heart they were kindly disposed.*

—Alexis de Tocqueville, *The Old Régime and the
French Revolution*

Royal justice in the eighteenth-century Sarladais existed on the periphery of a predominantly self-regulating society in
which royal judicial action was still often viewed as intrusive. For cases
below a certain level of gravity, official justice competed with various
modes of conflict resolution internal to the social group and the larger
village community. The impulse toward the informal resolution of disputes arose, not only from a sense of Christian duty and a conviction
that the methods of popular justice were more appropriate, but also
from a distrust and fear of royal justice. Many people therefore avoided
involvement with the royal judicial system and even rebelled against its
interference. They perceived official justice as linguistically foreign, cul-
turally antithetical, financially ruinous, and primarily controlled by
local elites using it for self-advancement. To comprehend this deep-
seated, longstanding resistance to royal justice in the Sarladais, one
must understand the fundamental jurisdictional and legal limitations
within which the Sénéchaussée of Sarlat functioned.

Alongside royal justice existed seigneurial justice—essentially the
privately owned right of a seigneur to exercise judicial functions through

a tribunal. Although reduced in number and somewhat circumscribed in power, seigneurial tribunals in the late eighteenth century still exercised considerable authority and played a significant role in the lives of the populace. In theory, at least, three levels of seigneurial justice existed: low, medium, and high. In civil matters, the right of low justice allowed the seigneurial judge to adjudicate affairs concerning seigneurial dues as well as personal matters between the seigneur and his vassals involving up to fifty sous. In criminal matters, the tribunal ruled on offenses for which fines could not exceed ten sous. Low justices therefore handled very minor affairs, holding their sessions usually once every three months, when they judged accumulated peasant claims and disputes over the enforcement of seigneurial rights.

In civil matters, tribunals of middle justice handled property disputes and cases involving the rights and duties owed the seigneur, with the right to condemn subjects to the fines specified in the *coutumes*. The coutumes were not uniform in the powers given to tribunals of middle justice in criminal affairs. Several coutumes specified that fines could not exceed sixty sous, while others conferred wider powers. In any case, by 1789 inflation had seriously eroded the real value of fines in criminal cases and damages in civil cases. By failing to increase the monetary limits, the Crown had effectively reduced the competence of tribunals of low and middle justice to the most minor affairs. Tribunals of high, middle, and low justice were nonetheless empowered and obligated by royal law to apprehend all delinquents found in their jurisdictions, imprison them for twenty-four hours, and initiate proceedings. If the offense merited greater punishment or a larger fine than the tribunal could impose, the tribunal was obliged to conduct the prisoner, along with the case transcript, to the next highest jurisdiction.[1]

Tribunals of high justice possessed more extensive powers. The judge had the right to adjudicate all civil matters between the seigneur's subjects and those disputes between the seigneur and his subjects concerning seigneurial rights. He could not preside over cases involving the seigneur alone. In criminal matters, the right of high justice included the power to adjudicate all sorts of offenses committed in the jurisdiction, provided they were committed by domiciled persons (not vaga-

1. Diderot (ed.), *Encyclopédie*, IX, 99; Julius R. Ruff, "Crime, Justice and Public Order in France, 1696–1788: The Sénéchaussée of Libourne" (Ph.D. dissertation, University of North Carolina at Chapel Hill, 1979), 51.

bonds and *gens sans aveu*) and were not included among the serious offenses classed as *cas royaux*. These tribunals could in theory condemn the accused for all sorts of afflictive punishments, and since the death penalty could be handed down, seigneurs had the right to maintain a pillory, a scaffold, and a gibbet. In reality, however, few offenses meriting the death penalty were not classed as cas royaux. As a result, seigneurial justice in the eighteenth century, like royal justice, was probably seldom bloody in practice. Banishment, the *carcan* (iron collar), whippings, and fines were the penalties most often handed down for insults, blows, wounds, and scuffles.[2]

By the end of the Old Regime, the distinctions between the three levels of seigneurial justice were effaced, and the actual authority of seigneurial tribunals was relatively limited. All final sentences were subject to appeal before the sénéchaussée or the parlement. Moreover, the appeals process could be more complicated, leading from one high justice to another and then to a royal *prévôté* before ever reaching the sénéchaussée. In some instances, a case made its way through eight different jurisdictions before reaching final judgment. During the early stages of royal encroachment on seigneurial prerogatives, few seigneurs objected, and many actually welcomed the development. Justice rendered by private tribunals involved the risk of liability for the seigneur and the judge if a superior court overturned the ruling. Owing to this circumstance and the rising cost of maintaining and staffing a court and prison, many municipalities and seigneurs willingly abandoned their judicial powers to royal officials.[3]

Representatives of the Crown used two devices to expand the authority of the royal courts: cas royaux and *prévention*. The Crown declared that because the king represented the common good and owed security and protection to his subjects, certain civil and criminal offenses that directly challenged these interests could be tried only in his courts. For a long while the Crown refused to enumerate these cas

2. Diderot (ed.), *Encyclopédie*, IX, 98. Also see Pierre Goubert, "Le Paysan et la terre: Seigneurie, tenure, exploitation," in Labrousse *et al.*, *Des derniers temps de l'âge seigneurial*, 123. For a complete listing of civil and criminal cas royaux, see Roland Mousnier, *Les Institutions de la France sous la monarchie absolue* (2 vols.; Paris, 1974, 1980), I, 404, II, 265–67.

3. John P. Dawson, *A History of Lay Judges* (Cambridge, Mass., 1960), 68; Goubert, "Le Paysan et la terre," in Labrousse *et al.*, *Des derniers temps de l'âge seigneurial*, 123.

royaux—to do so would have meant, in effect, to limit them. The Ordinance of 1670 finally specified the following criminal cas royaux: treason, sacrilege with breaking and entry, rebellion, unlawful assembly, sedition, popular disturbances, counterfeiting, and kidnapping.[4]

The right of *prévention* permitted royal judges to claim cases over which seigneurial judges were fully competent. This right was designed to assure the prosecution of offenses by allowing a royal judge to claim competence simply by warning or notifying the subordinate judge that he intended to do so. Unless the seigneurial judge began proceedings within twenty-four hours of a crime's commission, the royal judge could claim competence over it, in virtually any affair. In practice, however, seigneurial tribunals were left a real but limited sphere of action, especially in civil cases.[5]

Although by the end of the eighteenth century the Crown had succeeded in limiting the jurisdiction of seigneurial and municipal tribunals, many still remained active. In eighteenth-century Brittany, an estimated 90 percent of judicial business was handled by seigneurial tribunals, of which approximately 3,905 existed in 1769, or 3 tribunals to each parish. Twenty years later, approximately 2,500 tribunals still existed in Brittany alone, of which one-third were courts of high justice.[6] The city of Le Mans in 1753, with 2,036 houses, fell under the jurisdiction of 29 seigneurial tribunals, without counting the resident sénéchaussée. The Rouergue encompassed 600 such tribunals; the Sénéchaussée of Angers held 29, that of Saumur 19.[7] In 1764 the séné-

---

4. Mousnier provides a more complete list of criminal and civil cas royaux, the latter including affairs concerning the royal domains, churches, hospitals, academies, religious orders, taxes, the rights of royal officers, ecclesiastic bénéfices, and the freedom of the Gallican church (*Les Institutions de la France*, I, 392, II, 265–67). Also see Marcel Marion, *Dictionnaire des institutions de la France aux XVIIe et XVIIIe siècles* (1923; rpr. Paris, 1976), 73–74.

5. Pierre-Jean-Jacques-Guillaume Guyot *et al.*, *Répertoire universel et raisonné de jurisprudence civile, criminelle, canonique et bénéficiale* (17 vols.; Paris, 1784–85), XIII, 537.

6. J. Dawson, *A History of Lay Judges*, 79; John Mackrell, "Criticism of Seigneurial Justice in Eighteenth-Century France," in John F. Bosher (ed.), *French Government and Society, 1500–1850: Essays in Memory of Alfred Cobban* (London, 1973), 124. Also see André Giffard, *Les Justices seigneuriales en Bretagne au XVIIe et XVIIIe siècles* (Paris, 1903), 307.

7. Raoul Aubin, *L'Organisation judiciaire d'après les cahiers de 1789* (Paris, 1928), 46–47; Paul Bois, *Paysans de l'Ouest* (Abridged ed., Paris, 1971), 174; Mackrell, "Criticism of Seigneurial Justice," 124–25.

chaussées of Périgueux, Sarlat, and Bergerac contained 158, 109, and 32 separate seigneurial and municipal tribunals respectively, or a total of 299 for the entire Périgord.[8]

An examination of the daily workings of seigneurial tribunals reveals their continued importance in the lives of the populace. A *seigneurie* carried with it the right of justice exercised over the property belonging to the seigneur as well as over the hereditary holdings of peasants otherwise free of seigneurial obligations. Implicit in this right was the seigneur's obligation to maintain at his own expense a courtroom, a clerk's office, and a prison, as well as the appropriate personnel to staff them. He paid for the subsistence of foundlings discovered within the jurisdiction until they reached an age of self-sufficiency. The seigneur was also bound to subsidize a portion of the costs of prosecuting crimes committed within his jurisdiction that were seized by royal judges exercising the right of *prévention*. Although seigneurial judges habitually shunned criminal cases because of their high cost and low return, tribunals welcomed civil cases and continued to act in a notarial capacity, registering all sales, exchanges, donations, and successions; protecting minors; and nominating tutors and curators. With each act, they levied fees.[9]

Although the criminal competence of seigneurial tribunals was limited in scope and in monetary fines levied, these lower courts played a significant role in the lives of the peasantry. Abel Poitrineau discovered that whereas many seigneurial courts in the lower Auvergne settled cases at the rate of only one per year, others ruled on approximately thirty-five cases each per year. Some courts held hearings every week and examined three or four cases each session. In addition to the seigneurial judge's authority in civil cases, he possessed police powers: care of the roads, fire prevention, protection of vineyards and meadows, sanitation of streets and fountains, and enforcement of regulations barring drinking in cabarets during religious services. Within the

---

8. Bussière, *Etudes historiques,* I, 160–84. Vicomte de Gourgues, in *Dictionnaire topographique du département de la Dordogne comprenant les noms de lieu anciens et modernes* (Paris, 1873), lvi–lviii, gives the figure of 108 for the Sénéchaussée of Sarlat in 1789. Pierre Goubert estimates the total number of seigneurial and municipal tribunals in France at between 20,000 and 30,000 (*Les Pouvoirs* [Paris, 1973], 82, Vol. II of Goubert, *L'Ancien Régime,* 2 vols.). In contrast, Mousnier estimates that 70,000 to 80,000 tribunals were active (*Les Institutions de la France,* I, 401).

9. Goubert, "Le Paysan et la terre," in Labrousse *et al., Des derniers temps de l'âge seigneurial,* 123–24.

tribunal's criminal competence were fighting, insults, disputes over wages, minor hunting and fishing misdemeanors, and depredations by livestock. Through his police powers, the seigneurial judge had control over many aspects of social and economic life, and as an agent of the seigneur, he assured the prompt and exact payment of seigneurial dues. In conflicts between the seigneur and his vassals, the tribunal functioned as both judge and plaintiff.[10]

Seigneurs commissioned judicial officers after a brief inquiry into their qualifications and morals; judges did not have to possess degrees in law. Seigneurial notaries and *sergents* (bailiffs), the latter sometimes illiterate, generally came from the ranks of *praticiens,* those who understood judicial methods and were capable of guiding a case through the various steps of prosecution. Clerks, *sergents,* and prosecutors were all required to know the basics of legal practice and the guidelines for composing legal documents. *Praticiens* even substituted as judges when men with university degrees were unavailable, and often simultaneously held the same office in several courts.[11]

The seigneurial offices of *procureur fiscal* (public prosecutor) and judge were paid at a modest rate and frequently in kind. The office of clerk was usually farmed out for a minor sum, in one case twelve livres per year. Although such offices were occasionally sold and became patrimonial, most seigneurs refused to sell them, thereby maintaining closer control over their court personnel. Qualified candidates were in great demand. In the Auvergne, wine merchants and cabaret owners sometimes acted as judges. Although answerable to the seigneurs they served, they still carefully promoted their own interests and ensured observance of the few privileges their office afforded. Overall, the reluctance of seigneurial officials to initiate criminal prosecution can be attributed to their limited legal jurisdiction and meager financial resources, the absence of fees and lowness of fines in criminal cases, and lack of interest on the part of the seigneur, for whom the possession of a court essentially represented a guaranty of payment of the dues attached to his other patrimonial rights.[12]

10. Poitrineau, *La Vie rurale en Basse-Auvergne,* 637–38. Also see Goubert, "Le Paysan et la terre," in Labrousse *et al., Des derniers temps de l'âge seigneurial,* 124. For a description of the functioning of tribunals in a variety of regions, consult Mousnier, *Les Institutions de la France,* I, 401–409.

11. Guyot *et al., Répertoire,* XIII, 229.

12. Poitrineau, *La Vie rurale en Basse-Auvergne,* 638–40.

Despite the obvious advantages to a seigneur of maintaining his own tribunal, the costs of keeping court steadily increased. Some ecclesiastic seigneurs in the Auvergne began to abandon their jurisdictions to the king in the eighteenth century owing to the growing expense of caring for foundlings. While some local seigneurial jurisdictions in Burgundy maintained their police powers and assured order in the villages, many others disappeared in the course of the century, ceding their place to municipal and royal courts.[13] The royal government may actually have been instrumental in slowing this trend. Whereas in the seventeenth century royal policy toward seigneurial justice was characterized by an aggressive attack on the private right to keep court, in the next century royal policy no longer contested that right and instead concentrated on rendering seigneurial justice more efficient. Criticism to this approach came from humanitarian writers and lawyers whose objections were mostly utilitarian in nature. Putting aside the earlier argument that justice in private hands was wrong in principle and should therefore be abolished, they stressed the corruption and inefficiency of the courts and the rapaciousness of their officers. Society needed cheap and efficient justice, they argued, yet seigneurs were concerned only with protecting their rights.[14]

The royal edicts of the last twenty years of the Old Regime designed to stimulate the seigneurial tribunals to undertake criminal prosecution were intermittent and rarely enforced. The edict of 1771 essentially reiterated the royal right of *prévention* by threatening seigneurs with the entire cost of prosecution if a royal judge seized upon a case normally within the competence of the seigneurial judge; if, however, the seigneurial judge held an inquest and issued an indictment before the royal judge acted, all costs of prosecution would be paid by the Crown. But because the edict was promulgated during the political tur-

13. *Ibid.*, 640. Overall, however, according to Pierre de Saint-Jacob, seigneurs defended their judicial rights and skillfully adapted them to the demands of a money economy (*Les Paysans de la Bourgogne du nord au dernier siècle de l'ancien régime* [Dijon, 1960], 408).

14. Mackrell, "Criticism of Seigneurial Justice," 129–31, 136–38. The Crown had ceased to patronize the school of royal lawyers that had long supported its claims, and could no longer rely on their services. By the eighteenth century, many of them had transferred their loyalties to the opposing side and defended the right of seigneurial justice as an inalienable property right. See William F. Church, "The Decline of the French Jurists as Political Theorists, 1660–1789," *French Historical Studies*, V (1967), 28–29; *De l'administration de la justice dans les campagnes* (N.p., n.d.), 6, 8–10.

moil resulting from the reforms of Maupeou in 1770, it remained largely unenforced—despite the exile of the parlements from 1771 to 1774—and was completely ignored after 1775, with the death of Louis XV and the disgrace of Maupeou.[15]

The next royal effort to prod the seigneurial tribunals into action was the edict of March, 1772, which permitted a seigneurial prosecutor—after summoning the accused—to send a brief of the case to the clerk of the sénéchaussée in whose jurisdiction the tribunal lay so that the king's prosecutor might continue the case at Crown expense. The edict thereby freed seigneurs of further expense in the hope that thereafter they would be less reluctant to initiate costly criminal proceedings and assume greater responsibility for policing the countryside. Although it is difficult to measure the effect of this attempt to revitalize seigneurial justice, one indisputable consequence was that many sénéchaussées were quickly swamped with *grand criminel* cases that afforded little remuneration. In 1781 the magistrates of the Sénéchaussée of Cahors, adjacent to that of Sarlat, complained to the prosecutor general of the Parlement of Bordeaux that "the Sénéchaux find themselves overloaded due to the obligation imposed on them to perform the onerous task of completing cases begun by seigneurial judges . . . with all the onerous and purely gratuitous burden of the multitude of cases that have been referred to them since the edict of 1772 . . . often for cases that never ought to have reached the Sénéchal since they were prévôtal in nature."[16] At least a handful of the tribunals of the Sarladais took advantage of the edict to transfer serious *grand criminel* cases to the sénéchaussée, where approximately 22 percent of all cases heard between 1770 and 1790 were continuances from lower-level courts. Far from falling into abeyance, these seigneurial tribunals instead appear to have been quite active during this period and even to have undergone some revitalization because of the edict of 1772.

When the nation was asked in 1789 to catalog its grievances in the form of *cahiers de doléances,* the populace often responded by focusing on the inconveniences and abuses of seigneurial justice: the multiplicity of jurisdictions, the poor distribution and inaccessibility of courts, the

15. Marion, *Dictionnaire,* 320; Mackrell, "Criticism of Seigneurial Justice," 127.

16. Edict of March, 1772, B 1598, ADD; magistrate quoted in Nicole Castan, *Justice et répression en Languedoc à l'époque des lumières* (Paris, 1980), 126; also see 151–53.

lack of proper facilities and personnel, the rapaciousness and ignorance of the officials, and the ubiquity of procedural irregularities and corruption.[17] But one must look beyond their complaints. Many seigneurial judges doubtlessly pocketed more of the fines than permissible, and notaries and clerks most certainly multiplied paperwork and wrote as largely as possible to increase their meager salaries. But minor judges were not necessarily ignorant and avaricious; moreover, notaries and clerks were essential, especially in regions of high illiteracy such as the Sarladais. Close to the villager, cheaper than royal justice, run by people well acquainted with local customs, and absolutely indispensable in providing everyday services—resolving conflicts, chastising offenders, and drawing up sales, successions, and leases—seigneurial justice was extremely useful to the peasants, though admittedly even more useful to the seigneur.[18]

In 1789 the territory of France comprised thirteen parlements and four sovereign councils of varying size. The Parlement of Paris, the largest of the realm, extended from Calais in the North to La Rochelle, Angoulême, and Lyon in the South, and included approximately ten million inhabitants. At the other extreme, the Parlement of Metz encompassed lower Lorraine and three bishoprics, with a total population of only 360,000. The Parlement of Bordeaux was the second largest of the kingdom, with more than two million people under its jurisdiction in Guyenne, Gascony, Limousin, the Périgord, and Saintonge. A similar disproportion existed among the bailliages and sénéchaussées: Whereas the Bailliage of Alençon in Normandy contained 46 parishes with 22,000 inhabitants, that of nearby Falaise included 242 parishes with

17. Marcel Marion, *La Garde des Sceaux: Lamoignon et la réforme judiciaire de 1788* (Paris, 1905), 254; Aubin, *L'Organisation judiciaire*, 48, 73, 81–82. The *cahier* (list of grievances) of the parish of Saint-Sulpice-de-Roumagnac, in the Sénéchaussée of Périgueux, near Riberac, concisely summarizes the abuses associated with seigneurial justice not only in the Périgord but in all of France (Marion, *Dictionnaire*, 321). Also see Duboscq, "Le Cahier des doléances," 60–65; Noël Becquart, "Le Cahier de doléances de la Roque-Gageac," *Bulletin de la Société Historique et Archéologique du Périgord*, CIII (1976), 207–209. Unpublished *cahiers* also exist for Saint-Avit-Sénieur and Saint-Cyprien.

18. Goubert, "Le Paysan et la terre," in Labrousse *et al.*, *Des derniers temps de l'âge seigneurial*, 124–25. Mousnier argues that seigneurial justices were generally active and prosperous and rendered valuable services (*Les Institutions de la France*, I, 404, 409).

approximately 100,000 inhabitants, and that of Mamers consisted of 56 parishes with 30,000 people. The Sénéchaussée of Sarlat comprised 205 parishes in the late eighteenth century, with a total population of about 115,770.[19]

Because almost all of the 400 to 450 bailliages and sénéchaussées that formed the electoral districts in 1789 were essentially amalgamations of disparate fiefs and often did not include entire parishes, difficulties arose in defining their geographic extent. Furthermore, their limits seldom conformed with those of financial and administrative units under the Old Regime, compounding the confusion. In certain jurisdictions existed enclaves of neighboring sénéchaussées, as in the case of the Sénéchaussée of Périgueux, which included an enclave of the Sénéchaussée of Angoulême. Because of this imprecision, courts were often involved in boundary disputes with neighboring jurisdictions. By 1525 the Sénéchaussée of Sarlat existed as a separate, sedentary court whose geographic extent remained virtually unmodified until its dissolution in 1790. After 1641, the Présidial of Sarlat shared the same geographic jurisdiction and personnel as the sénéchaussée, with only slightly different judicial competence.[20]

Two types of courts administered royal justice, *tribunaux ordinaires* and *tribunaux d'exception*. The "ordinary" courts were, in turn, divided into essentially three classes or degrees. At the lowest level existed *prévôtés royaux,* known in various regions as *vigueries, vicomtés,* and *châtelainies*. Although their competence surpassed that of seigneurial tribunals, it remained quite limited. Royal edicts of the sixteenth century had empowered these courts to hear in the first instance ordi-

19. Aubin, *L'Organisation judiciaire,* 82–83. Also see Gégot, "Etude par sondage de la criminalité," 110; Margot, "La Criminalité dans le bailliage," 188.

20. Etat des paroisses de la Sénéchaussée de Sarlat, B 3601, ADD. This document locates the town of Issigeac and surrounding parishes in the Sénéchaussée of Sarlat, yet later sources show them as part of the Sénéchaussée of Bergerac. See the map of Armand Brette in *Atlas des bailliages ou juridictions assimilées ayant formé unité électorale en 1789* (Paris, 1904) and that found in Germaine Chapgier-Laboissière, "Guillaume Gontier de Biran, subdélégué de Bergerac (1743–1766)," *Bulletin de la Société Historique et Archéologique du Périgord,* LIX (1932), 109–17, 146–62, 184–214, 236–65, 283–307. Noël Becquart also lists these parishes as part of the Sénéchaussée of Bergerac, in *Répertoire numérique des registres paroissiaux et de l'Etat Civil* (Périgueux, 1968). Whereas Brette lists 455 jurisdictions, Mousnier places the figure at closer to 400 (*Les Institutions de la France,* II, 259).

nary civil cases involving non-nobles and ecclesiastics as well as appeals from seigneurial justices within their jurisdictions, but not the cas royaux reserved exclusively for the bailliages and sénéchaussées. Whereas the competence of the superior ordinary courts expanded, that of these inferior courts diminished to the point that many had ceased to function by the eighteenth century. In recognition of this fact and in an effort to simplify the appeal of seigneurial cases originating within these inferior courts, an edict of 1749 abolished all such tribunals in towns where a bailliage or sénéchaussée already existed. In the eighteenth century, four inferior royal justices remained in the Sarladais, initiating cases and passing judgment before forwarding them to the Sénéchaussée of Sarlat.[21]

Above the prévôtés royaux existed the jurisdictions known as bailliages in the northern half of the kingdom and as sénéchaussées in the southern half, with numerous exceptions. Although royal baillis and sénéchaux had originally rendered justice personally, they eventually appointed lieutenants to act in their absence or illness. Thereafter, each lieutenant exercised justice in the name of the bailli or sénéchal, who retained the honorific privilege of presiding at all judgments but lost the right to vote and accordingly was no longer required to hold a law degree. The officers of the bailliages and sénéchaussées possessed the exclusive right to judge all civil and criminal cas royaux as well as all cases referred to them from lower courts in civil, criminal, ecclesiastic, municipal, seigneurial, and police affairs in their jurisdiction. As already noted, they possessed the right of *prévention* over all seigneurial and subordinate judges, even for offenses the latter could handle, provided that the seigneur did not act within twenty-four hours or the *prévôt des maréchaussées* within seventy-two hours. In addition, officers of the bailliages and sénéchaussées presided over *cas privilégiés*—cases involving offenses committed by ecclesiastics and meriting afflictive punishment, which ecclesiastic judges could not pronounce, as well as cases implicating nobles and clerics, those involving crimes committed by judicial officers, and those concerning offenses committed within the walls of the judicial palace and the royal prisons. With the exception of letters obtained by nobles, which could only be registered by the parle-

<hr />

21. Edmond Seligman, *La Justice en France pendant la Révolution* (2 vols.; Paris, 1901), I, 18; Marion, *Dictionnaire*, 453.

ments, the royal courts alone could register letters of remission or pardon and recall sentences of banishment and conviction to the galleys.[22]

All sentences pronounced by the sénéchaussées and bailliages were subject to appeal before the parlements, superior or sovereign ordinary courts that issued *arrêts,* or judgments in last resort. The number of sénéchaussée judges required for sentencing varied, depending on the nature of the affair. In a minor case judged without recourse to the "extraordinary" phase of criminal procedure, a single judge could pronounce the ruling. In a serious case ruled extraordinary, the presiding magistrate required the assistance of two colleagues, and in cases of duel, five other magistrates, all of whom signed the sentence. In summary, the sénéchaussées and bailliages not only initiated minor cases, cas royaux, and cas privilégiés but also reviewed sentences of minor cases pronounced by subordinate courts and continued cas royaux initiated by lower tribunals. By the eighteenth century, the bailliages and sénéchaussées were the most important courts in the kingdom and handled either in the first or second instance virtually all serious cases.[23]

Henry II in 1552 conferred upon sixty bailliages and sénéchaussées the power to receive appeals from neighboring jurisdictions and to make decisions no longer subject to appeal. These selected courts were designated as *présidiaux,* nine of which existed within the Parlement of Bordeaux. The présidiaux were intended to decentralize the judicial system by terminating relatively minor affairs at a lower level than the sovereign courts of parlement, resulting in more expeditious decisions and lower costs for litigants. The présidiaux were therefore empowered to judge civil matters in which the value in question did not exceed a capital sum of 250 livres or an annual income of 10 livres.[24]

As defined in the Ordinance of 1670 and confirmed by the Declara-

22. *Encyclopédie méthodique, ou par ordre de matières: Jurisprudence* (10 vols.; Paris, 1782–91), I, 709–10; Mousnier, *Les Institutions de la France,* II, 264–68; Adhémar Esmein, *Histoire de la procédure criminelle en France et spécialement de la procédure inquisitoire depuis le XIIIe siècle jusqu'à nos jours* (Paris, 1882), 32; Guyot *et al., Répertoire,* II, 77.

23. Mousnier, *Les Institutions de la France,* II, 251; *Encyclopédie méthodique . . .: Jurisprudence,* I, 717; Guyot *et al., Répertoire,* II, 86; Esmein, *Histoire de la procédure criminelle,* 24; Seligman, *La Justice en France,* I, 19.

24. Daniel Jousse, *Traité de la juridiction des présidiaux tant en matière civile que criminelle* (Paris, 1757), iv; Philip Dawson, *Provincial Magistrates and Revolutionary Politics in France, 1789–1795* (Cambridge, Mass., 1972), 33.

tions of May 29, 1702, and February 5, 1731, the présidiaux were empowered in criminal matters to judge in the first instance and last resort
(and in concurrence with the prévôtés of the maréchaussée) all cases
classed as *cas présidiaux* (or *cas prévôtaux*), which were defined according to the *qualité* of the accused and the nature of the crime. The
first category encompassed cases involving crimes committed by vagabonds and *gens sans aveu*, defined as "persons who have neither a profession, trade, fixed domicile, nor means of subsistence, and for whom
no one can attest to their good conduct and morals"; crimes committed
by recidivists; crimes committed by military men; and situations in
which beggars who were not vagabonds asked for alms with insolence,
pretended they were soldiers, carried false papers, feigned illness or a
handicap, gathered in groups of four or more, or were found carrying
firearms, swords, iron-tipped clubs, or other arms. All of the above persons could also be judged either before the sénéchaussée or in the police
tribunals of a municipality.[25]

Considered by the nature of the crime, the prévôtés and présidiaux
possessed jurisdiction over the following: theft on the highroads (ex-
cluding the streets of towns and their suburbs); armed theft with breaking and entry and public violence; armed theft with breaking and entry
that breached the walls, roof, or exterior doors and windows of a
house, even if done without arms or public violence; sacrilege accomplished in the same manner; sedition, popular disturbances, and unlawful assembly; the raising of troops without royal permission; and
counterfeiting. After 1731 premeditated murder was no longer considered a cas présidial. In all of the above cases, the présidial held the right
of *prévention* over the prévôté, but cases involving clerics and nobles
were not subject to judgment in the last resort by either court. Because
the Crown considered these cases by their nature and by the *qualité* of
the accused to be unworthy of judgment on appeal and meriting prompt
punishment, it empowered both sorts of tribunals to judge them, assuming that the more courts empowered to handle such offenses, the
quicker and more certain their repression. Finally, and not least among
its powers, each présidial reviewed and judged sovereignly the criminal

---

25. Jousse, *Traité de la juridiction des présidiaux*, 312. The présidiaux had previously handled cases involving crimes committed by deserters, but after 1731 only the
prévôts des maréchaussées did so (*ibid.*, 312–15).

competence of the prévôté, other sénéchaussées or bailliages, and municipal police courts within its jurisdiction.[26]

The présidial almost always judged in the first and last instance, unlike the sénéchaussée or bailliage, which judged on appeal in both the first and second instance. The sentences of the latter in minor criminal cases were subject to appeal at the request of the accused; in more serious cases, where the court pronounced sentences of afflictive or dishonorable punishment, review by the *tournelle* (criminal chamber) of the parlement was mandatory and automatic, for the sentence could not be carried out without confirmation by an arrêt. In theory at least, the présidiaux judged certain criminal cases in the last resort, despite frequent intervention from the parlements in practice. Whereas prévôtés judged sovereignly in all condemnations (after présidial review of their competence), the présidiaux did so only in condemnations to the *carcan*, whipping, banishment, and the galleys for less than life; death sentences and condemnations to the galleys for life were still subject to automatic review by the tournelle of the parlement.

Alongside the ordinary royal courts existed the extraordinary courts, the most important of which were the prévôtés of the maréchaussée. Since the prévôtés were basically military tribunals judging summarily without appeal, numerous abuses appeared, about which the intendants complained to the royal commissioners charged with the revision of the criminal code in 1670. Although many critics called for the outright suppression of these courts, the Crown adamantly favored their maintenance. The drafters of the 1670 ordinance did, however, tighten the jurisdictional limitations governing them. The présidiaux were thereafter required to review the competence of a prévôté within three days of the arrest of an accused in its jurisdiction, and the accused had to be interrogated in the presence of an accredited public prosecutor within twenty-four hours of arrest. Moreover, the ordinance required the constables of the maréchaussée to inventory the accused's possessions in the presence of at least two witnesses. Abuses nevertheless persisted.[27]

26. *Ibid.;* Ernest Laurain, *Essai sur les présidiaux* (Paris, 1896), 176–77.

27. Other extraordinary tribunals were the Grand Conseil, the Chambres des Comptes, the Cours des Aides, the Cour des Monnaies, and the courts of the Eaux et Forêts and the Admiralties (Mousnier, *Les Institutions de la France,* II, 251; Marion, *Dictionnaire,* 318–19; Laurain, *Essai sur les présidiaux,* 166–67). The president of the

The Declaration of 1731 further distinguished between types of cas prévôtaux and described in detail the police functions of the mounted constables of the maréchaussée, who were responsible for the maintenance of public order and possessed a general right to arrest any culprit caught in the act. They policed the towns, countryside, highroads, fairs, and markets; supervised cabarets; regulated travelers and persons from outside the region; and enforced regulations concerning land and river transport. Upon demand, they also performed escort duty for the transportation of prisoners and the shipment of tax revenues to Bordeaux. Because the prévôté possessed wide police powers yet relatively restricted judicial competence, many cases passed through this tribunal before being referred to the sénéchaussée. The Prévôté of Sarlat, for example, whose twelve constables patrolled a jurisdiction of approximately 116,000 inhabitants, served as a sort of clearinghouse for a large proportion of the cases that came before it: Of the surviving 37 cases handled between 1770 and 1790, 22 were subsequently referred by présidial judgment to the Sénéchaussée of Sarlat, 3 to seigneurial tribunals, and 2 to the présidial. Of the remaining 10 cases, only 7 reached definitive sentence by the prévôté.[28]

Fifteen of the 22 cases referred to the sénéchaussée for continuance involved theft. In most of the cases, constables had responded to public outcry by arresting a suspect very often apprehended by the victim himself, aided by his relatives and neighbors. In some instances the accused was then taken before the prévôté and interrogated to determine whether the case was actually within the tribunal's competence. Most cases apparently were not. In other instances the constables arrested suspects and seem to have conveyed them directly to the sénéchaussée or to the local seigneurial tribunal because the case was clearly outside the competence of the prévôté. In a typical case, a weaver arrived at a fair and attempted to sell a calf stolen the night before. He was captured by the calf's owner and a "troupe de gens," who imprisoned him

---

1670 commission acknowledged that prévôtal officers were responsible for the worst abuses of the criminal justice system (Esmein, *Histoire de la procédure criminelle,* 219–20).

28. Given the many restrictions on prévôtal competence, the study of such specialized jurisdictions reveals only a partial view of the general contours of criminality in a region. See J. Lorgnier and R. Martinage, "L'Activité judiciaire de la maréchaussée de Flandres (1679–1790)," *Revue du Nord,* LXI (1979), 594, 600; Cameron, *Crime and Repression.*

in the local château before turning him over to the constables of the maréchaussée, who then conducted him to the royal prison at Sarlat. Upon interrogating him, the prosecutor of the sénéchaussée/présidial decided the theft fell within the competence of the local seigneurial tribunal; he therefore sent the prisoner and a copy of the case to that court for prosecution. The case never returned to the sénéchaussée. Given the competing and overlapping competence of the different courts, it often took quite some time to determine which tribunal should prosecute a specific case.[29]

Alexis de Tocqueville shared the opinion of Revolutionary detractors of the maréchaussée. He asserted that although ordinary royal justice effectively protected the poor man against injury from richer and more powerful members of the community, when the individual came up against extraordinary tribunals—in which his adversary was the Crown itself—he met with biased judges, summary procedure, and a mere semblance of a trial. More recently, Iain Cameron has insisted that the bad reputation attached to the "booted justice" of the maréchaussée was largely undeserved. He argues that its notoriety was a carefully cultivated psychological weapon conceived to disguise and supplement its numerical weakness. "The maréchaussée," he concludes, "was a trick played on the populace by the ruling classes." Despite the Revolutionary critics' exaggeration of the abuses that derived from this combination of robe and sword, everyone agreed on the practical value of the maréchaussée as a police force, and the populace actually called for expansion in the number of its brigades. Recognition of its usefulness came in 1790, when the National Assembly expanded it, converting it into the Gendarmerie Nationale.[30]

The administration of criminal justice in the Old Regime was inefficient, expensive, and inherently selective in its daily functioning. In criminal matters, the Sénéchaussée of Sarlat handled two sorts of cases, *petit criminel* and *grand criminel,* a distinction that theoretically corresponds closely to that between *délits* (misdemeanors) and *crimes* (fel-

29. Requête du procureur du roy, May 16, 1770, Information, May 17, 1770, both in B 1545, ADD.

30. Alexis de Tocqueville, *The Old Regime and the French Revolution,* trans. Stuart Gilbert (Garden City, N.Y., 1955), 191–92; Cameron, *Crime and Repression,* 255–57.

onies). Contemporary jurists defined *crime* as "an evil action that directly harms the public interest or the rights of the citizen." Although in common parlance the terms *crime* and *délit* were used interchangeably, in their strict legal sense, *crime* referred to "an offense that concerned the public," whereas *délit* signified an offense "whose reparation concerned a private individual more than the public." In short, all *crimes* were offenses, but not all offenses were serious enough to be considered *crimes*.[31]

In theory, at least, legal action stemming from a misdemeanor generally gave rise to a petit criminel case, which began when a private individual filed a formal petition. If, after a preliminary inquest and interrogation, the presiding magistrate was satisfied that the offense was exclusively a private matter, he could order that it be *civilisé*—resolved orally in an *audience* (hearing) at which the magistrate awarded reparations in the form of damages. If, on the other hand, the magistrate judged that the offense somehow disturbed public order, he would recommend that it be treated as a *crime*.

Crimes generally gave rise to grand criminel cases, which were initiated by a lower-level court or, more rarely, by the sénéchaussée itself. Such cases were necessarily prosecuted by the king's prosecutor, who initiated the suit either unilaterally by his own petition or in response to a denunciation by a private party. Sometimes he joined with a private plaintiff in a suit already underway. Grand criminel cases were then pursued beyond the ordinary phase of criminal procedure into the extraordinary phase until sentencing either absolved or condemned the accused.

In practice, however, the division between petit and grand criminel was indistinct. There was no sure way to predict by the nature of a complaint whether it would result in a petit or grand criminel case. Plaintiffs tended to claim that the offenses allegedly perpetrated against them were *crimes* that merited public prosecution. But the records themselves do not distinguish between cases on these grounds. Not until the decision was made either to abandon or to continue a case did it become evident whether the case was petit or grand. The historian therefore can only classify cases as such in retrospect. For contemporaries, the distinction may have been only that of a filing system: Petit criminel cases were those that were abandoned (regardless of whether

31. Guyot *et al.*, *Répertoire*, V, 170.

the offense in question fell into the legal classification of a *crime* or a *délit*), whereas grand criminel cases were those that were continued into the extraordinary phase.[32]

Punishment and reparation were distinct in Old Regime France. Whereas a *délit* required only reparation, every *crime* carried with it two obligations on the part of the offender: first, to repair the harm done, and second, to suffer the punishment incurred by the *crime*. In cases involving *crimes*, even if the *partie civile* (private party) dropped his suit, the public prosecutor was obliged to prosecute if the *crime* merited afflictive, dishonorable, or capital punishment. The action to punish the *crime* could be initiated only by the officers of the king; the action to provide *réparation civile,* in the form of monetary reparations, was begun only by the partie civile. Misdemeanors generally resulted in privately initiated prosecution that could condemn the accused to damages and reparations but not to punishment.[33]

The seriousness of an offense and, consequently, the punishment it merited depended not only on its nature but also on the circumstances surrounding its commission. The degree of malice, the motive, the manner in which the offense was committed, the instrument used, the character and *qualité* of the accused and of the victim, the age and sex of the accused and of the victim, the time and place, and whether or not it was a second offense all factored into the gravity of the offense and the extent to which it threatened public safety. Moreover, although the law prescribed specific punishments for the most common crimes, all sentences were to a certain extent arbitrary. Judges could not pronounce sentences more severe than the law allowed, but they could exercise discretion within the prescribed limits, depending on the circumstances of the crime. An insult, for example, merited a heavier sentence if addressed to a social superior, especially if delivered in public. Moreover, those offenses most difficult to prevent were punished more severely than others.[34]

The treatment of theft provides a good example of the essentially arbitrary nature of sentencing. Legal treatises offered guidelines to help the prosecutor distinguish between simple thefts and aggravated thefts

32. Alexandre Mericskay discovered that the petit criminel archives of the Châtelet of Paris contain cases of both *crimes* and délits ("Le Châtelet et la répression de la criminalité à Paris en 1770" [Thèse de IIIème cycle, Université de Paris, 1984]).

33. Guyot *et al., Répertoire,* XIII, 64.

34. *Encyclopédie méthodique . . .: Jurisprudence,* III, 425.

(*crimes*). Broadly defined, theft was "any removal of movable property." Theoretically, a simple theft injured or harmed only private individuals, whereas an aggravated theft threatened public order. In general, theft was considered most serious when it abused social conventions and betrayed the trust on which society depended to function smoothly. Accordingly, a servant who stole from his master violated a sacred trust and therefore could be condemned to death on the gallows for even a minor theft. Consistent with this rationale, the thief who breached even the thinnest exterior wall or roof of a dwelling could be judged without appeal (*prévôtalement*), as could the thief who robbed the vulnerable traveler on a lonely highroad. Perhaps implicit in the above criteria is the fact that the royal courts did not expect to supplant self-regulation and seigneurial justice or to police society in a quotidian manner; prosecution was admittedly and necessarily selective, and punishments were accordingly harsh and exemplary. Since the relative seriousness of a theft and the severity of its punishment were subject to wide interpretation, one must look beyond the theoretical guidelines of legal treatises to the archival evidence to discover how theft was punished in practice.[35]

As a general rule, arbitrariness is a double-edged weapon that can exaggerate both the severity of punishment and the magnanimity of clemency. The more personalized (albeit official) justice of a traditional society projects the appearance of rigor for the sake of deterrence. Its spectacular severity is occasionally brought to bear on those guilty of atrocious crimes, but more often the great majority of delinquents benefit from its combined indulgence and powerlessness. Both traits disguise its inherent weakness and make such personalized, arbitrary justice more palatable to subjects who are the potential beneficiaries of that arbitrariness. As a result, a traditional ruler's subjects more easily accept such a regime than one in which the law is more precise but harsher and less responsive to the personal needs of individuals. In other words, judicial formalism is repugnant to traditional rulers be-

---

35. Diderot (ed.), *Encyclopédie*, XVII, 439–40; "Déclaration du roi sur les cas prévôtaux ou présidiaux du 5 fevrier 1731," *Recueil des édits, déclarations, et ordonnances du roi, arrêts du conseil, du parlement de Toulouse, et autres cours, etc. concernant l'ordre judiciaire, et les matières publiques les plus importants* (8 vols.; Toulouse, 1782–86), V, 32; Dominique Muller, "Les Magistrats français et la peine de mort au 18e siècle," *Dix-huitième siècle*, IV (1972), 86–87; Michel Foucault, *Discipline and Punish: The Birth of the Prison*, trans. Alan Sheridan (New York, 1979), 53–54; Arlette Farge, *Délinquance et criminalité: Le Vol d'aliments à Paris au XVIIIe siècle* (Paris, 1974), 32.

cause it diminishes the dependence of the individual on both the grace and the power of the authorities.[36]

In French jurisprudence, criminal procedure was closely associated with modes of civil adjudication to the extent that even in the eighteenth century civil procedure was still an appropriate form for some criminal litigation. A civil case, by definition, was one that had some civil objective, such as the payment of a bill or debt or the division of a succession. In contrast, a criminal case had as its goal the reparation of an offense, the punishment of a *crime,* or often both. Nonetheless, one could still choose to settle criminal offenses (except for *crimes*) via civil proceedings. What royal statutes had done, in effect, was to isolate the public interest in criminal prosecution and to entrust its supervision to the king's prosecutor. This was especially urgent in cases without private complainants. But in many cases the prosecutor and private complainant were joint complainants; the private party sought only civil reparations for the injury done him, whereas the king's prosecutor sought punishment for the *crime* that offended public order. The Crown actually welcomed the private complainant as civil plaintiff alongside the king's prosecutor, investigating simultaneously both the civil case of the partie civile and the criminal case of the king's prosecutor, because in such joint actions the civil plaintiff still bore the expenses. Only if a private complainant failed to come forward would the king's prosecutor consider initiating criminal proceedings solely at royal expense.[37]

French criminal procedure in the eighteenth century was composed essentially of six steps:

1. *Inquest.* The *information préparatoire* (preliminary inquest) was initiated either by a denunciation or by a petition of complaint from the king's prosecutor or a private party. In privately initiated cases, the partie civile was obliged at this time to pledge responsibility for all court costs that followed. A magistrate appointed as *rapporteur* (examiner) conducted the preliminary inquest and prepared a careful written record of his investigation to be used by a different judge who would finally decide the case. The initial inquest proceeded in the same

36. P. Henry, *Crime, justice et société,* 490–91; *Max Weber on Law in Economy and Society,* ed. Max Rheinstein, trans. Edward Shils and Max Rheinstein (Cambridge, Mass., 1954), 226–28.

37. John H. Langbein, *Prosecuting Crime in the Renaissance: England, Germany, France* (Cambridge, Mass., 1974), 225–26. Also see Daniel Jousse, *Traité de la justice criminelle de France* (4 vols.; Paris, 1771), II, 838 ff.

manner as an ordinary civil hearing, except that the witnesses could be heard in the presence of the partie civile and that their depositions were entirely written down by the court scribe. The examiner generally did not intervene, preferring the witnesses to speak freely. A completed dossier containing the petition or denunciation, the depositions, various *procès-verbaux* (official reports) of inspection, and reports by surgeons and other experts then was sent before the king's prosecutor, who reviewed the case and recommended further action: either dismissal of the case or the bodily arrest or summons of the accused to appear before the court. His recommendation was added to the dossier, which was then sent before the judge designated to hear the case.[38]

2. *Interrogation.* Until this stage, the case against the accused had been prepared without his knowledge. When the accused appeared before the judge to respond to the accusation, he did so without the aid of a defense counsel and without precise knowledge of the evidence. After being allowed to raise objections to the jurisdiction of the court, the accused was sworn in and asked to state his name, occupation, age, and residence. Although the main purpose of the interrogation was, in the judge's view, the gathering of incriminating evidence from the mouth of the accused, it did afford the accused his first opportunity to respond to the allegations made against him. The interrogation was rarely an insidious or a subtle trap designed primarily to force the accused to confess. Most interrogations were conducted in purely routine fashion, with the examiner content to organize his line of questioning along the same plan as the inquest, pursuing details and the chronology of events that may have come to light somewhat haphazardly.[39]

The transcript of the interrogation was added to the dossier and returned to the prosecutor for his review and recommendation. If the accused confessed or if the prosecutor believed that sufficient evidence had already been assembled, he would consult with the partie civile (if one existed) and make his motions for final penal and civil judgments. But the prosecutor also had the option of moving for one of two sorts of interlocutory decrees. He could move that the case be *civilisé* (con-

38. Diderot (ed.), *Encyclopédie,* XIII, 798; Esmein, *Histoire de la procédure criminelle,* 150.

39. Louis-Bernard Mer maintains that the accused did not hesitate to defend themselves, often with surprising energy, ability, and defiance ("La Procédure criminelle au XVIIIe siècle: L'Enseignement des archives bretonnes," *Revue historique,* CCLXXIV (1985), 20–23.

verted into a civil case) and prosecuted by means of ordinary procedure, leaving the parties involved the choice of continuing the case or settling informally, or he could recommend that it be ruled *à l'extraordinaire,* in which case the witnesses were recalled for confrontation with the accused. The recommendation of the prosecutor was routinely followed.[40]

3. *Recall and confrontation.* The extraordinary phase of criminal procedure—designed to provide a set of checks on the evidence in the dossier—was essentially defensive in function. If the prosecutor's recommendation that the case was worth pursuing was ratified by the judge's *règlement à l'extraordinaire,* he scheduled the *récolement* (recall). The recall of the witnesses before the judge in the Chambre de Conseil was actually the first time the judge examined anyone but the accused, the preliminary inquest having been conducted by the subordinate examiner. In the recall, the witnesses appeared singly and, after being sworn in, were asked to restate their testimony. If it conformed to the written deposition, the judge began the confrontation. A witness was brought into the presence of the accused and asked to confirm that the latter was the person of whom he had spoken in his deposition. If so, the judge then asked the accused to voice any objections he had to the witness before the latter's testimony was read. Objections having been waived or voiced and recorded, the clerk read the deposition. The accused was then asked whether it was true or false, and was invited to refute the charges against him and cross-examine the witness himself. The procedure was repeated for each witness.

This phase of the trial ostensibly provided the accused—technically deprived of a defense counsel under French criminal law—his only opportunity to learn the extent of the evidence against him and to conduct his own defense. Secrecy, however, was often difficult to maintain. Moreover, many accused apparently did have access to outside counsel—lawyers and legal practitioners—who visited prisoners and aided them in composing their *mémoires* (statements) and petitions,

---

40. If, after referring the parties to a civil hearing, the prosecutor was presented with new evidence incriminating the accused, he had the option of resuming the extraordinary phase of criminal procedure (Diderot [ed.], *Encyclopédie,* XIII, 404). In practice, 85 percent of all criminal cases examined in a study of eighteenth-century Breton archives ended either by *civilisation,* in adjournment, or in the condemnation of the accused to a lighter penalty. In other words, only 15 percent of criminal cases proceeded to the extraordinary phase (Mer, "La Procédure criminelle," 12, 25).

suggesting that legal counsel may not have been as prohibitively expensive as heretofore assumed.[41]

The recall and confrontation also served as a much-needed check on the procedures of the lower-level courts that most often conducted the preliminary inquest. Witnesses not uncommonly retracted or altered their original depositions as recorded by seigneurial scribes. In some instances, the sénéchaussée even summoned the seigneurial examiner responsible for the procedural irregularity, interrogated him, and ordered that the inquiry be repeated at his personal expense.[42]

After completion of the confrontation, the prosecutor again examined the dossier, which was by then often quite lengthy, and submitted his conclusions in writing. Definitive conclusions constituted a motion for final judgment and included a proposed sentence that the magistrate sitting in judgment could either accept, reduce, or augment. Provisional conclusions were motions for continuation of either of two sorts: the examination of witnesses for the defense or the use of judicial torture.

4. *Examination of defense witnesses.*   By law, if the prosecutor considered the defense of the accused well founded, he could recommend that the accused be allowed to name witnesses to testify on his behalf. The witnesses would then be summoned and heard, just as in the preliminary inquest. In practice, however, this seldom occurred, primarily because prosecutors did not usually allow cases conducted at royal expense to proceed if the evidence was not sufficiently damning.[43]

French criminal procedure contained an unquestionable prosecutorial bias. In France, the real or formalized duel between prosecution and defense—conducted orally in England—had early been replaced by a cumbersome written process patterned after Roman-canon inquisitorial procedure. By 1539, the jurists drafting the Ordinance of Villers-Cotterets had concluded that the only way to expedite this complex, lengthy, and expensive process was to entrust the defensive proof

41. Mer, "La Procédure criminelle," 19.

42. Esmein, *Histoire de la procédure criminelle,* 150; Langbein, *Prosecuting Crime,* 234. For an example of sénéchaussée action against seigneurial authorities, see Chapter IX herein.

43. In general, Old Regime judges exercised considerable caution in opening the extraordinary phase of a trial, in large part because most such cases were prosecuted at royal expense. See Julius R. Ruff, "The Character of Old Regime Justice: The Examples of the Sénéchaussées of Libourne and Bazas," paper presented at the Twelfth Annual Meeting of the Western Society for French History, October 26, 1984, pp. 13–14.

to the public officer conducting the prosecution. Confident that the recall-confrontation stage provided the accused adequate opportunity to refute the charges against him, they maintained that the granting of defense counsel not only would needlessly protract the proceedings and increase legal expenses but also would be superfluous.[44]

5. *Torture.* If the evidence against the accused in a capital case was substantial but not conclusive, the prosecutor might recommend and the judge order that the accused be subjected to torture. The form of torture known as the *question préparatoire* was designed to obtain full proof against the accused through extraction of a confession. After sentencing and prior to execution for a capital crime, the accused could also be subjected to the *question préalable* in an attempt to learn the names of accomplices.

The maintenance of torture in judicial proceedings well into the eighteenth century seems incongruous to modern observers, just as it did to many enlightened contemporaries. Traditional scholars have argued that the growing complexity of inquisitorial procedure and the inherent difficulty of satisfying the stringent set of legal proofs needed for conviction actually compelled judges to maintain torture throughout the Old Regime. The system of legal proofs, which required that a judge have certain kinds and quantities of evidence strictly defined by law before he could convict, was mechanical and meant to benefit the defense by making convictions more difficult. In practice, however, if a strong presumption of guilt existed in capital crimes, judges would resort to torture to produce a confession and thereby shorten the procedure, reducing court costs for lengthy capital cases. Torture, the argument continues, was essential to the smooth functioning of French criminal procedure and therefore continued unabated until abolished in 1780, and then only in response to a campaign conducted by able publicists, most notably Voltaire and Césare Beccaria. Subsequent to the abolition of torture, the argument concludes, French criminal courts found it virtually impossible to condemn manifestly guilty criminals; as a result, the inherent flaws in the Roman-canon law of proof became all the more apparent, paving the way for the reform of the entire system in 1789–90.[45]

44. Langbein, *Prosecuting Crime*, 234–38.
45. Esmein, *Histoire de la procédure criminelle*, 270; John H. Langbein, *Torture and the Law of Proof: Europe and England in the Ancien Régime* (Chicago, 1977), 4–5.

Recent research has called this traditional view into question. Indeed, the critiques of torture advanced by eighteenth-century publicists had been known for more than a century; moreover, the system of proofs was already regarded as antiquated at the time Voltaire made it the target of his barbs. It now seems clear that torture was abolished in 1780 because a new system of proof and an alternative form of punishment that made torture obsolete had already been developed both in theory and in legal practice. In cases where previously it may have been judged necessary to use torture to obtain a conviction, it was now possible to punish the accused without a formal conviction. This development liberated French criminal law from its dependence on torture, which could then be abolished without jeopardizing the functioning of the criminal courts.[46]

Prior to the Ordinance of 1670, criminal law required either of two kinds of evidence before a court could condemn an accused: two eyewitnesses or a confession. Because few cases were so clear cut, in cases where half-proof or strong circumstantial evidence existed, judges apparently resorted to torture to elicit a confession. But because the Ordinance of Villers-Cotterets stipulated that accused who did not confess under torture had to be released, hardy individuals who withstood their ordeal were greatly favored. To correct this imbalance, the Ordinance of 1670 permitted judges to assign penalties short of death to accused who refused to confess but against whom existed strong circumstantial evidence. Because punishment could thenceforth be administered on the basis of circumstantial evidence alone, torture became unnecessary and therefore declined throughout the eighteenth century.[47]

Both capital punishment and torture were already in deep decline when Voltaire and Beccaria focused the literate public's attention on the gore of public executions and on famous miscarriages of inquisitorial procedure such as the Jean Calas case of 1762. The decline was due, in great part, not only to the new system of proof but also to the new penal system that allowed various forms of imprisonment to replace traditional blood sanctions. In the sixteenth and seventeenth cen-

46. Mer, "La Procédure criminelle," 34–36.
47. Although "full and complete" proof was theoretically necessary before capital punishment could be pronounced, lesser punishment could be founded on lesser degrees of proof. See Guyot *et al.*, *Répertoire*, XIII, 563–64, 587–89; Ruff, "Crime, Justice and Public Order," 89–91; Langbein, *Torture and the Law of Proof*, 10–12.

turies, the Mediterranean states introduced the galley sentence, northern European countries founded workhouses, and England transported its convicts abroad. Although by the eighteenth century the galley fleets of France had long been superseded by sailing ships, the galleys still functioned as prison hulks for the accommodation of prisoners, who slept aboard at night and usually worked ashore by day.[48] The galley sentence afforded eighteenth-century French judges an alternative form of punishment for criminals convicted of relatively serious crimes who would otherwise have been subjected to torture and then either sentenced to capital punishment or released. The option of an intermediary form of sentencing combined with the subsidiary system of proof permitted the courts to punish serious crimes on the basis of persuasive circumstantial evidence. As a result of these developments, torture gradually became obsolete, and capital punishment relatively rare.[49]

Archival research confirms as much. The magistrates of the Sénéchaussée of Sarlat ordered the *question préalable* only once between 1770 and 1780, in a case of horse theft in which the accused evidently refused to name his accomplice. In 1763 the présidial subjected a coppersmith accused of counterfeiting to the *question préparatoire*, the last recorded instance of its application within the jurisdiction. As with every aspect of criminal procedure, the clerk recorded the details of the torture. After a preliminary interrogation in which the accused already seemed quite willing to confess and name his accomplices, a *brasselet* was applied to his right arm and given three turns while the questioning continued. A second brasselet was applied to his left arm and given three turns. Finally, after a surgeon's assistant had been called to witness further proceedings, the prisoner was tied to a bench and a stone placed across his lower back to increase the pressure while he was simultaneously stretched and questioned on discrepancies in his testimony. When the judges were satisfied, they ordered that the accused be unbound and placed on a mattress before a fire to recuperate from his ordeal. The clerk then reread the accused's testimony and asked him to

48. See Paul Bamford, *Fighting Ships and Prisons: The Mediterranean Galleys of France in the Age of Louis XIV* (Minneapolis, 1973), 174–75, 189–90, 234–38, 318. Also see André Zysberg, "La Société des galériens au milieu du XVIIIe siècle," *Annales: Economies, sociétés, civilisations*, XXX (1975), 43.

49. Langbein, *Torture and the Law of Proof*, 50–55. Also see Pieter Spierenburg (ed.), *The Emergence of Carceral Institutions: Prisons, Galleys and Lunatic Asylums, 1550–1900* (Rotterdam, 1984).

swear to its truthfulness, which he did. In light of the newly gathered information, the court issued a warrant for the arrest of his two accomplices. A growing body of literature corroborates that such examples of torture were already quite rare in other jurisdictions.[50]

6. *Final process.* The provisional conclusions of the prosecutor having been accepted, the dossier was again returned to him for his definitive conclusions, which he then submitted to the presiding magistrate. This magistrate, in turn, presented the dossier along with his own recommendation to the assembled court. Although it was possible at this point for the charges against the accused to be dropped, the case remitted to the ordinary phase, and the parties left to litigate any civil claims—including any action against the partie civile for wrongful accusation or against witnesses for false testimony—in reality, the case would never have proceeded to this stage unless the prosecutor was confident of condemnation. Having summarized the case in an oral presentation before his colleagues in the Chambre de Conseil, the presiding magistrate voted with them on the final sentence.[51]

The punishments inflicted on the condemned were of three main sorts: *peines capitales, peines afflictives,* and *peines infamantes. Peines capitales* took the life of the condemned or permanently deprived him of his rights and freedoms as a subject of the king (*mort civile*). The death penalty, the galleys for life, banishment from the kingdom for life, and life imprisonment were all forms of capital punishment. *Peines afflictives,* or corporal punishments, were those that afflicted the body of the condemned or deprived him temporarily of his freedom, such as the galleys for a specific period, flagellation, branding, the *carcan,* and the pillory. *Peines infamantes* dishonored the condemned. They included *amendes honorables* (public avowal and begging pardon), temporary banishment from the jurisdiction, and censure. Other, less

---

50. Procès-verbal de question, December 6, 1763, Décret de prise de corps, December 10, 1763, both in B 1667, ADD. The *question préparatoire* was applied only once in the Sénéchaussée of Libourne in the eighteenth century; the *question préalable* only six times (Ruff, "The Character of Old Regime Justice," 11). Mer discovered that from 1750 to 1780, 11 accused (of 6,000) were subjected to the *question préparatoire* in Breton courts. Only 1 of the 11 confessed ("La Procédure criminelle," 28–29). P. Henry found that between 1707 and 1806 a total of 51 (4.9 percent) incarcerated delinquents were tortured in the principality of Neuchâtel, with 68 percent of the tortures occurring during the first forty years of the period (*Crime, justice et société,* 270–73).

51. Diderot (ed.), *Encyclopédie,* XIII, 798.

serious punishments were warnings, mandatory almsgiving, and injunctions to be more circumspect in the future.[52]

Insufficient proof did not necessarily result in outright acquittal. Rather than being found innocent, an accused could be declared *hors de cours:* grudgingly freed yet kept under suspicion and unable to sue his accusers for civil damages. The court might also decide that the case should be *plus amplement informé,* which verdict either released the accused or detained him in prison up to a year pending the resumption of the case upon discovery of new evidence. Since such a verdict also entailed mort civile for the accused, it prevented him from holding office, from testifying in court, and even from making out his last will and testament.[53]

Although penalties could indeed be brutal, capital punishment was seldom pronounced and rarely implemented. In the sénéchaussées of Libourne and Bazas, from 1696 to 1789 the most common sentences (in 58 percent of cases) involved separation of the accused from society: banishment or incarceration in the galleys for life or a set term, or confinement in a *dépôt de mendicité* for male vagabonds or a *maison de force* for females. The death penalty was pronounced in 22 percent of the courts' guilty verdicts, but in one-third of those cases the accused was condemned *contumace* (in absentia). In addition, parlementary review of sénéchaussée sentences often resulted in attenuation of the penalty.[54]

The French criminal justice system rested on the principle of the delinquent's exclusion either by officially imposed temporary banishment or by self-imposed exile. The definitive separation of the delinquent from society by death, banishment for life, or life sentence to the galleys was much less common. Justice was incapable of taking in charge a condemned criminal that it did not wish and could not afford to keep for a long time. The system certainly did not envision the re-

---

52. Guyot *et al., Répertoire,* XIII, 62. For a more complete treatment of the subject, see Ruff, "Crime, Justice and Public Order," 93–96; Langbein, *Torture and the Law of Proof,* 51–60.

53. Ruff, "The Character of Old Regime Justice," 15; Marion, *Dictionnaire,* 387.

54. Ruff, "The Character of Old Regime Justice," 17–18; P. Henry, *Crime, justice et société,* 485–86. Mer found that in Brittany the relatively high proportion of death sentences in grand criminel cases in the first instance (one of three sentences) was moderated, after appeal, to one of ten condemnations confirmed and executed ("La Procédure criminelle," 31).

socialization or correction of the culprit. Moreover, self-exile can be seen as a chastisement imposed by popular justice: As long as a delinquent did not challenge order and morality in a serious manner, society permitted him the chance to elude the sanctions of official justice. The power to punish therefore remained divided between the authorities and their subjects, with the guilty obligingly exiling themselves by flight, and victims not only exacting retribution but also sometimes protecting culprits from public infamy.[55]

In its composition, the Sénéchaussée of Sarlat differed little from comparable courts in the rest of the kingdom. The lieutenant general was undoubtedly the most powerful magistrate, although gradually his powers were diminished by the creation of lieutenants criminal and civil. He presided over all civil and criminal judgments and distributed civil cases among the magistrates, who supervised their *instruction* and reported them to the court for judgment. He personally judged summary civil affairs involving a sum less than ten livres and possessed a deliberative voice in all cases. Exempt from the taille and the quartering of troops, he was considered the highest judge of the province below the sovereign courts of parlement.[56]

Generally, one of four parties policed the towns: a royal provost, the municipality itself, a seigneur, or the officers of the sénéchaussée. In Sarlat, the rights of police and local justice belonged to both the bishop and a group of magistrates called consuls. Petty civil cases were judged by two magistrates called *conjuges,* one named by the bishop, the other by the consuls. Although previously the municipality alone had been responsible for policing the town, by the eighteenth century Sarlat shared this right with an officer of the sénéchaussée—a counselor or assistant who also held the position of *lieutenant général de police, juge criminel de la ville, et banlieu de Sarlat.* The lieutenant general of police ensured the observance of Sundays and feast days, kept order in public ceremonies, controlled censorship, supervised municipal provisioning and sanitation, kept watch over the cabarets and lodging houses, and generally guaranteed public safety in Sarlat. Because this office combined wide police powers with considerable political influence, séné-

55. P. Henry, *Crime, justice et société,* 349–51, 484–86, 702, 706–707.
56. Laurain, *Essai sur les présidiaux,* 199–200.

chaussée and municipal authorities often struggled for its control.[57] But all three men who held the office between 1770 and 1790 were not only magistrates at the tribunal but also consuls or former consuls of the municipality. Indeed, little distinction seems to have existed between Sarlat's royal and municipal ruling bodies, which were dominated by the same elite.[58]

The lieutenant criminal of the sénéchaussée assigned criminal cases to the various counselors (magistrates) who were to present them to the court, distributing them usually on the basis of seniority. He, in turn, was assisted by a *lieutenant particulier,* who was also first counselor of the court. While serving as magistrates, counselors were forbidden to act as lawyers on behalf of private clients. Referred to as magistrates while they sat in hearings and in the Chambre de Conseil, they held a deliberative voice in all civil and criminal affairs. In the case of a counselor's absence or recusal, a lawyer connected with the court could serve as substitute. If a sénéchaussée was also a présidial, a minimum of seven counselors was necessary for criminal judgment in the last resort.

Connected with each court were at least two *avocats du roi* (king's lawyers) and one *procureur du roi* (king's prosecutor). Both of the king's lawyers were also counselors and, as such, took part in the hearings and attended the Chambre de Conseil, where they were assigned cases and collected fees. Acting in his official capacity, an avocat du roi represented the interests of the king in all cases pled orally in the *audience*. In the morning, before a hearing began, he and the procureur du roi conferred on the cases to be heard that day and came to their conclusions. In the event of disagreement in cases heard orally, the opinion of the lawyer prevailed, whereas in cases instructed in writing, that of the prosecutor held sway. During the hearing the lawyer spoke while standing, with his head covered and his hands gloved, and could not be

57. Escande, *Histoire de Sarlat,* 238; Marion, *Dictionnaire,* 441–42; P. Dawson, *Provincial Magistrates,* 51.

58. A deep rift developed in 1780 and 1781 between the officers of the *élection* and the prominent citizens of Sarlat, led by the officers of the présidial. The *élu* apparently attempted to force residents of Sarlat who owned land elsewhere to pay taxes in the parishes where the property was located—thereby depriving Sarlat of revenue on which it relied to meet its own tax assessment. When the Cour des Aides ruled in favor of the municipality, the consuls rang tocsins and the populace filled the streets to celebrate by humiliating the officers of the *élection* with songs and placards (Lettre de Meyrignac à M. l'Intendant, August 1, 1781, C 489, ADG).

interrupted even by the presiding magistrate. His report finished and his conclusions presented, he listened to his opponent's case. If, after this initial plea, the judges deemed the hearing to be sufficiently informative, they voted at once; if not, they requested that both parties prepare written *instructions* and that the case be continued according to the rules of written procedure. Unlike the other counselors, the avocats du roi could defend private parties in cases that did not involve the public interest. Whereas the lawyer was a legal expert who performed the most learned and intellectually demanding activities—pleading, instructing, consulting, mediating—the prosecutor was a procedural expert who learned his trade through a ten-year apprenticeship. Their division of labor, however, often broke down.[59]

Each court usually employed two *greffiers* (court clerks), one for civil cases and one for criminal. The greffier recorded all proceedings and sentences faithfully and accurately, assessed his own fees, recorded those assessed on their own behalf by the judges, and conserved a record of the above acts in a *greffe* (depot). Also connected with each court were several *huissiers* or *sergents* (bailiffs), who executed court orders, served writs, and apprehended persons summoned by the court. In all public ceremonies, they marched at the head of the magistracy.[60]

The total number of officers associated with a court varied according to the extent of its jurisdiction and the volume of its caseload. The Sénéchaussée of Sarlat in 1789 consisted of fourteen magistrates and two clerks, but also listed a total of twenty-two affiliated prosecutors and lawyers. Although the size of its magistracy had fluctuated somewhat in the course of the century, the tribunal was virtually the same size as in 1700.[61] The presence of a court not only conferred an important honor on a municipality but also constituted an essential source of

59. Lenard Berlanstein, *The Barristers of Toulouse in the Eighteenth Century (1740–1793)* (Baltimore, 1975), 5–6; Laurain, *Essai sur les présidiaux*, 227–28.

60. According to a schedule of rates for the assessment of judicial expenses that was part of the declaration of June 26, 1745, three sous could be charged per folio (folded) sheet—provided that it contained a minimum of twelve lines and twelve syllables to each line—exclusive of reimbursement for the stamped paper (Jousse, *Traité de la justice criminelle*, II, 835; Laurain, *Essai sur les présidiaux*, 243).

61. In 1700 the Sénéchaussée of Sarlat numbered sixteen magistrates and thirteen affiliated lawyers. Whereas the Sénéchaussée of Périgueux counted thirty-three magistrates in 1708, that of Sarlat consisted of twenty-two. See *Calendrier de 1789* (Périgueux, 1789); Ferdinand Villepelet, Introduction to *Inventaire sommaire des archives départementales de la Dordogne: Archives civiles, série B* (2 vols.; Périgueux, 1899), II, vii; Comte de Saint-Saud, *Magistrats des sénéchaussées, présidiaux, et élections* (Bergerac,

revenue, especially for towns like Sarlat that possessed a narrow economic base. The magistrates of the sénéchaussée numbered among Sarlat's richest citizens; they also monopolized social prestige and dominated municipal governing councils and administrative bodies. They and their households were not the sole contributors to the town's prosperity: Litigants often traveled far to plead lengthy civil cases and sometimes even established temporary residence in Sarlat for the duration of a case.[62]

The social rewards of judgeship in the sénéchaussées and présidiaux, although considerable, did not include ennoblement. Membership in a sénéchaussée held little attraction for most nobles, even though as judicial officers they were able to retain their noble status. Between 1770 and 1789, the offices of president and lieutenant general of the Sénéchaussée of Sarlat were always held by nobles, but below these upper echelons only five nobles numbered among the thirty individuals identified as officeholders. Of the fourteen officers in 1789, only three held the title of *écuyer* (esquire). That the judiciary of the sénéchaussée was predominantly non-noble was also true elsewhere in France.[63]

The magistrates occupied the highest position of honor in the provincial Third Estate. The magistracy as a whole was exempt not only from standing watch with the municipal guard and from the quartering of troops but also from paying the taille, *aides,* subsidies, gifts, and tolls assessed on the remainder of the Third Estate. Présidial magistrates wore red robes, symbols of their precedence over other royal officials. In all public ceremonies held in a cathedral, several stalls in the chancel were reserved for the court. When Te Deum masses celebrated in honor of the royal family were followed by *feux de joi,* the magis-

---

1931), 9–12. Also see Projet de rôle de la capitation des nobles et privilégiés de l'élection de Sarlat, C 2696, ADG; Escande, *Histoire de Sarlat,* 239.

62. Philip Dawson estimates that at the end of the eighteenth century the bailliages and sénéchaussées contained at least 2,700 magistrates—nearly half of all judges in the kingdom. The Sénéchaussée of Sarlat, with approximately 116,000 inhabitants and 14 magistrates in 1789, ranked among jurisdictions that were average or above average in the size of their judiciary—despite the Sarladais' predominantly rural and illiterate character (*Provincial Magistrates,* 35–39).

63. In 1789 only 6 to 7 percent of sénéchaussée magistrates in the provinces of Poitou and Burgundy were noblemen (P. Dawson, *Provincial Magistrates,* 71–72, 75). In contrast, Olwen Hufton found that the highest venal positions of judge, avocat du roi, and procureur du roi in the bailliage of Bayeux were all occupied by nobles in 1789 (*Bayeux in the Late Eighteenth Century* [Oxford, 1967], 59). See also Georges Lefebvre, "Urban Society in the Orléanais," *Past and Present,* XIX (1961), 50–51.

trates lit the bonfire according to their order of precedence. But to the sénéchaussée and présidial magistrates these honors were insufficient. Throughout the eighteenth century they unsuccessfully clamored for ennoblement, which they asserted would resolve the growing difficulty encountered in filling présidial positions.[64]

Because criminal prosecution was based on a cumbersome, lengthy written procedure, it proved complex and expensive to administer, owing in part to the large number of officials required. Magistrates received *gages,* official salaries that represented in the early seventeenth century an annual return of 3 percent or less on the capital initially invested in office. *Gages* varied according to the importance of the office and tribunal, but were generally minimal. By 1600 they had practically ceased to have significance for most counselors, either as a return on their investment or as an element in personal income. An inquest by Jacques Necker, director general of finances, showed that in 1778 the return on capital invested in offices of justice, police, finances, and the chancellery, after deducting all of the public taxes for which magistrates were still liable, amounted to approximately 1 percent.[65]

Magistrates also derived income from *épices,* fees assessed by the presiding judge and paid by the litigants. Determining the average income from épices is difficult since fees were distributed unevenly among the counselors. One-half to two-thirds of the fees belonged to the judge that reported the case, the remainder to those participating in the judgment. Fees were assessed in proportion to the complexity of the case, the number of sessions and witnesses involved, the volume of the paper work, and the duration of the case. Both the value and the number of individual cases that a counselor might report varied widely, depending on his seniority, talent, and learning—not to mention his ties to the lieutenant criminal who assigned cases. In general, more important cases and higher fees went to those with greatest seniority, who therefore might earn several times what the less fortunate majority earned.[66]

---

64. When, in 1678, the president of the Présidial of Sarlat tried to usurp the place of the lieutenant general in lighting the bonfire, he was reprimanded by a *lettre de cachet* (royal sealed letter) (Laurain, *Essai sur les présidiaux,* 250).

65. *Ibid.,* 63, 214; Jonathan Dewald, *The Formation of a Provincial Nobility: The Magistrates of the Parlement of Rouen, 1499–1610* (Princeton, 1980), 148–49. Counselors in the jurisdiction of Provins received fifty livres each in *gages* in 1717.

66. Laurain, *Essai sur les présidiaux,* 214; Dewald, *The Formation of a Provincial Nobility,* 151–52.

Complaints about abuses in fee charging were common. Because judges were only meagerly rewarded for expeditious decisions, they were probably tempted to prolong private civil cases unnecessarily. The drafters of the Civil Ordinance of 1667 had tried to minimize the number of civil cases instructed in writing; but Chrétien-François de Lamoignon, president of the Parlement of Paris, complained in his memoir of 1784 that almost no civil cases were judged in hearings primarily because written cases were much more lucrative. Prosecutors multiplied the procedural acts of private petit criminel cases for the same reason, he argued, and generally slighted grand criminel cases heard at royal expense in which no fees were assessed.[67]

Real fiscal inhibitions often prevented judges from prosecuting criminal cases. By the end of the seventeenth century the Crown did not actually allocate funds or even designate a special account for the prosecution of crime. Court expenses were reimbursed from a general fund that included revenues from fines and confiscations imposed by the courts and that normally was under the control of the local receiver of the royal domain. After reviewing a list submitted by each sénéchaussée of the expenses it had incurred in the prosecution of its public criminal cases, the intendant authorized the receiver to pay only within certain limits and for certain crimes. The intendant could authorize less funding than the amounts already committed by the court and could even disallow the costs for entire cases. Moreover, royal orders of council specifically forbade the disbursement of royal funds for minor criminal cases, reserving royal resources for the prosecution of serious crimes.[68]

67. Jousse, *Traité de la justice criminelle*, II, 803–804. To the *épices* one must add *vacations*, sums charged by judicial officials in payment for time spent in performing their functions. Although *vacations* were originally calculated on the basis of time actually spent, gradually officials assessed them arbitrarily. See Marion, *La Garde des Sceaux*, 15–16; Aubin, *L'Organisation judiciaire*, 153; John A. Carey, *Judicial Reform in France Before the Revolution of 1789* (Cambridge, Mass., 1981), 12–14, 44–47. For examples of abuses before the Parlement of Paris, see Marion, *Dictionnaire*, 549.

68. Jousse, *Traité de la justice criminelle*, II, 805–806, 812, 818–21. The Arrêt du Conseil of November 25, 1683, disallowed payment by the Domaine du Roy of the transportation costs of judges, procureurs du roi, greffiers, and bailiffs except in cases involving murder, rape, arson, theft on the highroad, and other crimes ordinarily punished by *peine afflictive* or *peine infamante*. Since the public prosecutor alone could call for such punishments, the arrêt meant, in effect, that the royal domain would only subsidize the prosecution of grand criminel cases (Guyot *et al.*, *Répertoire*, XIII, 64; also see VII, 173).

Given these financial restraints, the ordinary royal courts simply could not prosecute all criminal cases that came to their attention and clearly did not expect to do so. Instead, they spent most of their time and resources prosecuting minor criminal cases in which private parties paid the expenses. This structural weakness of the criminal justice system was especially critical in the prosecution of theft. Although the procureur du roi was technically required to prosecute all crimes committed within a jurisdiction, the sénéchaussée could expect scant recompense from fining or confiscating the property of the impoverished offenders normally hauled before the court for stealing food, clothing, or agricultural tools. The fear of unrecoverable expenses crowded out and eliminated cases involving petty delinquents, especially poor thieves, who were no less guilty than more solvent ones. Of course, the same was true for seigneurs and private individuals, who likewise found little financial incentive in prosecuting paupers. Because it was virtually impossible to recuperate expenses incurred in the exercise of criminal justice, judicial bodies charged with its implementation tried to avoid the responsibility.[69]

Despite complaints about the arbitrary and exorbitant assessment of judicial fees, the overall income of magistrates from *gages* and épices seems to have been quite low. The financial situation of the judiciary was so serious that in the eighteenth century the présidiaux especially fell into decay as inflation eroded their competence and recruitment of new members became increasingly difficult. To hold judicial office in the eighteenth century, an individual therefore needed a sizable private fortune. Magistrates were most often landed proprietors and lenders of money for whom judicial office was an important yet subsidiary investment. In the regions of Picardy and Beauvais, their fortunes were commonly founded on land and *rentes,* the latter increasingly important as the return from land rose in the eighteenth century. A typical judicial family possessed at least a vineyard supplying it with wine and often a garden providing fresh produce. But the magistrate's essential revenues

69. N. Castan, *Justice et répression en Languedoc,* 217; P. Henry, *Crime, justice et société,* 343. Despite the overall decline in the eighteenth century of judicial business before the Parlement of Paris and the Cour des Aides, grand criminel cases before the parlement actually increased steadily in the 1760s and continued to do so until the end of the Old Regime. See Colin Kaiser, "The Deflation in the Volume of Litigation at Paris in the Eighteenth Century and the Waning of the Old Judicial Order," *European Studies Review,* X (1980), 320.

came from his farms and pastures, generally entrusted to carefully supervised sharecroppers, as was often the case in the Sarladais. The revenue from one farm normally sufficed to support the household, the remaining income being channeled toward other investments. Throughout the seventeenth century and well into the eighteenth, revenue from judicial office was secondary and often insignificant in the overall income of magistrates.[70]

Proprietors and rentiers nonetheless purchased judicial offices to achieve the prestige, rank, and political power accompanying them, often passing on the office to a son or son-in-law. Moreover, one cannot discount the value of exemptions from many fiscal charges. Finally, magistrates possessed through the exercise of their functions an unseen but considerable advantage: By the registration of civil contracts and mortgages, they were in a perfect position to survey the financial situation of their jurisdiction. Because they knew which landowners were in difficulty and what property was encumbered with debts, they could easily aggrandize their own holdings. For these reasons, a family would purchase and jealously guard an office that was expensive to acquire, financially unrewarding, and personally demanding.[71]

Although the magistrates of the sénéchaussées did not issue from a single occupational category, one should not hesitate to qualify them as "bourgeois." They generally came from families that had been engaged in the practice of law, the administration of seigneurial justice, the collection of tax payments, or the management of landed estates. But owing both to their origins and to their meager professional income, many magistrates sought supplementary income in the accumulation of offices. Indeed, their considerable political influence is further explained by their tendency to hold several offices simultaneously in the *élection,* prévôté, royal finances, and seigneurial courts. This was especially true of lesser court officials as well as the lawyers and prosecutors affiliated with the court, for whom the accumulation of offices was an economic necessity. Lawyers also placed their expertise at the disposal of seigneurs anxious to defend existing seigneurial rights or to discover

70. Between the sixteenth and the eighteenth centuries, inflation eroded the monetary limits on the présidial's competence by 80 percent. See Mousnier, *Les Institutions de la France,* II, 262; P. Dawson, *Provincial Magistrates,* 82–83, 89, 93, 98–99; Laurain, *Essai sur les présidiaux,* 210, 213; Pierre Goubert, *Clio parmi les hommes* (Paris, 1976), 129–31.

71. Goubert, *Clio parmi les hommes,* 133–34; Hufton, *Bayeux,* 60.

lapsed ones. Fifty percent or more of the lawyers connected with the Sénéchaussée of Toulouse in the last half of the eighteenth century presided over seigneurial courts, placing them in a strategic position to encourage litigants to appeal to the sénéchaussée, where they could plead the case themselves.[72]

As much was true of the judiciary of the Sénéchaussée of Sarlat. Among the principal judges in 1789, the lieutenant criminal was also the civil and criminal judge of the seigneurial tribunal of Terrasson. Whereas the *lieutenant particulier* of the sénéchaussée held the same position in the *élection*, the *assesseur* (adjunct magistrate) had previously been royal prosecutor of the *élection* in 1776–77. One of the seven counselors had earlier been a consul of Sarlat, as well as the *procureur sindic* (prosecutor) of the *cours consulaire* (municipal court) in 1773; another counselor had in 1764 been lieutenant in the *élection*. A third had served as *élu* in 1763 and been appointed by the bishop as civil judge to the cours consulaire in 1764. Of the fourteen lawyers inscribed on the Tableau des Avocats in 1789, one had been a consul (and later served as deputy of the Third Estate to the National Assembly). Two of the nine prosecutors affiliated with the court in 1789 also held other positions: One was concurrently royal prosecutor of the prévôté; the other had been a consul. All three of the lieutenants general of police were concurrently or had previously been consuls. The clerks and bailiffs of the tribunal frequently doubled as clerks for the consuls or the prévôté. In fact, the chief clerk of the prévôté in 1789 also held the position of clerk for the consuls, was a notary for the municipality, and occasionally acted as clerk for the sénéchaussée.

The judiciary was united by a strong sense of solidarity, reinforced through intermarriage and sharpened by constant quarrels over precedence and prestige between immediately inferior and superior echelons of officers. Kinship ties were common in the Sénéchaussée of Sarlat well into the eighteenth century. Sons often succeeded their fathers in office, the most striking example being the Gérard family, seven members of which held the office of lieutenant general from 1572 to 1750. Nor was

72. Aubin, *L'Organisation judiciaire,* 75, 183. For a definition of the term *bourgeois,* see Goubert, *Clio parmi les hommes,* 123–24, 126. Prosecutors in the Bailliage of Bayeux averaged between 200 and 300 livres annually, bailiffs between 50 and 222 livres, depending on the court. Prosecutors therefore used their office not so much for income but as the basis for careers as moneylenders, estate agents, and rent collectors (Hufton, *Bayeux,* 64–66; Berlanstein, *Barristers of Toulouse,* 24).

it unusual for father and son, uncle and nephew, to hold office simultaneously; royal authorization was necessary but easily acquired. If a
magistrate died and left his office to a son still in his minority, relatives
found a *prête-nom* (stand-in) for him until he reached the required age
or obtained an exemption. Once in office, a magistrate might continue
in his functions until the age of seventy-five or eighty. François Delmon,
sieur de Talissac, replaced his father as *lieutenant particulier et assesseur criminel* on October 8, 1724, and remained in office until 1779.
Jean-Baptiste de Rupin, sieur du Breuil, replaced his brother as lieutenant in 1721 and held office until 1780. Louis de Pignol, écuyer and former *capitoul* (municipal magistrate) of Toulouse, was royal prosecutor
from 1730 to 1779, and his brother, Raymond de Pignol, écuyer and
sieur de la Contie, served as counselor from 1758 to 1785. Both longevity in office and kinship ties bound members of the sénéchaussée in a
close network and effectively maintained continuity of membership.[73]

Although royal criminal justice was inefficient, expensive, and therefore tangential to the lives of the majority, it was not as brutal or arbitrary as Enlightenment reformers depicted it to be. Nor was it a mono-
lithic monster devouring all suspects that came into its clutches. Its
day-to-day operations were hindered by a number of factors. Prohibitively long distances to the seat of royal justice, rural isolation inten-
sified by linguistic barriers and social distinctions, entrenched habits of
informal dispute settlement, and the relatively high cost of legal action
all combined to discourage victims from looking to the sénéchaussée
for redress of their grievances. And the distinctive character of Old Regime criminal procedure and the underfinancing of royal criminal justice discouraged royal magistrates from prosecuting serious crimes
when they could earn higher fees by judging civil cases. Ludicrously inadequate (by modern standards) police and police-support resources
further impeded effective law enforcement. Given these obstacles, involvement in the royal judicial system was almost entirely voluntary or
simply a question of bad luck for the suspect who happened to be
apprehended.

The magistracy of the Sénéchaussée of Sarlat struggled with the limi-

73. Goubert, *Clio parmi les hommes,* 123–25, 127; P. Dawson, *Provincial Magistrates,* 110, 340–41; Saint-Saud, *Magistrats,* 7–8; Berlanstein, *Barristers of Toulouse,*
146, 170.

tations of the criminal justice system, as did royal magistrates throughout the realm, and somehow managed to acquit themselves conscien-
tiously and astutely. The famous miscarriages of justice publicized by
Enlightenment reformers were uncharacteristic of the normal functioning of the courts. The judicial officers of the sénéchaussée were cul-
tured, educated men of modest social distinction, stable economic fortunes, and considerable political influence (at least locally) who, in the
main, exercised their functions with punctiliousness and even objec-
tivity.[74] Even so, the obstacles facing the court, combined with the
availability of alternative forms of redress, compelled the Sénéchaussée
of Sarlat to restrict its activities to a limited geographic and jurisdictional sphere on the periphery of society.

74. Mer, "La Procédure criminelle," 32–34, 36–37; Ruff, "The Character of Old
Regime Justice," 20–21.

III

Crime and Royal Justice
in the Sarladais

So long as the peasants refrain from arson and mur-
der, so long as they pay the taxes and do not poison
people, they may do as they please among themselves,
and as they have not a vestige of religious principle,
the state of things is shocking.

—Honoré de Balzac, *The Peasants*

Research on crime and criminality in Old Regime France has long been dominated by the theoretical distinction made between crimes against persons and crimes against property. According to the received doctrine, spontaneous violence against persons is the characteristic form of criminal activity in traditional societies, whereas premeditated crime against property (primarily theft) is most characteristic of modern capitalist societies. Therefore, the argument runs, as a society modernizes, so too does the character of its criminality modernize, evolving from predominantly violent in nature to property oriented. The fundamental reason for this transition from traditional to modern criminality is the emergence of private property in modern capitalist society as the basis of social organization and therefore as the object of keener aspirations and covetousness.[1] The wide acceptance of this argument can be explained both by the need to impose some pattern on the confused mass of material found in the judicial archives and by its adaptability to both Marxist historiography and modernization theory. But this unidimensional approach is unsatisfactory because it ignores the social, political, financial, and legal circumstances that

1. Pierre Deyon, *Le Temps des prisons: Essai sur l'histoire de la délinquance et les origines du système pénitentiaire* (Paris, 1975), 77–78.

95

shaped the creation of the criminal data. Moreover, the limitations of the analytical categories of "crimes against persons" and "crimes against property" quickly emerge when one employs them in the analysis of crime and criminality in the Sarladais.

Upon the publication in 1826 of the first French national criminal statistics, it was observed that crime in the urban, educated regions of the North was directed primarily against property while passionate crimes of violence predominated in the South. This generalization has subsequently been incorporated into modern history textbooks of Old Regime France, one of which observes that south of an imaginary line from Geneva to Saint-Malo existed a primitive, violent form of criminality that stood in sharp contrast with the more modern, property-oriented crime of the North and Northeast. Although this conclusion is based on several regional studies of crime and criminality performed over the last twenty-five years, one must ask if this sort of generalization is valid and useful.[2]

Closer examination of the research based on the criminal court records of Norman bailliages reveals that the transition appeared clearly in some areas, while in others the level of violence remained constant throughout the eighteenth century. Even within this relatively advanced region, a distinct geographic differentiation existed between urban milieux turned toward the outside world and more isolated rural areas, where violence persisted much as it had for centuries. Historians also have come to appreciate that the restricted legal jurisdiction of the bailliages and the limited popular acceptance of all royal courts meant that traditional criminality studies were not as revelatory as had been assumed. Social historians interested primarily in the study of deviance have therefore expanded the scope of their research to include documents produced by alternative agencies and institutions. Others, however, have persisted in the study of royal criminal court records while reducing the magnitude of their claims for the data. In short, researchers

---

2. *Ibid.*, 80; Emmanuel Le Roy Ladurie (ed.), *L'Age classique des paysans, 1340–1789* (Paris, 1975), 550–51, Vol. II of Georges Duby and Armand Wallon (eds.), *Histoire de la France rurale*, 4 vols. See the studies of Bernadette Boutelet, Jean-Claude Gégot, Marie-Madeleine Champin, and Alain Margot conducted under the direction of Pierre Chaunu and published in *Annales de Normandie* from 1962 to 1972. For a more recent summary, see Isser Woloch, *Eighteenth-Century Europe: Tradition and Progress, 1715–1789* (New York, 1982), 171–73.

have acknowledged that although royal criminal court records do not provide a truly representative picture of deviance in Old Regime society, they do reveal a great deal about the means by which certain offenses came to be criminalized and about the relationship of royal justice to society as a whole.[3]

More recently, historians have asserted that in the backward and sparsely populated regions of the Southwest and Massif Central and even in more advanced areas such as the jurisdiction of the Sénéchaussée of Libourne, the pattern of criminality remained clearly preindustrial well into the nineteenth century: Crimes of violence predominated and royal justice remained extraneous to the lives of the great majority of the populace outside the large urban areas, particularly to the nobility at one end of the social hierarchy and to the mass of the peasantry at the other.[4] But to what extent, if any, did the modernization of crime occur in the Sarladais at the end of the eighteenth century? Did crimes against property increase in number or in proportion to crimes against persons? What was the nature of criminal cases involving violence, and how did they find their way before the court? As we address these questions, the relationship of the Sénéchaussée of Sarlat to the society onto which it was grafted emerges much more clearly.

Between 1770 and 1790, public prosecutors and private plaintiffs brought at least 477 criminal cases before the Sénéchaussée of Sarlat (some initiated, others transferred), for an annual average of 23 cases in a jurisdiction containing approximately 116,000 inhabitants. In the nearby sénéchaussées of Libourne and Bazas, the rate of reported crime was equally low: 25 offenses per 100,000 for the district of Libourne and 26 per 100,000 for that of Bazas.[5] In reality, the annual caseload of the Sarlat tribunal ranged from a low of 8 cases in 1781 to a high of 36

3. Cameron, *Crime and Repression*, 191–211; Deyon, *Le Temps des prisons*, 68–69.

4. Le Roy Ladurie (ed.), *L'Age classique*, 551; Timothy J. A. Le Goff and D. M. G. Sutherland, "The Revolution and the Rural Community in Eighteenth-Century Brittany," *Past and Present*, LXII (1974), 96–119; Ruff, *Crime, Justice and Public Order*, 183.

5. For comparison, present-day indictable crime rates are around 3,000 offenses per 100,000 or more in most European countries; the United States reported 5,521.5 offenses per 100,000 in 1979. See Bruce Lenman and Geoffrey Parker, "The State, the Community and the Criminal Law in Early Modern Europe," in Gatrell, Lenman, and Parker (eds.), *Crime and the Law*, 16–17; Ruff, *Crime, Justice and Public Order*, 44–45.

FIGURE I

Distribution of Criminal Cases Before the Sénéchaussée

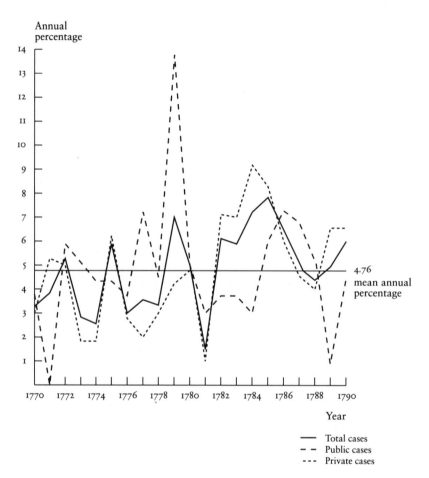

cases in 1785. Of the cases for this period, 450 are currently included in the bundles of court records housed in the Archives Départementales de la Dordogne in Périgueux, and an additional 21 cases are among the briefs of sénéchaussée cases forwarded to the Tournelle of the Parlement of Bordeaux. Sentences exist in the departmental archives for 6 other cases whose dossiers are found neither among the records in Périgueux nor among the appeals in Bordeaux. As a result, the combined records reveal the existence of at least 477 criminal cases heard by the sénéchaussée during this period, 474 of which specify the charge against the accused.

The distribution throughout the twenty years in question of the criminal cases with known offenses reveals that during the first twelve years of the period the annual percentage of all cases was well below the mean percentage of 4.76 percent (Figure 1). After 1781, the caseload increased until 1787, when court activity decreased somewhat before reviving again in 1789 and 1790.[6] The reasons for the sharp decline in caseload in 1781 remain unclear. At first glance, one might guess that the vicissitudes of record survival account for the variations in Figure 1. Yet a comparison of the sénéchaussée cases with those appealed to the tournelle attenuates that argument: The distribution of the 73 appeals from Sarlat to Bordeaux closely corresponds to the distribution of the 450 sénéchaussée cases currently housed in Périgueux, allowing for an average interval of one year between a case's inception and its appeal. The decline in caseload in 1781 is therefore reflected in a subsequent drop in the caseload of the tournelle approximately one year later. Moreover, record linkage of tournelle appeals with the original dossiers was successful for 79 percent of the cases. Both facts suggest that the 1781 decrease in the caseload of the Sénéchaussée of Sarlat represents a real drop in court activity and not an apparent decline owing to record loss.

To explain these variations in the criminal caseload, one must first distinguish between the public cases (29 percent of the total) and the privately initiated cases (71 percent). As mentioned in the previous chapter, criminal proceedings were initiated either by the royal prosecutor, who was theoretically obliged to prosecute all offenses that could become grand criminel cases, or by private parties, who generally sought reparation for less serious offenses. In public cases, the crown financed the costs of prosecution from a general fund under the control of the local receiver of the royal domain. Because the intendant authorized the receiver to disburse royal funds only for the prosecution of serious crimes, the sénéchaussée clearly could not concern itself with every offense committed within its jurisdiction. Even for serious offenses classified as *crimes*, the prosecution of all offenders regardless of their ability to defray court costs through fines and confiscations would

6. The criminal court archives of the Sénéchaussée of Sarlat are located in Series B 1544–B 1604 and B 1636–B 1642, ADD.

have quickly drained the general fund. Because it was very difficult to recuperate expenses from either the accused or the Crown, royal and seigneurial judicial bodies charged with the implementation of criminal justice generally sought to avoid the responsibility.[7]

Of the various factors capable of disrupting the efficient operation of a criminal justice system, lack of finances is easily the most telling and most immediate in its impact. Examples abound of how the inadequacy of financial resources determined whether police agents would arrest suspects and whether royal prosecutors would initiate proceedings against those apprehended. In April, 1773, for instance, Subdelegate Meyrignac ordered the apprehension of a poor bordier named Calotte accused of assaulting a soldier. But the constables of the maréchaussée complained to the subdelegate that he should not waste their time, insisting that even if apprehended, Calotte would be unable to pay the expenses of their mission or indemnify the victim. Indeed, when Calotte was finally captured early the next month, he was ordered to pay only six livres in damages to the victim and six livres to the constables, the latter sum being grossly insufficient to cover the costs they incurred in performing their duties. The poverty of the accused evidently precluded a harsher penalty; in fact, Calotte reportedly had to borrow money even to pay the twelve livres.[8]

When the prévôté of the maréchaussée in June, 1781, found two young women guilty of vagabondage and condemned them to three years' confinement in a *maison de force,* the subdelegate objected to the intendant that the sentence was highly unrealistic since the nearest *maison de force* was in Bordeaux. He further complained that the limited space and insalubrity of the royal prison at Sarlat made it unsuitable for the women's lengthy confinement. To make matters worse, the présidial then condemned three additional women to similar terms of confinement (one for life). But when the subdelegate asked the judicial officers of the maréchaussée to show more restraint in their arrests and sentencing, they retorted that legally they had little latitude to do otherwise. The poorly paid constables of the maréchaussée were also notorious for supplementing their meager income—sometimes by means of

7. Soman, "Deviance and Criminal Justice," 9–11; N. Castan, *Justice et répression en Languedoc,* 115–16.

8. Lettre de l'Intendant à M. de Meyrignac, April 26, 1773, Lettre de l'Intendant à M. de Meyrignac, May 17, 1773, both in C 478, ADG.

part-time jobs (mostly as *cabaretiers*) but frequently through graft.[9]

Given its financial limitations, the sénéchaussée understandably spent most of its time prosecuting cases in which private parties paid the expenses. Only 29 percent of its caseload from 1770 to 1790 consisted of public cases heard at royal expense. In the sénéchaussées of Libourne and Bazas, royal prosecutors in the course of the century pursued less than one-quarter of the cases for which the plaintiff is known.[10] Focusing on the twenty-year period between 1770 and 1789, one perceives that the Sénéchaussée of Sarlat prosecuted a total of 132 criminal cases at royal expense, or an average of 6.6 cases annually. Of those 132 cases, 74 were thefts (56 percent), 25 were homicides (19 percent), and the remainder were assorted crimes against the king's authority and public order or crimes against morality. Although court costs generally could not be recuperated in public cases of theft, the sénéchaussée handled an average of 3.7 such cases annually between 1770 and 1789. One can only assume that the magistrates felt reasonably confident that the intendant would consider the cases in question worthy of prosecution at royal expense.

The number of cases of theft before the tribunal in a given year had an essentially unknown but assuredly tangential relationship to the actual rate of delinquency in the Sarladais. In any given year the number of theft cases varied from none (in 1771 and 1789) to thirteen (in 1779).[11] Modulations in the caseload reveal little about fluctuations in actual incidence: The fact that the court prosecuted no thefts in 1771 and 1789 does not, of course, mean that no such crimes were committed during those years. Contemporaries readily admitted that the entire criminal justice system rested on the principle of occasional arrests and harsh public punishments for those few who were guilty of atrocious crimes. Their ordeal, it was hoped, would impress the populace with the king's power and restore order by deterring would-be

9. Lettre de Meyrignac à M. l'Intendant, August 14, 1781, Lettre de M. Pouzal, procureur du roy en la maréchaussée, July 3, 1781, both in C 489, ADG; Cameron, *Crime and Repression*, 28–37.

10. Ruff, *Crime, Justice and Public Order*, 45–47.

11. Seven additional cases for theft were initiated by private parties but ruled to be *vols simples* that concerned only the individuals involved and were therefore continued at private expense. Altogether, the sénéchaussée heard 81 cases of theft, or approximately 18 percent of the total caseload of 446 public and private cases with known offenses. Because Revolutionary disturbances affected the normal functioning of the sénéchaussée in 1790, figures for that year have been excluded from these calculations.

criminals. As a general rule, the severity of punishment stands in inverse relationship to the efficiency of justice. But this does not necessarily imply that sentencing under the Old Regime was uniformly severe and executions always spectacular.[12]

One must look beyond the selectivity that derived from legal criteria and financial limitations to examine the actual process by which certain offenses were criminalized. Of the 74 public cases of theft heard between 1770 and 1789, the court heard only 11 (15 percent) in the first instance and heard the remaining 63 cases (85 percent) in the second instance, as referrals from prévôtés or from lower-level tribunals. Most of the 11 cases of theft initiated directly before the sénéchaussée were committed within the parish of Sarlat itself. Of the 63 public cases of theft referred to the sénéchaussée, 15 (20 percent of the total) were first instructed before a prévôté, and 48 (65 percent) were first handled by a seigneurial or municipal tribunal. The dependence of the royal tribunal on these lower tribunals is all the more evident when one remembers that fully 88 percent (122) of the 138 public cases that came before the sénéchaussée between 1770 and 1790 had already been prosecuted to some degree by lower-level courts or exceptional tribunals—confirming that the royal court played an essentially passive role of reviewing and continuing felony cases begun elsewhere.[13]

But the most striking feature in the complex selection process by which some incidents of delinquent behavior became criminalized was the fact that the society of the Sarladais was to a large degree self-policing. Aside from the few suspects unlucky enough to be caught in the act by the constables of the maréchaussée, the majority of the offenders apprehended were delivered to royal and seigneurial authorities by the populace itself. It appears that members of the community informally and perhaps unconsciously singled out those delinquents who would become criminals. Popular justice therefore served as a kind of court of first instance that resolved petty disputes and thefts, usually allowing only serious crimes to reach the sénéchaussée. In turn, royal justice essentially acted as a higher court of appeal or referral for affairs involving truly serious offenses such as murder, which, if left to in-

12. P. Henry, *Crime, justice et société*, 347–48, 490–91.
13. For a fuller description, see my article "The Selective Prosecution of Crime in Ancien Régime France: Theft in the Sénéchaussée of Sarlat," *European History Quarterly*, XVI (1986), 3–24.

formal mediation or private vengeance, might have touched off endless feuding.

In private criminal suits, on the other hand, proceedings began only after the private party pledged to defray the costs of prosecution. As a result, an injured party considering legal action necessarily weighed the potentially high cost of a lawsuit against the advantages. He carefully assessed not only his own financial situation but also that of the accused, for there was little point in prosecuting a poor man who could not afford to pay court costs or reparations. The decision to bring suit against an adversary was, in essence, a calculated risk. The cost of initiating criminal action was relatively modest: A petition of complaint could cost as few as three or as many as twenty livres, depending on its length and complexity. But the total cost of legal action for a privately initiated suit could vary wildly, depending primarily on the stubbornness of the adversaries and the point at which they negotiated an out-of-court settlement.

Should the case proceed until official action terminated it (short of the extraordinary stage) via court judgment or an interlocutory decree, expenses could attain 100 livres or more. In 1785, for example, Jean Delmas of Sarlat brought suit against Antoine Lasserre on charges of *assassinat* (assault). It seems that Lasserre, who had been denounced by Delmas and fined for carrying firearms, attacked Delmas one evening outside a cabaret in order to "make him pay." Delmas petitioned the court, a surgeon reported on the injuries, and witnesses testified at the inquest. But before the accused was even summoned, the adversaries apparently negotiated a settlement out of court. The total court costs amounted to 87 livres 16 sous. In a similar private suit in 1784, this time for verbal violence (*insultes et menaces*), expenses amounted to 79 livres, although again the accused was never summoned or interrogated. Expenses in 1783 for another private suit of comparable length, again for verbal violence, totaled approximately 70 livres.[14]

In contrast, a single public case that proceeded into the extraordinary phase could cost the Crown several hundred livres. The figure of 1,000 écus was advanced by administrative, military, and judicial au-

14. Plainte, November 18, 1784, Information, November 22, 1784, and Etat des frais, n.d., all in B 1583, ADD; Plainte, February 16, 1785, Procès-verbal, February 16, 1785, Information, February 21, 1785, Etat des frais, n.d., all in B 1585, ADD. Procès-verbal, September 13, 1783, Etat des frais, n.d., both in B 1581, ADD.

thorities as an average cost of criminal proceedings reaching the Tour-nelle of Toulouse from the eastern part of Languedoc, where distances increased expenses.[15] Indeed, simply sending the thirteen dossiers of a lengthy case of theft to the Tournelle of Bordeaux in 1772 cost 21 livres—at a time when a domestique in the Périgord earned annual wages of 60 livres and a journalier earned 5 sous per day, plus bread. Overall, then, the great majority of the populace probably found the legal services of the sénéchaussée to be discouragingly, if not prohibi-tively, expensive. They knew that although the cost of initiating criminal proceedings was not necessarily expensive in and of itself, the conse-quences of such action were uncertain and could prove ruinous, espe-cially for individuals lacking the knowledge, experience, and French-language skills needed to compete in the legal arena.[16]

The division of cases into the two categories of public and private indicates that the overall increase in caseload was due primarily to an increase in privately initiated suits after 1781, as illustrated in Figure 1. One conceivable explanation for this increase in private cases is a sud-den crime wave to which private individuals responded, but this is highly unlikely. A slight increase in public cases for serious offenses occurred only after 1784, whereas the increase in private cases began three years earlier and peaked in 1784. Only in 1785 and 1786 do the two overlap. A more plausible explanation is that private individuals for a variety of reasons were more inclined after 1781 to use the royal court to prosecute relatively minor offenses that they previously settled informally.

The breakdown of cases according to type of offense confirms that the typological distinction between serious and lesser offenses clearly coincides with the division between public and private cases (Table 1). Minor offenses against persons were almost entirely privately prose-cuted, as were relatively minor offenses against property. On the other hand, 100 percent of homicides and 90 percent of thefts were public cases. Crimes against morality and even those against the king and pub-lic security were also predominantly prosecuted as private cases (71 per-cent and 65 percent, respectively). Most significantly, for the period as a whole, almost 60 percent of all cases involved crimes of violence

---

15. N. Castan, *Justice et répression en Languedoc*, 115–16.

16. To some extent, the above conclusions apply to civil legal action; unfortunately, investigation into civil litigation at the local level in France remains to be done.

against persons, and only 25 percent of the total caseload involved crimes against property. Figure 2 illustrates that the proportion of crimes against persons (89 percent of which were private cases) fluctuated greatly before 1781, after which date it increased somewhat for the remainder of the period, with the exception of a brief decline below the mean in 1786 and 1787. On the other hand, Figure 3 reveals that the proportion of crimes against property (68 percent of which were public cases of theft) also fluctuated yet gradually declined after 1781, with only a temporary resurgence in 1786 and 1787. The criminal court was clearly spending more of its time prosecuting minor offenses at private expense. Crimes against morality, which constituted 4 percent of the total, fluctuated throughout the period without any discernible trend. Cases involving offenses against the king and public security constituted 11 percent of the total and were clustered during the disorders associated with the dearth of 1773–74 and the revolutionary disturbances of 1789–90. Both the breakdown of cases according to offense and the distribution of offenses throughout the period confirm that the overall increase in the caseload of the sénéchaussée was due to the fact that more private individuals were initiating criminal proceedings at their own expense to prosecute violent but nonfatal offenses against persons.

Violent crimes against persons—aside from fatal violence—were of two sorts, verbal violence (insults, menaces, calumny) and nonfatal physical violence (battery). Figure 4 illustrates the movement of both categories of offenses during the period and suggests that whereas the prosecution of verbal violence was relatively infrequent before 1781, afterwards it became increasingly common, to the point that in 1783 such cases constituted 48 percent of private suits and 39 percent of the total caseload of the sénéchaussée. Private suits stemming from battery were more common throughout the period, but also increased significantly in the 1780s. In 1784, both types of offenses made up nearly 81 percent of the private suits being prosecuted and 72 percent of all cases heard by the court.

Analysis of the caseload according to the type of offense and the public or private nature of the case reveals that in this relatively backward region, private cases stemming from violent offenses against persons, far from declining, constituted a growing proportion of the caseload of the sénéchaussée. Although on the surface this development suggests the enduring strength of a preindustrial pattern of crime, other

TABLE I

Criminal Cases with Known Offenses Before the Sénéchaussée

Offense	No. of cases	% of subtotal	% of total cases
Crime against persons			
Verbal violence	81	28.72	17.09
Battery	176	62.41	37.13
Fatal violence	25	8.87	5.27
Subtotal	282		59.49
Crime against property			
Damage to property	21	17.50	4.43
Fraud	9	7.50	1.90
Theft	90	75.00	18.99
Subtotal	120		25.32
Crime against morality (prostitution, rape, seduction)	21		4.43
Crime against the authority of the king and public security	51		10.76
Total	474		100.00

Sources: Plaintes et informations criminelles du Sénéchal, procès-verbaux, et interrogatoires, B 1544–B 1604, Sentences criminelles du Sénéchal, B 1636–B 1642, Sénéchaussée: Requêtes, informations, et sentences, B 3613, all in ADD; Tournelle de Sarlat, Series B, ADG.

discernible trends suggest that this interpretation of the data is inaccurate. Indeed, that the absolute increase in caseload can be attributed in the main to a significant rise in private suits suggests the opposite. Throughout the first twelve years of the period, serious offenses (public cases) fluctuated greatly in their deviation from the mean; but during the three-year period when private cases increased (1782–84), public cases were well below average, suggesting that the surge in private suits was not due to a crime wave. That the offenses in question were relatively mundane incidents of assault and battery arising from the routine interaction of the inhabitants of the Sarladais only reinforces this argument. The most plausible explanation for this increase lies in the obvious fact that in the 1780s more individuals were prepared to involve the royal court in the resolution of their minor conflicts, suggesting a

No. of public cases	% of offenses	No. of private cases	% of offenses
0	0.00	81	100.00
7	3.98	169	96.02
25	100.00	0	0.00
32	11.35	250	88.65
0	0.00	21	100.00
1	11.11	8	88.89
81	90.00	9	10.00
82	68.33	38	31.67
6	28.57	15	71.43
18	35.29	33	64.71
138	29.11	336	70.89

more modern attitude toward royal justice. Paradoxically, however, this apparent movement toward the acceptance of official, legal methods of settling disputes resulted in more cases of violence against persons, a pattern of ciminality that suggests—according to current wisdom—stasis if not regression.

Although the statistics cited above are suggestive, the evidence they provide remains inconclusive owing to the small number of cases involved and the brevity of the period in question. But an investigation into the identity of the private plaintiffs and the proportional share of litigation initiated by different socioprofessional groups reinforces this hypothesis. Between 1770 and 1790, 461 plaintiffs initiated 338 private suits. The documents indicate the titles of address or *qualité* claimed by 173 plaintiffs, who can thereby be divided into three broad but dis-

FIGURE 2

Crimes Against Persons

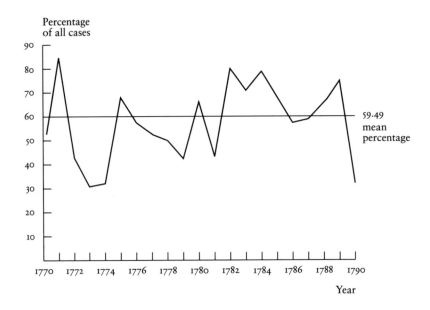

FIGURE 3

Crimes Against Property

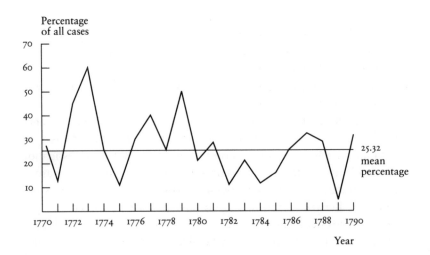

FIGURE 4

Violent Crimes Against Persons

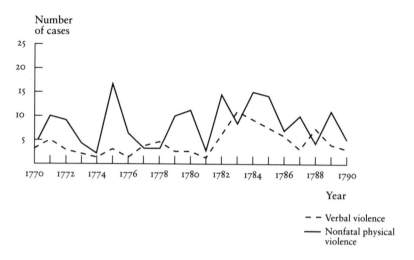

Year

- - Verbal violence
— Nonfatal physical violence

tinct groups: nobles, non-nobles, and artisans.[17] The proportionate share of nobles who initiated suits before the sénéchaussée during this period increased from almost 13 to 19 percent (Table 2). Non-nobles (primarily bourgeois) generated the greatest share (80 percent) of court business throughout the period, while artisans (designated as "master" or "apprentice") continued to initiate private suits in relatively low proportion (7 percent overall). Only on the part of the nobility can one discern a greater degree of participation, especially from 1786 to 1790.

The documents further specify the occupations of 314 (68 percent) of the 461 plaintiffs. Table 3 shows their distribution into socioprofessional categories and the degree to which each category's participation in private suits varied from one period to the next. The most significant movement occurred in the agricultural sector, with an absolute increase

17. Although by the eighteenth century a person's title was not as reliable an indicator of status as in previous centuries, the following analysis is based on a strict interpretation of the records. Only those persons were counted as nobles who bore the title *monsieur, messire, noble, comte, écuyer, chevalier, marquis,* or *baron;* and their wives and daughters, *madame* and *mademoiselle.* Those grouped in the non-noble category were persons referred to as *sieur, maître, bourgeois,* or *conseiller du roi;* and their wives, *dame.* Artisans for whom the documents specified a title (only 17 percent of those with artisan occupations) were divided into *maîtres* and *garçons.* See Roland Mousnier, *Les Hierarchies sociales de 1450 à nos jours* (Paris, 1969).

in the number of persons initiating private suits and a doubling of this group's proportionate share of cases from 14 to over 27 percent in the course of twenty years. Artisans, tradesmen, and shopkeepers, on the other hand, declined as plaintiffs both in numbers and in relative importance, whereas those engaged in commerce remained fairly constant in numbers but fluctuated somewhat in relative importance (between 13 and 22 percent). Members of the liberal professions generated the largest share of private cases in the 1770s and accounted for 40 percent of such cases from 1786 to 1790. The remaining groups only intermittently initiated criminal proceedings and never to any significant ex-

TABLE 2

Qualité *of Plaintiffs in Private Cases*

Time period	No. of plaintiffs	Plaintiffs with known *qualité* (No.)	(%)	Qualité					
				Nobles (No.)	(%)	Non-nobles (No.)	(%)	Artisans (No.)	(%)
1770–75	124	47	37.90	6	12.76	36	76.60	5	10.64
1776–80	79	24	30.38	2	8.33	21	87.50	1	4.17
1781–85	141	60	42.55	7	11.67	50	83.33	3	5.00
1786–90	117	42	35.90	8	19.05	31	73.81	3	7.14
Total (Average)	461	173	(37.53)	23	(13.29)	138	(79.77)	12	(6.94)

SOURCES: See Table 1.

TABLE 3

Socioprofessional Status of Plaintiffs in Private Cases: An Overview

Time period	No. of plaintiffs	Plaintiffs with known status (No.)	(%)	Agricultural sector (No.)	(%)	Artisans, tradesmen, shopkeepers (No.)	(%)
1770–75	124	80	64.52	11	13.75	26	32.50
1776–80	79	58	73.42	9	15.52	13	22.41
1781–85	141	96	68.09	24	25.00	21	21.87
1786–90	117	80	68.38	22	27.50	9	11.25
Total (Average)	461	314	(68.11)	66	(21.02)	69	(21.97)

SOURCES: See Table 1.

tent. The most significant feature emerging from an analysis of the court's clientele is the somewhat increased participation of noblemen and members of the agricultural sector.

A further breakdown of the three most important broad occupational categories discloses that within the agricultural sector small landowners and sharecroppers were primarily responsible for that sector's increase in private cases (Table 4). The share of large landowners (seigneurs, propriétaires, and fermiers) also increased, but to a lesser extent. As might be expected, agricultural employees (*valets*, bordiers, and journaliers) continued to initiate very few private suits. Within the commercial sector, wealthy traders and wholesale merchants (négociants) came to constitute a larger share of plaintiffs in private cases, while lesser merchants declined somewhat in importance. As for the liberal professions, various *hommes de loi* along with assorted royal officials took advantage of their skills and familiarity with legal procedures to generate 35 percent of private suits (in which the status of plaintiffs is known) between 1786 and 1790.

The above analysis of the *qualité* and socioprofessional status of private plaintiffs, although by no means conclusive, does provide a clearer picture of what occurred during these years. The overall increase in cases heard by the Sénéchaussée of Sarlat between 1770 and 1790 evidently was due largely to the initiation by private individuals of an increasing number of relatively minor offenses of verbal and physical violence. Partly because no evidence points to a greater incidence of such offenses but mostly because their nature argues against such an explanation, the increase in private prosecution of minor violent offenses against persons can be attributed to the growing inclina-

Socioprofessional Status

Traders and merchants (No.) (%)		Liberal professions (No.) (%)		Military (No.) (%)		Religious (No.) (%)		Miscellaneous (No.) (%)	
10	12.50	26	32.50	2	2.50	4	5.00	1	1.25
13	22.41	17	29.31	2	3.45	2	3.45	2	3.45
14	14.58	28	29.17	0	0.00	4	4.17	5	5.21
14	17.50	32	40.00	2	2.50	0	0.00	1	1.25
51	(16.24)	103	(32.80)	6	(1.91)	10	(3.18)	9	(2.87)

TABLE 4

Socioprofessional Status of Plaintiffs in Private Cases: A Breakdown

Time period	Plaintiffs with known status	Agricultural sector					
		Proprietors and leaseholders (No.) (%)		Small landowners and sharecroppers (No.) (%)		Agricultural employees (No.) (%)	
1770–75	80	4	5.00	6	7.50	1	1.25
1776–80	58	2	3.45	3	5.17	4	6.90
1781–85	96	10	10.42	10	10.42	4	4.17
1786–90	80	7	8.75	13	16.25	2	2.50
Total (Average)	314	23	(7.32)	32	(10.19)	11	(3.50)

SOURCES: See Table 1.

tion of individuals to involve official, royal justice in the settlement or at least the pursuit of their petty disputes and feuds. Moreover, the *qualité* and occupation of plaintiffs in private suits altered in some degree. In the early years of this period, artisans and members of the liberal professions were equally active in the initiation of suits, between them generating 65 percent of the total (Table 3). By the end of the period, persons from the agricultural sector and négociants had supplanted the artisan group, which by then had fallen into fourth position. The growing participation of persons from the agricultural sector is perhaps the most significant development in the evolution of the court's clientele. Not only seigneurs, propriétaires, and fermiers but also small peasant proprietors and sharecroppers began to have recourse to royal justice to resolve conflicts previously settled either by informal mediation or by the direct action of those involved. Finally, more noblemen were apparently among the propriétaires who took advantage of the services afforded by the royal court.

The preeminence of the liberal profession is readily understandable. Given the preindustrial nature of the Sarladais economy in the eighteenth century, the bourgeoisie was composed largely of members of the liberal professions, men who were educated, literate, accustomed to dealing with written records, and therefore sufficiently skilled and strategically placed to use the courts to their own advantage. In addition to speaking the patois used exclusively by the majority of the populace, they could read and write French, the language of officialdom. In

Traders and merchants				Liberal professions			
Traders		Merchants		Medical profession		Legal practitioners and royal officials	
(No.)	(%)	(No.)	(%)	(No.)	(%)	(No.)	(%)
0	0.00	10	12.50	0	0.00	26	32.50
4	6.90	9	15.52	4	6.90	13	22.41
7	7.29	7	7.29	2	2.08	26	27.08
7	8.75	7	8.75	4	5.00	28	35.00
18	(5.73)	33	(10.51)	10	(3.18)	93	(29.62)

contrast, literacy was extremely low among the general populace of the Périgord: Approximately 10 percent of men and 7 percent of women in rural milieux could sign in the 1777–86 period, and in urban centers such as Sarlat, the literacy figures were only somewhat higher—19 percent of men and 10 percent of women.[18] Members of the liberal professions undoubtedly always formed the core of the court's clientele and, not surprisingly, generated 40 percent of its private cases (in which the status of plaintiffs is known) by 1790.

But how can the growing participation of the nobility and peasantry be explained? It is implausible that people began insulting each other or resorting to violence more frequently in their disputes. Furthermore, improved police work can easily be ruled out as a factor in the increase of private cases. Throughout the period, three brigades of four cavalrymen each were responsible for patrolling the highroads and markets of the entire jurisdiction, which contained more than 100,000 inhabitants. In most instances, private citizens themselves pursued, apprehended, and then held the accused until the authorities arrived. Given the preponderant role of private citizens in the prevention and prosecution of crime, one cannot assume that the increase in criminal cases was due to the increased incidence of offenses in the community. Nor had royal justice become any less expensive. Members of the agri-

18. Jean-Pierre Poussou, "Recherches sur l'alphabétisation de l'Aquitaine au XVIIIe siècle," in François Furet and Jacques Ozouf (eds.), *Lire et écrire: L'Alphabétisation des français de Calvin à Jules Ferry* (Paris, 1977), 332–33.

cultural sector across France did, however, become wealthier (in varying degrees) during the latter half of the eighteenth century because
of rising grain prices and easier commercialization of their products,
which may have contributed somewhat to the growing litigiousness of
Sarladais nobles and peasants. More probable is either that the populace grew increasingly intolerant of certain offenses and therefore more
willingly cooperated with the authorities, or that people simply became
more skilled at or at least accustomed to using the court's legal services
to their own advantage.[19]

Royal justice had been superimposed on a network of popular justice that included revenge and traditional modes of reconciliation via
arbitration and restitution. Throughout the eighteenth century, the two
systems coexisted in what can be characterized as a *modus vivendi*.[20]
Unofficial forms of conflict resolution had always been available to the
populace. In minor offenses such as verbal abuse and physical attack
and even in more serious offenses such as manslaughter, opposing parties frequently agreed to resolve their differences, usually through the
mediation of a third party, and to drop any civil or criminal proceedings begun by either party. Occasionally they went before a notary to
formalize the agreement.[21] But in truly serious matters and for offenses
committed by outsiders—immune to the informal sanctions of a local
community—offended parties preferred to appeal directly to the royal
courts, which by the end of the Old Regime served as auxiliary courts
for the informal tribunals of popular justice.

Did popular justice become less attractive as an alternative? Yves

19. Pierre Goubert, *The Course of French History*, trans. Maarten Ultee (New
York, 1988), 246–48; Ernest Labrousse, "Aperçu de la répartition sociale de l'expansion
agricole," in Labrousse *et al., Des derniers temps de l'âge seigneurial,* 481–87.

20. Soman, "Deviance and Criminal Justice," 20–23; Deyon, *Le Temps des prisons,* 79–80; Spierenburg, *The Spectacle of Suffering,* 10–11.

21. Soman, in "Deviance and Criminal Justice," 15–18, noted the need for systematic research to measure the extent to which notarial settlements served as a means not
only of terminating legal disputes but also of avoiding them. The sénéchaussée records
occasionally contain copies of notarial settlements and frequently refer to them. More
often, however, cases were simply not pursued and ended without any hint of how they
may have been resolved. Record linkage in the Sarladais is impossible owing to the incomplete nature of the notarial records. Nicole Castan, working exclusively with judicial
archives, found that 7.48 percent of the 4,092 criminal cases appealed to the Parlement of
Toulouse between 1779 and 1790 mention a prior informal transaction or one in progress (*Justice et répression en Languedoc,* 15). Among the cases that came before the Sénéchaussée of Sarlat, 9 percent refer to a prior or ongoing attempt at informal settlement.

Castan maintains that traditional forms of dispute settlement became less effective in other areas of France as a result of the gradual erosion of communal solidarity by the greater mobility of the populace, the advance of social differentiation, and the progressive integration of local communities into regional economies. Although it is difficult to assess the impact of these trends on the Sarladais, we do know that by the end of the Old Regime the peasants of the region displayed a smoldering resentment toward the nobility, perceived by them as a superfluous class unable and unwilling to protect them as it had done in the seventeenth century, when both groups united to resist royal fiscal agents.[22]

In the course of the eighteenth century, nobles and peasants alike had capitulated to royal authority. Neither group at that time appealed to royal justice, but for different reasons. Peasants could ill afford royal justice and therefore rarely appeared before the courts except as defendants. In their own disputes, they had little alternative but informal arbitration, which, unfortunately, was unreliable—especially when the parties involved were of unequal status and had divergent interests and opinions. Moreover, peasants could neither force their social superiors to submit to arbitration nor make them abide by the final ruling. If all else failed, they had recourse to direct action: ambush, assassination, arson, mutilation, vandalism, and poaching. Likewise, nobles tended not to resort to the lower royal courts to resolve local conflicts with peasants. They preferred either to use more personalized methods to exert their considerable political and economic influence or to work through seigneurial courts more susceptible to their control.[23]

Some historians have argued that the social unrest and economic depression of the final years of the Old Regime brought significant changes in popular justice. Growing numbers of beggars strained traditional sources of charity. When denied charity, they often resorted to threats and occasionally even to theft and violence. The result, these

22. Y. Castan, *Honnêteté et rélations sociales,* 56; Boutier, "Jacqueries en pays croquant," 760–86. Iain Cameron concurs that eighteenth-century peasants in the Périgord were more antagonistic to seigneurial dues and, in certain circumstances, to the tithe than to the taille ("The Police in Provincial France: The Maréchaussée of the Auvergne and the Guyenne, 1720–1790" [Ph.D. dissertation, University of Reading, 1976], 808). Also see Bercé, *Histoire des croquants,* 632–33.

23. For a theoretical overview of this process, see Torstein Eckhoff, "The Mediator and the Judge," in Vilhelm Aubert (ed.), *The Sociology of Law* (Baltimore, 1969), 172–75.

historians claim, was an increase in serious crimes and a climate of fear in which rural dwellers desperately sought protection. These circumstances, it is argued, significantly eroded popular confidence in self-regulation and convinced nobles and peasants to appeal to the royal courts during the waning years of the Old Regime.[24]

But no one of these factors taken in isolation can adequately explain the increase in private suits for petty physical and verbal violence before the sénéchaussée. The peasant proprietors and sharecroppers of the Sarladais who had recourse to royal justice were not prosecuting vagabonds for theft or extortion, but were prosecuting persons of equal or superior social status for minor offenses previously settled extralegally. This phenomenon is linked not only to the question of the continued vitality of infrajudicial forms of dispute settlement but also, perhaps, to the dissemination of the ideal of the *homme civilisé,* a somewhat extended version of the *honnête homme,* the human type that represented the true ideal of court society. *Honnêteté* can be described as a set of values and a form of interpersonal behavior previously restricted to the royal court and salons that dominated the intellectual and social life of the aristocracy. The ideal emphasized civility, politeness, self-control, and propriety in one's economic and personal relations. By extension, the process of *civilisation* involved more than the refinement of manners: It implied the creation of an orderly, rational, internally pacified society or state. The impulse toward moderation and standardization in interpersonal relations, like the desire for legal codification and linguistic uniformity, was therefore intimately linked to the gradual process of economic and political modernization underway in even the more remote regions of the kingdom.[25]

But we must proceed with caution. The perceptible yet slight increase in private recourse to the Sénéchaussée of Sarlat for misdemeanors cannot be explained by a social crisis in Old Regime France. Al-

24. For a general description of this process, see Olwen Hufton, *The Poor of Eighteenth-Century France, 1750–1789* (Oxford, 1974), 201–202. Also see Olwen Hufton, "Attitudes Towards Authority in Eighteenth–Century Languedoc," *Social History,* III (1978), 281–302. Nicole Castan outlines a more general crisis on the eve of the Revolution (*Justice et répression en Languedoc,* 7–8, 46, 126–27).

25. Norbert Elias argues that there is a direct connection between social and political structure and the individual's personality structure (*The Development of Manners: Changes in the Code of Conduct and Feeling in Early Modern Times* [New York, 1978], 39, 48, 201–202, Vol. I of Elias, *The Civilizing Process,* 3 vols. Also see Y. Castan, *Honnêteté et rélations sociales,* 56–57.

though one could, perhaps, characterize the modification in behavior evident during this period as a shift in mentality, one cannot easily explain the former by the latter without slipping into a circular argument. In fact, it can be argued that the measurable increase in private suits for verbal and petty physical violence came about without any significant change in mentality on the part of the court's new clients. Most litigants in such cases were simply adding legal recourse to a panoply of tactics that ran the gamut from revenge to restitution. Their goal was not so much the peaceful resolution of disputes via official methods or the advancement of predictability in human relations, but the traditional goal of restoring social equilibrium or of humiliating and ruining their opponent. In other words, recourse to royal justice was often simply another means of attaining vengeance in a society still dominated by the concept of *honneur*, not *honnêteté*. One must therefore examine the day-to-day workings of popular justice and consider the practical advantages plaintiffs believed they could gain by involving the royal courts in their disputes to explain why the criminal caseload of the Sénéchaussée of Sarlat increased in the 1780s.

IV

Dispute Settlement
in Public Cases

Thus, authority was either non-existent or weak, except in those cases—which naturally are very rare—where justice is forced into action by the blatant gravity of the case.

—Honoré de Balzac, *The Black Sheep*

Criminal litigation was undoubtedly an atypical means of resolving disputes in the Sarladais. Disputants rarely pressed their claims so far as to require resort to a royal court of law; one or the other invariably offered a satisfactory settlement or proposed the use of some infrajudicial procedure to settle the dispute before it reached the sénéchaussée. The choice of a method for resolving disagreements was logically influenced by the advantages and disadvantages of the alternatives available. Many people apparently shunned seigneurial courts during this period, perhaps because of their reputation of being inefficient, corrupt, staffed by poorly trained personnel, and plagued by procedural irregularities. More important, seigneurial tribunals were by nature controlled and too often manipulated by seigneurs solicitous of their own interests. Individuals who seriously wished to challenge the social hierarchy therefore looked elsewhere for the redress of their grievances.

Traditional modes of dispute settlement constituted an alternative system of justice replete with informal agents, laws, and rules of procedure. This system had long coexisted with royal justice in a relationship that was intrinsically antagonistic yet often mutually beneficial in practice. Each judicial system offered its services to the populace, but with important differences. Dispute settlement involved mediation and arbitration by a third party who did not rule in favor of one disputant at the expense of the other but instead appealed to the mutual interest of both parties and emphasized the future benefits to be gained from restoring social equilibrium. Because mediation reinforced the notion that compromise was the preferred method of settlement, it necessarily implied the undesirability of appealing to outside authority to rule on the applicability of norms in a given incident.

In contrast, litigation by nature leads to a decision that makes clear who is right or wrong in accordance with standards independent of the disputants' will. As a result, judicial decisions emphasize the differences that divide disputants and exacerbate the conflict between them. Anthropologists have pointed out that in many traditional societies, where the role definition of each individual is highly contingent upon that of others, relationships between people of roughly equal status are expected to be characterized by harmony. Social pressure strongly insists that disputes not arise and, when they do, that they be solved via compromise and mutual understanding. When people are socially organized in multiple groups and involved in relationships that embrace many interests and endure into the future, attempts to regulate conduct by appeal to outside authority or universalistic norms can be threatening. In short, because litigation fixes individual rights by means of impersonal, objective standards, it effectively destroys the social fabric. Resort to litigation in traditional societies is therefore often condemned as morally wrong, subversive, and rebellious.[1]

Although antagonistic in principle, the relationship between popular and royal justice in the Sarladais was highly complementary in practice. As noted previously, popular justice acted as a court of first instance that filtered out many petty disputes and thefts but generally allowed serious offenses to reach the courts; in turn, royal justice acted as a court of appeal or of last resort for affairs involving serious crimes. Some inhabitants of the Sarladais also resorted to official justice in their petty disputes, using litigation or the threat of litigation as a point of leverage to gain a quicker or more favorable extrajudicial settlement.

Popular justice manifested itself most visibly in opposition to foreigners and other outsiders who threatened to upset the equilibrium of the local community. One can best examine its functioning in the

---

1. Takeyoshi Kawashima, "Dispute Resolution in Japan," in Aubert (ed.), *Sociology of Law,* 184–86; Max Gluckman, "The Judicial Process Among the Barotse of Northern Rhodesia," *ibid.,* 165–66; Eckhoff, "The Mediator and the Judge," *ibid.,* 172, 180.

defense of honor, wherein individuals and families avenged affronts through direct but measured violence; in the defense of "territory," wherein youth groups and other collectivities ritually chastised offenders of public morality by means of rough music and charivaris; and in the defense of the traditional equilibrium of communal rights and duties that applied to economic relations, wherein individuals and groups acted with the tacit approval of the populace.

The informal resolution of conflicts generally occurred through reconcilement or conciliation. Reconcilement is the process by which parties confer with each other to restore harmony or create harmonious differences; it often involves adjustments of demands after the assessment of the parties' needs and relative power. Given a disparity in power, a decision might in reality be imposed on an inferior, although agreed to by the latter. In contrast, conciliation is essentially the settlement of disputes through a third party and includes two categories: mediation and arbitration. Whereas in mediation the third party offers suggestions that have no binding force, in arbitration the third party can render a decision on the merits of the dispute. In practice, however, mediation and arbitration are often undifferentiated, especially when the third person who intervenes is of higher status than the disputants. In such cases, suggestions for reconcilement can, for all intents and purposes, be regarded as imposed. As a general rule, the greater the power of the go-between, the more the mediation takes on the coloration of arbitration. The go-between must, however, avoid the principles implicit in a judicial settlement: He cannot make any clear-cut decision on who is right or wrong, or inquire into the existence and scope of the rights of the parties. Go-betweens therefore often decide to "punish" both parties to a dispute.[2]

Historians have long known that criminal statistics for Old Regime France reveal more about royal justice than about society since autoregulation successfully dealt with delinquents and resolved disputes. But relatively little is known about how this process of dispute settlement functioned or the degree to which it affected official litigation.[3] At first glance, the criminal court records of the Sénéchaussée of Sarlat seem

2. The terminology and definitions used here are based on those of Kawashima in "Dispute Resolution in Japan," in Aubert (ed.), *Sociology of Law*, 191–92.
3. N. Castan, *Justice et répression en Languedoc*, 53–70.

to be the wrong place to look for evidence of informal dispute settlement. The decision to turn to royal justice was, however, often closely linked to the decision to reach a settlement, and disputants often used the threat or reality of legal action to persuade an opponent to settle informally. Therefore judicial records can be an excellent source for learning about instances of conciliation that either preceded, coincided with, or followed criminal litigation. The judicial records reveal the circumstances in which informal settlements were reached, the rules by which they were conducted, the social and mental structures from which they arose, and the manner in which this process may have been evolving.

In the Sarladais, the impulse to seek informal settlements was strong and spontaneous. Christian doctrine reinforced the social imperative of peace between neighbors, and curés were known to deny the sacraments to those who persisted in their differences.[4] Community and family solidarity discouraged the interference of outsiders in private affairs, especially in delicate matters involving honor. Families preferred informal settlements not only because they calmed antagonisms and repaired wrongs by the mechanism of the social group but also because official criminal prosecution did irreparable damage to family and personal honor. Culprits and their families avoided official justice in the hope of avoiding public shame; victims, in the hope of gaining immediate compensation. Moreover, the victim by his toleration made the culprit and his family beholden to him, which could prove useful in the future.[5]

In addition to being "foreign," royal justice was often inaccessible and, when available, potentially ruinous in light of the uncertain outcome. But popular distrust and avoidance of royal justice was rooted in more than fear of financial ruin, xenophobia, and the inaccessibility of the courts. The most decisive factor was arguably sociocultural: Community members preferred informal dispute settlement because judicial decisions punished and humiliated only one party to a dispute and thereby upset the tenuously balanced equilibrium of the rural community. The continued cohesion of the social group thus engendered reluc-

4. *Ibid.*, 16 ff.
5. For comparison of the Sarladais on this point with the Swiss principality of Neuchâtel, see P. Henry, *Crime, justice et société*, 696.

tance to have recourse to official justice and maintained the process of extrajudicial settlements—which, in turn, served to safeguard the traditional community from the encroachments of the modern state.

Of the 477 criminal cases heard by the Sénéchaussée of Sarlat between 1770 and 1790, 43 (approximately 9 percent) contain references to attempts at extralegal settlements (successful and unsuccessful) undertaken before or during the sénéchaussée case. The figure of 9 percent refers to all attempts to head off or settle disputes, whether reconcilements or conciliations, but is undoubtedly an underestimate of the number of attempts made at informal settlement. In comparison, Nicole Castan found that of the 4,092 criminal cases appealed to the Parlement of Toulouse during the same period, 306 (7.48 percent) mention a prior or ongoing settlement.[6]

A number of variables determined whether a case made reference to an informal settlement. Disputants who settled before a notary sometimes submitted a copy of the act to the court and requested that charges be dropped and the case be terminated. But the informal resolution of cases often left no trace in the records. Many cases were simply discontinued.[7] Moreover, many references to informal mediations concern multiple attempts made prior to litigation—attempts that obviously failed to discourage delinquent behavior or to resolve longstanding differences between the parties involved. Because chance also entered into whether or not a case contained references to a settlement, one cannot assume that cases failing to mention settlements were not resolved extralegally.

As seen in Table 5, settlement attempts increased slightly in number and maintained essentially the same relative importance through-

6. N. Castan, *Justice et répression en Languedoc,* 15. In the judicial records of the sénéchaussée, informal settlements are most often referred to as *accommodements, cessions, arrangements, assouplissements, compositions, arbitrations, médiations, traitements,* and *accords.* In some cases, although no term is used to describe the desired result, the intent of the parties is quite clear: "conclude their affairs amicably" or "settle the affair."

7. In practice, 85 percent of all criminal cases examined in a study of eighteenth-century Breton archives ended either by *civilisation,* adjournment, or condemnation of the accused to a lighter penalty (Mer, "La Procédure criminelle, 12, 25). Julius Ruff found that in the sénéchaussées of Libourne and Bazas only one in seven cases was carried through to a criminal verdict. More important, only 5 percent of private plaintiffs' cases culminated in a criminal court verdict ("The Character of Old Regime Justice," 12–13).

TABLE 5

Frequency of Informal Settlement Attempts in Public and Private Cases

Time period	No. of cases	Settlement attempts (No.)	(%)	No. of public cases	Settlement attempts (No.)	(%)	No. of private cases	Settlement attempts (No.)	(%)
1770–75	112	11	9.82	32	6	18.75	80	5	6.25
1776–80	104	7	6.73	47	6	12.77	57	1	1.75
1781–85	135	13	9.63	26	2	7.69	109	11	10.09
1786–90	126	12	9.52	34	3	8.82	92	9	9.78
Total (Average)	477	43	(9.01)	139	17	(12.23)	338	26	(7.69)

Sources: See Table 1.

out the period. Whereas public cases mentioned informal settlements less frequently as the period progressed, the proportion of private cases referring to settlements increased somewhat. Indeed, of the limited number of settlement attempts (43) referred to in the records, approximately 60 percent appeared in private cases. This increase must be viewed in conjunction with the absolute increase in the number of private suits in the second half of the period and with their increasing importance in relation to the entire caseload. Taken as a whole, the findings extracted from the records by no means reveal whether individuals in society at large were attempting settlements more or less frequently; they may, however, suggest that settlements were increasingly less successful in heading off litigation, especially in private cases. Cases involving violence had undoubtedly been settled informally before this time, but had left no trace in the judicial records simply because the incidents never came before the court.[8]

The informal settlements mentioned in public cases for felonies necessarily occurred before litigation and relate to transgressions prior to the one resulting in legal action. In other words, these earlier informal settlements had successfully obviated legal action until the most recent transgression. Why did such efforts fail to prevent recourse to official justice in the latest incident? The great majority of the settlements in public cases concern cases of theft, which—like all felonies—

8. P. Henry speculates that the publicity surrounding violence may have made it more difficult to settle such cases discreetly (*Crime, justice et société,* 694–95).

could not be compounded without permission of the court. In some cases of theft, the failure of an attempted settlement directly resulted in the criminal proceedings in question. Other cases refer only to past settlements that had nonetheless failed to persuade the accused to alter his behavior.

In the 74 public cases of theft heard by the sénéchaussée from 1770 to 1789, the defendant was tried on an average of 3.6 counts of theft. Many of the thefts had occurred over the preceding years—up to fourteen years, in one case—and had been settled informally. A number of examples illustrate the normal functioning of dispute settlement and the process by which such thefts eventually led to legal action. In February, 1781, a weaver was captured and turned over to the local seigneurial tribunal for the theft of wood supports from a shed, followed by arson to conceal the theft. Although the weaver denied the recent theft and arson, he readily admitted in his interrogation that he had stolen the supports of his house, but from someone else. He ingenuously admitted that in the course of several years he had stolen wood for heat, food for his table, and assorted agricultural implements for his own use. At the same time, he scrupulously denied not only the theft five years earlier of a plowshare (for which the local police had made him pay restitution) but also the theft of a cauldron he had reluctantly returned to its owner as part of a settlement designed to avoid prosecution. In the earlier instances, the weaver had benefited from the tolerance of his neighbors and local authorities and from the relative impotence of royal justice. When he finally exhausted the goodwill of the community and was dragged before the sénéchaussée, the court convicted him of "various thefts" and "of being accustomed to stealing for quite some time"; it sentenced him to be whipped and branded.[9]

In a similar case in 1785, a bourgeois went before the prosecutor of a lower-level court to denounce a thief he and his neighbors had captured. The bourgeois declared that "for a long while now he and the inhabitants of his village had suspected the accused of stealing fruit and of housebreaking, so they all agreed to keep the accused in sight." When the bourgeois subsequently realized that he had been robbed of money left in the pocket of his trousers hung on the bedpost as he slept, he alerted his neighbors. "As word of this theft spread," he continued, "everyone suspected the accused and took new measures to protect

9. Interrogatoire à Beaumont, December 19, 1780, B 1574, ADD.

their goods." But the very next morning a wagoner discovered that overnight someone had broken into his house and stolen bread. The following morning, when a sharecropper discovered that someone had taken a shirt from his *valet de ferme* and various articles from his barn, he immediately suspected the same man. So the bourgeois and the other victims assembled to track down the accused. They discovered him hidden in the straw of a barn and, upon searching him, found the stolen property. After claiming their goods, as they had done in the past, they decided this time to turn him over to the local authorities. Accused of at least ten instances of theft committed during the previous ten years, he was convicted by the sénéchaussée and sentenced to be branded and to serve on the galleys for twenty years.[10]

But the detailed history of how two young thieves gradually exhausted a community's fund of patience and toleration best illustrates the workings of informal dispute settlement and the manner in which seigneurial and royal courts not only tolerated such arrangements but also served the function of auxiliary courts of appeal for popular justice. Jean Dumon, known as "Sanspareil," and Jean Lavergne were young *travailleurs* arrested by the seigneurial court of Peyruzel in 1774. When the court interrogated them and held an inquest, it discovered that acting together or separately Dumon and Lavergne were responsible for at least ten thefts in the previous fourteen years.

Lavergne's career of delinquency began with an incident in 1760, when he was sixteen years old. While engaged as a domestique for Jean Mianes, a *praticien,* he discovered as he swept the stable a cloth sack containing the sizable sum of ten *louis d'or* (between 200 and 240 livres). Without mentioning his discovery to anyone, he took his leave before his tenure of employment expired. When Mianes and his father-in-law discovered that the money they had hidden in the stable was missing, they suspected Lavergne but had neither proof nor knowledge of his whereabouts. About six weeks later, they learned that Lavergne was employed in the next parish and had made himself conspicuous by loaning two louis to a friend. That evening, Mianes and a neighbor set out to find Lavergne and discovered him asleep in the barn of his current employer. Only when they threatened to have the boy hanged did he admit taking the money and agree to return it. After retrieving the

10. Interrogatoire, June 2, 1785, B 1584, ADD; Tournelle de Sarlat, July 18, 1785: Dénonciation faite à Moliere (December 11, 1784), B, ADG.

money from the home of his brother, Lavergne went with his captors to a tavern, where the boy returned the coins to the *praticien.* Mianes seemed quite satisfied and even promised Lavergne a reward. No criminal charges arose from the incident, and no real harm was done to either party. The money was returned, their agreement sealed with a drink, and both parties seemed satisfied.[11]

One suspects that the incident would never have come to light if Lavergne had not subsequently been involved in other thefts. Four or five years later, he was suspected of breaking into Mianes' wine cellar. Again the victim took no action against him. In 1772, another of his employers found a stolen shovel concealed in the straw of Lavergne's bed; he berated Lavergne but took no further action. Later that year, however, the same employer—one of the more prosperous men of the parish, a man named Lagrandie—surprised Lavergne and Dumon shaking walnuts from his trees and collecting them in their hats. With the aid of his *valets de ferme,* Lagrandie apprehended them and locked them in his barn. The next morning he marched them off toward the nearest judicial seat, announcing that he intended to turn them over to the tribunal of Peyruzel. The threat of prosecution was enough to induce Lavergne to plead with Lagrandie for his freedom and to promise to pay whatever was necessary to avoid being taken to court. In response, Lagrandie halted the party alongside the road and released Dumon, whom he knew to be pitifully poor and therefore incapable of paying damages. He then took Lavergne before a bourgeois, who informed the thief that a settlement would cost him forty-eight livres plus six livres in expenses. When Lavergne balked at the sum, the bourgeois reminded him that "he would be better off paying fifty livres than being taken to court."[12] As a result, they reached an *accommodement* (settlement) in which Lavergne reluctantly agreed to sell a calf to raise the required amount. In exchange, Lagrandie agreed not to press charges.

When Dumon was arrested in 1774 and confessed to the above theft of walnuts, he thereby implicated Lavergne, leading to the latter's arrest. During his interrogation, Lavergne vainly protested that he had already avowed publicly the theft of the nuts and paid restitution to the victim, therefore absolving himself of further liability. He insisted that

11. Information à Peyruzel, December 24, 1774, Interrogatoire, January 28, 1775, both in B 1558, ADD.

12. Interrogatoire, January 27, 1775, *ibid.*

the only reason Lagrandie had released Dumon and not him was that "Lagrandie apparently realized that [Dumon] was unable to pay."[13] But the sénéchaussée did not recognize the validity of the informal settlement reached between Lagrandie and Lavergne. In this as in all public cases, the accused was tried not only for the specific crime that resulted in prosecution but also for all others of which he may have been guilty and that came to the attention of the court.

Jean Dumon had an even more eventful career of petty theft that apparently began in 1764, when Joseph Lapeyre allowed Dumon, his mother, and two younger brothers to sleep in his corn crib. Dumon repaid the kindness by stealing the chain Lapeyre used to tether his calf. A few days later, word of mouth informed Lapeyre that Dumon had sold the chain to a *laboureur* in the next parish. Lapeyre visited the *laboureur,* who eagerly related how he had been approached while plowing by a boy who looked like a beggar, carrying a short chain. The boy explained that his father had died, leaving him only an iron chain that he wished to sell. They agreed on the price of eight sous, and the plowman told the boy to go to his house, where his wife would pay for the chain. So that she would know the boy had not come under false pretenses, the *laboureur* gave Dumon his knife to show her as a token of his trust. But when the boy took the knife to the house and presented it to the woman, he said he had just sold her husband a pair of chains for twenty-four sous. She accepted him at his word and paid the amount. That evening, when the *laboureur* returned from his day's plowing, his wife asked to see the pair of chains he had purchased. When he replied that he had bought only one chain, she said that it had better be a good one because she had paid the boy twenty-four sous. Although furious, the *laboureur* knew it was useless to pursue the culprit, who had long since made his escape.

Lapeyre and the *laboureur,* having exchanged stories, resolved to follow Dumon to his home parish, where they found him sleeping in a field. They beat him until he admitted the theft of the chain, but then could not decide how to settle the matter. Both victims eventually recognized that each of them would have to take a loss on the affair, so Lapeyre paid the *laboureur* twelve sous in exchange for the chain. But they took no legal action against Dumon.

Dumon's career of petty theft was far from finished. Four or five

13. *Ibid.*

years later, in about 1769, he stole a hoe and a pewter plate from Lagrandie, whose relative prosperity made him the logical target of recurrent thefts. When Lagrandie confronted him with the theft, he admitted stealing the plate and selling it to a miller for twelve sous that he then lost playing skittles, but denied the theft of the hoe. To settle the affair, Lagrandie purchased the plate from the miller but resigned himself to the loss of the hoe; in exchange, Dumon agreed to work for Lagrandie for two summers without pay—a penalty that far exceeded in value the twelve sous Lagrandie paid to recover the pewter plate.

Evidently Dumon had not yet learned his lesson, nor had his precarious economic situation improved. In 1772, he was not only apprehended for stealing walnuts but also suspected of stealing a mattock from a *travailleur*. One year later he stole a pewter plate again, this time from Lapeyre. As with the stolen chain, word of mouth alerted Lapeyre that Dumon had committed the theft and could be found in the adjoining parish. He therefore alerted the seigneur of Peyruzel, who instructed the judge of the tribunal to accompany the victim and verify ownership of the plate. Despite the involvement of ecclesiastic and seigneurial authorities, no formal action was taken: Dumon was reprimanded, and the stolen plate returned to its owner.

Within the year before his arrest in 1774, Dumon was implicated in two other thefts, one of a hatchet from a *laboureur,* the other of two measures of canvas from the *valet de ferme* of a sharecropper for whom both Dumon and Lavergne had previously worked. On Saint Martin's Day (November 11), 1773, the sharecropper caught Dumon leaving his barn with the canvas and forced him to admit the theft. But Dumon insisted that he did not deserve to be beaten because he had only taken the cloth at Lavergne's instigation. This came as no surprise to the victim, for everyone had seen the two drinking together and, knowing the shady reputation they shared, as well as their relative poverty, had assumed they carried on some sort of "mauvais commerce." When the sharecropper only reproached Dumon and warned him not to trespass again, Dumon apparently believed he had been treated fairly and proposed they both go to the cabaret to shell walnuts and drink a bottle of wine. They agreed and set off for the cabaret.[14]

Finally, in December, 1774, Dumon committed the theft that irrevocably crossed his victim's threshold of toleration. On the way home

14. Information à Peyruzel, December 24, 1774, B 1558, ADD.

from a cabaret where he had drunk too much, Dumon stole a skirt dry-
ing on a window ledge at the home of his perennial victim, Lagrandie.
Lagrandie at once suspected Dumon and sent his *valets* to retrieve the
skirt and apprehend the culprit. When the *valets* accused him of the
theft, Dumon readily confessed and offered to tell them where he had
hidden the skirt if they would release him. The *valets,* apparently acting under their master's instructions, refused to bargain with Dumon
and forced him to reveal where he had hidden the skirt. Having recovered the stolen article, the *valets* locked Dumon in the stable of the
château of Peyruzel and notified the prosecutor of the seigneurial tribunal. The next day, owing to the disrepair of the prison, the prosecutor ordered Dumon's transfer to the nearby prison at Domme. But
before the transfer, the prosecutor took advantage of Dumon's capture
to obtain his confession and to implicate Lavergne. Although Lavergne
was in no way involved in the theft of the skirt, Dumon—plied with
wine before and during his interrogation—named him as an accomplice in the theft of the walnuts from Lagrandie in 1772. On the strength
of that denunciation and in light of Lavergne's own reputation for petty
theft, the prosecutor ordered Lavergne's arrest. At the inquest, witnesses and past victims willingly came forward to testify to the two
prisoners' recurrent depredations, all of which had been overlooked or
settled informally during the previous fourteen years.

The case of these two thieves incorporates nearly all of the character-
It is hardly surprising that Dumon, when apprehended for the theft
of the skirt, expected to bargain with his captors as he had done so
often before. Nor is it surprising that Lavergne kept insisting that he
should not be prosecuted for stealing a hatful of walnuts for which he
had long ago paid restitution. The pair nonetheless found themselves
before the Sénéchaussée of Sarlat, which finally convicted Dumon of
five counts of theft and Lavergne of one count. The court sentenced
Dumon to be whipped and branded, Lavergne to be banished from the
jurisdiction for three years.[15]

The case of these two thieves incorporates nearly all of the characteristics of informal settlements in public cases. Victims were not so much
interested in chastisement of the culprit as in reparation of the damage
done or restitution of the stolen objects. Through informal settlements
they had a better chance of recovering their goods and avoiding all expenses. Also at stake in many incidents was much more than the value

15. Sentence définitive, September 9, 1775, B 1637, ADD.

of the stolen object. Because a theft challenged the honor and esteem of the victim, he was motivated not only by the desire to recoup his material losses but also by the necessity of making the culprit acknowledge the theft and accept what was often a token punishment. After a settlement was reached, the victim was generally content—even if he had absorbed some economic loss—because his honor was restored, he had demonstrated his vigilance, and his neighbors had shown their solidarity with him by cooperating in the detection and capture of the culprit.

In all but one instance in the Dumon-Lavergne history of thefts the victim and culprit agreed to a settlement orally, without the intervention of a go-between. Only in the affair of the stolen walnuts did Lagrandie appeal to a bourgeois to arrange an accommodement. On a couple of occasions the parties involved proceeded to a cabaret to "boire chopine" together to seal their agreement, as was commonly done. The terms of each settlement ranged from moral to monetary penalties. As mentioned above, victims placed emphasis on forcing the culprit to confess his misdeeds. In payment for stealing a pewter plate, Dumon worked for Lagrandie during two summers without pay. On the other hand, Lagrandie forced Lavergne to pay him forty-eight livres in damages and six livres in expenses for the theft of walnuts. Finally, in each incident the culprit invariably received some form of physical chastisement from his captors.[16]

The Dumon-Lavergne case reveals the lengths to which villagers went to resolve thefts informally before taking legal action. The fear of incurring legal expenses sometimes prompted victims to allow even thieves caught in the act to go free, for local judges often refused to imprison a suspect unless his captor pledged to provide all of the prisoner's food during his captivity.[17] Nor can one discount the fear of retaliation from a suspect still at large or from his relatives. But people were also aware of the retributive nature of royal justice and, preferring less drastic measures commensurate with the offense, opted for settle-

16. For examples of settlements in thefts occurring in the principality of Neuchâtel, see P. Henry, *Crime, justice et société*, 690–93.

17. Cameron, *Crime and Repression*, 179–83. Cameron, working exclusively from prévôtal records, has concluded that of all offenses on the statute books, theft was least tolerated. He does, however, qualify this generalization by stressing that whereas villagers showed little mercy to vagabonds, whom they apprehended and often beat before delivering to the constables of the maréchaussée, they were more tolerant of transgressions by their neighbors. He also found that in the Périgord such intense community spirit was breaking down. See p. 181.

ments that alleviated social tensions and restored the delicate balance of honor and esteem in the community. Finally, one must view this reluctance to have recourse to royal justice in light of the ambiguity surrounding many thefts: Everyone at one time or another stole a handful of grapes or a hatful of nuts from his neighbor, and the person who objected vociferously to such a minor infraction also risked ostracism.

Seigneurial officials were just as reluctant as private individuals to prosecute petty thieves from whom they had no hope of recuperating expenses. To avoid the trouble and expense of prosecuting minor offenses, they often tolerated, encouraged, and even arranged informal settlements. Only when a petty thief had repeatedly proven himself recalcitrant did it prove worthwhile for a victim to denounce him to the authorities. The decision did not necessarily hinge on the value of a stolen item or on the technical gravity of the theft. Very often it seems that a certain threshold of toleration had been crossed by the most recent theft, triggering a concerted response. The latest incident may have precipitated legal action, but members of the community and both seigneurial and royal officials knew well that the thief was being prosecuted just as much (if not more) for earlier thefts. The most recent theft simply provided the pretext for purging the community of an incorrigible. Historians of Old Regime France who study penalties in relation to crimes should therefore proceed with caution: A penalty often reflected a desire to punish an entire history of delinquent behavior as well as the crime of the moment.

The jurisdictional contest between royal and popular justice was especially intense in the area of theft. Whereas a high percentage of homicides undoubtedly resulted in public cases before the sénéchaussée, only a small proportion of thefts ever reached the court. The evidence suggests that in the Sarladais the attitude of the populace toward theft was highly ambivalent during this period. Everyone seemed suspicious of his neighbor, and often with good cause. Minor thefts, although commonplace, were highly resented. As a result, when someone was caught in the act or even just suspected of a theft and denounced, his neighbors often would readily participate in the inquest, recalling the slightest suspicious actions of the accused. The suspect could then be turned into a scapegoat for as many thefts as possible. This impulse was pronounced if the alleged culprit was an *étranger*, whom members of the community could conveniently blame instead of running the risk of falsely accusing their own neighbor of the theft. When the excitement of the initial inquest had subsided and neighbors had reflected on the probable fate of the accused, they sometimes retracted or substantially revised their testimony. A community would more frequently close ranks and come to the defense of a native son accused of theft— usually to head off legal action, but sometimes only after the case had reached the sénéchaussée. Depending on the nature and circumstances of the accused and his offense, the populace would welcome or resist official intervention.

A growing readiness to have recourse to royal justice may, in some cases of theft, be characterized as the lowering of a threshold of toleration for such criminal action. But the nature and the limits of that threshold varied considerably. In some instances, the accused seems to have stolen from the same person once too often. Usually thieves were careful to distribute their exactions among a wide cross section of the community, but inevitably wealthier individuals were recurrent targets. In such cases, victims previously willing to settle matters informally refused to compromise on the latest recurrence of the offense. In March, 1778, for example, a young *travailleur* named Jean Bescombe stole two oxen from the barn of Jean Peyrounel. Upon discovering the theft, Peyrounel enlisted the aid of two neighbors in pursuing Bescombe, whom they found trying to sell the oxen at a nearby fair. They apprehended the thief and turned him over to the *valets de ville* of Saint-Martial, who conducted him to the municipal prison. There the prosecutor plied Bescombe with wine until he confessed. When the thief threw himself at the feet of his victim and begged forgiveness, Peyrounel stood fast, saying that he had often warned and threatened and even beaten Bescombe for previous offenses. This time he refused to settle informally and left the thief in the hands of the seigneurial authorities.[18]

In other cases, however, the most recent theft resulted in prosecution not because a certain numerical or monetary limit was attained but because the thief eventually stole from someone who did not share the popular toleration of petty theft. Jean Delmon (without profession) had stolen numerous objects of considerable value before finally being prosecuted for a lesser theft. In October, 1778, he stole thirty-six livres, a pistol, and a snuffbox from a *valet,* who pursued him and made him return the stolen articles. Early in 1779, on Holy Thursday, Delmon stole twenty-two sheep from the métairie of a bourgeois landowner and

18. Information à Saint-Martial, March 30, 1778, B 1566, ADD.

managed to sell them in two lots. When the owner followed Delmon's trail, he met the first and then the second of the two buyers and persuaded them to join him in pursuit of the culprit, whom they apprehended on Easter and forced to return the money. The owner, having recovered his sheep, and the two buyers, having been reimbursed, did not bother to prosecute the thief. Undeterred, Delmon on the night of May 6 quietly entered the room of Jean Fauvel, a merchant, and stole fifty-three livres from his trousers, hung over a chair at the foot of the bed. The next day, the merchant and two friends confronted Delmon with the theft and, searching him, discovered the money hidden in his shoes. Apparently content with the recovery of the money, they took no further action. Two days later, however, Delmon stole twenty sheep from the métairie of a bourgeois named Rivière. Rivière apprehended Delmon while trying to sell the flock at a local fair and had him arrested and imprisoned by the town police, who turned him over to the constables of the maréchaussée. They, in turn, transferred him to the seigneurial tribunal of Monferrand, which prosecuted the initial phase of the case before sending it to the sénéchaussée for continuance. The royal prosecutor finally concluded that Delmon was guilty of four counts of theft, for the four acts described above, and recommended that he be condemned to serve on the galleys for ten years.[19]

In this case, at least three incidents of theft had been settled informally before the fourth resulted in the arrest of the culprit. Because each theft occurred in a different parish and involved different victims, one cannot use the concept of threshold to explain why the last theft alone resulted in litigation. Nor does the relative seriousness of the theft explain why only the last victim had Delmon arrested. The only remaining explanation is that the last victim, Rivière, was not content with the return of his sheep and therefore appealed to official justice to punish the culprit. Delmon was taken before the court on this final occasion because he had the misfortune to steal from someone less interested in restoring social equilibrium than in punishing the thief.

In other instances, a general public outcry seems to have spurred the local prosecutor of the seigneurial tribunal to initiate proceedings against known petty thieves. The criminalization of the offense came about in some cases because the victims, although they did not for-

19. Interrogatoire, August 29, 1779, B 1570, ADD; Conclusions, September 13, 1779, B 1639, ADD.

mally denounce the thieves to the authorities, refused to settle the affair informally. Their obduracy was tantamount to public stigmatization of the accused—which eventually attracted the attention of the seigneurial authorities. This appears to have been the case in 1779, when a tailor and a master shoemaker from Terrasson were prosecuted for theft of poultry from an innkeeper who rejected an attempted settlement. On the night of February 21, the innkeeper and his wife apprehended François Boudy, the tailor, as he sat in a drunken stupor alongside the road. They were convinced he was the man they had just chased from their chicken house, and despite his protests, they gave him a *coup de baton* on the head before leading him off to the inn. Hardly had they arrived when Bertrand Rouby, the shoemaker, appeared at the door and tried to persuade them that Boudy did not steal their chickens. The two of them had been together the entire evening, he claimed. Rouby was suspiciously polite, continually tipping his hat—which appeared to have chicken feathers on it—and offered to buy a bottle of wine for all of them to share. Although the innkeeper and his wife steadfastly refused to drink with the two, they did eventually agree to release Boudy, who returned to the inn the next morning and renewed his pleas of the night before. Without confessing to the theft, he asked them to tell no one about the affair, saying "that such a rumor would dishonor him, that he would pay them handsomely for their hens, and although he had not taken them, he would make good for everything, and that although he did not have any money, the next day he would bring them a bedsheet." He also promised to bring them a pile of manure if they said nothing more about the incident. But the victims declined his gifts and again, significantly, refused to drink with him. Their steadfast refusal to settle the case informally undoubtedly allowed news of the theft to spread in the community; as a result, the prosecutor of the tribunal at Terrasson was warned by "clameur publique" of the theft and decided to initiate proceedings against the two suspects.[20]

In this case, the responsibility for the criminalization of the offense was shared by the victims and the seigneurial prosecutor. Although the innkeeper and his wife had not suffered prior losses from the suspects, they were angry enough to allow their accusation to be known in public. Because they had already beaten Boudy, it is doubtful that they

20. Information à Terrasson, February 24, 1779, B 1569, ADD.

would have bothered to denounce him formally. But at this point the role of the prosecutor and public opinion became crucial. In his request for permission to initiate proceedings, the prosecutor explained that word of mouth had informed him of "an infinity of thefts of all kinds of poultry committed at night" in and around Terrasson during the preceding months. The seriousness and recurrence of the thefts led him to perceive the thieves as a public nuisance; moreover, he regarded the latest theft as being all the more serious because it was committed during Lent, "demonstrating a formal disregard for religion, a dissolution of morals and conduct, and a determined inclination to theft." Given the gravity of the theft at night and the continued complaints of the inhabitants, the prosecutor felt impelled to rid the community of two suspected thieves. Boudy was charged with nine counts of theft. The sénéchaussée found both men guilty of the theft of the chickens and banished them from the jurisdiction for one year.[21]

Although seigneurial prosecutors often acted in concert with or as extensions of popular opinion, in other instances they took action despite the attempts of those involved to settle an affair amicably. A good example of such a case occurred in mid-May, 1772, a time of great economic distress in the Périgord. At that time Pierre Doublon, a grain merchant, purchased wheat at the Salignac market and loaded half of it onto a mule, which he then started down the road while he loaded his second mule. When he caught up with the first, he discovered that someone had stolen his grain. He notified the seigneurial authorities, who undertook a house-to-house search of the neighborhood until they found the stolen wheat at the home of Jean Bourianne, a *travailleur*. Bourianne admitted the theft and explained that he had taken the wheat "because of extreme poverty, he and his family dying of hunger."[22]

Notified of the recovery of his grain, the merchant declined to press charges and required only that Bourianne pay for the minor costs incurred by the bailiff and his assistants in their search. But despite the thief's agreement to do so, the prosecutor requested permission to initiate action against Bourianne because he considered the theft "a very serious case that merited exemplary punishment." Doublon and even

21. Requis en plainte du procureur d'office à Terrasson, February 23, 1779, Confrontation de Rouby à Sarlat, April 20, 1779, both in B 1569, ADD; Conclusions, May 4, 1779, B 1639, ADD.

22. Tournelle de Sarlat, July 7, 1773: Requis en plainte du procureur fiscal (June 8, 1772), B, ADG.

some of the witnesses recalled to confirm their testimony before the sénéchaussée were evidently moved by the plight of the *travailleur,* who had fled his village since the theft and reportedly stolen turnips in the next parish. One of the witnesses declared that before the theft of the wheat he had never heard the probity of the defendant questioned and added that "Bourianne is extremely poor, that poverty made him act as he did in the one and the other case, if the second was indeed true." [23]

Doublon apparently felt strongly enough about the affair to re-affirm his desire to settle informally. In February, 1773, he therefore acceded to Bourianne's request and instructed a notary to prepare an official declaration, stating, "In order to do justice to the truth, [the victim] certifies that he is content, paid, and satisfied that the grain he had complained had been taken eight months ago by Jean Bourianne . . . was returned to him in its entirety at that time, that he renounces any claim or right he may have to prosecute the said Bourianne, promising not to do so in the future, and that the above declaration was requested by the said Bourianne." But because the theft was technically a felony and threatened public order, a private party's disclaimer of his right to reparations did not dissuade the royal prosecutor, who was intent on punishing the offender. In May, 1773, the sénéchaussée found Bourianne guilty of the theft and banished him from the jurisdiction for three years. [24]

The role of the seigneurial prosecutor could be pivotal in determining the success or failure of an attempted settlement. If a prosecutor believed the offense did not really threaten public order and had not been committed by a known offender, he was inclined to allow informal dispute settlement to operate—especially if the seigneur's treasury was depleted at the moment. The maréchaussée's records of interrogations for repeated thefts sometimes reveal that past offenses had been settled informally with the knowledge and complicity of local seigneurial authorities. In 1770, for example, Antoine Juge, a bordier, was accused of stealing four livres plus some flour from a sharecropper. When apprehended, he admitted stealing the flour and returned it to his victim, but denied that he had taken the money. Nonetheless, the next day Juge's wife quietly brought to the sharecropper an iron pot, a frying pan, and a pick—all in compensation for the stolen money. The share-

23. *Ibid.;* Récolement, February 25, 1773, B 1552, ADD.
24. Tournelle de Sarlat, July 7, 1773: Acte de notaire (February 15, 1773), B, ADG.

cropper was apparently satisfied and said no more about the affair. About nine years earlier, a miller had reported that someone had stolen flour and a bedsheet from him. The judge at Montignac issued a search warrant, and the *valet de ville* discovered the stolen goods in Juge's house. The articles were returned to the miller, and Juge was forced to pay the expenses of the search; but no legal action was taken against him—no doubt because he and his family were known to have lost their crops to hail that spring and to be suffering from hunger.[25]

The 1770 interrogation of Leonard Audebert, a sharecropper, revealed that he had stolen a sack of grain in the summer of 1769 from the courtyard of a *praticien* and had hurriedly taken it to a miller to be ground into flour. The next day, as news of the theft spread, the miller reported milling about the same amount of grain for Audebert as the amount that was missing. When the prosecutor and bailiff of the tribunal of Auriac searched Audebert's house, they found part of the flour hidden in the bed, the remainder having been kneaded into dough and baked by his wife. They seized both the flour and the fresh bread and returned them to the owner. Audebert, who freely admitted the theft, was imprisoned overnight in the Château LaFaye, but released the next morning.[26]

In both of the above instances, the seigneurial authorities were fully aware of the commission of thefts within their jurisdictions and aided in the recovery of the stolen goods. But at that point they, too, were content to let the parties settle informally. In other words, seigneurial authorities evidently ignored their legal obligation to prosecute what royal statutes classified as serious crimes and even acted as go-betweens to arrange settlements that obviated litigation. Their action was influenced, on the one hand, by the desire to avoid prosecuting persons too poor to pay expenses and, on the other hand, by their need to respond to popular pressure when offenders seemed to abuse public toleration. They more often acted as extensions of the popular system of dispute settlement than as subalterns of official justice.

Informal settlements were less frequent in cases of theft with violence (*vol-assassinat*), owing primarily to the greater gravity of the offense. Royal statutes defined such theft as a capital crime. Also, victims of *vol-assassinat* were reluctant to accept restitution and forgive the of-

25. Interrogatoire à Sarlat, September 9, 1770, B 1546, ADD.
26. Information à Sarlat, September 19, 1770, *ibid.*

fense: Judicial records refer to only one case in which the victim agreed to settle the affair extralegally.[27] Likewise, in public cases of homicide few attempts were made to head off legal action. Of the twenty-five cases of homicide prosecuted by the Sénéchaussée of Sarlat from 1770 to 1790, only one case of accidental manslaughter was settled out of court: The accused paid reparations to the victim's family and obtained letters of pardon. By means of a notarial act of cession, the family relinquished any further claims or intention to prosecute in return for an unspecified monetary settlement.[28]

The prevalent popular ambivalence toward theft contrasts sharply with the clear concurrence between royal and popular justice in cases of homicide—even to the extent that both popular opinion and the Crown recognized only accidental homicide as pardonable. Among all cas royaux, homicide was the one crime least often settled informally, in part because it was difficult to conceal from the authorities charged with its prosecution, in part because of its longstanding relegation to royal jurisdiction, but primarily because of its intrinsic gravity. In such cases, the relatives of the victim demanded and actually welcomed the retribution promised by royal justice.[29]

27. Interrogatoire de Verliac, January 12, 1778, B 1566, ADD; Sentence, June 15, 1778, B 1638, ADD; Tournelle de Sarlat, June 22, 1778: Extrait mortuaire (March 5, 1779), B, ADG.

28. A commoner who obtained *lettres de rémission* (granted for involuntary homicide or legitimate self-defense) had to have a third party present them to the sénéchaussée after he was imprisoned. He was obliged to notify the partie civile of his intention to submit the letters so that the latter could make an objection to the court if desired. In most cases, the accused not only informed but offered compensation to the partie civile before submitting the letters. As a result, the court rarely objected to the registration of the letters. See Guyot *et al.*, *Répertoire*, VIII, 183–86; Plainte, September 17, 1787, B 1593, ADD.

29. Spierenburg, *The Spectacle of Suffering*, 10–11.

V

Dispute Settlement in Private Cases

For a French population of twenty millions the law is nothing but a sheet of white paper nailed to the church door or pinned up in the mayor's office.

—Honoré de Balzac, *The Peasants*

As a rule, the more successful a society is in attaining a smooth social functioning, the less need it has to call on official law. In fact, it can be argued that individuals have recourse to law only because less stringent methods of social control have failed to hold members of the community in line or in harmony. Therefore the extension of the importance and sphere of activity of observable law in more highly developed societies is not in itself an index of social "progress" but rather an index of that society's greater complexity and hence of the norms or imperatives to be observed, as well as an indicator of the increasing difficulty in obtaining adherence to such norms.

Although the frontier between the spheres of official and popular justice in the Sarladais remained virtually static in public cases from 1770 to 1790, it may have been shifting in private cases. Given the relatively stagnant, backward nature of the Sarladais and the small number of informal settlements discovered, it would be incautious to conclude and impossible to prove that the populace had decisively abandoned its traditional attitudes to royal justice and moved toward a more modern, individualistic approach. But the fact that the absolute increase in royal caseload in the 1780s stemmed primarily from the greater number of private suits, plus the fact that prior or ongoing settlements were mentioned with greater frequency in private cases (Table 5), suggests the

Table 6

Informal Settlement Attempts in Private Cases of Verbal and Physical Violence Against Persons

Time period	Cases of Verbal Violence			Cases of Physical Violence		
	No.	Settlement attempts (No.)	(%)	No.	Settlement attempts (No.)	(%)
1770–75	13	0	0	44	4	9.09
1776–80	11	0	0	34	1	2.94
1781–85	35	3	8.57	53	7	13.21
1786–90	22	5	22.73	38	4	10.53
Total (Average)	81	8	(9.88)	169	16	(9.47)

Sources: See Table 1.

beginnings of such a tendency.[1] References to settlements in private cases, which were relatively rare in the 1770s, appear in greater numbers in case records of the 1780s. Twenty of the 26 settlement attempts described in private cases during the twenty-year period involve cases initiated in the 1780s, during which decade references to settlements in cases of verbal violence also appear for the first time (Table 6). But one cannot conclude from this evidence that the practice of dispute settlement was more or less common in society. To the contrary, the mention of this practice in the records may even suggest that in such cases informal settlements were deliberately being used not as final solutions but as preliminary skirmishes, or preludes to legal action.

Records of privately initiated suits involving physical violence against persons contain 16 of the 26 references to settlements, most of which referred to previous attempts at conciliation that failed to neutralize the tension between two parties. The mounting tension had eventually culminated in violent outbursts, which gave rise to criminal litiga-

---

1. In contrast, Nicole Castan argues that in Languedoc during the last half of the eighteenth century, the authority of the Crown made significant inroads into traditional modes of conflict resolution in the area of public cases for felonies (*Justice et répression en Languedoc*, 24). Also see Elisabeth Claverie, "L'Honneur: Une Société de défis au XIX siècle," *Annales: Economies, sociétés, civilisations*, XXXIV (1979), 755; P. Henry, *Crime, justice et société*, 694–95.

tion. The origins of such violence were many, but it generally derived from boundary disputes, disagreements over business dealings, and insults to family honor. Occasionally, even attempts to mediate long-standing conflicts sparked violence. In one case, an innkeeper's efforts to mediate an affair resulted in his own involvement in a brawl when the victim resented the terms of settlement he suggested as go-between. The meal that was intended to be a feast of reconciliation turned into a free-for-all after the victim again complained about the terms.[2]

An attempted settlement provided the setting for violence in another, similar case. A bourgeois named Dujarric brought civil suit before the seigneurial tribunal of Coulonges against his neighbor, a *clerc* named Jean Boutié, accusing Boutié of encroaching on his meadow. The judge advised the parties to settle the dispute informally and even offered to accompany them to the meadow, not as judge, but "in the capacity of arbitrator." Both men agreed to abide by his decision, so on March 19, 1770, Dujarric—accompanied by his lawyer, a royal notary from Montignac, and the judge—met Boutié and his son in the meadow "in order to work together for an accommodement." But when they measured the boundary between Dujarric's meadow and Boutié's, which adjoined it, they discovered that there had been no encroachment. The argument that followed soon degenerated into insults and scuffling.[3]

Two lawsuits arose from this unsuccessful attempt at settlement. On March 21, Dujarric and his lawyer brought criminal suit before the sénéchaussée for *excès-réels* (personal assault) and *injures*. Dujarric claimed that Boutié had called him "foutade, foutèze, et foutrasson" and then kicked the lawyer in the chest with his sabots while his son held the lawyer by the hair. In their countersuit, Boutié and his son accused the lawyer of holding Boutié by the hair, dragging him into a ditch, and punching him. In July, after both sides had conducted inquests and all of the accused had been interrogated, the royal prosecutor ruled that only Dujarric's suit was valid. He ordered Boutié to go to Dujarric's home and ask him for pardon in the presence of the four

2. Interrogatoire de Bertrand, March 16, 1771, Interrogatoire de Daubige, May 23, 1771, both in B 1547, ADD.
3. Tournelle de Sarlat, January 12, 1772: Interrogatoire de Jean Boutié (April 9, 1770), B, ADG.

witnesses of the inquest; furthermore, he warned Boutié not to repeat the offense and sentenced him to pay thirty livres in damages, plus all expenses.[4]

Dujarric, with the aid of his lawyer, had achieved at least a limited victory over his neighbor. Although his goal in initiating a suit before the tribunal of Coulonges had clearly not been the restoration of social equilibrium, he had agreed to arbitration of the dispute at the insistence of the judge. But one suspects that his true intent was best expressed by his lawyer, who was heard to say, "I would not begrudge fifty livres in order to ruin this f. peasant." In fact, Boutié had been reluctant to go to the meadow for the attempted settlement because he suspected Dujarric might have been drinking with his friends and would cause trouble. Only because he did not wish to displease the judge did he agree to appear.[5] In this instance, the attempt at settlement not only failed to head off legal action but actually sparked the confrontation that resulted in two lawsuits before the royal court.

The majority of the settlements mentioned in private suits involving nonfatal physical violence preceded legal action and were intended to avert it. A single example illustrates how this process both worked and failed to work. In 1775 Jean Frances obtained an arrest warrant against two of his neighbors. Soon afterwards, he terminated the suit "by means of a composition" at their request, hoping that his restraint and the reparations they paid would inspire in them a more moderate spirit. But the two men continued to slander him in the parish, spreading rumors that he had stolen a calf and plow. As a result, many people came to regard him as a known thief and shunned or harassed his wife and children. Years later, the two men saw Frances asleep outside a cabaret and gave him a light blow on the head with a *baton*, saying, "You know very well that someone stole Delfaut's calf." Before he could reply, they continued on their way. Frances then filed a petition, in which he argued that the blow, albeit slight, had been meant as an insult and had seriously injured him and his family: "The plaintiff cannot hope for either honor or tranquility if he does not obtain reparation."[6] Because he realized that his enemies would not be intimidated

4. Tournelle de Sarlat, January 12, 1772: Conclusions définitives du procureur du roy (July 7, 1770), *ibid.*

5. Tournelle de Sarlat, January 12, 1772: Interrogatoire de Boutié, fils (April 17, 1770), *ibid.*

6. Plainte, June 25, 1783, B 1580, ADD.

by the seigneurial court or restrained by informal sanctions, this time he took his suit directly to the sénéchaussée. His petition was the first and last act of the case, suggesting that his recourse to royal justice was merely a tactic—and a successful one—designed to pressure the accused into settling informally out of court before legal costs accumulated any further.

The continuum of alternatives available to disputants emerges from the records: If an informal settlement did not guarantee security, satisfaction, or monetary reparation, then adversaries appealed to royal justice; if the court did not provide satisfaction, they then resorted to the more direct methods of intimidation and vengeance. Disputants used all of these tactics in a case of violence in 1782. Returning from the market in Sarlat, a miller named Antoine Pouch, his father, and a bourgeois named Dutheil encountered Etienne Grenaille, a merchant with whom Pouch had earlier quarreled over the sale of two pigs. As they passed one another on the road, Grenaille, who was on foot, struck the legs of Pouch's horse with his *baton*. Fearing that his horse was wounded, Pouch dismounted, his hat falling to the ground. When he bent over to retrieve it, Grenaille hit him over the head with his *baton*. The two grabbed each other by the hair, but Pouch's father intervened and separated the combatants. Dodging rocks thrown by Grenaille, Pouch and his father then turned their horses and returned to Sarlat to lodge their complaint against the assailant.[7]

Dutheil, the bourgeois, continued on his way, leaving Grenaille standing in the road. Realizing the implications of his actions, Grenaille ran after Dutheil and explained that he had acted rashly because he was "a bit drunk" but now wished "to settle the affair." Dutheil accepted the twenty-four livres Grenaille pressed into his hand and said he would approach Pouch on Grenaille's behalf. But when he did so, Pouch and his father refused to drop their suit, stating that they "preferred to have recourse to justice." Informed of their refusal, Grenaille took the only course of action remaining open to him: He brought his own suit against them, claiming he had acted in self-defense.[8]

Because the two parties were antagonists of long standing (they are described as "brouillés," or on bad terms), an informal settlement was

7. Information, September 16, 1782, B 1577, ADD.
8. *Ibid.*, Interrogatoire d'Antoine Pouch, October 5, 1782, Plainte d'Etienne Grenaille, September 8, 1782, both in B 1577, ADD.

probably doomed. The violence that erupted between them, while not premeditated, was surely undertaken deliberately. Limited, ritualized violence was viewed as a normal if not acceptable means of expressing, and sometimes resolving, petty differences. Since onlookers were generally quick to intervene in a scuffle, the reaction of witnesses to the above incident is revealing. Two weavers decided to intervene, but only when blood began to flow. Dutheil prevented them from doing so because, as he later testified, the fight was nearly finished and "did not appear to be very dangerous." The two must have agreed, for when Pouch's father tried to grab a *baton* from one of them in order to attack Grenaille, they resisted and left the scene.[9]

Settlements in private cases involving *assassinat*—physical assault of a more serious nature because it entailed design or premeditation— tended to be made in writing via notarial acts of cession. The criminal court records of this period contain four acts of cession, which can be defined as any legal instrument by which one person transfers to another some form of property, whether movable or immovable. Legal rights, being a form of property, could be bought or sold with whatever stipulations the two parties agreed upon. In the adaptation of this form of notarial act to the out-of-court settlement of lawsuits, no mention was ever made of the unwritten agreement between the accused and the go-between. The latter, after acquiring the rights to the lawsuit, would drop all charges.[10]

In a typical example, a wigmaker named Jean Perier from Paris was accused of attacking Madeleine Roudel. Although the incident does not seem to have been serious, Roudel and her mother, assisted by the considerable skills of their lawyer, managed in their petition to depict the incident as "un véritable assassinat" committed by a rascal who would surely have killed Roudel if neighbors had not intervened. Quite alarmed, Perier contacted a bourgeois merchant of Sarlat named Lamarche and asked him to arrange a settlement with the mother and daughter. The next day, Lamarche joined the plaintiffs in a notary's office, where they ceded their criminal case to him in the presence of witnesses: "Together they cede to Sieur Lamarche all the damages and interest that may have been awarded to the said Roudel, even all the costs and expenses that they incurred to date against the said Perier,

9. Plainte d'Antoine Pouch, September 7, 1782, *ibid.*
10. Guyot *et al.*, *Répertoire*, III, 26.

desisting purely and simply from the said proceedings, circumstances and dependencies of the said damages and interest, costs and expenses etc., assigning them to the said Lamarche in their stead and place so that he may do as he wishes with them, the said Mother and daughter promising on their part not to pursue the matter." The transfer was made in exchange for two hundred livres, paid in cash by Lamarche. A copy of the act was drawn up and delivered to the court, and four days later Perier surrendered himself to the authorities at the royal prison in Sarlat. Three days later, Lamarche appeared before the court as the cessionary of the plaintiffs and requested that all charges be dropped and the prisoner released. No record exists of the agreement made between the accused and the go-between.[11]

The financial status of the disputants was of crucial importance in their assessment of whether and when to reach a settlement. In 1784, a sergeant of the seigneurial tribunal of Auriac who was accused of *assassinat* waited three months before attempting to settle out of court. Because by then not only he but the plaintiff was growing extremely concerned about rising court costs, the latter was willing to accept the sergeant's offer and even settle for a loss in the affair: Although his expenses already amounted to 480 livres, he agreed to an award of 400 livres. In the act of cession, the plaintiff ceded all rights in his criminal case to a merchant. The merchant subsequently dropped all charges, and the accused was released under judicial oath.[12]

Insults and defamation were of course widespread during this period, but were generally overlooked or handled informally. Private cases involving verbal violence were admittedly scarce, but their number and relative importance did grow in the 1780s. Seventy percent of these cases were initiated in the last ten years of the period. So, too, did the frequency with which these cases referred to informal settlements grow. It is virtually impossible to determine whether popular tolerance of verbal violence actually decreased or individuals in the community simply began to appreciate the value of legal recourse in the harassment of their adversaries. The result was the same. The plaintiffs in these

11. Acte de cession, November 7, 1783, Controlé à Sarlat, November 13, 1783, Plainte, November 20, 1783, all in B 1581, ADD.

12. Acte de cession, February 5, 1785, Plainte d'Hyvert, February 5, 1785, both in B 1583, ADD. The records contain two other examples of cessions: Plainte de Pierre Maigne, November 7, 1787, and Acte de cession, November 7, 1787, both in B 1593; Plainte, June 22, 1789, and Acte de cession, June 22, 1789, both in B 1597.

cases—even more so than in cases of minor physical violence—were motivated not so much by the high ideals in their petitions as by the desire to use the courts to humiliate and ruin an opponent, "pour lui faire manger son bien." The object of legal action was to make the accused "pay" in one manner or another: occasionally by a court-awarded decision, but most often by means of an out-of-court settlement. The somewhat higher frequency of references to informal settlements in such cases may therefore be significant.[13]

Most references concerned failed attempts to terminate lawsuits in their early stages, before expenses mounted. If an individual bothered to initiate litigation over an insult, he was not always eager to accommodate the first overture made by an opponent anxious to settle informally. Because recourse to royal justice was essentially a financial gamble, he often preferred to wait in order to drive up the stakes. In some cases, the animosity and obstinacy of the disputants doomed them to lengthy litigation and ruinous court costs. But the great majority of cases of verbal violence were either discontinued or settled out of court, leaving no trace in the records.[14]

The increasing number of private parties that began to use the courts for the prosecution of insults, defamation, and menaces in the 1780s employed a variety of tactics, both official and unofficial. In a dispute in which insults were exchanged (usually in some public place), one of the parties often would call on the others present to note how he was insulted because, he would loudly proclaim, he intended to bring suit. His adversary then might try to cajole him into smoothing over the incident. If that did not work, he would ask a third party to intervene and propose a settlement either to avert a lawsuit or to resolve it quickly if begun. If an adversary was ill disposed to settle amicably, his opponent might employ threats to intimidate him into settling out of court, or he could always initiate his own countersuit to be used as a bargaining chip in future negotiations. Recourse to royal justice was simply the most recent addition to a panoply of tactics employed by adversaries in their traditional disputes. That more and more private parties used the courts in the 1780s to prosecute petty verbal and

13. In the nineteenth-century Gévaudan, requests for *arrangements* (accommodations) generally occurred before justice intervened (Claverie, "L'Honneur," 755–56).

14. Only one case of verbal violence in this period refers to an informal mediation by a bourgeois (Procès-verbal, May 19, 1790, B 1599, ADD).

physical violence suggests the growing acceptance of royal justice as a reliable strategy in adversarial relations.

The alternation and merger of official litigation (civil and criminal) with unofficial methods of dispute settlement are illustrated in the following case. A dispute began in February, 1783, when Barthelemi Rougier, a calf merchant from the Auvergne, sent his son to the Périgord to collect bills due for past purchases. When the son arrived in Montignac, he contacted Jean Labrousse de Borédon, seigneur de Murat, who owed Rougier 215 livres; Guillaume Ladoux, a merchant-tanner; and a man named Lapendrie. The men invited Rougier's son to dine with them at a cabaret in order to settle their affairs behind closed doors. After dining, they proposed a game of cards. It lasted all afternoon and into the evening; meanwhile, they plied the young man with liqueur and expensive wine. As a result, he not only lost the 60 livres in cash he had with him but also signed over the receipts the three owed his father for a total of 550 livres.

When the game ended about midnight, the young man stumbled away to the home of a shoemaker with whom he was staying. He arrived "drunk as wine itself, swearing, raving, and throwing himself on the ground, crying that he had lost all his money." The shoemaker tried to put him to bed, but Rougier's son again threw himself on the ground and swore that he would never go home again and might as well drown himself. To calm him, the shoemaker brought him to the local sergeant to lodge a complaint. But the sergeant expressed little sympathy and offered less hope of recovering the money. Evidently he had warned Rougier's son not to play cards in Montignac the previous year, when he had lost eighteen livres to the same three men! By the next day, the entire town had heard the news, and the young man dejectedly left for his home in the Auvergne. Upon arriving, he told his mother what had happened and, fearing the consequences, departed for Spain without even seeing his father. Rougier decided to go to Montignac himself to reproach the three and to demand payment of what they owed. When he arrived, Labrousse and Lapendrie invited him to dine and afterwards showed him the receipts signed by his son. When Rougier stated that he did not intend to honor them, Lapendrie relented and agreed to pay what he owed, but Labrousse refused to pay.[15]

15. Information, September 17, 1783, Procès-verbal, September 13, 1783, both in B 1581, ADD.

In late April, Rougier returned to the Périgord. He dined with Pierre Delbonne, a merchant from the parish of Auriac, and related what had happened to his son. He also stated that he was prepared to bring civil suit against the three and asked Delbonne to assist him by drawing up a petition requesting a hearing before the Sénéchaussée of Sarlat. When they arrived in Montignac the next day, Rougier attended the local fair while Delbonne went off to have the petition prepared. In the cattle market along the river, Rougier encountered Labrousse, who poked him in the stomach with a *baton* and called him a "bugger of a scoundrel." Labrousse had already heard that Rougier intended to bring suit, and said that he would cut Rougier's throat if he did so. At that point, Delbonne and others intervened and warned Labrousse not to harm Rougier, but Labrousse replied, in a voice loud enough for all to hear: "He's a f. rascal and I'll skin him. I don't give a f. about him and his protectors or about the petition he has had drawn up against me." Meanwhile, Rougier slipped away.[16]

But as Rougier retreated along the riverbank, the merchant-tanner Ladoux, one of the three debtors, intercepted him and managed (with some difficulty) to persuade him to come have a drink at a nearby caba- ret. No sooner had they arrived, however, than Labrousse entered. He and Ladoux forced Rougier to climb into the loft, where they could talk in privacy. Labrousse again threatened to kill Rougier if the latter refused to give him a final receipt for his debts; but Rougier fell to the floor, weeping, and told Labrousse that he would sooner die than squander his children's inheritance. Ladoux and Labrousse began to grow concerned about the commotion Rougier was making, so they de- scended the steps to show those present that they had not harmed Rou- gier. They then ordered wine and forced him to drink with them, warn- ing him not to speak ill of them or they would cut his throat. Finally, they threatened to hang him from the nearest tree if he made trouble, brought suit against them, or told anyone what they had said in the attic.

Rougier refused to be intimidated and continued his civil suit against them. At this point, Ladoux began to waiver in his resolve, es- pecially when fellow merchants from the area pressured him to settle

16. Procès-verbal, September 13, 1783, Information, September 17, 1783, both *ibid.*

the affair. When first approached, he replied angrily that if Rougier continued to slander him he would hang Rougier from a tree. When approached a second time, he admitted that Rougier would do well "to settle the affair, but if he didn't he would drag him behind his horse." Finally, when the merchant Delbonne urged him to settle, Ladoux relented and agreed to pay his debt. He tried to persuade Labrousse to do the same, but Labrousse refused and decided to change his tactics. Instead of repeating his threats, he went before the sénéchaussée and brought criminal suit against Rougier for calumny and insults.[17]

With this move, Labrousse shifted the ground of battle, not only from popular justice to royal justice, but also from civil to criminal proceedings. The effect on Rougier was dramatic. When he learned that Labrousse planned to bring suit against him, he approached Labrousse's elder brother, asking him "to end this affair." The elder brother agreed and enlisted the aid of two men: Jean-Baptiste Desvignes, a lawyer in parlement and judge of the seigneurial jurisdiction of Montignac; and Dujarric, a bourgeois of Montignac. Desvignes was related to the younger Labrousse by marriage and was the uncle of Ladoux. Dujarric and Desvignes approached Labrousse and proposed a settlement, but he refused Rougier's terms. So the elder Labrousse reported back to Rougier: "We were unable to end the affair, but stay here a few days longer and suspend your complaint against my brother. Perhaps then we will be able to bring the two of you to terms." Rougier agreed to remain in Montignac because the comte de Saint-Exupéry, chevalier, lieutenant des maréchaux de France, and seigneur de Fraysse, had seen the inquest of Labrousse's suit before the sénéchaussée and advised Rougier that he risked being summoned. Sufficiently frightened and fearful for his reputation, Rougier asked the go-betweens to try again, which they did without success. Having exhausted popular modes of dispute settlement and sensing that his civil suit did not represent enough of a threat, Rougier decided to initiate his own criminal suit against Labrousse and Ladoux for insults and menaces. The court records do not indicate how either suit was resolved. Whereas Rougier was summoned and interrogated, Labrousse was never summoned. But at the point when the case was evidently discontinued, Labrousse had

17. Procès-verbal, September 13, 1783, Information, September 17, 1783, both *ibid.*; Plainte du Sieur Jean Labrousse, July 6, 1783, B 1580, ADD.

accumulated 132 livres and Rougier 70 livres in court costs. Both cases were undoubtedly settled out of court shortly after Rougier's interrogation.[18]

This case graphically illustrates the fusion of popular modes of dispute settlement with official, legal methods in private cases involving verbal violence. In most such cases the plaintiff had recourse to the court not so much because he expected to win the case and impose a unilateral decision on his opponent as because he hoped to use litigation as a point of leverage in attaining a favorable informal settlement. Accordingly, the criminal lawsuit was often not the culmination of failed informal negotiations but simply an attempt by one party to outflank his opponent in an ongoing contest. Therefore, initiating a suit against one's opponent did not end informal attempts at conciliation but actually touched off a new round of activity. Only if the opponents displayed unusual stubbornness would court costs multiply to the point where neither side could afford to lose.

The role of go-betweens in informal settlements is particularly illuminating. In the Sarladais, seigneurial officials seem to have played the most active role in the conciliation process. Positioned on the frontier between the realms of popular and official culture, they often served as intermediaries between the outside world and the mass of the peasantry, which was isolated by an oral culture and the *langue d'oc*. In practice, seigneurial officials seem to have acted as agents of popular justice as often as they did in their official capacity as extensions of royal justice: They frequently appear in the records actively working to arrange settlements in a wide variety of affairs, especially in thefts committed by indigents from whom they would never recuperate expenses. Their occasional involvement in affairs that otherwise might have become profitable private lawsuits is therefore all the more significant.

In at least one case, seigneurial officials encouraged a settlement in order to avoid offending relatives and local *notables*. Two young bourgeois tried to take liberties with an innkeeper's wife, who fled to a neighbor's house to escape their advances. The next day, she went to Montignac to bring suit before the seigneurial tribunal for attempted rape. But the judge refused to receive her petition under the pretext that he was related to the two accused; he sent her to see a prosecutor, who

18. Procès-verbal, September 13, 1783, B 1581, ADD.

refused her petition on the same grounds. Stating that she would take her case directly to Sarlat "in order to obtain justice," she returned home, where "a little while later the judge visited her to propose that she not go to Sarlat but instead end this affair." When she insisted on continuing, the judge reluctantly advised her to see the prosecutor of the Montignac tribunal, who, he said, would accept her petition. But when she went to see him, he referred her to still another prosecutor, who also refused to help her! Intent on bringing suit and convinced that the seigneurial officials of the Montignac tribunal were encouraging her to settle informally only to protect the accused, she brought her complaint directly to the sénéchaussée.[19]

The most visible of those few noble seigneurs who remained active in the process of conciliation was the comte de Saint-Exupéry. His reputation as a benevolent seigneur and go-between impressed Inspecteur des Manufactures Latapie, who delivered a letter to the elderly count in 1778. Latapie recorded in his journal of inspection that the count was a "simple man" who "acted selflessly" for his peasants: "He spends his days on his domain, ministering to the poor, settling all of their conflicts, and extending hospitality to his neighbors. Moreover, nothing equals the respect in which Monsieur de Saint-Exupéry is held in the Périgord and especially in Terrasson. Everyone dreads his passing, which unfortunately is not too far off, since he is more than eighty years old."[20]

The records refer to an earlier attempt by the comte de Saint-Exupéry to mediate a dispute between two feuding noblemen, both of whom he ordered to appear at his château to explain the reasons for their disagreement and to settle their differences. His intervention did succeed in temporarily calming their dispute, but two years later their hostility erupted in violence and resulted in a criminal suit before the prévôté. In the inquest, witnesses testified that the two were known to be hopelessly "brouillés" and said they believed "that sooner or later they would kill each other."[21] Overall, however, noble seigneurs seem to have played a relatively minor and probably decreasing role in in-

19. Plainte de Jeanne Glane et Pierre Borderie, February 25, 1785, B 1585, ADD.

20. Latapie, "L'Industrie et le commerce en Guienne," 433. In contrast, Georges Bussière reports that peasants in the vicinity disliked the count and, in late 1789, assembled to call for the return of property they believed he had wrongfully seized (*Etudes historiques,* III, 241–42).

21. Information devant la Maréchaussée de Sarlat, February 7, 1775, B 1684, ADD.

formal settlements unless acting in some official capacity. In general, seigneurial court officers, curés, and persons simply described as "bourgeois" were much more active as go-betweens in infrajudicial settlements.

The role of curés is also instructive, for they were sometimes consulted not only in questions requiring discretion but also in more mundane matters of theft and property disputes. In a public case of theft with breaking and entry in 1773, for example, the victim first reported the crime to the curé of Condat. Even when they themselves were victims of crime, curés sometimes chose to settle informally. In 1783 the seigneurial judge of Salignac ordered the arrest of Jean Archimbal for the theft of five altar cloths. Only the most recent of the thefts, from the church in Montignac, had resulted in legal proceedings; other thefts came to light in the course of the inquest held at Salignac and its continuation before the sénéchaussée. But the first of the thefts, in April, 1782, had not gone undetected. Archimbal, who had previously been convicted and branded for smuggling in the vicinity of Toulouse, was a jack-of-all-trades who had been employed as an agricultural worker, shepherd, wool and flax carder, and woodworker. At the time of the crime, he was employed in the vineyards near Archignac, where he entered the parish church and stole two altar cloths. When he attempted to sell them to a gunsmith whose shop was near the church, the shopkeeper recognized them and alerted the curé. The curé and his *valet* confronted Archimbal in the *boutique* and forced him to follow them back to the rectory, where the *valet* took Archimbal to the cellar and searched him. Archimbal reluctantly unfastened his trousers and removed from around his waist the stolen altar cloths. He then "fell on his knees before the curé and asked pardon. The curé said he would pardon him on the condition that he left the country and went overseas." Although his order of banishment may seem harsh, the alternative in store for the thief before a royal court would have been much more severe. Archimbal agreed, the curé pardoned him, and no further action was taken against him until ten months later, when Archimbal repeated his crime.[22] In the first case the curé not only pursued and apprehended the culprit but also acted as informal prosecutor and judge in his "trial." Although there was no real mediation by a third party,

22. Récolement à Sarlat, May 21, 1773, B 1554, ADD; Interrogatoire à Sarlat, December 1, 1783, B 1582, ADD.

the termination of the incident was accomplished in the traditional manner of informal settlements: In exchange for the return of the stolen goods and a confession of guilt, the accused was pardoned and spared legal prosecution.

Although sometimes involved in bitter controversy with members of their flocks, curés could also be instrumental in attempting to resolve differences and avert legal action in minor affairs of family honor and property disputes. In one such case, a curé intervened on behalf of sharecroppers in danger of eviction in 1787. Two négociants of Sarlat had brought suit against their sharecroppers to force them off their land, but the curé of Sarlat arranged a compromise whereby they were allowed to stay in exchange for paying the legal expenses of the plaintiffs. One year later, however, the sharecroppers still had not paid the plaintiffs' court costs and proclaimed to all who would listen that the two had employed false witnesses against them in the trial. As a result, the two merchants initiated criminal proceedings against them for insults.[23]

Curés rarely attempted to interfere in litigation already underway but rather limited themselves to averting legal action. The curé of Saint-Crépin (aided by a brigadier of the maréchaussée), for example, intervened in a delicate family matter in 1788 and persuaded one of his parishioners, a sharecropper, not to bring suit against an elderly merchant who, the sharecropper feared, would dishonor his daughter. According to the terms of the settlement, the father agreed not to bring suit if the merchant (described as "old, white-haired, and married") would stop pursuing the sixteen-year-old girl. When the merchant violated the terms of the settlement and continued to bother the girl, her family felt justified in resorting to threats and actual violence. The sharecropper and his son limited themselves to menaces, but the girl's mother was less restrained and attacked the merchant, throwing rocks at him as he fled. The merchant retaliated by bringing suit against the family for insults and violence.[24]

Some curés took seriously their Christian duty to preserve and restore harmony among their parishioners. They opposed litigation and did not hesitate to intervene, even when unsolicited, to order disputing

23. Plainte, August 20, 1788, B 1595, ADD.
24. Interrogatoire à Sarlat de Jean Albie, July 2, 1789, Interrogatoire de Jeanne Paget, September 10, 1789, both in B 1597, ADD.

parties to settle their differences; they were even known to use informal methods to settle serious crimes that involved them personally. Their role in crime detection and conflict resolution was accepted by the populace, whose first impulse often was to report theft or even murder to the curé.[25] Furthermore, royal justice formally recognized the centrality of curés and called on their aid in the solution of serious crimes. By means of a *monitoire,* a judge would request that a bishop issue an injunction to be read by curés on three consecutive Sundays, calling on parishioners to reveal what they knew about a specific crime under pain of excommunication. Those who came forward were then assigned to testify in the sénéchaussée inquest.[26]

The traditional role of the curés as go-betweens was destined to diminish as individuals in the community came to appreciate the benefits of legal recourse and combined official tactics with the informal modes of dispute settlement. Also, eighteenth-century Périgourdin curés, like seigneurs, were becoming more preoccupied with their financial situation. As they began to supervise more closely the collection of the tithe and press for its extension to new crops such as maize, they increasingly came into conflict with their parishioners. An equally serious source of conflict was their campaign to purify popular religious practices. Both developments eventually led to the alienation of the curé from his flock, which thenceforth would logically have regarded him less as a peacemaker and more as a troublemaker. It seems likely, then, that mediation of disputes by curés decreased over this period. Unfortunately, insufficient documentation exists to quantify such a transition in the Sarladais.[27]

The increase in private suits and the amalgamation of official and popular tactics may have accentuated the role of bougeois in informal settlements. In most of the cessions examined, the go-between was literate, acquainted with legal contracts and therefore capable of supervising the drafting of a written settlement, and wealthy enough to supply the capital so rare in an economy that still relied heavily on barter. All of these attributes made merchants and members of the liberal pro-

25. See Révélations devant les curés des paroisses de la Cassaigne et de Jayac, B 1558, ADD.

26. Guyot *et al., Répertoire,* XI, 584–89; Marion, *Dictionnaire,* 383.

27. Nicole Castan argues that the role of curés in dispute settlement was definitely diminishing in Languedoc (*Justice et répression en Languedoc,* 43).

fessions logical go-betweens in private suits. Their role as go-between was no longer to avert legal action and maintain internal social equilibrium but to use legal maneuvers to achieve a settlement more akin to the sentences of royal justice than to the compromises of popular justice.

In a typical example, a nobleman brought suit against a commoner in 1790 for insults and violence. The accused, apparently moved by revolutionary fervor, had spread "seditious remarks about the nobility" and particularly the plaintiff. When the two met at an inn in the parish of Saint-Julien, they had begun to argue, and the defendant had insulted the nobleman, saying "f. noble, f. fish merchant, you'll pay for this." The noble explained in his petition that he was bringing suit to repress such disorderly conduct and disrespect from a man who was "evil and brutal." But when the assigned witnesses arrived in the *auditoire* (hearing room) on May 19, the plaintiff failed to appear. After waiting five hours, the judge and clerk sent for the nobleman, who declared to the court "that his affair was in mediation and a compromise would be reached via the decision of M. Maraval de Berbiguière, bourgeois." [28]

Another example illustrates not only the entanglement of legal and extralegal tactics employed in private cases but also the hazards encountered by one bourgeois in acting as go-between. Jean Berbesson, non-noble seigneur of Marence, prided himself on being the "enemy of all litigation" and was known to work amicably with his neighbors to settle disputes. In November, 1785, he was mediating between Jean Marcary and the son of a nailmaker, who were involved in a ruinous civil suit. A bourgeois fermier named Fonpeyre suspected Berbesson's motives and warned him not to intervene, but Berbesson ignored this warning and invited the two disputants to meet at his home "to reach a conciliation." When they arrived, he had them drink together and finally managed to reconcile their differences. Meanwhile Fonpeyre, who had heard of the plans for a settlement, met with two accomplices outside Berbesson's house. The three fired shots at Berbesson's horse in a nearby meadow and then set their dogs to chase the wounded animal. When Berbesson emerged from the house, Fonpeyre approached and tried to shoot him, but Berbesson escaped by deflecting the gun barrel.

28. Procès-verbal, May 19, 1790, B 1599, ADD.

The next day he had a surgeon verify the injury to his horse. He then brought suit against all three for damage to property and attempted *assassinat.*[29]

In response, Fonpeyre resorted to a variety of tactics. He at first appealed the arrest warrant against him, but when the sénéchaussée confirmed it, he began his own suit against Berbesson before the seigneurial tribunal of Terrasson. When Berbesson, in turn, appealed that case, the sénéchaussée ruled in his favor and annulled it. After the failure of these legal maneuvers, Fonpeyre paid two men to shoot Berbesson. When that failed, in 1787 Fonpeyre and his brother tried to bribe the witnesses in the sénéchaussée case into retracting their testimony at the time of the recall. Thwarted in their attempt, they spread the rumor that Berbesson himself had bribed the witnesses. In 1789 Berbesson countered by adding to the charges in his original suit the accusation of "subornation of witnesses and defamation."[30]

In its definitive sentence, the sénéchaussée rejected Fonpeyre's case at Terrasson as "purely recriminatory" and declared the three accused duly convicted of trespassing on Berbesson's land with firearms and, in an act of defiance, of intentionally wounding his horse. All three were reprimanded and fined a total of three hundred livres in damages to be donated, with the consent of the plaintiff, to the poor of the parish, plus all expenses. They were acquitted of the remaining charges against them.[31] The whole spectrum of tactics employed by disputants can be found within this case: civil suits, settlements, vengeance by direct action against an opponent's person or property, criminal suits, countersuits, appeals, bribery of witnesses, rumor mongering, and intimidation. Ironically enough, the man who prided himself on being the "enemy of all litigation" found himself involved in expensive litigation for four years.

In sum, the role of traditional go-betweens was confined to resolving differences and averting litigation; once one of the disputants decided to have recourse to royal justice, their involvement came to an end. Seigneurial officers were active primarily in arranging settlements in public cases such as thefts. Although they were less inclined to settle

29. Tournelle de Sarlat, August 19, 1786: Plainte (November 16, 1785), B, ADG.
30. Tournelle de Sarlat, August 19, 1786: Note (February 6, 1786), B, ADG. Also see Plainte, April 21, 1789, B 1598, ADD.
31. Plainte, April 21, 1789, Interrogatoire de Fonpeyre, March 5, 1789, both in B 1598; Sentence définitive, May 23, 1789, B 1642, ADD.

private disputes, they occasionally did so. Noblemen and curés maintained their traditional role as go-betweens in rural communities, but they were perhaps increasingly perceived to be less essential as individuals came to appreciate the benefits of recourse to official justice. Economic strains were further testing if not sundering the few remaining ties of reciprocity that united seigneurs and curés with their peasants.[32]

The real beneficiaries of the increase in private suits were the rural bourgeois (primarily legal professionals and royal officials) who dominated the peasantry with their property, wealth, education, and official connections. As already mentioned, in private suits involving verbal violence, the great majority of references to informal settlements during this period concerned efforts to settle litigation already underway. Legal recourse was used more and more to increase the concessions gained when an informal, out-of-court settlement was finally reached. Merchants and especially legal professionals were the logical choices for this new style of mediator, who, unlike the traditional go-between, went to work only after legal action was initiated.

Informal settlements were generally oral agreements referred to as *accommodements* and were similar to informal contracts of sale. In the hustle and bustle of the market could be heard the voice of the *accordeur,* who acted as go-between in the haggling over prices, speaking first in the ear of one party and then in that of the other. Once the agreement was concluded, the parties all went to a cabaret to "boire chopine."[33] A good description of the protocol for such sales can be found in two private cases that came before the sénéchaussée in 1777. On a Saturday, the eve of Pentecost and a market day in Sarlat, a merchant named Monturel brought to market two pair of oxen he wished to sell. The first serious inquiry came from Bernard Magueur, a cattle merchant of Sarlat. The two haggled over the price and then went to a cabaret with three other persons, one of whom was the accordeur, to dine and discuss the deal. But neither party found the compromise price of 850 livres proposed by the accordeur satisfactory, and so they parted amicably. Upon reflection, however, Magueur returned to the market one

32. In the Périgord the tithe represented the essential part of curés' incomes, which rose an average of 50 percent in the final twenty years of the Old Regime—significantly faster than the cost of living. The tithe was therefore the source of much conflict (Mandon, "Les Curés en Périgord," 283, 509–11).

33. Fayolle, *La Vie quotidienne en Périgord,* 107–108.

hour later to renew negotiations. As he approached, he saw two bourgeois named Couserant, father and son, standing behind Monturel's oxen. Not realizing they were already negotiating for the animals, he renewed his bargaining. The accordeur again proposed the price of 850 livres and, "because he wished to reconcile the two parties, took each by the hand and made them touch as a sign of the transaction they should conclude." The Couserants objected and accused Magueur of interfering in their negotiations. When Magueur claimed he had been the first to bargain for the oxen and therefore had priority, the Couserants grew angry. The son, using the *tu* form to address Magueur, called him a "f. greenhorn" and pushed and kicked him. The elder Couserant joined in, calling Magueur a "j. f. [jean foutre] and a bankrupt," at which Magueur turned to those gathered around them and said: "Messieurs, I want you all to remember that he called me a bankrupt. Now he must prove that it is true." The opposing parties then stormed off to bring their respective suits for "insults and violence." [34]

Infrajudicial settlements proceeded along much the same lines. The go-between was most often referred to as an *arbitre,* but the term *accordeur* was also common. Although the records do not specify that parties to a settlement actually touched hands or used the expression "tope la" employed in Languedoc when a deal was struck, it was common practice for all concerned to share a bottle of wine in a ritual gesture of agreement and reconciliation. Among the peasantry, negotiations were most often held in a cabaret, but even when they were held in the home of a seigneur, food and drink accompanied or followed the settlement. Although in normal circumstances Périgourdins needed little encouragement to drink wine, the successful resolution of a dispute and the restoration of social harmony still warranted special celebration.

Reliance on notaries to record the terms of a settlement was apparently deemed necessary only when cases involved serious offenses such as accidental manslaughter or attempted *assassinat.* In these instances, cessions fulfilled the dual purpose of compensating the victim and protecting the accused from further prosecution, and the cessionary served

34. Interrogatoire de Magueur, May 28, 1777, B 1564, ADD. On May 16, 1778, the court finally decided in favor of Magueur and ordered the elder Couserant to retract his accusation and declare that he now recognized Magueur as an "honnête homme." He was also sentenced thirty livres in damages, plus expenses (Sentence, May 16, 1778, B 1564, ADD).

not only as go-between but also as technical adviser and source of capital. Nicole Castan found that parallel with the declining influence of curés and seigneurs as go-betweens there occurred in Languedoc a growing reliance on the notarial act, especially in cases involving financial and legal questions. In the Sarladais, however, the few notarial acts referred to in the criminal court records were exclusively for the above-mentioned cessions. Because they constituted only five of the forty-three known examples of settlements, one cannot conclude that notarial acts were replacing informal, oral agreements in the Sarladais as they may have been doing in Languedoc during the same period.[35]

The terms of informal settlements were both moral and material in nature. Intrinsic to the moral reparation of theft was the culprit's admission of guilt and request for pardon, preferably in the presence of the victim and witnesses. Thefts upset not only the distribution of goods within a community but also the equilibrium of honor: The victim suffered both material loss and a lowering of esteem in the eyes of his neighbors if he allowed the offense to go unpunished. It was therefore essential for him to call on his relatives and friends to help him pursue and apprehend the culprit. By reclaiming the stolen goods and forcing the culprit to admit his misconduct and accept punishment, often in the form of a token beating, the victim demonstrated his vigilance, made a show of solidarity with his relatives and neighbors, and thereby restored his lost honor. In cases of insult and calumny, the attack on a person's honor was much more direct and obvious. The victim who wished to avoid permanent loss of status was obliged to make the culprit proclaim his retraction in public or at least before carefully chosen witnesses. Because of its wide social repercussions, no offense or dispute was a purely private affair; consequently, any retraction or punishment necessarily had to be in the public view to fulfill its purpose— the restoration of social harmony.

Material reparations were either in money or in its substitutes— bread, labor, manure, or other goods—even for strictly moral (immaterial) transgressions. The object, of course, was to make the culprit "pay" for the damage done to his victim, for even a symbolic or token payment could effectively restore the delicate equilibrium of honor within the community. The ultimate purpose of infrajudicial settlements was punishment not as retribution but as a form of reparation

35. N. Castan, *Justice et répression en Languedoc*, 48.

enabling the injured party to save face and the contrite culprit to gain readmission into the social body—an occasion for all to celebrate their solidarity. The terms of payment often minimized the handling of money in this cash-poor society. Those without money promised to pay when the harvest came in or agreed to work in exchange for damages, and victims had little choice but to accept such terms. Persons without resources or property who repeatedly transgressed nevertheless ran the risk of being turned over to royal justice.

The increase in the 1780s of private suits revolving around minor offenses of verbal and physical violence suggests that the populace may have begun to welcome the involvement of the Crown in the regulation of private disputes. But the plaintiffs in such cases did not abandon other modes of dispute settlement; rather, they combined and alternated formal and informal tactics in an effort to obtain more favorable out-of-court settlements. The intervention of bourgeois in the settlement of ongoing litigation seems to have increased, and it is logical to suppose that mediation and arbitration by nobles and curés dedicated to averting litigation decreased. But this hypothesis remains virtually unprovable on the basis of research in the criminal court records. Available evidence does suggest, however, a shift from a traditional to a more individualistic attitude toward official justice in the Sarladais.

VI

Vengeance and the Defense of Honor

It is public scandal that constitutes offense,
and to sin in secret is not to sin at all.

—Molière, *Le Tartuffe*

The essential component of law is the legitimate use of physical coercion by a socially authorized agent; the use or the possibility of use of organized force effectively raises the legal order above simple custom. But the privilege of applying force does not necessarily belong only to an official with legal office; rather, the offended party may become the private prosecutor and judge. In such cases, he often does not act solely on his own, his family's, or his clan's behalf; he may enjoy the approval or tacit support of the remainder of the community. The support of the offended party by the community, albeit the tacit support of opinion and not overt action, denotes that its members believe the actions of the offender somehow contravened the standards of the community as a whole. The individual or collectivity acting as a private prosecutor in self-regulating societies therefore represents the general social interest as well as a private interest.[1]

Agents of popular justice in the Sarladais survived as enforcers of customary law, acting either in conjunction with or in opposition to royal law. Whereas infrajudicial dispute settlement resolved conflicts by peaceful compromise, vengeance refused all compromise and intended to chastise the offender. The agent of vengeance was most often the offended party himself or his surrogates—relatives, friends, and neighbors. Although the vengeance of popular justice, like that of royal justice, was retributive in nature, a crucial difference distinguished the

---

1. E. Adamson Hoebel, *The Law of Primitive Man* (New York, 1974), 22–27.

two. The goal of royal justice was to manifest the absolute authority of the king over the culprit; in contrast, the goal of popular justice was to redress the balance of honor or esteem upset by the offense. In this respect, vengeance shared with dispute settlement the primary goal of popular justice: the maintenance and restoration of social equilibrium.

Royal retribution was fraught with political significance. According to royal law, any offense or *crime,* quite apart from the damage it produced, offended the sovereign, from whom all justice emanated. The intervention of the king in public cases, then, was neither an arbitration between two adversaries nor even primarily an attempt to guarantee the rights of individual victims. Instead, royal justice was the sovereign's direct reply to the subject who had offended him and required that he avenge the affront to his person. Consequently, public execution was, in the words of Michel Foucault, a ceremony by which the injured sovereignty reconstituted itself.

> Its aim is not so much to reestablish a balance as to bring into play, as its extreme point, the dissymmetry between the subject who has dared to violate the law and the all-powerful sovereign who displays his strength. Although redress of the private injury occasioned by the offense must be proportionate, although the sentence must be equitable, the punishment is carried out in such a way as to give a spectacle not of measure, but of imbalance and excess; in this liturgy of punishment, there must be an emphatic affirmation of power and of its intrinsic superiority.[2]

In short, the ceremony of punishment was an exercise in political terror designed to impress upon the populace, through the body of the criminal, the unrestrained power of the sovereign. The retributive nature of royal justice as outlined by Foucault must be viewed within the context of the accelerated expansion of royal power in the seventeenth century. The expansion of the King's Law was an essential element in that aggrandizement. Because every crime constituted a rebellion against the King's Law and every criminal was, to an extent, guilty of *lèse-majesté,* a public execution was more than an act of justice; it was a political operation that manifested and reaffirmed royal power in all its vengeful excess.[3]

In contrast, the purpose of popular justice was to redress the bal-

---

2. Foucault, *Discipline and Punish,* 48–49.
3. *Ibid.,* 53–54. The public execution as it was still ritualized in the eighteenth century was infrequently practiced. See Ruff, *Crime, Justice and Public Order,* 60–63.

ance of honor through the direct but measured chastisement of the offender by the offended party. Its methods were controlled and proportionate to the offense, not gratuitously excessive. The choice between mediation and vengeance via direct action was sometimes a function of the seriousness of the offense. When the social wound was too grievous, the offended party could not be assuaged by compromise; in such cases, the balance of solidarity was upset so drastically that the diplomacy of dispute settlement could not restore the peace. But sometimes vengeance came into play in relatively minor affairs that were not even crimes. In these instances, royal justice was rejected or ignored as inapplicable. Because vengeance, unlike mediation, was intended not so much to avert recourse to the courts as to provide an independent alternative to royal justice, it can, in some respects, be seen as the democratization of the judicial function.[4] In the Sarladais, rich and poor persons of varied *qualité* and socioeconomic status—and not just members of the *classes populaires*—resorted to direct action wherever royal justice was unavailable, uncertain, or unsatisfactory.

The direct action of vengeance usurped the right to chastise offenders and therefore represented an open challenge to the jurisdiction of the royal courts. As a result, it could not be tolerated by royal officials except out of weakness. The relationship between the two rival systems can be characterized as truly symbiotic only in those few instances where royal law and popular custom did not converge. The marriage of an elderly widow to a young eligible bachelor or the beating of a man by his wife was an affront to popular sensibility but generally did not constitute a violation of royal statutes. In such a case, the authorities were inclined to tolerate the rough music and charivaris staged to punish the offenders so long as they did not disturb public order. Although the relationship of royal justice to popular justice remained intrinsically antagonistic, in practice royal authorities could extend their jurisdiction only in partnership with individuals in the community who were anxious to free themselves from the restrictive bonds of popular justice.

Private individuals and groups assumed the role of informal prosecutor and judge in various circumstances. The defense of honor was a frequent cause of such action; in fact, Yves Castan found that much of the litigation in eighteenth-century Languedoc had its origins in affairs of honor. A relatively minor incident that arose from a longstanding

4. N. Castan, *Justice et répression en Languedoc,* 82.

disagreement over property illustrates how such cases were soon trans-lated into affairs of honor. On August 19, 1783, a drawn-out feud be-tween two neighboring families came to a head. Early that morning, a small pig belonging to a peasant named Jean and his wife, Marie, es-caped from the courtyard of their farm and wandered onto the prop-erty of their neighbor, Vilatte. When he saw the pig, Vilatte set his dog after it and also began to throw stones to chase it away. By the time Jean and Marie were alerted by the commotion and came running, they found that their pig was seriously hurt and could hardly move. Marie cried out to Vilatte, "Come back here, come back here, you bugger, look at our pig that you almost killed." When Vilatte finally appeared, she told him that if the pig died, they would make him pay for it. Fur-thermore, she added, since he chose not to live in a neighborly fashion, they would kill any of his animals that wandered into their yard. Vilatte replied, "Don't play the Great Lady with me, you're a nobody and no one is afraid of you." He added that she, her mother, and her sisters were all worthless, and he called her "a tart and a trollop." She retorted in anger that he had no right to say such things because her family had much more honor than his had ever had. Both of them elaborated on this theme for quite some time. One witness later politely described the gist of their words: "They uttered to each other thousands of invectives on the subject of their ancestry."[5]

Jean and Marie finally stormed off, carrying their wounded animal in their arms. Realizing the implications of what had happened, Vilatte followed them and pleaded with them not to pursue the matter. He even promised to pay damages if the pig really was hurt, but Jean and Marie refused his offer. That same day they went before the royal court and brought suit against Vilatte for "atrocious insults." They argued that the nature of Vilatte's insults, especially his imputations against Marie's sexual conduct, had "troubled the harmony of their marriage." They therefore felt obliged to seek satisfaction in the form of repa-rations.[6]

Although the above incident had its origins in a longstanding prop-erty dispute, it quickly turned into an affair of honor. *Honor* can be defined as the value of a person in his own eyes, his self-esteem; more important, honor is also the esteem in which a person is held by his

5. Y. Castan, *Honnêteté et rélations sociales*, 82; Information, August 20, 1783, Plainte, August 19, 1783, both in B 1580, ADD.

6. Information, August 20, 1783, Plainte, August 19, 1783, both in B 1580, ADD.

peers. In other words, honor is not only a person's estimation of his own worth or claim to pride but also the acknowledgment of that claim by society. In effect, people extort from one another validation of the image they cherish of themselves. Individuals and families in the Sarladais struggled to defend an integrity that derived primarily from inherited social status and secondarily from conduct. The degree of honor was relative and therefore served as the basis of precedence in society. This fact lent a certain competitive aspect to the ongoing struggle for honor within a community. An individual needed to be constantly vigilant and sufficiently powerful to enforce his claim, thereby ensuring that he received the respect, precedence, and social status that he was due.[7]

Anthropologists have pointed out that in western Europe in general, precedence is recognized or deference is accorded by various demonstrations of respect centered on the head. Forms of address and gestures normally associated with the head—which may be bowed, touched, covered, or uncovered—either confirm or deny the individual's claim to honor. In the words of the British anthropologist Julian Pitt-Rivers, "The head of the person honoured is used to demonstrate his status whether it is adorned, dressed in a distinctive manner, prohibited to be touched or even chopped off."[8] Even where society has outlawed physical violence, it has retained the ritual slap on the cheek as a challenge to settle an affair of honor. Moreover, it was no accident that in early modern France the execution of persons deemed worthy of respect was by decapitation, a right reserved for noblemen until the guillotine of the French Revolution graciously extended the privilege to all citizens. Both words and actions were significant in this code of honor because they were expressions of attitudes that asserted, accorded, or denied honor. Any verbal or physical affront created a situation in which the equilibrium of honor was upset.[9] To correct the imbalance, the offended party demanded an apology (a verbal act of self-humiliation) or made the offender "pay" through physical violence. Only when the insult was corrected was the equilibrium of esteem restored.

7. Julian Pitt-Rivers, *The Fate of Shechem, or the Politics of Sex: Essays in the Anthropology of the Mediterranean* (Cambridge, Eng., 1977), 1–4; Claverie, "L'Honneur," 746–48.

8. Pitt-Rivers, *The Fate of Shechem*, 4–5.

9. The common people in Italy at one time believed that the person committing an affront enhanced his own reputation in direct proportion to the humiliation of the offended party (*ibid.,* 4).

In a relatively closed social community, the implications of this code of honor were many and profound. Although recourse to litigation was used occasionally as a means of avenging and restoring lost honor, many inhabitants of the Sarladais persisted in regarding recourse to royal justice in this circumstance as an act of cowardice. Also, appeal to outside authority was tantamount to breaking solidarity and was an act of treason against the moral authority of the community. Even victory in a court of law did little to redeem one's lost honor. Moreover, going to the courts for redress and protection meant advertising the offense and proclaiming one's vulnerability. The delays of litigation only gave the offender more time to gloat over the public humiliation of his opponent.[10]

Submission of affairs of honor to any form of arbitration, even by the king, was considered a weakness. In explanation, Pitt-Rivers argues that an individual's honor was essentially his share of sacredness. God, the personification of ideal qualities, was the ultimate source of the honor that stretched in a hierarchy from God through the king (whose legitimacy depended on divine sanction) and then down through the ranks of the social structure to those who had no honor at all (*gens sans aveu*). But the monarchy gradually forbade direct appeal to God and took on the responsibility of arbitrating claims of honor. Although the sovereign was, in one sense, the guardian and bestower of all honor, in another sense he was the usurper of honor since he claimed the right to arbitrate in regard to it. Individuals with a highly developed sense of honor were therefore reluctant to submit the settlement of affairs of honor even to a royal court. The change from the period when the law prescribed the judicial combat to that when the duel was made illegal hence corresponds to the gradual extension of the competence of the state in judicial matters.[11]

In the case immediately in question, Vilatte challenged his neighbors by attacking their two most prized possessions: their property (in the form of the pig) and their good name (in the form of Marie's reputa-

---

10. In eighteenth-century Paris, commoners sometimes had recourse to police commissioners to stop rumors and provide proof of innocence. But the restoration of honor via public justice was a double-edged sword since it exposed the transgression to public view (Arlette Farge, "Familles: L'Honneur et le secret," in Roger Chartier [ed.], *De la Renaissance aux Lumières* [Paris, 1986], 598–600, Vol. III of Philippe Ariès and Georges Duby [eds.], *Histoire de la vie privée*, 5 vols.).

11. Pitt-Rivers, *The Fate of Shechem*, 3, 9–10, 13, 15–16.

tion). Jean, in order to defend his honor, show he was not a coward, and defend his wife against accusations of sexual misconduct, was obliged to seek satisfaction. In this case, he did so by recourse to royal justice; but in many affairs of honor, offended parties preferred vengeance through direct violent action. Honor was worth fighting for, whether in a court of law or at the local tavern. The preoccupation with reputation was common to all social classes, including the lowliest sharecroppers. In fact, members of the lower orders seem to have been particularly defensive in their relations with persons of superior rank and were quick to assert that they had just as much *honneur* or *honnêteté*.

Honor was part of one's person and could not be violated with impunity. Individuals and families from every social level valued their good reputation and honor, without which the humblest could not easily gain employment. Public arrest and incarceration followed by public punishment were most ignominious, for they conferred infamy on the criminal and his entire family. This desperate struggle to protect honor also explains the length to which families would go to help their relatives escape. In the villages of the Sarladais, where men and women lived in close proximity and shared a common economic and physical insecurity, the spoken word was all-powerful and could create wounds and cause serious conflicts. Through words, the individual measured and remeasured his position vis-à-vis his fellows and carved out a space for his personal and familial honor. But his honor was mutable and depended on the opinion of others, who were also trying to distinguish themselves. The individual had to be constantly vigilant about the esteem of others, for his reputation was the only means of guaranteeing the exact place that he claimed in the social hierarchy. Within this context, every insinuating, provocative, or even evasive word about someone's reputation could bring immediate consequences.[12]

Insults were designed to thrust the target beyond the margins of respectability and social integration. But the constituent elements of an individual's honor differed between men and women. The essential characteristic of manliness was fearlessness, a readiness to defend one's

12. Jean-Louis Flandrin, *Families in Former Times: Kinship, Household and Sexuality in Early Modern France,* trans. Richard Southern (Cambridge, Eng., 1979), 46–47; P. Henry, *Crime, justice et société,* 696–701; Farge, "Familles," in Chartier (ed.), *De la Renaissance aux Lumières,* 591–94.

own pride and that of one's family. Power in its various aspects was frankly equated with sexual potency, and the merging of the two elements found expression in both the language and the ritualized violence accompanying affairs of honor. The sexual content of the insults was not as overt as one might expect: Even when people used terms like *bougre* and *jean foutre,* it is not certain that they did so with sexual connotations foremost in mind. A man who allowed an insult to his honor to go unchallenged was nonetheless deemed to have lost his masculinity and to have forfeited his standing in the community of adult males. In the same manner, a man who failed to challenge an insult to his wife's honor effectively admitted he was a cuckold. Accusations of theft were also treated seriously, for they challenged a man's integrity and honesty in everyday dealings with his peers. The primary responsibility of every adult male was to defend his own honor and that of his family—in particular, the sexual honor of his mother, wife, and daughters.[13]

In 1785 Jean Lacombe and his wife, Toinette Carsenac, brought suit against Pierre Lavergne and his wife, Elisabeth Lavialle, and their daughter for insults. In the heat of an argument over business dealings, the accused had called Toinette "a trollop, a whore, a bad sort, and worthless." In a more general slander of the entire family, Lavergne's wife had told the curé that Toinette came from a family of scoundrels and that her brother had barely escaped being hanged. Furthermore, she had spread the rumor in public that Toinette had gone to another town to give birth to a bastard child. Finally, Lavergne's daughter had been heard to say that "the husband is cuckolded and content" and that "his wife was skilled at the trade of making babies." In response to their insults, Toinette had first retaliated by confronting Lavergne's wife in public, calling her a "f. *bougresse,* whore, and trollop," and throwing stones and threatening to kill her. She and her husband had then taken legal action and even rejected the offer of a settlement, arguing that "when the insults are so serious and amount to absolute defamation, when they attack the honor and reputation of a married woman, they cast a shadow upon a household" and therefore could not be overlooked in exchange for thirty livres.[14]

13. Julian Pitt-Rivers, *The People of the Sierra* (2nd ed.; Chicago, 1971), 89–92; Farge, "Familles," in Chartier (ed.), *De la Renaissance aux Lumières,* 595–96.

14. Interrogatoire d'Elisabeth Lavialle, August 22, 1785, Interrogatoire de Guillaume Lavergne, August 22, 1785, and Plainte, September 7, 1785, all in B 1586, ADD.

The power to impugn the honor of another depended on the relative status of the contestants. In theory, at least, an inferior did not possess sufficient honor to resent the affront of a superior; in practice, however, many inferiors did. Likewise, a superior could safely ignore the affront of an inferior, though he might decide to punish him for his impudence. If he decided to punish the inferior, he did not need to abide by the rules that normally governed affairs of honor. If, for example, a commoner failed to use the proper form of address or lift his hat when greeting a nobleman, the latter could safely overlook it. Treating such behavior as a challenge to his honor was tantamount to recognizing the other's equality with him. A man, then, was answerable for his honor only to his social equals, and a butcher could still boast to a bourgeois "that he was an *honnête homme* and that when it came to honor, he had as much as he." [15]

The imperative to defend one's reputation was particularly pressing for persons engaged in commerce, who could be ruined if insults went unchallenged. A bourgeois who brought suit against his sharecroppers because they accused him of stealing their grain characterized their accusation as being "of the utmost seriousness for a man of honor." [16] In 1786, a merchant named Jean Rochette brought suit against Guillaume Delbreil for "heinous insults" that he believed would surely harm him. When the two quarreled over an unpaid wager, Delbreil called him a "f. rascal and f. loup-garou" and repeated the insult several times in a crowded cabaret. Rochette asked Delbreil to recant these accusations "because of the harm that the label of loup-garou could cause him." In the late eighteenth century and well into the nineteenth, popular superstition still held that loups-garous (or *léberons,* in patois) were persons condemned to roam the fields at night as werewolves. In a more figurative sense, the epithet was used to taunt merchants regarded as "bloodsuckers." The witnesses who testified in the inquest agreed with Rochette that the accusation was indeed serious. One of them explained to the court that "the words made an impression on the minds of many present because *loup-garou* is an evil expression that dishonors the person to whom it is given." Another witness agreed that "being called loup-garou dishonors the person in question, who is regarded

15. Pitt-Rivers, *The Fate of Shechem,* 10; Mousnier, *Les Hierarchies sociales de 1450 à nos jours,* 32–39; Interrogatoire d'Armand Delprat, July 3, 1783, B 1580, ADD.
16. Plainte, September 4, 1789, B 1597, ADD.

askance to the point of doing him harm." The final witness averred that the term brought such dishonor that people even avoided drinking after someone so described.[17]

Merchants were especially sensitive to insults that challenged their probity. Pierre Arbelat, a cattle merchant who sold a calf at the Domme fair, went to a cabaret to drink with the buyer and close the deal, "as is the custom." But a disagreement over the cost of the drinks led to an argument and the intervention of the *sergent royal* of Domme, who grabbed Arbelat by the hair and shook him. Arbelat later explained: "This man began to say publicly and in a loud voice that the plaintiff was a rogue, a thief, and a bankrupt. He added that his [the plaintiff's] father was as much of a knave and thief as he was and that he had per- jured himself and stolen or caused the loss of two *louis d'or*." In his petition, the merchant emphasized that because these "heinous insults proffered against his reputation and honor" were uttered "before the public," he was forced to seek reparation. In a similar suit, another insulted merchant explained why he felt obliged to take legal action: "The petitioner cannot dissemble these calumnies without appearing to merit them, and we all know how important it is for a merchant to keep his reputation pure and intact and how any malicious rumor can harm his well-being."[18]

The criminal court records contain numerous examples of sym- bolic attacks on men's probity and power (including their virility) in the form of violence directed against heads, hair, and hats. When men fought, a combatant generally seized his opponent by the hair not least of all for practical reasons—in order to sling him to the ground or other- wise immobilize him so that the attacker could better kick him with his sabots or beat him with his *baton* or even drag him by the hair into the mud. But the main object, of course, was to render him powerless and humiliated, to emasculate him at least symbolically. In a typical ex- ample, a nobleman and a merchant began insulting each other late one evening after playing cards at a café in Sarlat. Each then knocked the

17. Information, August 29, 1786, B 1590, ADD. In a dispute over fishing rights in 1754, one man said of the other: "He was a werewolf, and when he ate his soup, he was seen to have spit four dog's feet into it" (Cocula, *Les Gens de la rivière de Dordogne*, 628). For a summary of local superstitions about werewolves, see Georges Rocal, *Le Vieux Périgord* (Périgueux, 1926).

18. Plaintes, July 7, August 30, 1784, both in B 1583, ADD.

other's hat off, grabbed him by the hair, and struck him in the head with his *baton* before onlookers separated them. The nobleman was armed with a saber but refrained from using it; he did, however, take the merchant's hat to present to the court as evidence of the assault.[19]

In 1772, three young noblemen who had made sexual advances toward the wife of a tavern owner and then attacked her husband when he came to her defense were forced by their relatives to agree to an out-of-court settlement of one hundred écus. Afterwards, wishing to punish the tavern owner for his insolence, the young men attacked him, held him on the ground by his hair, and beat him with their *batons*. One of the three then took out his knife and cut the tavern owner's hat into two pieces. Helping the victim to his feet, the young men handed him only half of his hat, warning him never to tell anyone what had happened.[20] In a similar incident, a *valet de ferme* and a bourgeois who were shelling walnuts at a crowded veillée one winter evening in 1779 began to quarrel. The bourgeois warned the other not to pursue his servant girl, who was also present, and tried to hit the *valet* with his *baton*. The *valet* grabbed his opponent's cap and threw it to the ground, drew his knife, and—in a gesture of defiance—cut the cap into pieces. In response, the bourgeois turned his wrath upon his servant, calling her a "f. worthless trollop," and told her to return to his house. Given the gravity of his insults and the large number of people present, she felt obliged to bring suit against her master.[21]

In contrast to male honor, female honor derived almost exclusively from a woman's shame, her sense of sexual virtue and propriety. Whereas imputations of weakness and dishonesty dishonored men, unanswered accusations of sexual promiscuity brought dishonor upon women. Feminine honor was primarily associated with conjugal fidelity. By protecting her sexual honor, a married woman safeguarded the reputation of her entire family. Moreover, because her actions in other

19. Plainte de M. Mtre. Philibert Marie Angélique de Bonnin, February 19, 1771, Plaintes de Gérard Lescure, February 18, 23, 1771, and Information, March 8, 1771, all in B 1547, ADD. On the significance of hats in public life, see Michael Sonenscher, *The Hatters of Eighteenth-Century France* (Berkeley, 1987), 12–17.

20. Plaintes, March 17, August 1, 1772, B 1552, ADD. Stymied by the wall of silence that the accused managed to organize, the court called for a monitoire that did produce testimony: Révélations du monitoire, October 4, 1772, *ibid.*

21. Plainte de Marguérite Cabanet, November 6, 1779, Information, November 24, 1779, both in B 1570, ADD.

respects were her husband's or father's social and legal responsibility, a woman could pronounce words and commit acts forbidden to men, and often acted as the most aggressive defender of the family's threshold.[22] This distinction also reflects the relative spheres of male and female influence within the family. Whereas the man was preeminent in the conduct of the family's formal social and economic relations with the outside world and possessed legal responsibility and authority over its members, the woman played the predominant part in the home and was responsible for the moral standing of the family within the community. In other words, the husband's manliness (honor) and the wife's virtue (shame) were complementary and combined to confer upon their children moral qualities regarded as virtually hereditary.[23]

The criminal court records accordingly show that ritualized or symbolic violence against women was not aimed at their heads, as with men, but most often at their bellies. Men who attacked women generally hit them with their fists or *batons,* or kicked them in the flanks, the *reins* (loins), or *bas ventre* (lower belly). Male threats against females also frequently centered on their reproductive capacity. In a typical example, a tavern owner and his wife forbade a former soldier known as a troublemaker from returning to their establishment. When he did so anyway and the woman refused to serve him, he called her a hussy, *bougresse,* and whore. He opened his knife and menaced her, saying "one hundred times that she would die only by his hand and that he wanted to disembowel her from her mouth to her navel."[24] In another incident, some cattle merchants became involved in an altercation with an ambulatory merchant and his wife who had come from Agen to Sarlat to sell their merchandise during the cattle market. The attackers

22. Y. Castan, *Honnêteté et rélations sociales,* 79; Nicole Castan, "La Criminalité familiale," in André Abbiateci *et al., Crimes et criminalité en France sous l'ancien régime, 17e–18e siècles* (Paris, 1971), 92–93.

23. Although in practice the simple division of space between the house for women and the fields for men must be qualified, social norms, especially in the South, assigned women to the home. The qualities that made her a *bonne ménagère* were reflections of her household, reputation, and honor (Martine Segalen, *Mari et femme dans la société paysanne* [Paris, 1980], 124–25, 127, 133). Also see Pitt-Rivers, *The People of the Sierra,* 112–15. Claverie emphasizes the long collective memory of Gévaudan villagers, who seemed to know every family's intimate history and believed that traits were transmissible and hereditary ("L'Honneur," 747–48).

24. Plainte, July 6, 1779, B 1570, ADD.

directed their blows at different parts of the pair's anatomy: They hit the man on the head with their *batons* but kicked his wife "in the lower belly and thighs" and tore her bodice while calling her "trollop, whore and *bougresse*." (She, in turn, threw stones at her opponents.) The surgeon who examined the couple's wounds remarked that the woman, who was more than four months pregnant, would undoubtedly lose the child she was carrying.[25]

Affairs of honor involving women invariably stemmed from the seduction of a daughter or the slandering of a wife. In 1783, for example, a young man seduced the daughter of a merchant. Her father argued in his petition to the court that it was scandalous "that such an evil man [had] brought shame upon a respectable family" and condemned his daughter, who had forgotten her duty, "to spend the rest of her life in tears and humiliation." Because, the merchant said, their family honor was their only fortune, he had decided to prosecute for damages. Another father argued in 1789 that the most precious possession of his daughter was "her honor and virtue." The consequences of her weakness, he added, were socially irreparable: "scorn and probable shunning by her own family and the public."[26] There was no quicker way to arouse the indignation of a man than to challenge the virtue of the women of his family.

Central to the concept of honor is the notion of balance or equilibrium, a notion that derives in large part from the fragile material base of a world in which commodities are limited. There was only so much material wealth to go around in the eighteenth-century Périgord: If one person prospered, it was at someone else's expense. The concept of limited good also lay at the core of popular religion, the goal of which was to appease angry gods and balance evil with good to restore equilibrium in the universe. The notion of balance pervaded many aspects of popular mentality and placed a premium on maintaining the status quo if at all possible and restoring it when upset.[27] As applied to honor, this rationale resulted in a distrust of outside authorities, whose

25. Information, July 18, 1779, Rapports du chirugien, July 21, 1779, both in B 1570, ADD. Also see the countersuit of one of the pair's opponents, a cattle merchant: Plainte, July 20, 1779, and Information, July 21, 1779.

26. Plainte, September 2, 1783, Récolement, January 29, 1784, both in B 1581, ADD; Tournelle de Sarlat, June 20, 1789: Plainte (February 7, 1789), B, ADG.

27. Peter Burke, *Popular Culture in Early Modern Europe* (New York, 1978), 176.

decisions were based on a logical but anonymous criminal code. Judicial decisions were by nature concerned with determining who was right and who was wrong, and ruled in favor of one party at the expense of the other. By contrast, autoregulation placed a premium on compromises appealing to the mutual interests of the parties. Mediation and arbitration were therefore preferable to royal justice, which irritated wounds and upset social equilibrium. Stated more generally, in a society wherein social relations continue to be characterized by deference and authority and the give-and-take of reciprocal relationships, judicial decisions based on fixed law codes are incompatible with the social order. And the only way that an individual who wishes to break with that traditional order can do so is precisely by appealing to outside authority to support his claims.

Another consequence of the notion of balance is that even when offended parties take direct action to restore the upset balance of honor, they do so with limited, controlled violence. An excess of violence only tips the balance of honor too far in the opposite direction and then requires redress by the other party. In similar fashion, absolute victory is undesirable and only provokes the vanquished party (and jealous neighbors) to work to limit the gains of the victor. Accordingly, vengeful violence in the eighteenth-century Périgord was not only highly ritualized but also carefully measured. Although the language of violence preserved much of the brutality of an earlier age, acts of violence were rarely gratuitously brutal or truly spontaneous. Combatants often threatened to cut off each other's limbs or to cut their opponent into pieces and throw him into the well or river, whichever was nearby, in a kind of ritual ablution reminiscent of the seventeenth-century *chasse aux gabeleurs* (hunt for taxmen). The records reveal that one peasant even threatened to make lard of a *feudiste* (expert on fiefs). But since the object of vengeful violence was to make the offender "pay" only in proportion to the gravity of the original offense, combatants armed with knives, sickles, or other potentially lethal weapons generally avoided using them. Firearms were illegal, scarce, and—even when available—shunned in favor of nonlethal weapons, except in self-defense. Along the Dordogne River, for example, in the different scuffles and skirmishes in which boatmen were involved, those who were armed generally fired their guns into the air to intimidate their foes or only used the gun stocks as clubs. Significantly, the firing of guns directly at assailants seems to have been confined to travelers or other outsiders who—either less prudent or less sure of themselves—took the initiative of violence.[28]

Violence in the Périgord was endemic yet measured. A cattle driver who saw a *laboureur* use his scythe to take a swing at his opponent, a domestique named Mandegon, later testified that he had reproached the assailant, saying: "You acted like a real rogue by going after Mandegon with your scythe. You could have taken a *baton* to fight each other with."[29] When a métivier who was shaking walnuts from his trees heard his brother call out for help, he picked up a hatchet lying on the ground. But a fellow worker warned him to "leave the hatchet where it is, because armed with such a weapon you cannot know what might happen." He further advised the man to stay where he was because his brother and his opponent "would arrive at a settlement between them." The métivier heeded at least part of the warning, for after using the hatchet to cut himself a *baton*, he left the hatchet behind as he ran to his brother's aid.[30]

The ubiquity of violence in Old Regime France has led many historians to conclude that peasants of that time were brutal, passionate, uncivilized, and quick to resort to violence at the least provocation.[31] Indeed, Nicolas Desmarest of the Académie des Sciences remarked during his 1761 tour of the Périgord that "the peasants are wild, vindictive, quarrelsome, always going about with iron-tipped *batons,* and lazy." When called upon to report on the mores of their parishioners in 1838, Périgourdin curés described the peasants as proud, litigious, and extremely solicitous of their honor. The curé of Mialet wrote: "If they promise something, they are slaves to their word. They will hold to it by the Saint of honor." According to the curé of Savignac, "They give themselves over easily to anger and nurse grudges in their hearts for a

---

28. Cocula, *Les Gens de la rivière de Dordogne,* 638–39. Violence in Parisian taverns was also controlled and deliberate in nature. Weapons were notably absent. See Thomas Brennan, *Public Drinking and Popular Culture in Eighteenth-Century Paris* (Princeton, 1988), 32–33, 35, 52–53.

29. Plainte, July 5, 1775, Information, July 7, 1775, both in B 1559, ADD.

30. Plainte, October 3, 1783, Information, October 6, 1783, both in B 1581, ADD. See especially the testimony of Pierre Ourly, *travailleur,* and of Jean Lafaurie, domestique.

31. Robert Mandrou speculated that chronic undernourishment may have accounted for the volatility of the populace (*Introduction à la France moderne, 1500–1640: Essai de psychologie historique* [Paris, 1974], 47, 86–88).

long while. Vengeance for them is a pleasure." [32] Violence was a fact of everyday life and to a large extent condoned precisely because individuals consciously employed it to redress the balance of honor continually being upset by failures to observe the rules of courtesy and deference that governed interpersonal relations. [33]

Vengeance was the exaction of retribution for an affront. Witnesses, the representatives of public opinion, were essential ingredients in an affront: A remark that would dishonor a man if said to his face would not necessarily dishonor him if said behind his back. Since a person's honor was essentially his social personality, the extent of the damage to his reputation was determined in large part by the range of public opinion within which the damage was broadcast. An affront delivered in public demanded public apology or humiliation to repair the harm done, as can clearly be seen in a case brought before the sénéchaussée in 1781. Charles Lafon and his wife had been involved in a conflict with Jean Chaux and his family for years; they had even previously taken the Chauxs to court. In April, 1781, Lafon was guarding his livestock when Chaux approached and asserted that Lafon's animals had damaged his vineyard. Lafon excused himself, said that his animals had not caused the damage, and claimed that Chaux's own pig had caused it. Chaux then knocked Lafon down, grabbed him by the collar, and kicked and beat him. When Lafon's wife came to his aid, Chaux's elder son seized her and "gave her hard kicks to the lower belly." [34]

Not content with the damage they had inflicted, the next day, a Sunday, Chaux and his family waited for Lafon's wife outside the parish church. When she emerged from church after vespers, the Chauxs insulted her in a loud voice and hounded her through the streets to her home. In their petition to the court, Lafon and his wife emphasized that being insulted on the public square was as serious as being assaulted

---

32. Notices sur les paroisses du diocèse, 1838, 3 V5 38, ADD; Remarques de Desmarest. See especially the reports for Savignac, Cubjac, Mialet, and Thiviers.

33. In addition to honor-related violence should be noted the popular proclivity for violence as distraction. Such violence often occurred in the evenings, upon leaving cabarets or veillées. See P. Henry, *Crime, justice et société*, 600–602; N. Castan, *Justice et répression en Languedoc*, 184. During debates over the abolition of *lettres de cachet* in August, 1790, some delegates to the Constituent Assembly argued that familial honor was linked to barbarity and popular credulity, and that guilt was a stain on the individual only (Farge, "Familles," in Chartier (ed.), *De la Renaissance aux Lumières*, 611–13).

34. Pitt-Rivers, *The Fate of Shechem*, 5–7; Plainte, May 1, 1781, B 1574, ADD.

the previous day. Moreover, they pointed out, these two most recent incidents were part of a long history of acts of vengeance directed against them in retaliation for their legal action against Chaux. No better setting could be desired for their ritual chastisement than the public square of the village on a Sunday afternoon, a market day.

An incident that occurred in 1783 in the square of Montignac provides another good example of vengeance as public theater. Early one morning, the local schoolteacher appeared at his door wearing only his nightshirt. His neighbor, the Chevalier Duverdier, a nobleman, greeted him "in the tone of *honnêteté* and familiarity that reigned between them." The schoolteacher politely returned his greeting, and the two began to discuss the theatrical presentation of the previous evening, at which the teacher's students had acted out a farce based on Molière's satirical play *Les Précieuses ridicules.* But when the teacher glanced down at his pocket watch, the nobleman lifted his *baton* and said he was going to make the teacher "pay" for his deeds. The teacher managed to deflect the first blow (breaking his thumb in the process) and tried to escape, but Duverdier advanced and hit him three times. When the teacher fell, Duverdier kicked him. The teacher managed to stand up and stumble across the public square, in full view of the many people watching from their balconies and windows. Seeing no other escape from Duverdier, who kept advancing on him, he retreated into the river, crying out for help. By then some bystanders also began to call for help, so the nobleman backed off, swearing in a voice loud enough for all to hear that the teacher would pay for his actions and promising that he would "take his life in one manner or another." But most onlookers apparently sympathized with the nobleman. In fact, one member of a group of nobles observing the spectacle from the bridge encouraged Duverdier "to redouble his blows" and menaced the teacher with his fist, "crying out in public that it was not enough, that this was how to punish rascals." [35] Having administered the beating, Duverdier proudly showed off the bloodstains on his stick.

The inquest revealed that the assault on the teacher, which had been planned the day before, was intended as a public punishment and was not really considered an affair of honor between equals. It seems that local nobles believed they had been ridiculed in the farce prepared

35. Procès-verbal, September 19, 1783, Informations, September 19, 29, 1783, all in B 1581, ADD.

by the teacher and presented by his students. They first considered bringing suit against him for defamation, and went before the seigneurial judge of Montignac the very evening of the play. But they apparently rejected litigation and opted for direct action, for the next day they met on the bridge to discuss their plans. One of them favored throwing the teacher off the bridge, but they finally agreed that Duverdier, the boldest of the group, would administer the public chastisement the next morning. The twenty-six witnesses to the assault who later testified at the inquest either were openly sympathetic with the nobles or tacitly approved of their action. Duverdier had cautioned people not to leave their homes if they heard a commotion. Those immediately involved in the conspiracy, of course, agreed with the assessment offered by one of them, who said the teacher was "a joke, a rogue, and that he deserved much worse." [36]

Even the widow of the former seigneurial judge, one of the few people who realized that the farce was based on Molière's comedy, emphasized in her testimony that the characterization was rather broad and blatantly satirized prominent members of the community. In her opinion, Duverdier had acted rashly by beating the teacher in public; instead, she said, "he should have given him twenty *coups de baton* when no one was watching." Such a beating would, perhaps, have seemed more like a punishment and even less like a duel between equals, but an ambush under cover of darkness would nevertheless have been much less satisfying. Despite Duverdier's threats, he did not intend to kill the teacher—though he could have easily done so. Instead, the point was to punish the teacher and make him "pay" for his insult. And since the offense was delivered in the form of a theatrical presentation, what better way to make him "pay" than in a comparable performance on the public stage of the town square? Considering that vengeance was essentially a social act that assumed greater meaning the larger the audience, the nobles must surely have felt satisfied with the outcome—at least until the victim appealed to royal justice.

In this respect, the case cited above is not only typical but also significant. Individuals initiating private lawsuits before the royal court were often the targets of punitive action or vengeance. If a substantial amount of privately initiated litigation in eighteenth-century France

36. Informations, September 19, 29, 1783, both *ibid.*

had its origins in affairs of honor, such litigation was typically brought by individuals who chose to separate themselves from the social body and appeal to royal justice for protection. They chose not to abide by the rules of the game of honor—or at least sought to modify them by introducing modern tactics. For such individuals, the bonds of communal solidarity had become a form of bondage that prevented them from leading their lives as they saw fit. In other words, the informal sanctions of the community prevented them from challenging the social hierarchy and from pursuing their own private (often economic) interests as they wished.

Among the reasons some individuals and groups took direct action, even when royal justice was readily available, was the hope of avoiding the snares of official justice and the risk of incurring expenses. François Coustans, involved in a dispute over grazing rights with a *laboureur* who rented a meadow from the seigneur of Marsillac, was heard to explain why he preferred direct action to legal recourse. When his son allowed himself and his flock to be chased from the meadow, Coustans was angry that his son had not attacked the *laboureur*. He told everyone that personally "he did not wish to get involved [in a lawsuit] because he owned property that might be consumed by legal costs. But he would have preferred that his son break [the *laboureur's*] bones, because he had nothing to lose." [37]

Individuals chose to settle their own affairs even when royal justice was available and inexpensive, as in public cases that clearly would be prosecuted at Crown expense. Much theft was settled infrajudicially or tolerated on the condition that it was committed by a known member of the community, justified by need, and free from aggravating circumstances. Even when accused thieves were finally brought before the court, popular reaction was sometimes ambivalent. Victims may have been willing to recount the long list of depredations suffered at the hands of the suspect, but when face to face with him in the confrontation, they sometimes equivocated—especially when an accused "accidentally" fell into the hands of justice because caught in the act by constables of the maréchaussée, or when he was denounced for a first offense by an overly zealous victim.

In one such instance, a public case for theft with assault also impli-

37. Plainte, August 6, 1771, B 1550, ADD.

cated one of the suspects' brothers (Bernard Gautier) and his brother's wife (Marie Lalba), who owned the cabaret where the two thieves were staying when they committed their crime. The seigneurial prosecutor of Larche called for the arrest of the husband and wife, who were brought before the court. The witnesses called to testify at Larche seemed willing to cooperate and dredged their memories to recall potentially suspicious actions that might explain the pair's involvement. But the husband and wife succeeded in extracting themselves from the tentacles of justice when the case proceeded before the sénéchaussée. Gautier challenged the testimony of almost every witness and asked each of them directly if they had not always known him and his wife to be "honnêtes gens." Of the eight witnesses recalled, five willingly admitted that Gautier was known in the community as an honest man and that his wife also enjoyed a good reputation. One of them added that he had not been paying attention at the inquest and claimed that the judge at Larche must have made a mistake in recording his testimony. Gautier's vigorous self-defense, combined with the witnesses' own lingering doubts, cleared him and his wife of the charges against them. The sénéchaussée acquitted them both, with all expenses being compensated.[38]

The populace of the Sarladais seems to have recognized the preeminence of royal justice in instances of homicide—although it is likely that the twenty-five cases of homicide (approximately 5 percent of all cases) that came before the sénéchaussée in this period do not represent the total committed within the jurisdiction.[39] Unlike thefts, homicides could not easily be overlooked. The records do not refer to a single instance of unprosecuted, infrajudicially settled homicide; moreover, premeditated murder as a form of private vengeance seems to have been rare during this period. The intrinsic gravity of the crime, the difficulty of concealing even accidental homicide, the depth of emotions stirred, and the general consensus that blood feuds should be avoided combined to minimize under-reportage of this crime. Moreover, in support of this argument lay the perception that if blood vengeance had to be

---

38. Tournelle de Sarlat, June 22, 1778: Sentence (June 28, 1777), B, ADG.

39. Ruff found 36 cases of homicide (3 percent of all cases) in the nearby sénéchaussées of Libourne and Bazas in combined samples for periods analyzed from 1696 to 1789 (*Crime, Justice and Public Order*, 70). Persons prosecuted for homicide constituted 5.3 percent of all those prosecuted in the principality of Neuchâtel (P. Henry, *Crime, justice et société*, 573–74).

exacted, the Crown was the agent best suited to do so. In instances of homicide, intervention by an outside authority was not only allowed but welcomed as the only way to save the community from being further rent asunder by feuding.

In several notable exceptions, however, the populace sharply contested royal jurisdiction by either passively or actively resisting the apprehension of suspects and the investigation of homicides. These incidents revolved around divergent opinions of what, exactly, constituted accidental or justifiable homicide. One example concerned Jean Coustans, a man known by his neighbors to be violent, brutal, quarrelsome, and often inclined to mistreat his wife. When word spread in the parish of La Cassagne that Coustans' wife and sister-in-law had killed him, people therefore received the news with mixed feelings. But the overall consensus was that the two were justified in their actions and deserved either a pardon from the king or, if one was not forthcoming, communal protection from the authorities.[40] This opinion seems to have been shared by all, from the mother of the victim to the royal notary and local countess. Because the inquest held by the seigneurial justice of Coussanges produced little evidence, royal authorities called for a monitoire when the case was referred to the sénéchaussée.

Only from the testimony given before the curés of La Cassagne and Jayac can one reconstruct the facts of the case. On May 31, 1774, Marie Gaubert, wife of Jean Coustans; her sister-in-law, Marie Sambat (married to Coustans' elder brother); and a neighbor named Catherine Demous had just finished washing linen and were folding it when Coustans, who was called Bouygue, entered "drunk as wine" and began to insult them. Demous decided it was time to leave and headed for the door, but as she was leaving she heard a scuffle. Turning, she saw that Coustans held his wife by the neck and had begun to strike her. When Gaubert called out to her sister-in-law for help, Sambat laid the Coustans' child on the bed, grabbed a pickax, and, to separate them, hit Coustans over the head. He cried out, "Do not kill me, I will never do it again," but she struck him twice more and he fell, unconscious, behind the wash kettle. His wife, "seeing that Bouygue still had a pulse, wanted

40. The power of a husband to chastise his wife, which had been quite considerable from the thirteenth to the end of the fifteenth century, was greatly diminished by the eighteenth century (Flandrin, *Families in Former Times*, 126–29).

to finish him off with her knife, saying that if he came to, he would surely kill both of them."[41] Sambat prevented her from doing so and said that it was impossible for him to recover. She then made Gaubert leave the house, locked the door, and took the child with her to guard the sheep.

Left alone but locked out of the half of the house where her husband lay wounded, Gaubert discovered how to accomplish her original intention. Because she and her husband had shared the same house with her husband's brother and wife for the last few years, she was able to go to her own side of the house, climb the ladder to the attic, and descend into her sister-in-law's side, where her husband still lay unconscious. She then took up the pickax and struck Bouygue until she thought he was dead. Just before sundown, her brother-in-law returned from the fields and discovered that Bouygue, although gravely wounded, was still alive. He said to Gaubert that "since you wish to kill him and since he will die all the same, it would be better to strike him on the chest with the pickax to finish him off." Gaubert then administered the final, fatal blow. When Sambat returned from the pasture, she said to her sister-in-law: "Oh, my poor dear, what have you done! You have put the noose around my neck and put it around yours as well. Since you have done this unfortunate thing, you had better turn his neck so that the blood does not come out and carry him to your bed while I go speak to the curé." But Gaubert replied bitterly that "he does not deserve to be in my room or upon my bed, but deserves to be dragged onto the highway."[42] So she wiped the blood from the face of the cadaver, and together they dragged it outside to the edge of the road, where passersby later discovered it.

The neighbors' reactions to the death reveal their basic sympathy for the two women. Before this incident, it was general knowledge in the parish that Bouygue often beat his wife, as well as his sister-in-law if she intervened. Demous revealed to the curé that because Sambat had risked her life several times before, people in the parish had earlier advised her and Gaubert to defend themselves, saying "that when they would kill him, they would be doing no more harm than killing a flea." Because Bouygue was regarded as a bad sort who was often drunk and

41. Révélations devant le curé . . . de La Cassagne, June 19–29, 1774, Révélations devant le curé de Jayac, June 30, 1774, both in B 1558, ADD.
42. Révélations devant le curé . . . de La Cassagne, June 19–29, 1774, *ibid.* See especially the testimony of Catherine Besses.

quarrelsome, the news of his death did not seem to surprise anyone. Nor was much attempt made to keep it a secret. Sambat especially spoke about the incident to all who would listen, saying that she deeply regretted it and wished it had not taken place in her home. She and Gaubert were heard sympathetically, and Bouygue's reputation seems to have been blackened as the news spread. By the time the story reached the next parish of Jayac, it had been embellished considerably, so that various persons reported that Bouygue's wife killed him because he had wished to "eat" or "burn" his own child.[43]

Given such obvious public support for the two women, it is not surprising that the official inquest met with a wall of silence, which could only be cracked by a monitoire threatening those who withheld information with excommunication. The records contain evidence of the wide-ranging support for the culprits and of the efforts made to thwart their capture and prosecution by the authorities. While most people scrupulously avoided direct involvement, some did not hesitate to encourage and help the pair. All seemed to agree that the king should pardon them. When it appeared likely that they would be prosecuted for murder, a local *notable* advised Sambat to leave the area because "he was not able to protect her," and the countess of Couzage arranged to find a wet nurse to care for Gaubert's child in her absence. Even Bouygue's family did not seem angered by his death. Although his brother was concerned that the murder would dishonor his family, the victim's mother was heard to say that her two daughters-in-law would do better to stay with their children than to flee. Community efforts to protect the two women were apparently successful, for neither was ever apprehended.[44]

The moral sanctions and the official laws of a society often prescribe codes of behavior that are far from identical. An action may not be considered morally wrong even though it is clearly illegal. What has been referred to as a distrust of formal justice is in reality often no more than a reflection of this distinction.[45] Without at least the tacit compliance of the populace, royal justice was severely handicapped in its enforcement of official law; in cases in which the majority of the commu-

43. Révélations devant le curé . . . de La Cassagne, June 19–29, 1774, Révélations devant le curé de Jayac, June 30, 1774, both *ibid.*

44. Révélations devant le curé . . . de La Cassagne, June 19–29, 1774, Révélations devant le curé de Jayac, June 30, 1774, Récolement, March 29, 1775, all *ibid.*

45. Pitt-Rivers, *The People of the Sierra,* 178.

nity refused to cooperate with the authorities, it was virtually powerless because of the absence of an effective police force. When no consensus existed between official and popular conceptions of justice, royal authorities could rely only on bailiffs and the constables of the maréchaussée. But these few royal agents hardly sufficed to intimidate a determined populace intent on protecting its relatives and thwarting royal justice.[46]

The most striking incident involving large-scale active resistance to royal justice occurred in 1780 in the parish of Millac, along the Dordogne River, and again originated with accidental or justifiable homicide. Antoine Pébeyre had quarreled with Armand Delmas Vivans over an unpaid debt, and Delmas vowed to make Pébeyre "pay" in one way or another. He saw his chance early on the morning of January 4, when he found Pébeyre stealing cabbages from his garden. Delmas first considered shooting him, but rejected that course of action—perhaps concluding that it was too drastic. Instead, he grabbed his *baton,* shouted "thief," ran after Pébeyre, and gave him a blow on the head that felled him instantly. Delmas' brother-in-law, Jean Crouzel, was awakened by the commotion and, looking out his window, saw Delmas trying to revive the victim. When Crouzel asked what had happened, Delmas explained that he had caught a thief and showed his brother-in-law the cabbages Pébeyre had already cut. Crouzel turned away, but his wife, Petronille, who was Delmas' sister, examined the victim and saw that he was gravely wounded. Delmas began to lament "that he was lost, that he had only hit Pébeyre once, which could not have killed him." Petronille weighed the alternatives open to them and concluded: "What shall we do? We must finish him off or he will bring suit against us and make us 'eat' our property." So the brother and sister took a *baton* and struck Pébeyre until they were certain he was dead. They then called their domestique and carried the body up to the house. The next day, the cadaver was found alongside the road.[47]

Public reaction almost unanimously favored the assailants. The seigneurial jurisdiction of Carlux initiated proceedings, but an inquest produced little evidence. In February, royal authorities therefore appealed to the bishop of Cahors for a monitoire. The response was en-

46. In Neuchâtel, both official justice and society regarded violence that accidentally led to death with indulgence: Only 14 of the 88 accused were ever arrested; the rest escaped (P. Henry, *Crime, justice et société,* 576–77).

47. Révélations à Carlux, February 6, 1780, Révélations à Millac, February 3, 1780, and Révélations à Peyrillac, n.d., all in B 1571, ADD.

couraging: Five people came forward in the parish of Carlux, five in Peyrillac, and sixty-four in Millac, where the crime occurred. But their testimony, although copious, was hardly substantive. Most of what they said was hearsay and endlessly repetitive. Those directly involved in the case or related to the accused evidently ignored the threat of excommunication. A majority of the individuals who testified were sympathetic to the accused, and one person reported that a woman who knew the three said "she prayed they would escape punishment." Those few members of the extensive Delmas family who came forward were cousins and in-laws who only repeated what the others said. The general consensus was not that it was permissible to kill someone stealing cabbages but that the death was the accidental consequence of acceptable, violent retaliation administered without excessive force. Here again, as in affairs of honor, the assailant's motive was more important in the eyes of the populace than the actual result of his act.[48]

The relatives of the assailants obstructed justice in more active ways. The day after the incident, the surgeon involved in the case, Géraud Sarret, was on his way to Millac to draw up his report on the death when he met on the road Armand Delmas Michailou, the uncle of Delmas and Petronille. When Michailou asked Sarret if he knew who was responsible for the murder, the surgeon admitted he had heard it was Michailou's nephew. The uncle then offered to buy him a bottle of wine and asked him "to tone down his report as much as possible," to which the surgeon replied that he would follow his conscience. Michailou, who was the fermier of Madame de Millac, then suggested that "after the authorities had drawn up their *procès-verbal*, [Sarret] should conduct them to the château of Millac to refresh themselves, where he [Michailou] would pay for everything."[49]

Michailou's efforts to dissuade the authorities evidently were in vain, for the seigneurial judge of Carlux initiated proceedings against the three suspects. Moreover, by attempting to protect his relatives, Michailou only succeeded in implicating himself in the crime. When word reached Millac that all four were to be arrested, the brother, sister, and domestique fled the area. Only Michailou remained—despite the warnings of his friends and relatives—explaining that he could not

48. Julian Pitt-Rivers, "Honour and Social Status," in J. G. Peristiany (ed.), *Honour and Shame: The Values of Mediterranean Society* (London, 1965), 27–28.

49. Révélations à Peyrillac, n.d., B 1571, ADD.

leave behind his wife and children. On the evening of August 19, four bailiffs arrived in Millac and quietly arrested him in his home at 11:00 P.M. Because of the late hour, they conducted their prisoner to the home of the curé for safekeeping until morning, when they would conduct him to the royal prison at Sarlat.[50]

At this point, the previously passive resistance to royal authority became active. Michailou's wife, daughter, and son, along with their servant, quickly spread the news of the arrest to their neighbors and relatives, asking them to lend a hand in his rescue. Some persons responded "that it was not their affair," and others, like Jean Crouzel, promised to help but then stayed at home. A cousin ordered his son to tell anyone who came to the door that he was not at home; he then hid in the attic until the next morning. But many members of the Delmas clan responded to the call. When royal authorities later asked a nephew why he had participated in the rescue, he responded "that he did so because he was related, that his aunt, the wife of the fermier Delmas, told him that blood was thicker than water."[51] Apparently many other relatives felt the same way.

By sunrise, a crowd of thirty people—primarily women, but a few men and children too—had assembled outside the home of the curé, where some of the women had kept vigil during the night. As morning approached, the crowd divided into three groups, two of which waited at the crossroads near the château while the third blocked the road to Sarlat. One of the women signaled the others when the four bailiffs and their prisoner prepared to leave. Two deputies positioned Michailou between them and, in lieu of shackles, tied each of his wrists to theirs with handkerchiefs. As they approached the crossroads known as Bas Dujardin, the three groups converged and surrounded the sergeant and his deputies. The nephew of the prisoner seized the sergeant and demanded by what right they were taking his uncle. Others seized the officer and his deputies by the hair and held them by the arms while they untied Michailou and led him away to his freedom. Only two persons responded to the bailiffs' cries for help—Pébeyre's widow and a bourgeois. Once the crowd was certain that Michailou had escaped, it began to disperse and released the officers, who were shaken and bruised but otherwise unharmed.

50. *Ibid.*, Information à Sarlat, August 20, 1780, B 1574, ADD.
51. Interrogatoires, August 22–23, 28, September 8–9, 13, 1780, all in B 1571, ADD. See especially that of Pierre Delmas on September 9, 1780.

The sénéchaussée could not afford to overlook such a direct challenge to its authority. The same day, it initiated criminal proceedings against the participants on the charge of "rebellion against justice and abduction of a criminal."[52] With the aid of Pébeyre's widow and the bourgeois who witnessed the rescue, the court eventually identified twenty-two persons in its suit. Eleven were members of the Delmas family, and three were employed as their domestiques; the remainder were inhabitants of Millac. When interrogated, many of the accused denied participation in the rescue and said they did not know who was involved besides the wife and family of the prisoner. The domestique of Pierre Delmas admitted being there but insisted that he had only gone to retrieve his sister-in-law. When Anne Cestares denied taking part in the rescue, the examiner asked skeptically why she had spent the entire night outside the home of the curé. She replied that she had simply been out taking a stroll.

The most active participants were all women, with the exception of Michailou's nephew and his shepherd. The other men implicated in the event insisted that they were only watching from a distance and had come because Michailou's wife had dragged them there by the arm. After ten months, Michailou's wife and her two children surrendered to the authorities. In her interrogation, she admitted organizing the rescue but claimed she had done so only because she believed Pébeyre's widow had ordered his arrest. She insisted that if she had known that "la justice" had ordered the arrest, she would not have acted as she did.[53]

The above incident graphically illustrates that popular justice still contested the jurisdiction of official justice over certain forms of homicide. Because moderate direct action was deemed acceptable in the defense of honor, the protection of property, and self-defense, the occasional accidental death of a victim of violence was understandable and perhaps even excusable in the eyes of the populace. In similar fashion, popular attitudes differed sharply from the official position that a man who found a thief in his house and killed him (either intentionally or accidentally) was liable for damages to the thief's relatives unless he could prove the thief's intent to kill him. The populace rejected this line

52. Procès-verbal, August 20, 1780, Information, August 20, 1780, both in B 1574, ADD.

53. Interrogatoires, August 22–23, 28, September 8–9, 13, 1780, all in B 1571, ADD; Information, August 20, 1780, Interrogatoires, August 20, June 26, 1781, all in B 1574, ADD; Interrogatoire, April 28, 1781, B 3613, ADD.

of reasoning, knowing that in the uncertainty and passion of struggle, blows even with nonlethal weapons might result in death.[54] In short, both royal law and popular custom authorized "legitimate" self-defense, but differed in the degree to which they allowed mitigating circumstances. In instances where official and popular interpretations did not concur, the populace of the Sarladais did not hesitate to obstruct justice or take the law into its own hands.

54. Plainte, January 17, 1782, B 1576, ADD.

VII

The Defense of Territory

*Wherever you may be in the country, sure though
you may feel that you are quite alone, you are the
cynosure of some pair of eyes under a cotton night-
cap. Some laborer drops his hoe to look at you, some
vine-dresser straightens his bent back, some little maid
leaves her goats, or cows, or sheep, scrambles up a
willow tree to watch your movements.*

—Honoré de Balzac, *The Peasants*

Recourse to direct action remained viable and highly
visible in incidents of collective violence undertaken by groups in defense of familial, professional, social, or geographic "territory." Necessity dictated that the inhabitants of the Sarladais protect and regulate
themselves through reliance on an interplay of social solidarities. They
accordingly surrounded themselves with successive circles of human relations: family, extended family or clan, professional organization, age
group, and community. Each subgroup asserted and protected its own
sense of exclusivity, while certain designated groups also assumed responsibility for policing and chastising transgressions against the entire
community. Via these groups, social sanctions were enforced not
through a formally ordained agent or institution but through the action
of representatives from the community, whose members thereby escaped the guilt that such action individually performed would have
entailed.[1]

The family was the basic grouping that afforded each individual

1. Pitt-Rivers, *The People of the Sierra*, 169; Muchembled, *Culture populaire*,
46–51.

the self-definition, support, and integrity needed to enter the contest of honor constantly waging in the public arena. Because a person's reputation depended primarily on his birth, the defense of any single member's honor or shame was necessarily a cause of concern for the entire family. The family took precedence over all other loyalties and seldom faltered in the face of criminal proceedings. In many respects, criminal cases were often just hidden interfamily feuds that emerged into the open after informal, peaceful means of settlement failed. A simple argument or scuffle was never a personal matter but always a cause of concern for both families involved, if not the entire community. Equally important as the conjugal family was the extended family or clan, which incorporated several nuclear units in different stages of the family cycle and therefore provided more consistent support and protection. Everyone knew his relatives, and not only because the Church forbade marriages between persons related in the fourth degree. As seen with the Delmas clan of Millac, in some villages almost everyone was related to some extent. The solidarity of the clan best expressed itself in opposition to outsiders, be they other clans or royal officials.[2]

Notwithstanding the crucial importance of kinship, the customs regulating community life pertained primarily to membership in the urban neighborhood or rural village. This was the case in regard not only to political and agricultural life but also to private and family life.[3] In the Sarladais, as elsewhere in early modern France, various forms of association beyond the family or clan—usually but not always age groups—collectively supervised morality and exercised functions of popular justice. Adolescent males, who were not yet drawn through marriage or trade into other primary forms of association, not only protected members of their group from outsiders and enforced conformity within that group but also exercised the same function for the community at large. Their justice normally displayed itself as xenophobia, and their actions often took the form of punitive expeditions.

The role of *les jeunes gens* as watchdogs of the entire community was well defined by custom. Young men chastised transgressions of values and challenges to the territorial integrity and harmony of the parish by means of rough music and charivaris, as well as mock battles with

2. Flandrin, *Families in Former Times*, 35–36, 45–47.
3. *Ibid.*, 35–36.

groups from rival parishes. Although forbidden by ecclesiastic and civil statutes since the sixteenth century, the practice of the charivari persisted. In eighteenth-century France, the ritual may even have been extended to censure a wider range of practices. Using symbolic action and language, the young men of the neighborhood or village acted as a group to exercise the right of social control over the young women of the community. They praised virtue, censured transgressions, regulated meetings between lovers, and intervened in nuptial ceremonies through rites such as that of the *barrière,* especially when a young bride was marrying an outsider or when the marriage was not to their liking. The young men might erect a barrier of straw sheaves or barrels or use a simple ribbon to block the path of the bride's nuptial cortège. The procession was allowed to continue to the church only after paying a suitable fee. During the formal celebration of carnival at Sarlat, couples who had married the previous year were required to pay a token tribute in proportion to their wealth, and the most notable of the newlyweds also had to furnish items that figured in the carnival games.[4]

Communal supervision of relations between the sexes did not cease after the wedding. Unfaithful wives, complaisant cuckolds, and husbands chastised by their wives were called to order by charivaris and rough music, which produced disharmony in sound and gesture in response to a situation that compromised social harmony. The watchdogs of popular morality also had recourse to the *azouade,* in which an offender (or a surrogate) was made to promenade on a donkey, usually seated backwards. In performing this rite, youth groups were often assisted by men and women from the neighborhood or village, with the closest neighbor playing a major role in the donkey ride in recognition of his duty of surveillance over his neighbors' conduct. In contradistinction to the honor paid during Sarlat's carnival to those married for the first time was the dishonor bestowed on a widow who insisted on marrying again, signified by the presentation to her of a pierced earthenware pot. Although this symbolic act took place as late as 1791, the city fathers' tolerance for carnival apparently began to wane in the

---

4. N. Castan, *Justice et répression en Languedoc,* 62; André Burguière, "The Charivari and Religious Repression in France During the Ancien Régime," in Robert Wheaton and Tamara K. Hareven (eds.), *Family and Sexuality in French History* (Philadelphia, 1980), 88–91; Cocula, "Trois Siècles de carnaval à Sarlat," 7–8, 14–15; François Lebrun, *La Vie conjugale sous l'ancien régime* (Paris, 1975), 42–43.

1780s. Beginning in 1783, they divorced themselves from the proceedings and allowed a youth group, La Belle Jeunesse, to organize the festivities, which continued to be staged annually throughout the century.[5]

Many inhabitants of the Sarladais maintained their carnival traditions well into the next century. In 1836 the young men of Villefranche-de-Belvès took advantage of carnival to oblige a man beaten by his wife during the previous year to ride backwards on a donkey. The youths of Monpazier forced a cuckold to wear horns and parade with them around town accompanied by his wife. The curés of Domme and Cénac reported in 1838 that their parishioners still practiced these carnival customs as well. Despite the efforts of ecclesiastic and civil authorities as well as the lawsuits of the targets of such popular actions, charivaris and donkey rides still took place in the Sarladais as elsewhere in France in the nineteenth and even the twentieth centuries.[6]

In Languedoc, youth groups were increasingly active at the end of the Old Regime because demographic growth swelled the ranks of the young and brought greater competition in marriage and entry to the trades. The result may have been an increase in resentment and rivalry that multiplied judicial cases of violence and disorder. Little evidence exists to confirm or deny that the same phenomenon occurred in the Sarladais between 1770 and 1790. The records contain nine such cases, in seven of which private individuals intolerant of self-appointed agents of popular custom had recourse to official justice. Five cases involved either battles (most often referred to as *rixes*) between rival parish youth or other disturbances by youth groups, and were evenly distributed throughout the period. The Crown initiated legal action in two of these instances, when village brawls resulted in the death of a participant. In contrast, all four of the cases arising from charivaris were privately initiated and occurred within the last five years of the period.[7]

The young men of the Sarladais had few activities to occupy them during the long winter evenings. The only planned social activities aside from the *fêtes baladoires* (parish fêtes) were the veillées held in

5. Cocula, "Trois Siècles de carnaval à Sarlat," 15–16; Escande, *Histoire de Sarlat*, 105; Burguière, "The Charivari and Religious Repression," in Wheaton and Hareven (eds.), *Family and Sexuality*, 90–91, 104–105.

6. Fayolle, *La Vie quotidienne en Périgord*, 104–105. See the reports for the parishes of Domme and Cénac: Notices sur les paroisses du diocèse, 3 V5 38, ADD; Flandrin, *Families in Former Times*, 35–36, 123–27.

7. N. Castan, *Justice et répression en Languedoc*, 62.

cabarets or private homes and stables, where people passed the time shelling walnuts, spinning and carding wool or flax, shelling maize, telling stories, exchanging the latest news, and singing songs with or without the accompaniment of bagpipes and vielles. It was not unusual for thirty or more persons to gather at such vigils, where a few men would use mallets to break walnuts and pass them along to others, who extracted the kernels for use in making oil. Merchants sometimes organized walnut-shelling vigils, providing food and drink in exchange for the labor. The vigils not only afforded a practical means of enlivening tedious work while conserving expensive fuel used for heat and light, but also provided the setting for young people to meet members of the opposite sex under close parental supervision.[8]

When Inspecteur des Manufactures Latapie toured the area in 1778, he lodged with the Sieur Joubert in Montignac. In their discussion of the mores of the Périgord, the son of Joubert asserted and Latapie readily agreed that popular customs were better preserved in the Périgord than elsewhere in the Guyenne. Latapie remarked in his journal that the best occasion to hear the many varied songs of the region was at the veillées.

> The renowned time for songs is when they break walnuts, a time they call *nougailla*. A good part of the village assembles on successive nights in each house, around a large table. There they pass the evening until midnight singing songs in patois. Each young woman in particular is obliged to sing her song. There are a great many satiric songs and many romances that recall occurrences in the region. When they find a very small walnut, they pass it around, exchange kisses with the girls, and drink another round. These assemblies are always followed by some kind of meal and brought to a close by serving crepes.

When a vigil finally concluded and people departed, the young men often made their way home in groups, singing songs, shouting at passersby, and scuffling with rival groups.[9]

The authorities apparently maintained a benign attitude toward youth groups and tolerated their behavior unless damage was done or

---

8. Rocal, *Le Vieux Périgord,* 13–15. The veillée constituted one of the essential elements of peasant social life and was practiced in the Limousin, as in the Périgord, in a relatively pure form until World War I. It survived in modified fashion until the end of World War II (Corbin, *Archaïsme et modernité en Limousin,* 299–301).

9. Latapie, "L'Industrie et le commerce en Guienne," 430–31. Also see Fayolle, *La Vie quotidienne en Périgord,* 162–63.

someone complained. On March 15, 1780, during the carnival season, the municipal prosecutor of Sarlat decided to take action against a group of young "libertines" who had caused "disorders and scandals" that disturbed public tranquility. The prosecutor argued that the municipality had to stop these young men who indiscriminately insulted members of both sexes, blasphemed, fired pistols, and beat on people's doors and windows, defying them to come out. The young men went too far when, after making their normal commotion in the streets, they threw stones at a statue of the Virgin placed in a niche above the street. The prosecutor argued that their motive was "to insult the piety of neighbors who kept a lighted candle in the niche where the statue was placed." Because this act not only disturbed public order but also attacked religion, the prosecutor initiated proceedings against eight youths for "unlawful assembly and blasphemy." [10]

The testimony of the neighbors confirmed that for the last three weeks several young men had passed down their street at night and awakened everyone with their rowdiness. Witnesses claimed that on the night in question, twenty or thirty youths threw stones at the house of Pascal Gillet, called Pascalou, a man known to be "alienated in spirit." Pascalou apparently had been the target of previous attacks, for he kept a supply of stones in his attic to throw back at the youths. The eight accused were either apprentices or tradesmen between the ages of sixteen and thirty. The eldest, a wigmaker, explained that they had all gone to help shell walnuts, but since there was not enough room for them, they went through the streets singing instead, as they had on previous nights. He testified that as they approached the house of Pascalou, they were met by a hail of stones and even a vase thrown from the roof. All of the accused claimed that Pascalou, not they, had damaged the statue. They affirmed their devotion to the Blessed Virgin and agreed that a person would have to be insane or born without religion to throw stones at the statue. Upon referral to the sénéchaussée, the royal prosecutor ordered the release of the four accused who had been imprisoned and the payment by the others of a total of four livres to purchase bread for the other prison inmates. The court then dismissed all charges against the eight. [11]

10. Requis en plainte du procureur sindic, March 15, 1780, B 1572, ADD.

11. Information, March 15, 1780, Interrogatoire, May 8, 1780, both in B 1572, ADD.

The royal prosecutor obviously viewed the offense differently than did the municipal prosecutor—or at least was not subject to the same pressure to respond to the complaints of neighbors; therefore, he chose to drop the case, which would otherwise have continued at Crown expense. In general, private parties were more inclined than the Crown to take the initiative in prosecuting the quasi-judicial actions of youth groups. During the festive season of Twelfth Night in 1785, two groups of young men clashed on the Place du Palais in Sarlat. A young bourgeois was injured in the scuffle, and a pistol shot was fired that pierced the hat of another young man, the son of a négociant. The two brought suit against ten youths for assault. The accused, all between the ages of seventeen and twenty-one and either the sons of artisans or apprentices, had been drinking and then gone for a walk in the streets, where they met the plaintiffs and two of their friends wearing masks. A fight ensued, and a shot was fired. Later that night the two groups clashed again, this time armed with *batons*.[12]

A number of reasons may explain why the incident resulted in a criminal case before the royal courts. In addition to the normal injuries sustained in such scuffles, a shot was fired, which violated the rules of ritualized combat and represented a potentially serious escalation of the conflict. The incident also involved two young bourgeois, who came from a social group more prone to be intolerant of rowdy behavior even during the festivities of the carnival season. The occurrence of material damage or personal injury provided an additional incentive or excuse for a claimant or the Crown to repress such actions and make the offenders pay for their excessive behavior. Overall, royal authorities took action against youth groups only on two occasions during this period, in 1777 and 1782, when clashes between youths from rival parishes resulted in death.

Young men played a special role as defenders of their parish. In the Sarladais, the parish fête was a major source of popular entertainment, and the youth of each parish made the rounds of the fêtes held in the neighboring parishes, as did virtually everyone within walking distance. The abundance of wine and the heightened festive spirit invariably led to many incidents of individual and collective violence. Whereas in the Auvergne the young men of the parishes apparently

---

12. Plainte, January 2, 1785, Interrogatoire, April 15, 1785, B 1585, ADD.

went to the fêtes primarily to battle the constables of the maréchaussée, in the Agenais and the Périgord they went to fight each other. Young men in the Sarladais did harass strangers and bait persons considered "alienated in spirit," but their favorite amusement seems to have been pitched battles with the youth of neighboring parishes. For example, when peasants of the parish of Azérat (in the Sénéchaussée of Périgueux) staged a dance in the local cabaret, a visitor from Thenon began to play his bagpipes out of time with the dancing. The youth of the two parishes began a general melee that the constables of the maréchaussée were unable to quell.[13]

While traveling from Cahors to Monpazier, Latapie stopped on April 20, 1778, for vespers in Sauveterre, on the boundary between Quercy and the Périgord. The curé warned him that because it was a feast day, he would witness an activity typical of the region. Latapie wrote: "Here they refer to the fêtes [at] which the peasants gather together as "bottes," and the day after Easter is one of the great fêtes of Sauveterre. None of the peasants from the neighboring parishes miss going there, and their gatherings are normally brought to a close with battles with *batons*. There are always many wounded and even deaths. It is bizarre to hear them speak of these things in such a cold-blooded fashion, as if it was a simple thing."[14] The majority of the inhabitants of the Sarladais and perhaps even some curés evidently viewed such combats without alarm, and the constables of the Guyenne maréchaussée were also reluctant to intervene. As late as 1838, the curé of Lalinde reported the continuance of the traditional combat held between his parishioners and those from Saint-Front, who disputed their right to cut wood on the knoll across the Dordogne River from Lalinde. Royal authorities only intervened in such interparish combats when fatalities occurred or when private parties brought suit.[15]

Pitched battles between parishes constituted another facet of the ingrained yet generally controlled violence prevalent in the daily lives of the majority of peasants, some of whom took advantage of these occasions of ritualized violence to settle private scores. Although the participants limited their weapons to stones and *batons*, serious injuries were

13. Cameron, "The Police in Provincial France," 790–91, 797.

14. Latapie, "L'Industrie et le commerce en Guienne," 391.

15. See the notice for Lalinde in Notices sur les paroisses du diocèse, 1838, 3 V5 38, ADD.

often inflicted. In 1777, the youth of Biron attended the *fête votive* of the parish of Gaugeac held on the feast of Saints Peter and Paul. When the youth of the two parishes clashed, Pierre Poujade of Biron received a blow on the head and died a few days later of his wound. In the public case for murder that resulted, the court asserted that the accused, a *travailleur,* had purposely sought out and attacked Poujade with the intention of killing him. The accused, who fled the region but finally surrendered to justice seven years later, denied any such intent and claimed that he did not even know the victim. He admitted that "upon being struck by stones thrown by the troop and being forced to defend himself, he struck the first person in front of him, but without any intention of killing him, only of defending himself." Given the confusion that generally reigned in such combats, his assertion sounded plausible to the court, which registered the *lettres de grâce* (pardons) he had obtained and dropped all charges.[16]

But the court possessed far more substantive evidence in a similar case that occurred in 1782. On the feast of the nativity of Notre Dame, the parish fête at Saint-Pompon attracted crowds from the surrounding district, including young men from the parishes of Saint-Laurent and Campagnac-les-Quercy. The youth of Saint-Laurent formed a troop of about thirty persons and apparently attended the fête with the express purpose of battling their rivals from Campagnac. They accordingly disrupted the dancing held on the public square of Saint-Pompon and chased the youth of Campagnac through the streets, attacking them with *batons* and stones on at least two separate occasions. During the second attack, several inhabitants of Campagnac were injured, notably Jean Lacombe, who died from a blow to the head. The seigneurial prosecutor of Saint-Pompon initiated criminal proceedings against ten young men from Saint-Laurent for the crime of murder. When the case was referred to the Sénéchaussée of Sarlat, the royal prosecutor added to that charge the crimes of "riot, sedition, and unlawful assembly."[17]

Of the ten accused, only one allowed himself to be captured, primarily because he was confident that he could prove he had not taken

16. Interrogatoire de Delpit, November 24, 1784, Entérinement des lettres de grâce, November 24, 1784, both in B 1583, ADD.

17. Interrogatoires de Lafon, February 3, 1783, July 21, 1784, Interrogatoire de Lasvigne, September 13, 1787, all in B 1591, ADD. Also see Conclusions du procureur du roy, July 2, 1784, B 1641, ADD.

part in the battle. Subsequent testimony confirmed his claim, and both he and another accused were acquitted by the court. The primary suspect, Gérard Vergniolle, was a wool comber, and the other accused with known occupations were a blacksmith, shoemaker, woodworker, chimney sweep, *valet de ferme,* and *laboureur*—all of whom were judged in absentia. The court convicted Vergniolle of murder and condemned him to be hanged; it found the others guilty of being accessories to the crime and convicted each to three years in the galleys. The court was much more lenient than the royal prosecutor, who recommended that six of the accused be hanged and the other two be sentenced to nine years each in the galleys.[18]

The harshness of the sentences can be explained by several factors. First, the combat resulted in the death of an older man of considerable wealth, a merchant who was the father of two children.[19] Second, the violence was premeditated and indiscriminate in its attack on any inhabitant of Campagnac who happened to be attending the fête. Finally, the accused failed to surrender to justice. The court invariably dealt more harshly with those judged *en contumace* because it considered flight tantamount to an admission of guilt and an implicit challenge to the jurisdiction of the court. Judges accordingly rewarded compliant offenders with lighter sentences. When, five years later, another of the culprits (the blacksmith) surrendered to the court and presented *lettres de grâce,* the court registered them without objection. In general, neither the maréchaussée nor the sénéchaussée made much effort to repress the violent activities staged by youth groups in the defense of their "territory." Owing to insufficient funding, inadequate policing, and the absence of vociferous complaints from private parties, the authorities evidently intervened at Crown expense only in exceptional circumstances.[20]

In 1786 and 1787, private individuals who refused to accept the customary role of youth groups in the enforcement of public morality initiated four private suits against youths who staged charivaris. A fifth case

18. Sentence définitive, July 21, 1784, Conclusions, July 2, 1784, both in B 1641, ADD.

19. The two petitioned the court for 15,000 livres apiece in damages from the accused. See Plainte, September 13, 1787, B 1591, ADD.

20. Plainte de Gabriel Lasvigne, September 13, 1787, *ibid.;* Charles Tilly, *The Contentious French: Four Centuries of Popular Struggle* (Cambridge, Mass., 1986), 178–80.

referred to an earlier charivari that did not directly result in legal action. Four of the incidents occurred in rural parishes; the fifth took place in a faubourg of Sarlat. All of the charivaris had their origin in classic circumstances: Two were organized when young men were outdone by young women, another when a man was scolded by his wife within earshot of his neighbors, another when a young man married an older widow, and another when a widower with two children married a younger woman. Neighbors and youths in each instance staged a charivari to remind those who had contravened social custom that their affront to popular morality had not gone unnoticed. To restore the impugned honor of the community, the offenders were made to "pay" in moral humiliation, monetary tribute, and sometimes physical pain. Generally, the offenders paid in material terms by purchasing food and drink for the participants in the charivari, who then celebrated the triumph of popular morality and the reparation of social harmony.[21]

The charivari was a hazardous instrument of social control. When everything proceeded according to the script and the actors played their prescribed roles without protest, popular justice was peacefully administered by its informal agents without the intervention of the authorities. But the criminal court records contain evidence that in the Sarladais, as elsewhere, charivaris sometimes turned into ugly, vengeful affairs that magnified divisions in the community. When, on the one hand, the persons who staged the charivari refused to observe the protocol that governed the ritual or, on the other hand, the target of such action denied their claims to jurisdiction over his private life, then the incident could easily lead to violence and eventually private recourse to royal justice.

The first incident that gave rise to criminal proceedings occurred in the parish of Peyrignac, near Montignac. Antoine Larfeuil, a bourgeois, was returning from hunting with a friend when the two passed a field where a considerable number of harvesters of both sexes were engaged in a test of strength. In his petition, Larfeuil explained what happened next.

> A few of the harvesters tried in their excessive gaiety to convince the plaintiff to engage in a contest with a large young woman who was among their number. He did not permit himself to do so until he realized that his re-

21. For a description of charivaris in the nineteenth century, see E. Weber, *Peasants into Frenchmen*, 399.

fusal might cause trouble. Goaded on by the gestures of the harvesters and especially by the young woman, he linked arms with her in the way she showed him. The result was that he fell to the ground first. This was a subject of much joking that he took in good spirits, despite the crudeness sometimes involved in these sorts of games. But the populace and the children carried things much too far.

The following Sunday the inhabitants of Peyrignac began a charivari that included the blowing of horns, the beating of pots and pans, and the shouting of insults. After vespers, a crowd of approximately fifty men, women, and young men surrounded Larfeuil when he left church and accompanied him home. At that point, two of Larfeuil's friends, a clerk and a bourgeois, urged him "to give this troop of people an écu and a pail of wine to make them stop the charivari." But he said he would do nothing of the sort, and the noise continued into the evening.[22]

Larfeuil and his brother finally asked a guest at their home, Joseph Martial, an avocat en parlement, to intervene with the crowd. He agreed to do so and went out into the street, where he offered to buy the participants' horns for an écu on the condition that they cease their noise and permit him to sleep that night. The young men rebuffed his offer and said they would accept money from Larfeuil only. So Martial called out to Larfeuil: "Give them an écu so they can drink to your health and promise that everything is finished." At the urging of his neighbors, Larfeuil begrudgingly paid the money so that the local cabaret owner could prepare something for the crowd to eat and drink. He further acquiesced when they asked for a bucket of wine. The participants then retired to the cabaret and left Larfeuil, his guest, and the neighbors in peace.[23]

But the revelers apparently were dissatisfied with Larfeuil's reluctant recognition of their right to levy tribute from males who yielded to female authority. The very next Sunday, a group waited for him outside church and made even more noise than before. Martial advised Larfeuil to go to the curé, but he replied that it would be useless, "since the curé himself was involved, and that he had also been told that the curé's own valet was the ringleader in this new troop of hornblowers." His obduracy evidently prompted the young men to escalate their action, for "they formed the plan to seize him, dress him in a ridiculous man-

22. Plainte de Larfeuil, July 22, 1786, Information, July 24, 1786, both in B 1589, ADD.

23. Plainte de Larfeuil, July 22, 1786, Information, July 24, 1786, both *ibid.*

ner, mount him on a donkey, and promenade him through three or four neighboring parishes."[24] Although Larfeuil evaded the crowd outside the church, they continued their charivari into the evening, blowing on horns and beating pots and pans like drums until after midnight. Then someone fired two musket shots that fell into Larfeuil's courtyard—a departure from protocol significant enough to persuade him to have recourse to royal justice.

Witnesses described those who took part in the charivari as "a crowd . . . composed of men, women, and young men." But the most active participants were clearly *les jeunes gens*, including boys of twelve to fourteen years. The crowd undoubtedly also contained several of the harvesters who had witnessed Larfeuil's humiliation. Four of the ten accused were identified as a carter, a tailor, a weaver, and a domestique. Testimony reveals that all of the witnesses had advised the plaintiff to meet the demands of the crowd. Although one of them, a bourgeois, had reproached members of the crowd for their actions, he had still advised Larfeuil to pay what they requested. Even the avocat en parlement believed initially that conciliation was the best course. Only when the troop rejected Larfeuil's tribute, returned the next Sunday, and fired two shots did the avocat agree with the plaintiff that legal recourse was the best course of action.

The reaction of the authorities is unclear. In his petition to the sénéchaussée, Larfeuil reminded the court that royal ordinances had long prohibited such public license, and that the authorities should repress charivaris with "the greatest severity not only to shelter citizens who find themselves targets of such action from derision and insult—but also to prevent the violence and harm that can accompany such disorders."[25] Legal treatises did emphasize that charivaris were contrary to public order and tranquility and were therefore outlawed throughout France, in some regions since the sixteenth century, but the practice was nevertheless deeply rooted and difficult to eradicate. The frequency with which royal ordinances and police regulations reiterated their prohibitions suggests that the practice was far from extinct by the end of the century.[26]

24. See especially the testimony of Joseph Martial in Information, July 24, 1786. Also see Plainte de Larfeuil, July 22, 1786, both *ibid.*

25. Plainte de Larfeuil, July 22, 1786, *ibid.*

26. On April 12, 1780, the Parlement of Paris pronounced against the instigators of a charivari (Guyot *et al., Répertoire,* III, 271–73).

The theoretical proscription of such activities surely had little impact on the Périgord, where royal authorities took little initiative to repress them. Latapie remarked during this trip through the Sarladais in 1778: "The practice of running the donkey, a very grotesque bacchanalian practice meant to humiliate solemnly any man who lets himself be beaten by his wife, is still vigorous in the Périgord, as is the horned bacchanal, in which persons declared cuckolds are held up for ridicule. There are also other practices with different purposes, for example those against young women who have given public proof of their weakness."[27] Royal ordinances had also long forbidden the holding of public dances, fêtes baladoires, fairs, and markets on Sundays and the feasts of patron saints. But because such activities were an integral part of popular culture, they continued to flourish in the Sarladais throughout this period and well into the next century.[28]

The ambivalence of local authorities toward manifestations of popular justice is best illustrated by a case resulting from an incident that occurred in the isolated parish of Marquay in 1787. Word spread quickly when Raymond Lachèze, a *laboureur,* was outdone by a young woman. The next morning, the feast of Saint Roch, a dozen young men seized Lachèze while he was spreading sheaves of wheat on the threshing floor, bound him, and conducted him to the home of Pierre Malbech. Along the way, they met the wife of another *laboureur,* who warned them not to harm Lachèze. When they threatened to seize her donkey by force, she agreed to loan it to them. For more than two hours, they kept their victim at Malbech's home, where they taunted him while dancing and singing. Others from the parish soon heard of the revelry and joined them there, until they decided to take Lachèze to a cabaret in the next village.

The troop assembled and, preceded by a man playing bagpipes, set out for the cabaret with everyone singing. Lachèze endured some rough treatment along the way and agreed to pay for everything once they arrived at the cabaret. Upon arrival, the eating, drinking, singing, and dancing recommenced. So, too, did the mockery. The revelry lasted all afternoon and into the evening. When the cabaret owner seemed reluc-

27. Latapie, "L'Industrie et le commerce en Guienne," 431.
28. Guyot *et al., Répertoire,* VII, 348. Also see E. Weber, *Peasants into Frenchmen,* 399–406.

tant to serve the participants more wine, they forced their captive to pledge to pay all expenses by threatening that otherwise "they would make him mount the donkey they had outside the door." Later that night, when the revelers (by then quite drunk) finally emerged from the cabaret and began to argue about where next to take him, Lachèze took advantage of the scuffle that ensued to escape, bruised and badly shaken.[29]

The reaction of the local authorities was significant. The very next day, Lachèze brought his petition to the Sieur Lacombe, judge of the seigneurial jurisdiction of Commarque. But the judge refused to accept his petition, saying that Lachèze had no cause to complain; moreover, the judge told him, even if his suit was heard, he would be unable to pay the legal expenses involved. Lachèze insisted and displayed his bruises and rope marks, but "the Sieur Lacombe laughed in his face, told him that it was a bagatelle, and that the accused had treated him as he deserved." The judge then had him shown to the door and told him not to return. But Lachèze, who was determined to bring suit, went to the prosecutor of the same tribunal to lodge his complaint. The prosecutor reacted in similar fashion: "He made fun of the petitioner, laughed in his face, and sent him away as a fool, asking him if he had finished with his comedy." He added, "You have not made people laugh enough . . . now you wish to make them laugh even more?"[30]

Rebuffed at the local level, Lachèze went directly to the royal prosecutor of the Sénéchaussée of Sarlat, who willingly accepted the petition. In the subsequent suit, a witness testified that he had overheard the curé of Marquay discuss the victim's case with the judge of Commarque, who again had argued that since the incident was only trivial teasing, Lachèze should have met the crowd's demands. When called to testify, the curé insisted that he knew nothing about the incident. That Lachèze persisted in bringing suit is quite remarkable given the expense of prosecution and the obstruction by local seigneurial authorities. His petition focused on the rough treatment he had received, and the testimony of witnesses corroborated his claims that the twelve accused, most of whom were domestiques and *laboureurs,* treated him harshly.

29. Plainte, August 18, 1787, Information, September 3–6, 1787, and Interrogatoire, November 7, 1787, all in B 1593, ADD.

30. Plainte, August 18, 1787, *ibid.*

But it is equally clear that most inhabitants of the parish, including the curé, regarded the incident as too mundane to warrant the victim's charges.

Charivaris could easily degenerate to unacceptable levels of violence if victims raised the slightest protest to the participants' demands. In the small village of Le Repaire, near Tayac, for example, neighbors overheard a dispute in which Jean Delpeyrat yielded to his wife. As word spread rapidly that he had allowed himself to be overruled, almost all the men of the village and a few from a nearby village decided to stage a charivari. The next three nights they appeared outside Delpeyrat's home with pots, pans, cauldrons, and horns, and noisily serenaded him. Delpeyrat, in his petition, emphasized that he did not mind the chiding he received, but believed the men went too far in demanding that he mount a donkey and ride it through the parish. He nonetheless told them he would pay for all the wine they wanted if they went the next day to the local cabaret, "where they would receive satisfaction."[31]

On Sunday, seventeen participants gathered at the cabaret, including a *travailleur,* tailor, sharecropper, and *laboureur.* At first, everything proceeded smoothly. The revelers brought along a donkey in case Delpeyrat proved uncooperative, but he held to his promise and bought them as much wine as they wanted and even drank with them until evening. But when he attempted to leave, they protested and insisted that he stay. At that moment, Delpeyrat's wife appeared to fetch her husband. When she berated the men for their behavior, they grew angry, seized husband and wife by the hair, threw them to the floor, and beat them until the victims' neighbors finally intervened. The following day, Delpeyrat and his wife had a petition drawn up to present to the sénéchaussée and then called a surgeon to verify their injuries.[32]

Delpeyrat, whose occupation is unspecified in the records, does not seem to have been particularly intolerant of popular disciplinary action. He matter-of-factly acknowledged the group's "jurisdiction" and prepared to play his role in the affair so long as the men of the parish acted with moderation. Only when he thought that they should have

31. Plainte, August 21, 1786, B 1590, ADD.
32. Plainte, August 21, 1786, Rapport du chirugien, August 23, 1786, and Information, August 23, 1786, all *ibid.*

been satisfied did he resist their demands that he stay longer and drink with them. His wife's appearance could not have come at a worse moment and must have confirmed in their minds the necessity of censuring Delpeyrat's submissiveness. Given the drunkenness of the participants, violence was perhaps inevitable. This incident graphically demonstrates that revelers were extremely defensive of their right to stage such actions and reacted violently when challenged or in any way thwarted.

The belligerence of youth groups emerges most clearly in an incident that occurred in January, 1787. Upon learning that a young man intended to marry a widow, the residents of the Sarlat suburb of La Bouquerie made plans for a charivari. For several nights, a troop composed of "all the women of the suburb" plus several "masked young men" paraded through the streets with their pots, pans, and horns. Then Sabine Delmond, the young man's sister-in-law and the wife of a merchant named Jardel, invited the prospective bride and groom to dine at her home. The crowd again paraded through the streets but stopped this time outside Delmond's home, where it continued its charivari. When no one inside responded, the participants pounded on the front door until Delmond finally opened a window and asked them to leave. The leader of the group, a woman named Campagnac, also known by the sobriquet "Merde de Poule," called her a "hussy and *bougresse.*" Delmond responded by dumping a bucket of water on the group. The enraged crowd tried to force the door, but abandoned their enterprise when neighbors complained about the commotion. The next morning, Campagnac encountered Delmond at the local fountain, where the two exchanged insults in public. Specifically, Campagnac berated Delmond for condoning her brother-in-law's marriage to the widow by inviting them to her house. Delmond replied, "F. merde de poule, vous me f." Delmond then brought suit against Campagnac and other participants in the charivari.[33]

This incident clearly took a turn for the worse when those who had offended public morality refused to acknowledge their culpability or recognize that members of the community were entitled to stage a charivari and exact tribute from them. Had Delmond responded by offering a bucket of wine rather than dumping a bucket of water on the

33. Plainte, January 16, 1787, Information, January 16–17, 1787, both in B 1592, ADD.

troop, it might have dispersed peacefully. Instead, the frustrated crowd felt obliged to defend its prerogative. When Delmond opened the window and told the noisemakers to leave, Campagnac replied, "We intend to exercise our right to hold a charivari." She repeated as much when one of the neighbors told the revelers to go home, saying to him "that they were not leaving and that she meant to exercise her rights." [34] But neither Campagnac nor the troop she led gained much satisfaction or even recognition of the customary right to discipline offenders. Instead, those persons offended by their action appealed to royal justice, the only ally available to individuals anxious to free themselves from the moral economy of the popular classes.

The above cases suggest that a sizable portion of the populace actively participated in such informal rituals, tacitly approved of them, or at least tolerated them. Curés and seigneurial officials generally advised persons unfortunate enough to find themselves targets of such actions to endure the humiliation and satisfy the demands of the participants. In effect, they advised the victims to recognize the primacy of popular justice by a symbolic act of submission. Of course, participants were also known to use threats of further violence against their targets and even against bystanders who tried to thwart them. But although local *notables*—primarily members of the professional classes and secondarily merchants—tolerated the charivaris, they do not seem to have taken an active role in them. In fact, many of them may have shared Latapie's view that such practices were "barbarisms" that should only begrudgingly be tolerated in the lower classes. His feelings emerge clearly from remarks made while stopping over in Montignac.

> We all regret what we call "the good old days," but I have never known quite why. The man who is less civilized is more ruthless, and he appears to become gentler and more indulgent the further he is removed from his primitive state of savagery. The men who appear to me to combine the most social virtues are these worthy gentlemen and well-off bourgeois who, having received an *honnête* education, have chosen to settle on their estates or in their villages, where they dispense their revenue. It is they who probably constitute the most useful and respectable class of the State.

The *notables* described by Latapie were conspicuously absent from the ranks of the agricultural workers, sharecroppers, and *cultivateurs* who

---

34. Information, January 16, 1787, *ibid*. See especially the testimony of Catherine Vergnolle and Antoine Arène.

ordinarily conducted charivaris in the rural parishes, and from the young tradesmen and apprentices responsible for them in the towns.[35]

Private individuals sometimes manipulated traditional forms of popular action in their own interests or took advantage of the temporary disorder thus created. In 1764, the mother of a young man whose son had been injured in a previous contest between youth groups incited the young men of her parish to attack their rivals from the next parish and afterwards invited the group to her home to eat and drink. In similar fashion, the curé of Sainte-Croix-de-Monferrand chose the night of carnival in 1777 to demolish the well of a nobleman who denied him the right established by tradition to draw his water there.[36] Private parties also used charivaris to cloak their own desires for vengeance. In December, 1770, for example, the leading family of the parish of Saint-Avit-Sénieur used popular tactics to harass the vicar, who was known for his opposition to music and dancing. Their feud apparently originated, at least in part, in the intervention by the cousin of the Sieur Bouysson, a seigneurial judge, against the vicar's brother in a lawsuit. In retaliation, the vicar refused to perform the marriage of the daughter of one of the judge's sharecroppers.

On the morning of the projected marriage, the wedding party was delayed. The judge asked the vicar to wait, but he started mass without them and afterwards, when the bride and groom approached the communion rail, refused to perform the marriage. When he insisted that they return the following day to be married, the enraged members of the wedding party returned to the home of the groom's father, where a reception had been planned. Because it was a Thursday and the meats that had been prepared could not be eaten on Friday, the wedding party decided to hold the reception anyway, even though the bride and her parents were obliged by custom not to remain in the house of the groom. After supper, they danced to the sound of the fiddle and drum. The judge interpreted the vicar's refusal as a direct affront and was overheard saying at the reception that he remembered the time when he would have given the vicar twenty lashes with a whip or run him through with a sword. He instead opted for a safer course of action. That evening, as guests prepared to leave, he said to them: "Messieurs

35. Latapie, "L'Industrie et le commerce en Guienne," 431.
36. Plainte, September 10, 1764, Interrogatoires, September 15, 1764, May 8, 1765, all in B 1546, ADD; Interrogatoire, December 10, 1782, B 1578, ADD.

of Saint-Avit, let us go to the home of the curé and vicar of Saint-Avit, who do not like the sound of the customary drum. We must go there and beat it under their window for two hours so they can grow accustomed to it. We must continue to do the same thing every evening until Carnival." So the wedding party assembled and, led by the drummer, took the road that led by the vicar's house.[37]

From that day forward, the feud assumed a more serious tone. The vicar, of course, interpreted the drum beating beneath his window as a provocation. He was heard to brag that he had already exacted his vengeance by refusing to perform the marriage, but retaliated further by including thinly veiled references to the Bouysson family in his Sunday catechism. On the first Sunday after the drum beating, he implied that the judge's wife engaged in scandalous behavior and was worse than a procuress. The next week, he insinuated that she was a thief because she sent grain and oil to her mother in Bergerac against the wishes of her husband. When the Dame Bouysson heard of these insults, she decided to accompany her son and servants to catechism the next Sunday. Significantly, the vicar began that morning's lesson with a sermon against the "sinister effects of dancing." When pushing and shoving among the boys in front disrupted the lesson, the vicar reprimanded the judge's son. The Dame Bouysson came to her son's defense and accused the vicar of slandering her, saying that if it were not for God she would avenge herself then and there in church.

When her husband and his brother heard of the incident, they saw it as a further affront to their family honor and at first discussed killing the vicar. The brother, a member of a cavalry regiment, decided to pay the vicar a personal visit and arrived with a saber at his side, two pistols in his belt, and a whip in hand. He warned the vicar never again to mention the Bouysson family in his sermons, but the vicar denied doing so and said that the inhabitants of the parish were all "rabble." In contrast, the judge took a more peaceful course of action and reported the vicar's conduct to the bishop. His wife agreed to this tactic on the condition that if official justice did not provide the vengeance she desired, she would have her brother-in-law slay the vicar even as he stood at the altar with the Holy Sacrament in his hands.

While awaiting the outcome of this action, her brother-in-law con-

37. Information, December 27, 1770, Interrogatoire, February 27, 1771, both in B 1547, ADD.

ceived of another means of retaliation. On leave from his regiment, he had learned that a young man was interested in enlisting. He seized this pretext to stage a recruitment drive that consisted of going to the various cabarets and public squares around town accompanied by a drummer, who would drum as the brother-in-law danced. In making their rounds, they effectively circled the parish church—where the vicar was trying to conduct catechism—and arrived back where they began, outside the sacristy door. This final act of provocation spurred the vicar to bring suit the next day against Bouysson and his wife, son, and brother for menaces, insults, and disorder in the church.[38]

This case not only illustrates how individuals adapted and distorted popular tactics for their own ends but also suggests the extent to which nobles, at the summit of the social hierarchy, still shared the same culture as the *classes populaires* and could unite against a clergyman who inveighed against unorthodox practices. Bouysson, a seigneurial judge and an avocat en parlement, maintained residences for his family both in Saint-Avit and in Bergerac, where family members stayed during the wine harvest. Despite their elevated social and economic status, they joined in popular festive rituals. At the wedding reception, the Dame Bouysson herself played the violin for the guests and led the dancing. When she and her son attended the catechism, she laughed and joked with her servant when the vicar warned against dancing. On the day the vicar refused to perform the marriage, her son and a friend fired their pistols in the church, as was the custom at weddings. During the catechism, he seldom sat in the family pew with his mother but stood with "a crowd of peasants" in the front.

Nor was he or his mother reluctant to use strong language to insult the vicar. When reprimanded in catechism, the young man called the vicar a devil, and his mother took up the refrain, pounding on the pew with her fists and chanting, "He is not a vicar but a devil." But much of what was said between them and the vicar was unintelligible to the others present because it was spoken in French, whereas the catechism was always conducted in patois. A few days later, the young man was heard at the communal oven to exclaim: "I do not worry about the curé or the vicar or give the devil about them. Let them go f. themselves."[39]

38. Information, December 27, 1770, Interrogatoire du Sr. Carrier, February 27, 1771, both in B 1547, ADD.

39. Information, December 27, 1770, *ibid.*

The judge and his brother undoubtedly shared the Dame Bouysson's sense of outrage and desire for vengeance, but also knew that they would be legally liable for all physical and verbal violence done to the vicar. They therefore limited themselves to direct action in the form of popular customs that disguised their true motives while assuring the further provocation of the vicar. In other words, although they were intent on vengeance, they were prudent enough to accomplish it in a moderate albeit unofficial manner.

The use of charivaris and battles between youth groups to settle private scores was not uncommon in the Sarladais, but cannot be said to represent a wider trend encompassing the adaptation and redirection of popular rituals toward more modern goals, as apparently occurred in Languedoc.[40] The appearance in the criminal court records of a handful of cases in which private plaintiffs objected to popular judicial sanctions must, however, be viewed in conjunction with the decision by more and more private individuals in the late 1780s to use the royal court to prosecute relatively minor offenses of verbal and physical violence. Seen in this light, these few cases may be interpreted both as germs of an incipient intolerance of popular interference in private affairs and as harbingers of a wider acceptance of royal justice as the only legitimate arbiter in interpersonal relations.

Beyond the nuclear family, the extended family, and the youth groups, every person belonged to a parish or village that served as a further means of self-definition and self-protection. This sense of solidarity, or *esprit du clocher,* rooted in proximity and reinforced by frequent contact, was the final form of association that united individuals. Although this sense of communality was undoubtedly less intense in the eighteenth century than previously, it still manifested itself in collective action, primarily in opposition to external threats. At such moments, virtually the entire populace of a village could be mobilized by the ringing of the tocsin and directed against *étrangers* and scapegoats perceived to threaten the community. But fewer and fewer occasions elicited such large-scale collective action, and the degree of participation by some sectors of the community was gradually dwindling. Although the inci-

40. Nicole Castan argues that in Languedoc in the late eighteenth century the number of judicial cases concerning charivaris and brawls increased as members of the popular classes used these rituals to protest new agricultural practices (*Justice et répression en Languedoc,* 62). Also see Tilly, *The Contentious French,* 30–34.

dents of collective action that occurred during this period preserved the ritual gestures, language, and goals of the seventeenth-century revolts of the Croquants, they no longer equaled those revolts in intensity, even during the disorders of 1789–90.[41]

In 1776, for example, the inhabitants of the village of Saint-Julien-de-Lampon who assembled to defend their rights of usage over an island in the Dordogne River asserted their claim in traditional fashion. Their dispute with the inhabitants of LeGard concerning the island of Bourgnol began at least seven years earlier, at a time when the villagers of LeGard, located across the river, possessed the rights of usage over most of the island while only three inhabitants of Saint-Julien still enjoyed use of a small portion of the island. But in the intervening years, the river gradually shifted its course, and the portion of Bourgnol belonging to Saint-Julien began to grow in size. As it did, the people of Saint-Julien became more accustomed to cutting hay and gathering osier on the island. When the inhabitants of LeGard responded by chasing them away and claiming use of the entire island for themselves, the people of Saint-Julien began to defy them by grazing their flocks on Bourgnol.

Their rivalry came to a head on Friday morning, August 17, feast of Saint Roch, when the son of one of the Saint-Julien villagers who had previously enjoyed full rights to a portion of the island took his flock of goats to graze there. Several persons from LeGard challenged him and threatened to kill both him and his goats if he returned. When the youth returned to Saint-Julien and repeated his story, the challenge generated a demand for retaliation. On Sunday, rumor spread quickly that the inhabitants of LeGard and nearby Calviac had just rung their tocsins to assemble their parishes on the island. So after vespers a few people in Saint-Julien rang the church bell under their own authority, and a large crowd armed with *batons*, pitchforks, and barrel staves gathered in the square. Before setting off for the island, they stopped for drinks at the home of the youth who had been chased away. When they arrived at the banks of the Dordogne, the men crossed over to the island, leaving the women and children on the shore. When they discovered that—contrary to rumor—the island was virtually deserted, they gathered on the shore opposite LeGard and began to dance, menace the villagers, and taunt them to come join them. But the villagers of

41. Bercé, *Histoire des croquants*, 695.

LeGard declined, so the men of Saint-Julien proceeded homeward, stopping off for another round of drinking to celebrate their successful assertion of their claims.[42]

This relatively tame and festive manifestation of communal solidarity in opposition to a chimerical external threat involved a sizable proportion of Saint-Julien. More than one witness described the crowd as numbering at least 200 people in a parish with approximately 850 inhabitants.[43] A private suit brought by seven inhabitants of LeGard named nine defendants, primarily persons from Saint-Julien who, currently or formerly, possessed rights of usage over a portion of the island. In their petition, the plaintiffs contended that the accused had illegally rung the tocsin to mobilize their fellow parishioners to act in what was essentially their own private interest. But the wide support accorded the collective action suggests that it resulted from more than private manipulation—that it was the parish's response to a threat to its traditional rights of usage and even its integrity. (One cattle merchant excused himself from participating because he was threshing his grain.) Although no confrontation actually resulted, the collective action was judged a success by its participants: Wine flowed, people danced, and communal solidarity was celebrated and reinforced.

Such incidents appear to have been consonant with traditional collective actions against outsiders. But some members of the community did not accept that interpretation and instead viewed these actions as transgressions of their legal rights, which they then called on royal justice to defend. Moreover, plaintiffs argued that such incidents were not spontaneous, legitimate manifestations of popular outrage but the result of the manipulation of the popular tradition by a few cynical ringleaders. From the scant evidence contained in the above cases, it is virtually impossible to discern the relative accuracy of these conflicting interpretations. In some cases, the most vocal and active participants or organizers were indeed persons who had a personal stake in the outcome, and it should come as no surprise that many people engaged in different forms of collective action had less than altruistic motives for

42. Continuation d'information, September 7, 1776, B 1563, ADD.

43. The Abbé Expilly lists Saint-Julien as having 170 *feux* (hearths) in 1779. If we use the standard multiplier of 5 persons per hearth, the parish had approximately 850 persons. See Abbé Jean-Joseph Expilly, *Dictionnaire des Gaules et de la France* (Paris, 1779). According to the census of 1806, the parish counted 834 persons (Recensement général de la population [1806], 6 M10, ADD).

their participation.[44] But other members of the community were capable of being mobilized precisely because they were predisposed to identify their own interests with those of the so-called ringleaders. What does emerge clearly from the above is that some victims of popular judicial sanctions rejected the jurisdiction of popular justice over their personal affairs and singled out for prosecution those participants who could most easily be accused of disturbing public order for their own private purposes. In other words, they came to perceive the defense of "territory" either by youth groups or by the entire community as not only intolerable but also illegal.

44. Olwen Hufton, *The Poor of Eighteenth-Century France, 1750–1789* (Oxford, 1974), 361.

VIII

The Defense of Economic Rights and Privileges

The suffering that such widespread disorders caused is attenuated when we reflect that in the midst of the license these unhappy people were not ferocious. There were no murders, and if they were capable of several profanations, it was never anything to make nature blush.

—Curé Pontard, vicar of Sainte-Marie-de-Sarlat, in his appeal to the National Assembly, February 3, 1790

On both a large and a small scale, the peasants of the Sarladais still resorted to the punitive sanctions of popular justice to defend the traditional equilibrium of economic rights and duties as they perceived them. Custom and usage existed before and outside official law and took precedence in the eyes of the populace. Transgressions of traditionally observed communal rights therefore occasionally triggered large-scale collective actions. On a more mundane level, individuals reacted equally violently and in ritualized fashion to official attempts to seize property for debts or foreclosure. They tended to view bargains and contracts not simply as commercial transactions but as part of the network of human intercourse that held society together. Hence the concept of the "just" price. Merchants who overcharged or landlords and traders who insisted that established contracts and debts took precedence over the welfare of the community therefore violated popular moral sensibilities as well as local interests.[1]

Depending on the specific nature and circumstances of the chal-

---

1. Charles Tilly, "Food Supply and Public Order in Modern Europe," in Tilly (ed.), *The Formation of National States in Western Europe* (Princeton, 1975), 432.

lenge, popular contention in the Sarladais either resembled the normal defensive actions typical of a relatively static rural society or, upon occasion, possessed a pronounced anticapitalist or antiseigneurial orientation.[2] A total of twenty-nine incidents during this period can be construed as involving to some degree the assertion of traditional rights of possession or usage against the strict legal definition of proprietary rights. Violent disputes over grazing rights as well as clashes with bailiffs and sequestrators were probably quite common; they nonetheless constituted a small proportion (approximately 6 percent) of the private suits initiated before the court. Their relatively even distribution throughout the period further reinforces the view of the Sarladais economy as stagnant.[3]

Popular resistance to seigneurialism expressed itself in the Sarladais most often in the defense by individuals and groups of customary rights of access, grazing, and gathering against both bourgeois and noble seigneurs anxious to manage their holdings profitably. Violent resistance by peasants who wished to challenge seigneurial efforts to maintain or expand their feudal rights was not peculiar to the last years of the Old Regime. But aside from the antifiscal revolts of the sixteenth and seventeenth centuries, mundane peasant contentiousness rarely interested the royal bureaucracy. As a result, the historian must examine local judicial archives—both civil and criminal—to discover not only the increasingly modern and sophisticated litigation challenging seigneurialism but also the more traditional violence carried out by individuals and groups resisting the payment of feudal dues or the commissioning of *terriers* (registers of landed property).[4]

Between the great plains of northern France and the Midi of Languedoc, where commercial agriculture had long since made consid-

2. N. Castan, *Justice et répression en Languedoc,* 66–67; Tilly, *The Contentious French,* 20, 23–24. For a summation of the arguments surrounding the question of the peasantry's anticapitalist mentality, see Peter M. Jones, "Georges Lefebvre and the Peasant Revolution: Fifty Years On," *French Historical Studies,* XVI (1990), 645–63.

3. In the districts of Libourne and Bazas, resistance to judicial authorities was a constant of rural life, regardless of changes in government, and did not denote popular rejection of the institutions of the Old Regime (Ruff, *Crime, Justice and Public Order,* 155–60).

4. Peasant communities in Burgundy increasingly used civil litigation before bailliages to challenge the seigneurial right to collect feudal dues. See Hilton Lewis Root, "Challenging the Seigneurie: Community and Contention on the Eve of the French Revolution," *Journal of Modern History,* LVII (1985), 652–81; Boutier, "Jacqueries en pays croquant," 762–63.

erable inroads, existed a group of provinces characterized by weak agricultural productivity, narrow economic horizons, low peasant revenues, and a precarious existence for the inhabitants. In mountain economies especially, seigneurialism maintained great importance and profitability. Economic blockage and the relative absence of innovations made the Southwest at the end of the Old Regime a haven of small and moderate peasant proprietors as well as "la terre classique du métayage." Although there does not seem to have been an absolute augmentation in seigneurial dues in the region in the last half of the eighteenth century, harvest dues were, in the words of Peter Jones, "exceedingly onerous and . . . extensive." Moreover, sharecropping leases apparently shortened in term, peasant indebtedness deepened, and the nationwide rise in agricultural prices also prompted some landowners to raise the rates of tenant farmers and sharecroppers. Some proprietors adopted more sophisticated estate-management methods of verification and collection of dues and rents. Such proprietors were not true capitalists in the sense of entrepreneurs seeking to maximize their profits by exploiting salaried labor. Their essential goal, aside from maintaining their dominant position, was the simple augmentation of *rente,* ideally seigneurial *rente,* that required no investment. To this end, however, they carefully revised their *terriers,* required more frequent legal verification (by a notary) of the extent of peasant indebtedness, and entrusted the collection of dues to skilled agents capable of keeping accounts and maximizing profits. As a result, the weight of "seigneurialism" may have been more keenly felt.[5]

Protests in the *cahiers de doléances* of 1789 and the presence of litigation in the criminal court archives attest to popular resistance to such practices. The *cahiers* of the Périgord testify that the payment of seigneurial dues was an occasion of continued contestation in which peasants felt they were duped and victimized. To them, the mutations in the collection of seigneurial dues—regardless of their legality—constituted violations of customary usage, the true foundation of popular law in their eyes. More specifically, the *cahiers* of the Périgord record

5. Marcel Marion, "Etat des classes rurales au XVIIIe siècle dans la généralité de Bordeaux," *Revue des études historiques,* LXVIII (1902), 342–43; Boutier, "Jacqueries en pays croquant," 777–79. Root calls for a reevaluation of the thesis that new estate-management policies sparked antiseigneurialism ("Challenging the Seigneurie," 680–81). Jones further argues that the "seigneurial reaction" was very real albeit extended over a longer period than previously thought (*The Peasantry,* 44–45, 48–49, 54–57).

complaints that dues paid in kind and remitted on the feast of Saint Michael (September 29) frequently were not collected by seigneurs until April or May, when scarcity had driven prices higher. Furthermore, peasants often had to travel long distances to pay their dues, only to have a portion of their grain rejected for being of poor quality. The curé of Sauveterre in the contiguous diocese of Agen observed that seigneurial dues were collected fraudulently by bailiffs who used sieves to reduce a sack of grain by two-thirds, collecting only the finest. "Let us not forget to say," he added, "that all of this is done in the name of the seigneur, who instead of being the father of his vassals becomes a tyrant." One of the *cahiers* of the Périgord similarly requested "that seigneurs be required to accept their dues in grains such as they are gathered in the fields that are subject to their rates."[6]

Resistance also greeted the efforts of Périgourdin landowners to restrict customary rights of grazing (*vaine pâture*), gathering, gleaning, and transit or to reclaim already scarce common lands for private use. Although contemporary agronomists agreed that the elimination of such traditional rights would promote long-term agricultural progress, the immediate effect was harmful to the well-being of Périgourdin peasants who supplemented their meager incomes by collecting nuts and grazing their livestock on parish lands, fallow fields, and cultivated fields after harvest. The result was continual tension and conflict between landlords and peasants, who viewed such claims as usurpations and took direct action to defend their rights. To them, the seigneurs and their agents had become "bloodsuckers of their vassals, whom they hardly allow to breathe, instead of being their protectors."[7]

The assertion and protection of traditional rights took many shapes and forms. Several cases that came before the sénéchaussée stemmed directly from the basic ambiguity of proprietary rights in a communal society. The Dordogne River, for example, was the subject of conflicts because of its simultaneous use by various parties and the confusion of rights and customs that pertained thereto. People along the Dordogne felt entitled to keep whatever the river brought them in floods or they fished from it: wood, flax, hemp, ears of maize, and so on. Because

6. N. Castan, *Justice et répression en Languedoc*, 69; Keith Michael Baker (ed.), *The Old Regime and the French Revolution* (Chicago, 1987), 216; Becquart, "Le Cahier de doléances," 209.

7. From the *cahier* of Savignac-de-Miremont (Dordogne), quoted in Marion, "Etat des classes rurales," 350.

those who lived along its banks believed that no one could legally claim ownership over the river and its natural resources, they actually welcomed the royal claim of dominion over the river as an important, long-awaited development that would rid it of feudal tutelage.[8]

Not everyone, of course, shared that view. In 1786, for instance, a raft of wood cut into planks for barrel staves broke apart and scattered wood along both shores of the Dordogne. Most notable among the many people who pulled wood from the river and claimed it as their own was a master surgeon, who conveniently overlooked the company mark on the staves and used them for his own barrels. The two négociants who owned the raft singled him out for prosecution on charges of theft, undoubtedly because he made the prospect of recovering costs more likely; the plaintiffs argued that their rights of ownership were infringed by the custom that allowed people to claim driftwood as their own. In similar fashion, it was not unusual for persons accused of stealing fruit or nuts, especially from trees growing along property lines and roads, to claim that their actions did not constitute theft in their own or the public's eyes. A young agricultural worker initially arrested for theft with breaking and entry was subsequently charged with having stolen fruit in the village. In his interrogation, he denied the theft of fruit and explained to the court: "It is true that he ate cherries and peaches belonging to his neighbors, but neither he nor his neighbors regarded that as theft, since his neighbors ate just as much from his father's cherry trees and peach trees. That is how things are done between neighbors." Where customary usage clearly conflicted with individual proprietary rights, the royal court emerged as the defender of private property when it could do so without jeopardizing public order.[9]

A proprietor who asserted his property rights too assiduously could, however, encounter the passive resistance of his neighbors or even find himself the target of collective action. Jean Cluzel, a weaver in Domme who also owned property outside a nearby village, apprehended three children eating grapes in his vineyard. When he took them before the consuls of Domme, who condemned the parents and masters of the children to pay a total of fifty sous in damages, the people of the village were outraged and vowed retaliation. Later that

8. Cocula, *Les Gens de la rivière de Dordogne*, 636–37, 689–90.

9. Plaintes, September 27, December 28, 1786, both in B 1590, ADD; Interrogatoire, June 16, 1773, B 1554, ADD.

month Cluzel chased several young shepherdesses and their flocks from his meadow and, in the process, injured one of the sheep. The shepherdesses ran to alert the village, and a crowd of women and children armed with clubs, pitchforks, and stones assembled. Finding Cluzel at work in his vineyard, they seized him by the shirt and struck him several times, calling him "knave, thief, and rascal," and shouting, "You're dead, you must die today." When nearby workers intervened and the crowd began to disperse, one of the shepherdesses said: "You can't let Cluzel go. Why don't you beat him and cut off his arms?" Several in the crowd replied that they would release him then but would avenge themselves sooner or later on his person or property. Before they could take further action, however, Cluzel brought charges against them before the sénéchaussée.[10]

Seigneurs who hired feudistes to survey their domains to facilitate the efficient collection of seigneurial dues received comparable treatment at the hands of peasants. Jean-Baptiste Taillefer, a doctor from Domme, made several attempts to survey his seigneurie, located on the floodplain of the Dordogne in the parish of Cénac. When his first attempt met with the united resistance of the tenants, Taillefer initiated criminal proceedings against them before the seigneurial tribunal of Domme. He argued in his petition that their resistance disturbed public order and interfered with his right to dispose of his property as he saw fit. But the tenants refused to be intimidated; they thwarted subsequent efforts to survey the land and collect feudal dues, and they refused to incriminate their fellows in the inquest. The doctor eventually appealed directly to the sénéchaussée, calling on royal justice to enforce the laws of the kingdom and guarantee him full enjoyment of his property.[11]

A brief history of the conflict reveals its classic dimensions. The Taillefer family purchased their domain in 1648, when a religious order of Domme decided to sell several of its holdings on the plain known as Bords. In 1777 Jean-Baptiste Taillefer, believing that his father had collected feudal dues "with a sort of laxity that several tenants unfeelingly abused," decided to put his accounts in order. He therefore hired Léonard Juge, notary and feudiste, "to verify each tenancy in particular and to prepare an acknowledgment of indebtedness for each."[12] Fearful

10. Plainte, September 16, 1772, Information, September 19, 1772, both in B 1552, ADD.
11. Plaintes, July 29, August 31, 1777, B 1565, ADD.
12. Plaintes, July 29, August 31, 1777, *ibid.*

that this project would threaten their well-being and certain that it contravened custom, tenants with holdings on the plain made every effort to prevent the feudiste from carrying out his commission.

On his first attempt to survey the domain, Juge stopped for a drink at a cabaret, where he encountered Jean Cluzel—the weaver who himself had been the target of popular violence five years earlier. Cluzel warned him that if he tried to survey the plain he would never leave it alive. When Juge advised him to consult a lawyer if he felt he had a legitimate complaint, Cluzel, who could speak from personal experience, replied that although he himself would not stop Juge, "they would send *la jeunesse,* who would kill him." Juge reconsidered and reported the incident to Taillefer, who initiated criminal proceedings against Cluzel for menaces. But the inquest held before the seigneurial tribunal at Domme produced no substantive evidence, for most of the witnesses present in the cabaret also held land on the plain and refused to cooperate.[13]

A second incident occurred on a Sunday, when Juge and Taillefer again attempted to survey the plain. They were spotted first by a mason, who forebade Juge to survey his land and warned him he would repent if he did. Juge grew angry and replied, "You have no right to forbid me my function, and your plot will be the first surveyed." The mason then tried to assault Juge, but his wife restrained him. Meanwhile, a crowd alerted by the commotion arrived on the scene and joined the mason in threatening Juge, crying out: "Kill him, the f. rascal, the f. knave. He's a rogue, and a j. f. You'd be better off making a lard of him." They chased both Juge and Taillefer back to Domme, jeering and shouting at them. Taillefer requested another inquest, which gathered more information than the first but still nothing of a substantive nature. The two witnesses that cooperated were tenants who had already paid their dues to Taillefer and possessed receipts to that effect. When they tried to dissociate themselves from the rest of the community, their neighbors threatened them with violence. One of them had agreed to have his land surveyed, but his neighbors had threatened to break every bone in his body and then kill him if he did so. The other tenant to testify had recently manured his field and was anxious to retain full use of it.[14]

---

13. Plaintes, July 29, August 31, 1777, *ibid.*
14. Continuation d'information à Sarlat, September 29, 1777, *ibid.*

Juge made one final attempt to survey the plain, this time early on a Thursday morning, but shepherds guarding their flocks saw him coming and raised the alert. Several people started toward him, shouting, "Kill him, kill him," and that "Juge was a thief and they had to throw him in the river." Juge took fright and fled to Domme. Convinced that little more could be accomplished before the seigneurial tribunal of Domme, Taillefer decided to initiate proceedings before the sénéchaussée against "this crowd of individuals who hold plots in the fief of the plaintiff and who seem to be set on eliminating his rights by terror and violence." [15] He named ten persons in his suit, one of them already embroiled in a civil suit with him over seigneurial dues. The case did not reach final sentencing, and its outcome is therefore unknown.

Disputes concerning rights of access were a constant source of litigation owing in part to the fragmentation of holdings that made it virtually impossible for some proprietors to reach their parcels without crossing a neighbor's land. Proprietors from the lowliest peasants to the highest rank seigneurs guarded their land jealously. In 1780 two *laboureurs* assaulted the Chevalier Duvignol when they found him crossing their land to reach his own. The chevalier brought charges and collected a total of 120 livres in damages from them. [16] In a similar case, a proprietor protested when Jean Audemon, seigneurial judge of Meyrals and Saint-Cyprien, crossed his land in order to harvest grapes in his own vineyard. The judge insisted that he had an established, traditional right of transit across the land, but the landowner disputed that right and called the judge "a thieving knave, a f. dishonest man." The judge, affronted by this outrage to his honor, said he would chastise the man then and there were he not armed with a pitchfork. Instead, he brought suit against the landowner for insults. When interrogated, the accused denied that he had insulted the judge and insisted that he would never even have considered doing so, "recognizing that the plaintiff is of a different *qualité.*" His newfound deference contrasted sharply with the defiance he showed when defending his own vineyard. [17]

Disputes over the right to gather walnuts and chestnuts or to graze pigs (*glânage*) also convey the enduring strength of customary usage as

15. Plainte, August 31, 1777, *ibid.*

16. Tournelle de Sarlat, April 7, 1784: Plainte (November 22, 1780), Sentence (February 13, 1784), B, ADG. Also see Plainte, December 20, 1780, B 1574, ADD.

17. Plainte, October 21, 1782, Information, October 27, 1782, and Interrogatoire, March 30, 1783, all in B 1578, ADD.

well as resistance to the strict enforcement of proprietary rights. In October, 1783, for example, a severe thunderstorm shook many walnuts from trees in the parish of Sergeac and created a ravine in a road separating the property of two neighbors. The next day, the servant of one of the landholders was collecting nuts floating in the ravine near a walnut tree whose branches extended beyond the neighboring property. When challenged by the tree owner's sister-in-law, the servant replied that she had the right to any windfallen nuts in the public road. The sister-in-law asserted that the nuts had not fallen in the road but had been carried there by the heavy rains and therefore really belonged to her. She forced the servant to surrender her basketful of nuts. When the servant told her master, he swore to take revenge and found the opportune moment several days later.[18]

Communal agricultural practices and commons were notably scarce in the rugged topography of the Sarladais, where small proprietors generally lived in concentrated villages but sharecroppers inhabited isolated farmsteads scattered across the uplands. Although attempts to enclose or divide village commons heightened tensions elsewhere in France, the criminal court archives of the sénéchaussée contain no bona fide examples of conflicts over commons within the jurisdiction. They do, however, record an incident occurring in the contiguous Sénéchaussée of Martel that graphically illustrates how popular justice was both mobilized to defend threatened communal rights and perhaps manipulated for personal gain. Early in 1785, several proprietors acquired a meadow in the parish of Saint-Michel-de-Bannières and empowered one of their number, a royal notary and prosecutor before the sénéchaussée, to act as their trustee or syndic. Problems soon arose because peasants accustomed to grazing their flocks in the field continued to do so, necessitating an edict from the Parlement of Bordeaux forbidding the parishioners of Saint-Michel to use the meadow.

The parlement's interdiction posed a special problem for a merchant named Moïse, whose own holding was entirely encompassed by the larger field, which he was therefore forced to cross to reach his own property. In early November, he led his seventy sheep onto the meadow, and others soon followed with their own flocks. In response, the syndic hired eight *laboureurs* to seize Moïse's sheep and transport them to a *parc de justice* (judicial detention compound) near Martel.

18. Plainte, October 3, 1783, Information, October 6, 1783, both in B 1581, ADD.

When they arrived at the meadow, the men were intercepted by Moïse, who offered to pay their day's wages and to treat them to drinks at a cabaret if they would only forget their mission and report that they had found no sheep. But they refused and proceeded to confiscate the flock. That evening, Moïse and several others he had assembled at a cabaret assaulted the syndic and his men when they emerged from another cabaret. The syndic later referred to the incident as an "émotion populaire," and the scuffle does seem to have involved quite a few people. Aside from Moïse, the most active among them were two butchers who grabbed the syndic by the collar and wig and threatened him until others intervened.[19]

In reaction to the syndic's suit against Moïse for "violence, menaces, and armed assault with illegal assembly," inhabitants of nearby villages led their combined flocks onto the meadow in open defiance of the owners. They responded by commissioning a royal bailiff and six assistants to seize all livestock found grazing on their property. When the agents arrived and began to gather the sheep, shepherds alerted the villagers of Saint-Michel, who formed a crowd of eighty persons armed with *batons,* stones, mattocks, axes, pitchforks, branches, and sticks of firewood. The crowd descended on the royal agents and threatened to hack them to pieces or shoot them if they tried to confiscate the flocks. The villagers shook their sticks and tools in the men's faces and poked them in the stomach until they retreated. Two days later, the syndic named eighteen persons in an additional petition to the court, charging them with unlawful assembly.[20]

The arrival of bailiffs sent by landlords to evict tenants and sequestrators sent by creditors to confiscate property occasioned what was by far the most ubiquitous form of popular contention in the Sarladais. Criminal cases resulting from such incidents are distributed relatively evenly throughout the period and convey a sense of the enduring popular distrust of proprietary law and the agents that enforced it. Resistance to a bailiff was generally a family affair. In a typical example, a royal bailiff commissioned to seize the furniture of the Izard family in the parish of Saint-Cybranet met with resistance on his first attempt. On his second try, he therefore brought along a locksmith to

19. Plainte, November 21, 1785, Information, November 22, 1785, both in B 1587, ADD.

20. Procès-verbal, November 24, 1785, Plainte, November 26, 1785, and Information, November 29, 1785, all *ibid.*

help him and his men gain entry. When the group arrived on July 1, 1786, the entire family mobilized to meet it. The eldest son tried to strike the locksmith with a hatchet, and his brother brandished a cutlass and threatened to cut off their heads. When the women of the household began to "crier justice," they attracted two neighbors armed with hoes, who came to their aid and forced the bailiff and his men to retreat.

Five weeks later, the same royal bailiff attempted to carry out another seizure of furniture in the parish. This time he found only the daughter of the *laboureur* at home and was able to confiscate an iron bedstead before the eldest son arrived, swearing. When he and his sister grabbed the bedstead, which the bailiff's assistants had already registered, the bailiff tried to explain to them that he was only executing the orders of justice. But the young man replied "that he did not give a f. about justice or anything it could do to him." Armed with a billhook, he forced them out of the house and down the steps, wounding one of the assistants, and threw stones at them as they retreated.[21]

The *cahiers* of 1789 testify to the widespread distrust and hatred of bailiffs and sequestrators by the rural populace of France. In the Périgord, the parish of Auriac requested "that there no longer be any confiscations for debts." The populace not only resisted bailiffs and sequestrators but also denounced the institutions that commissioned them: the sénéchaussée and the exchanges of Tulle and Bordeaux. In one revealing incident, two merchants obtained a legal writ authorizing them (or their agents) to take into custody the property of a miller until he complied with a court order to pay what he owed them. The merchants commissioned a royal sergeant from Montignac to post the summons in the miller's parish and to proclaim the seizure of his property. When the sergeant posted the summons on a Sunday after mass, the miller tore it down and (in the presence of a crowd) threatened to kill him. The sergeant warned the miller not to interfere because he was operating under orders from the sénéchaussée, but the miller replied "that even if they came from the devil he would not give a f. and that if they sent twenty constables of the maréchaussée, he would kill someone before he allowed his goods to be posted."[22]

21. Plainte, August 12, 1786, B 1589, ADD.
22. Aubin, *L'Organisation judiciaire,* 174–75; Plainte, June 26, 1775, B 1559, ADD.

The authorities were, of course, aware that the populace was highly resentful of such actions. During the difficult spring months of 1773 the subdelegate—in the interest of preserving public order—tried to attenuate the harshness of tax collection. He received so many complaints about seizures of poor people's property that he cautioned Certain, the collector of the taille, to review carefully his guidelines for authorizing confiscations. He advised Certain to target only those with the highest assessments, since concentrating on them would not only yield the highest return but also result in the least grumbling among the populace. "We are," the subdelegate wrote, "in circumstances where we must show humaneness in our operations, since a multitude of people in the countryside lack even the basic means of subsistence." Confiscating the goods of people with low assessments would only show favoritism to those with credit and wealth and make taxation most onerous for the poor, a policy "contrary to justice and the intentions of the King," he added. In contrast, the collector displayed little concern for those in arrears. When the curé of Couture in 1775 prevented two of his bailiffs from carrying out their duties, Certain complained to the intendant that "in the fourteen years that I have been receiver of the tailles or performed that function, it is only beginning in this year that I have seen that the curés are taking it into their heads to interfere with the bailiffs in their functions and to incite uprisings. I hope that M. the Intendant will restore order." The authorities often disagreed on the appropriate policy to follow in times of crisis but never wavered from their goal of maintaining or restoring order.[23]

Although most cases of rebellion against justice involved only one individual or family, some incidents aroused public sympathy and, as we have seen, mobilized neighbors and friends to join in pursuit of the legal agents. In 1774, two traders from Sarlat obtained a court order against the Sieur Baillot Duverdier, an impoverished nobleman who owed them 425 livres, and commissioned a bailiff to seize his furniture. The bailiff, who found Duverdier absent from his château, seized his furniture and persuaded a neighbor to allow his house to serve as temporary depot for the confiscated goods. But three weeks later, when the bailiff returned with his assistants to transport the furniture, the neigh-

23. Lettre à M. Certain, receveur des tailles, de Meyrignac, April 17, 1773, C 478, ADG; Lettre de Certain, receveur des tailles, à M. l'Intendant, August 29, 1775, C 481, ADG.

bor refused to open the doors of his house, forcing the bailiffs to seek court authorization to employ a locksmith. They returned two weeks later and began to remove the furniture despite the opposition of the neighbor's son and daughter-in-law, while the neighbor's daughter ran to the château to alert Duverdier. The nobleman grabbed his hat and gun and came running across the fields toward the legal agents, shouting, "I'm going to kill those buggers." The bailiff quickly mounted his horse and fled at a gallop, with his men running down the road after him. When Duverdier called for help, his domestiques and several masons he employed—as well as twenty people from his village—armed themselves with *batons* and pitchforks and pursued the agents all the way to the next village, crying, "Thief, thief." The bailiff argued in his petition (and the court agreed) that this action gravely disturbed public tranquility and, if left unpunished, would be detrimental to the respect and authority due the law and its agents.[24]

Resistance to bailiffs occasionally led to angry assemblies that evoked the language and ritual violence of seventeenth-century Croquants. When in 1778 a clerk from the parish of Saint-Julien-de-Castelnaud failed to repay a loan of 240 livres, his creditor obtained a writ of seizure on his property. The responsible bailiff and his assistants, unable to force entry upon their first visit, returned with a locksmith. The clerk's wife refused them entry, saying that for all she knew, they could be knaves come to cut her throat. Although intent on performing his duties, the bailiff could not find two persons, as required by law, to witness the execution of the ordinance because the neighbors refused to cooperate or even give their names. When the bailiff began to proceed anyway, calling to the woman several times in the name of the king and justice to open the door, she shouted "that someone would die before any furniture was removed."[25]

The locksmith finally forced the door, only to find that the woman had fled out the back. The bailiff and his assistants seized a walnut buffet, carried it to the home of a *laboureur* whom they had persuaded to act as depositor, and returned for more furniture. The debtor's wife meanwhile sought aid from her neighbors, whom she found threshing

24. Duverdier appealed the case directly before the Parlement of Bordeaux. See Procès-verbal, August 17, 1774, Information, August 20, 1774, Règlement à extraordinaire, September 25, 1774, and Interrogatoire, September 19, 1774, all in B 1557, ADD.
25. Procès-verbal, August 7, 1778, B 1567, ADD.

grain. They grabbed their flails and pitchforks and came running to the clerk's home, shouting: "They must die. Kill them. Where is the jean f. locksmith? We must kill him, too—cut his throat and throw him in the lake." They drove the legal agents from the house, threatening to beat them to death with the flails and leave them on the threshing floor. The bailiff and his men, fearing bodily harm, retreated to prepare their report. As they left, several among the crowd of approximately thirty people warned them that if they returned with any more ordinances they would have "their limbs [cut] off." [26]

The rituals, language, and goals of the punitive action taken by individuals and groups upholding their customary rights in the Sarladais between 1770 and 1789 were, at least on the surface, similar to those employed in the same area in the seventeenth century. Villagers assembled by the ringing of the tocsin or the beating of a drum seized their familiar weapons—flails, *batons,* pitchforks, stones—and threatened the targets of their rage with ritual dismemberment and ceremonial ablution. The targets of preference during this period were bailiffs, sequestrators, and feudistes, who were viewed as bloodsuckers and thieves representing a foreign world of officialdom and written (French) culture. Moreover, collective action retained certain carnivalesque elements: Music and dancing sometimes preceded or followed mock battles, and drummers and pipers often led crowds into action. The goal of popular sanctions remained the defense and restoration of communal solidarity by the chastisement (whether symbolic or actual) of the offender. When satirical sanctions elicited an admission of guilt and true penitence, the wayward son or daughter was readmitted to the social body. But large-scale insurrections, the final stage of such customary sanctions, were unknown. [27]

By the end of the eighteenth century, popular infrajudicial action in the Sarladais had changed in several important respects. Most important, the disorders of the last twenty years of the Old Regime were rarely directed against fiscal agents representing the king as had been the actions of the seventeenth-century Croquants. They were instead directed against persons actually residing in the rural world: landowners and seigneurs or their agents. Moreover, *notables,* seigneurs, curés, and rural bourgeois were all targets during the Revolutionary

26. *Ibid.*
27. Bercé, *Histoire des croquants,* 632–33.

disturbances of 1789–90. Within that group, seigneurs bore the brunt of collective action, but rural bourgeois were also targeted because they acted as fermiers, legal representatives (attorneys and notaries), fiscal agents, and judges for seigneurs.

The degree of solidarity that had formed the basis of the Croquants' large-scale violent resistance eroded in the course of the eighteenth century. In the Sarladais, the protection-allegiance bond between nobles and peasants continued to dissolve where it had not disappeared entirely. In short, the battle line between popular and official culture had shifted to within the rural community itself, isolating the château from the parish church steeple.[28] The revolts of 1789–90 issued from the internal antagonisms of rural society, the antagonism dividing seigneurs and peasants being only one example of the general opposition between those who paid rent in all its forms and those who collected it.

The destruction of the symbols that daily manifested seigneurial power inaugurated the Revolutionary violence. The peasants attacked the "foremost inhabitant of the parish" by attacking the symbols of his prerogatives: the church pews and family tomb that he held in the parish church (the theater par excellence of rural hierarchy) and especially the weather vanes that surmounted his château, a privilege in the Southwest restricted to holders of fiefs. Peasants rejected anything that had the least air of distinction, refused to lift their hats, omitted the particle in the seigneur's name, and claimed a fraternal embrace. The leveling was combined with jubilant provocation, and even in some places a tendency to "turn the world upside down," with the peasants now on top.[29]

The attack was not limited to symbols of power; it also targeted the practical economic foundations of the seigneurie, such as dues and fisheries. In some areas, peasants drained the ponds that provided fish for aristocratic tables yet caused fogs and fevers that plagued the peasantry. In many places they took possession of the château—by force if necessary—stripped it of consumables, and pilfered small objects. But the real goal of the visit was to make the seigneur admit their claims

28. Boutier, "Jacqueries en pays croquant," 769–71.
29. For an elaboration of the potentially subversive use of ritualized inversion, see Natalie Zemon Davis, *Society and Culture in Early Modern France* (Stanford, 1975), 124–51. D. M. G. Sutherland notes the folkloric elements in disturbances throughout France (*France, 1789–1815: Revolution and Counterrevolution* [Oxford, 1985], 101–103).

and recognize the legitimacy of their action. They required the prompt return of all titles, papers, and documents pertaining to agricultural rents, as well as receipts for payments in arrears, and even the restitution of firearms and fines unjustly collected.[30]

After the war against symbols of authority and the temporary seizure of châteaus, the peasants served public notice of their modification of the balance of power. Peasant actions therefore often ended in the planting of maypoles on the village square, a symbolic gesture crowning what had already taken place.[31] The constables of the maréchaussée of Périgueux sent to halt the erection of a maypole at Saint-Géral found that the inhabitants had planted before the church door a tall tree whose summit was shaped into a gallows, from which hung various symbols of authority including a writing desk and quill pen, and a placard with the inscription FINAL RECEIPT FOR RENTS. The tree was surmounted by the weather vane of the local seigneur.

This display of peasant potency in the heart of the community recapitulated the revolt that had just transpired by displaying the peasants' appropriation of the former means of domination, including justice. The peasant maypole—often decorated with a gallows—had taken the place of the seigneurial pillory. The peasants called into question everything they considered an abuse of power. The Vicomte de Noailles, in early February, 1790, described events to the National Assembly in the following manner: "In the Rouergue, Limousin, and Périgord, there are persons who have set themselves up as repairers of wrongs; they judge anew cases judged over the last thirty years and render sentences that they then execute." The agreement reached between the seigneur of Paulin (Périgord) and peasants, for example, in-

---

30. For descriptions of Revolutionary disturbances in the Sarladais, see Escande, *Histoire de Sarlat,* 277–84; Boutier, "Jacqueries en pays croquant," 761–62, 780–81; Mona Ozouf, *Festivals and the French Revolution,* trans. Alan Sheridan (Cambridge, Mass., 1988), 232–43. Also see Steven G. Reinhardt, "Ritualized Violence in Eighteenth-Century Périgord," in David Troyansky *et al.* (eds.), *The French Revolution in Culture and Society* (Westport, Conn., 1991).

31. Ozouf, *Festivals and the French Revolution,* 239–40, 243. Such collective maypoles were erected in Burgundy, Picardy, Orléanais, Guyenne, Languedoc, and Franche-Comté. The annual delivery of a maypole was often included in contracts made between villages and large proprietors. As early as 1257, a municipal charter stipulated that the inhabitants of a commune had the right to "quérir le mai" in the woods of the seigneur (Bussière, *Etudes historiques,* III, 259; Nicole Belmont, *Mythes et croyances dans l'ancienne France* [Paris, 1973], 93–95).

cluded a panoply of restitutions that the peasants required: three restitutions of land, two reimbursements of legal expenses, two returns of confiscated firearms, the cancellation of receipts for debts and arrears not paid, and four reimbursements of arrears of rents already paid (two of them going back twenty years).[32]

With the planting of the maypole, the peasants celebrated. Every revolt prolonged itself in festivities, a feast of bread and wine as well as rarer dishes such as an omelette with lard. The feasting began with *quêtes* (tours of collection) around the parish, as was traditionally done when a maypole was planted or during the Christmas or Easter season. Because generosity, a sense of *noblesse oblige,* was one of the social qualities expected of the *notable,* the peasant troops made their way to the best houses of the parish, including that of the curé. *Notables* willing to contribute to seasonal collections perhaps sensed the new political content of the exactions of 1790, which were more or less compulsory, and feared they represented a challenge to property rights.[33] The danger had always existed that the collections, when confronted with resistance, could become forced contributions. Peasant participants in the exactions of 1790 targeted those who possessed church pews and then characterized their exactions as just compensation for establishing equality in the new nation.[34]

The rites of revolt also took advantage of the specific sociability of youth, which did not stop with the frontier of marriage. Jean Boutier discovered that youths and young adults between the ages of fifteen and thirty-five (notably artisans) constituted the great majority of the participants in revolts in 1789–90. The planting of the maypole was one of the principal customs of cohesion practiced by unmarried young males, who were responsible for the violence that the community had formalized to regulate the integrity of the territory, marriage, the exchange of goods, and the enforcement of customary rights. Their actions had always had the potential to turn against traditional authority;

32. Boutier, "Jacqueries en pays croquant," 763–64.

33. Antifeudalism contained an implicit challenge to rights of private property in its challenge to agrarian individualism (Jones, *The Peasantry,* 80–81).

34. Boutier, "Jacqueries en pays croquant," 764–65. During the quêtes of the night of Holy Thursday, for example, "la jeunesse" went singing from door to door, requesting lard and chestnuts but especially eggs. If refused, they were known to scale walls and break doors and windows (Rocal, *Les Vieilles Coutumes,* 126–27; Belmont, *Mythes et croyances,* 83–84).

in fact, curés and *notables* had often complained about the insubordination and disrespect of a "republican" and "libertine" youth.[35]

The objectives of the collective violence made a wide consensus possible among the peasantry, but during these actions the social group as a whole was, in the words of Mona Ozouf, simultaneously "torn apart by confrontation and welded together by solidarity." The revolts of 1789–90 did not form around communal solidarity; they neglected and even contested the traditional leaders of the community. They had their origin in the antagonism felt between those who lived from the work of their own hands and those who lived off the work of others—in the first ranks of which stood the seigneurs.[36]

Both the disorders that occurred within the jurisdiction during the final twenty years of the Old Regime and the popular actions of 1789–90 were strangely attenuated versions of the peasant revolts of the previous century. Although a continuity of language, rituals, and goals is evident, the level of intensity was obviously lower. The seventeenth-century Croquants actually mutilated their victims before throwing them into a well or river, but eighteenth-century Périgourdin peasants only threatened to do so. Even during the disorders of the Revolution, popular action was notably nonviolent and directed primarily against the symbols of privilege. Peasants raised maypoles on which they figuratively executed symbols of seigneurial authority and forced nobles to touch hands and drink with them as a sign of their newfound equality, but the reports that arrived at the National Assembly of a Périgord in flames were unfounded.[37] The model of behavior that accepted collective violence as part of the habitual procedure of popular justice had been undermined, and the communal solidarity on which it depended had been challenged.[38]

The populace was nonetheless prepared to defend its customary rights by freeing an unjustly accused prisoner, defending communal

35. Boutier, "Jacqueries en pays croquant," 772–73.

36. Cameron, *Crime and Repression*, 252–55; Ozouf, *Festivals and the French Revolution*, 235.

37. One report was made to the Constituent Assembly by the Marquis Foucauld de Lardimalie, delegate of the second estate from the Périgord. Quoted in René Pijassou, "La Crise révolutionnaire," in Higounet-Nadal (ed.), *Histoire du Périgord*, 258.

38. For a summary of the disturbances of this era, see Yves-Marie Bercé (ed.), *Croquants et Nu-Pieds: Les Soulèvements paysans en France du XVIe au XIXe siècle* (Paris, 1974), 135–39. Also consult Cameron, *Crime and Repression*, 240–41.

grazing rights, or resisting the preparation of *terriers*. The mere threat of violence, joined with an impressive show of solidarity, usually prompted the authorities to capitulate—especially during the few grain disturbances that occurred in the Périgord during this period. The maréchaussée of Périgueux dealt with only six grain disturbances between 1720 and 1788, all of them occurring during times of great local or national distress—1739, 1758, 1764, 1768, 1770, and 1773—and generally during the classic riot months of spring. But as Iain Cameron has observed, hunger did not spontaneously ignite violence, and high grain prices did not automatically trigger disturbances. Of greater importance to the population was the violation of an unspoken trust, either by the movement of grain to another locality or by suspected hoarding and price fixing. Upon such occasions, the populace acted deliberately and in controlled fashion.[39]

In 1768 and 1770, for example, high grain prices caused unrest in Montignac when the populace suspected local merchants of hoarding and attempting to monopolize the grain trade. A succession of hard winters and summer hailstorms in the late 1760s, followed by the generally bad year of 1770, reduced thousands in the Agenais to begging, gave rise to grain riots in Bordeaux, and caused great hardship in the Sarladais. Times of dearth often forced the marginal poor of the Sarladais into individual criminal acts. Antoine Juge, an agricultural worker who lived in a shelter made of branches in the thickest part of the woods near Montignac and slept "under a pile of leaves," stole grain for his family in 1770 because he could not stand to hear his children cry from hunger.[40] This incident was followed by a rash of similar cases of theft of food directly motivated by *la grande misère* of 1771–72.

Peasants also threatened to take direct action to ensure that when grain did become available, it would be sold at a fair price. In March, 1770, the Prior Pomarel of the parishes of Brénac and Montignac reported to the intendant that "poverty is widespread in this region, grain is very rare, and the price is going up daily." When a Montignac merchant received five thousand pounds of grain, popular opinion and the municipal authorities constrained him to sell it immediately. Grain sent

39. Cameron, *Crime and Repression*, 234–37.
40. Procès-verbal, June 8, 1770, Interrogatoire, June 8, 1770, and Confrontation, December 3, 1770, all in B 1546, ADD.

by merchants from Brive was distributed under the supervision of the lieutenant criminal of police. According to Pomarel, the concern of the authorities was not unwarranted. "If the *archers* [police] had not been there," he wrote, "there would surely have been a riot."[41]

In the spring of 1773, a serious disturbance occurred in Bergerac, provoked in large measure by the appearance at local markets of traders who purchased grain for the Bordelais and the Agenais. This free movement of the grain trade not only drove prices up in the Périgord but also resulted in the alarming spectacle of boats loaded with local grain descending the Dordogne River to Bordeaux. As prices rose, tension increased in Bergerac to the point where the city fathers, the subdelegate, and the magistrates of the sénéchaussée called on the maréchaussée of Périgueux for aid and mobilized three hundred bourgeois militia to stand guard on market day. On May 22, the crowd demanded that grain be sold at three livres per measure, while the merchants insisted on five livres. To avoid violence, the authorities finally relented and forced the merchants to sell at three livres. The same day, a crowd laid siege to the grain store of a merchant named Grimet and forced the authorities to sell it at a reduced rate. Another crowd stopped a boat of grain on the river just outside of town and quickly distributed the contents before the constables of the maréchaussée arrived. Word of the forced sale of grain spread rapidly to the peasantry in the neighboring parishes. The next day, approximately two thousand men armed with *batons* surrounded the hôtel de ville and compelled the municipality to sell most of the grain remaining in town at a reduced price.[42]

When faced with popular disturbances, the standard procedure of the maréchaussée was to act prudently and yield when confronted with a large crowd, but to stand firm or take the offensive when opposition was weak. Accordingly, later that day constables charged a smaller group trying to break into a grain store and dispersed them, injuring forty persons. As the peasants left Bergerac that evening, they threatened to return the next day to burn the town. In light of this threat, the lieutenant des maréchaux, Gigounoux de Verdon, found it relatively easy to arouse in the Bergerac populace fear of a *jacquerie* (peasant revolt). The townspeople closed ranks behind the maréchaussée and or-

---

41. Lettre à M. de Farges, Intendant, March 6, 1770, C 475, ADG.
42. Cameron, *Crime and Repression*, 63–65.

ganized the defense of Bergerac, but their fears proved unfounded. Although rumors spread of rebellion in the countryside, the patrols of the constables met little resistance.

Verdon skillfully played upon the town dwellers' fears, arresting a few culprits and making an example of one of them by dragging her, bound, through the streets of Bergerac. He was greatly aided in his task by the rumors of a peasant offensive. According to his spies, peasants reportedly said: "They would get themselves cut to pieces or hanged, and they were no more averse to being killed than to starving. In that way, they would really have the bourgeois and the nobles, who would be forced to work their land for themselves." The lieutenant heard that women were planning to skin Grimet alive and put pieces of his skin on their rosaries. It was reported that one peasant returned home with a pound of meat purchased in Bergerac and bragged that it was a piece of the grain merchant. An army detachment finally arrived on May 28, guaranteeing that the next day's grain market would function without incident, and grain procured by the intendant expressly for the relief of the city began to arrive on May 31. The only other disorder occurred when peasants stopped boats loaded with grain for Bordeaux at several spots along the Dordogne and forced the sale of the contents at a price well below market value. But by early June, Bordeaux received shipments of grain from abroad and ceased to draw its provisions from the Périgord, easing shortages and lowering prices in the region. And so ended the last grain disturbance to occur in the Périgord before the onset of the Revolution.[43]

As a rule, the lower an administrator stands in an official hierarchy, the greater his knowledge of detail, the greater his involvement with the local community, and therefore the less his concern with enforcing the letter of the law. The power of the state always adapts itself to local reality. Authorities in small towns and rural areas of the Sarladais were accordingly reluctant to set the apparatus of justice in motion, since they had to live with the populace afterwards. In normal circumstances they had virtually no police force at their disposal, so they were understandably inclined to appeasement. Although the Crown supported the free movement of grain after 1765, local authorities were painfully aware of the practical consequences for the poor of higher grain prices. They did not welcome popular protest, but they understood its motiva-

43. *Ibid.*, 66–69.

tion and were reluctant to suppress it with severity. In years of poor harvests, the correspondence between the subdelegate of Sarlat and the intendant contained many special requests for exemptions from taxes and for relief shipments of grain. The subdelegate also complained in January, 1771, that when grain shipments did arrive, the traders in charge were guilty of profiteering. In his opinion, the free movement of grain only made it easier for local merchants to hoard supplies and organize monopolies.[44]

On at least one occasion, the authorities took a more active role in protecting the populace from shortages and monopolies. In July, 1770, the Sénéchaussée of Sarlat, alerted by several complaints and motivated no doubt by the near-riot that had occurred in the spring in Montignac, took the unusual step of initiating criminal proceedings against the judge and prosecutor of the tribunal of Montignac for embezzlement. Specifically, the royal court accused them of failing to enforce police regulations on weights and measures used for the sale of grain, cloth, wine, salt, and bread.

> In this year of calamity, these same officers carried their excesses to a degree difficult to believe and to the greatest prejudice of the people. Through their lack of attention and exactitude, they suffered and tolerated the sale in Montignac of bread that was improperly baked and that was, in a word, still dough. What is even worse is that the loaves that ought to have weighed two pounds weighed only one and one-half at most, and those that ought to have been one pound weighed only one-half pound or, at most, twelve or fourteen ounces. There was the same failing in the pricing of bread, which exceeded by far the price of the grain.

Moreover, the sénéchaussée charged, the judge and prosecutor knowingly allowed three merchants—one of them the brother-in-law of the prosecutor—to sell spoiled grain and to monopolize the sale of grain in and around the town. On market days, the merchants apparently had waited outside the city to intercept peasants bringing grain to market and had purchased it from them at favorable prices, thereby creating a shortage and driving prices even higher. The merchants then ordered the beating of drums to announce in the public square that ample grain was available in their storerooms—on the condition that it be ground into flour at the mill farmed out by one of them. The royal court cited

---

44. Spierenburg, *The Spectacle of Suffering*, 102–103; Lettre de Meyrignac à M. l'Intendant, January 2, 1771, C 476, ADG.

these abuses, which had continued for at least two years, as particularly scandalous because they jeopardized public tranquility in a year of
hardship.[45]

The rumor or threat of violence generally sufficed to spur the local
and royal authorities into taking preventive measures. By acceding to
the demands of the populace for price controls, they may have contravened the spirit of free trade in grain, but they also managed to avoid
major disturbances such as those in Bergerac. In the economic as well
as the political and social realms, the authorities recognized and tolerated popular practices they were powerless or disinclined to repress.
The populace, on the other hand, while still capable of mobilizing in
large numbers to enforce its concept of justice, did so in markedly less
violent ways than previously. The reality of the Bergerac disturbances
hardly equaled the violence threatened by the participants. In short, the
tradition of collective violence was on the wane well before individual
violence declined.[46]

Violence in the countryside was part of daily life. The brutality evident in family life, in disputes, in work, and in play manifests what
some have called an impulsive, "primitive" mentality. Neither the
Church nor education had yet managed to change behavior on a large
scale, instructing and training the populace in self-control. Nevertheless, one should not overemphasize the spontaneity and irrationality of
violence: Although ubiquitous, violence was seldom truly spontaneous
and, in the late eighteenth century, rarely excessive. Instead, a great
deal of the violence that surfaced in the judicial records of the Sarladais
was actually the controlled violence of popular justice.[47] Affairs of
honor still elicited acts of individual and familial vengeance to restore
the balance of esteem upset by some affront. The defense of territory in
its various forms was the special domain of collectivities, from youth
groups to entire parishes. New circumstances also gave rise to acts of
individual and collective violence in the late eighteenth century: Challenges to traditional rights of usage and the freeing of the grain trade
both prompted the populace to utilize customary sanctions to defend
its rights.

45. This case is cited in Villepelet, *Inventaire sommaire*, II, B 1545, p. 161.
46. Cameron, *Crime and Repression*, 240–41.
47. The gratuitousness of violence in the principality of Neuchâtel was also more
apparent than real (P. Henry, *Crime, justice et société*, 600–602).

But in all of these circumstances, collective violence gradually was attenuated and recourse to royal criminal justice slowly increased in the 1780s. In affairs of honor, offended parties were gradually learning the benefits of new legal strategies designed to make an opponent "eat his property." Members of the community who found themselves the object of charivaris often began refusing to submit to popular interference in matters of personal conduct. And the participants in collective disturbances confined their violence to threats and symbolic action, even more than did individuals involved in personal incidents of violence. In short, collective violence especially was on the wane, owing perhaps largely to the fact that large-scale collective actions represented more of a direct challenge to royal justice and posed a real threat to public order.

IX

Seigneurial Justice and Retaliation

True, the poor man was much better protected than is generally thought against high-handed dealings on the part of richer or more influential members of the community.

—Alexis de Tocqueville, *The Old Regime and the French Revolution*

The royal courts had long supplied a service that the majority in the Sarladais was unprepared or unwilling to utilize. As noted previously, however, recourse to the sénéchaussée increased in the 1780s as more individuals apparently defied communal solidarity and appealed to external authority to govern their private affairs. Those who opted for official justice evidently did so because the advantages outweighed the disadvantages. Any explanation of why they made their choice must therefore consider not only the attractions of royal justice but also the drawbacks of alternative forms of adjudication, namely popular and seigneurial justice. Seigneurial justice, for example, was relatively cheap and accessible, yet was inherently vulnerable to the influence wielded by local seigneurs anxious to protect the honorific and real privileges of the seigneurial regime.

The seigneurial and municipal tribunals of the Sarladais played an essential role in providing justice to the populace in the final years of the Old Regime. Of the 474 cases with known offenses heard by the Sénéchaussée of Sarlat between 1770 and 1790, 106 (22 percent) had previously been heard by a seigneurial or municipal tribunal. But whereas only 4 percent of private criminal cases were appeals or referrals, two-thirds of all public cases had already been initiated by a lower-level court. Moreover, the percentage for public cases actually increased throughout the period, while the percentage for private cases decreased. These trends readily emerge in Table 7, which depicts the percentage of sénéchaussée cases initiated by a lower-level tribunal in the four five-year periods of the study, omitting 1790, when seigneurial court activity was disrupted by the disorders of the Revolution. The data suggest that at least a handful of seigneurial and municipal tribunals in the Sarladais maintained an important if not steadily expanding role in referring public cases for felonies to the sénéchaussée. The dependence of the royal court on these lower-level tribunals becomes all the more evident when one remembers that an additional sixteen cases were referrals from various prévôtés of the maréchaussée, which acted as clearinghouses for cases that came before them. During the entire period (including 1790), 122 (88 percent) of the 138 public cases that came before the sénéchaussée had already been prosecuted to some extent by a lower-level or exceptional tribunal—confirming that the royal court played an essentially passive role of reviewing and continuing felony cases begun elsewhere.

Far from falling into abeyance, the seigneurial tribunals of the Sarladais appear to have been quite active during this period and even to have undergone some revitalization. Table 7 illustrates that the increase in the annual percentage of public cases first heard by a lower tribunal began in 1772, probably in direct response to the Crown's efforts, in its edict of that year, to free seigneurs of the expenses incurred in the opening stages of prosecution. The royal government's hope was that seigneurs would be less reluctant to initiate costly criminal proceedings and would assume greater responsibility for policing the countryside.[1] Yet one must remember that the above data reveal nothing about the overall prosecution of criminal and civil cases by seigneurial and municipal tribunals. In addition, only 40 of the 109 seigneurial courts known to have existed in 1764 referred cases to the sénéchaussée in the final two decades of the Old Regime. More than half of these 40 referred only one case to the royal court; the 5 most active tribunals generated 42 percent of the total number of referrals. But although the number of active seigneurial tribunals in the Sarladais was declining as the expense of keeping court grew and as inflation further reduced their legal competence, that decline was apparently arrested if

---

1. Mackrell, "Criticism of Seigneurial Justice," 127–31; N. Castan, *Justice et répression en Languedoc,* 126.

TABLE 7

Public Cases Referred to the Sénéchaussée from Seigneurial and Municipal Tribunals

Year	No. of Public Cases	No. of Referrals
1770	5	0
1771	0	0
1772	8	5
1773	7	5
1774	6	4
1770–74	26	14 (53.85%)
1775	6	3
1776	5	4
1777	10	9
1778	6	5
1779	19	10
1775–79	46	31 (67.39%)
1780	7	3
1781	4	4
1782	5	4
1783	5	3
1784	4	3
1780–84	25	17 (68.00%)
1785	8	6
1786	10	5
1787	9	7
1788	7	7
1789	1	1
1785–89	35	26 (74.29%)
Totals	132	88 (66.66%)

SOURCES: See Table 1.

not reversed by the edict of 1772. Research into the seigneurial court archives of the Sarladais can alone confirm or refute these tentative conclusions.

Contemporaries recognized that seigneurial tribunals hesitated to initiate public cases and preferred to concentrate on more lucrative privately initiated criminal suits and civil affairs. When in 1781 a young man wounded in a struggle with two merchant-tanners subsequently died, the prosecutor of the nearby seigneurial jurisdiction of Domme reluctantly initiated proceedings against the two for homicide—only because none of the victim's relatives did so and because he wished to avoid being saddled with the costs of prosecution if the royal prosecutor intervened first. The two accused—who had eluded capture—surrendered one year later after obtaining *lettres de rémission,* arguing in their petition to the sénéchaussée that they had acted in self-defense. They further contended that the relatives of the victim were ineligible for compensation since they had not requested to be made parties civiles until after the case was underway at the expense of the tribunal at Domme. In their petition to the sénéchaussée, the accused further remarked that "it is very well known that seigneurs of high justice are not very anxious to instruct in their own name and at their own expense criminal cases that lead to condemnation to death." [2]

The impulse toward private recourse to royal justice may derive at least in part from the inherent nature of seigneurial justice. Although the bulk of the cases handled by seigneurial tribunals were undoubtedly similar to the privately initiated suits being taken directly before the sénéchaussée (fights, insults, trespassing, depredations by animals), one cannot assume that private plaintiffs were initiating fewer such cases before lower-level courts. But there can also be little doubt that growing numbers of peasants and even sharecroppers were learning to appreciate the benefits of royal justice. The disadvantages of seigneurial justice were many: poorly trained personnel, limited legal jurisdiction, inability to pronounce anything but paltry fines, procedural abuses, and the use of the courts to safeguard the seigneurs' own interests. Finally, more and more seigneurs in some regions apparently were managing their private tribunals as business ventures from which they sought to derive maximum profits. Seigneurial tribunals therefore provided convenient but potentially unsatisfactory justice. [3]

Most criticism of seigneurial justice that developed in the course of the eighteenth century stressed the inefficiency and corruption of the tribunals and the rapacity of their officers. Examples of procedural irregularity and abuses of the rights of defendants did come to light when cases were transferred to the sénéchaussée for continuation. Seigneurial judges and prosecutors apparently used various kinds of pressure, for instance, to make prisoners admit their offenses and name their accomplices. When the owner of a stolen bullock apprehended—with the aid

2. Plainte, January 17, 1782, B 1576, ADD.
3. Poitrineau, *La Vie rurale en Basse-Auvergne,* 640; N. Castan, *Justice et répression en Languedoc,* 111.

of two neighbors—a young *travailleur* attempting to sell the animal at the local fair, they took him to the prison of the tribunal of Saint-Martial. There he was offered wine and cajoled into admitting the theft and begging for forgiveness.[4]

One of the worst offenders in this respect was the seigneurial court of Terrasson. In 1777, three young men were apprehended and prosecuted by the court for theft and vagabondage. Perhaps to simplify his work and to account for several unsolved cases of theft, the judge apparently attempted to bribe the three men into confessing. A witness recalled to verify his testimony explained "that while the accused were in prison, he had heard that the judge of Terrasson had made them drink and had promised them a pair of shoes to make them confess to certain thefts of which they were accused." Although the prisoners in this case resisted the offer of new shoes in exchange for an admission of guilt, others were not as stubborn. A mason accused of stealing wheat in 1771 signed an agreement to repay the victim two hundred livres for the stolen goods when the prosecutor of the jurisdiction of Belvès promised to release him in exchange. Despite his signing, the accused and his case were transferred to the sénéchaussée. In his interrogation, the mason claimed he was innocent of the theft. When shown a copy of his agreement to indemnify the victim, he explained that the prosecutor had come to his cell three separate times to persuade him to sign it. Only when promised immediate release did he sign. Given the conditions under which he was held, the accused added, he would have agreed in writing to pay a larger amount just to get out of prison.[5]

Seigneurial officers had many means at their disposal to build a solid case against suspects they were intent on convicting. The alteration or fabrication of testimony was the most effective way to accomplish this goal. In a case appealed to the tournelle in 1780, a *praticien* accused of theft claimed that a royal notary acting as prosecutor in the jurisdiction of Carlux fabricated the testimony of a woman already dead for five months. Experts called to analyze the document concurred that it was a forgery, and the notary and one accomplice were condemned to death by the tournelle, while another accomplice was sentenced to ten years in the galleys. But seigneurial officers generally

4. Information à St. Martial, March 30, 1778, B 1570, ADD.
5. Récolement, April 2, 1777: Temoin No. 26 de l'information, B 1564, ADD; Information, March 20, 1772, B 1550, ADD.

took less blatant measures to influence the outcome of cases. Witnesses recalled to verify their testimony were often quite surprised to hear the seigneurial court scribe's version of their testimony. Part of the problem arose from the fact that many witnesses testified in patois, which the scribe translated into French. The risk of both willful and unintentional distortion was great. In the only case of lewdness heard by the séné-chaussée during this period, the principal witness complained after hearing her testimony read back to her that she must have explained herself poorly or the judge at Belvès must have misunderstood, for her testimony required extensive revision.[6]

The tribunal at Terrasson seems to have been especially prone to the distortion of testimony. When Pélaud, a tailor accused of theft, confronted the witnesses against him, one of them described how the judge conducting the inquest asked him leading questions in an effort to establish Pélaud's culpability.

> When he had given his deposition, the judge of Terrasson asked him if he had not heard it said that someone from Pélaud's family had stolen a turkey from the Sieur Dubastit and that Pélaud's family enjoyed a bad reputation. The witness said "no," to which the judge replied "But you have heard it said now." The witness replied "yes," and that is what the judge put in his deposition—the hearsay about the theft of the turkey and the bad reputation of Pélaud's family. The witness declared that he had never heard it said that the accused stole anything from anyone and that aside from that, his deposition testimony is truthful.

Given the witnesses' imperfect understanding of the proceedings, many of them perhaps unwittingly allowed their testimony to be manipulated to meet the needs of the prosecution.[7]

As suggested above, the language barrier that separated the majority of the populace from the world of officialdom offered abundant opportunities for distortion and abuse. The patois of the Sarladais, although technically a subdialect of the Limousin dialect, was strongly influenced by that of the Auvergne as well, owing largely to the immigration of many families from that region. Variations even existed within the Sarladais between the patois of the Vézère region, which

6. Tournelle de Sarlat, August 19, 1780, à Bordeaux: Procès-verbal de déclaration du victim (January 30, 1779), Arrêt du parlement (May 11, 1781), B, ADG; Récolement, February 27, 1777, B 1564, ADD.

7. Confrontation de Boudy dit Pélaud, April 20, 1779, B 1569, ADD.

closely resembled that of the Limousin, and that of the Dordogne, which was closer to that of Quercy, Auvergne, and Languedoc. This linguistic complexity posed innumerable difficulties for the officials and commoners involved in royal and seigneurial judicial proceedings. The failure to understand French often prevented witnesses from testifying accurately. In 1775, for example, an inquest held to investigate an offense of insults and menaces was handicapped because many of the boatmen present when a nobleman and a trader quarreled could not understand what was said. One of the boatmen testified that the accused used "lots of words with f. and said certain other things that the witness could not understand because he spoke French, and the witness does not understand this language." [8]

An additional example of the confusion caused by linguistic and cultural differences can be found in the earlier-mentioned case of theft and vagabondage heard by the tribunal at Terrasson. The same judge who tried to extract confessions by giving the suspects wine and promising them new shoes also apparently distorted the testimony of witnesses confused by the technical language of the court. The confusion centered on the interpretation of the term *vagabond,* which was accorded a precise meaning by the royal statutes governing the repression of vagabondage and mendicity. The Declaration of August 3, 1764, defined vagabonds as "persons who for the last six months have not exercised either a profession or a trade, who possess no status or property for subsistence, and who cannot be vouched for or have their good conduct and morality certified by anyone worthy of respect." [9]

The responses of the witnesses called before the sénéchaussée to confirm their testimony—given in patois, translated into French, and then read back to them in patois—reveal that they had only an approximate idea of what *vagabond* meant as used by the judge at Terrasson. One witness, a merchant, protested that "he did not know the term *vagabond* when he gave his deposition and consequently did not know if the accused were such, because they lived in Terrasson." Another explained "that although she said she knew they were vagabonds, she did not know the full sense of the word." Yet another wit-

8. Marc Delbreil, *Le Dialecte sarladais ou patois du Périgord-Noir, ses origines, ses transformations* (Bordeaux, 1938), 23–25; Information, December 22, 1775, B 1560, ADD.

9. This definition is quoted in Jean-Pierre Gutton, *La Société et les pauvres: L'Exemple de la généralité de Lyon, 1534–1789* (Paris, 1971), 441.

ness told the court that when she had described the accused as vagabonds, "she only wished to say that the accused wandered about
[*vaguaient*] in the public square of Terrasson and performed odd jobs
for this person and that." A tailor who testified stated that when he had
said he knew the three were vagabonds, he had only meant "that they
were sometimes here, sometimes there, but that they ordinarily resided
in Terrasson." Even a *praticien* stated "that when he gave his deposition, he did not know the significance of the term *vagabond* and, consequently, whether the accused were such." [10]

Much more was involved in this case, however, than simply the
misunderstanding of legal jargon. Of the thirty-five witnesses summoned to the inquest in Terrasson, twenty-four were recalled before the
sénéchaussée. And of those twenty-four, fully nineteen modified their
testimony in such a way as to attenuate the gravity of the charges
against the accused. Many of the witnesses asserted that they must have
explained themselves poorly or the judge must have heard them incor-
rectly, because they had never heard it said that the accused were
known thieves until the judge suggested as much to them. An *ardoisier*
(tiler) testified that when the judge had asked him if he considered one
of the defendants to be "un honnête homme," he had replied simply
that he knew the suspect to be neither "honnête" nor "méchant." He
had not said, as his testimony stated, that the accused had a bad reputation and was known in public as a thief. One of the accused, Etienne
Lasserre, insisted in his interrogation before the sénéchaussée "that the
judge must have misunderstood his reply or inserted diverse things on
his own that he, the accused, would never have admitted to if he had
understood them even when they read his testimony to him." [11] His assertion seems all the more plausible because in the same interrogation,
Lasserre, after denying that he had confessed to several other thefts,
freely admitted that he had stolen wood and hay from a neighbor's
meadow—the crime for which he was arrested. It seems clear that the
judge and scribe at Terrasson had manipulated the testimony of witnesses and defendants to strengthen the prosecution's case.

But the motives of the witnesses who modified their testimony are
also suspect. In many respects, this case exemplifies the ambivalence of
community members toward the long-tolerated petty thieves in their

10. Récolement, April 2–21, 1777, B 1564, ADD.
11. *Ibid.;* Interrogatoire, May 17, 1777, B 1564, ADD.

midst. On the one hand, they shared the initial impulse to blame scapegoats for any and all thefts and losses recently occurring in the area. On the other hand, when they came to realize the gravity of the charges against the accused, they tended to vacillate. Although many witnesses could claim that they did not appreciate the significance of the terms used, few could pretend they did not know the gravity of the charge of theft. When recalled, the fifth witness lamely explained that he had said he knew the accused were thieves only because of their reputation for petty theft. A tailor insisted that he had not described the three men as known thieves; he nevertheless admitted having heard that Lasserre had stolen pumpkins and grapes when passing by the fields. Even the *praticien* contended that they were not really thieves—although they had taken a few armfuls of hay, straw, and wood.

In the past, neighbors had largely tolerated the defendants' petty thefts. One woman explained that she did not consider the accused thieves "par rumeur public" or otherwise, although she, too, knew that Lasserre had stolen hay and straw left in the fields and sold them at the market to support himself. In fact, her son had caught Lasserre in the act of stealing turnips and, after administering several *coups de baton*, had let him go. In short, many of the witnesses seemed to regret their earlier cooperation in the inquest. They conceded that the defendants were rumored to be petty thieves, but implied that such behavior did not really constitute theft—perhaps because it was common practice and similar to the customs of gleaning and collection of windfallen timber.

In some instances seigneurial tribunal officers blatantly influenced the testimony of witnesses. In 1777, a witness recalled by the sénéchaussée in a case of homicide revised and added to his earlier testimony, explaining that the changes were necessary because one of the seigneurial officers of the jurisdiction of Auriac had told him to depose in conformity with the other witnesses or he, too, would be named in the criminal charges. In another such case, the community of Domme finally found the opportunity to expel two young *travailleurs* who were apparently habitual petty thieves when, in 1781, they were implicated in an incident of theft on the highroad with assault and battery. When the initial inquest failed to produce sufficient evidence, the prosecutor of Domme at first called for a monitoire but later evidently resorted to bribery. According to both accused, several of the key witnesses were their sworn enemies and paid by the mayor and prosecutor of Domme to testify against them.[12]

The obvious disadvantages to defendants in seigneurial proceedings were inherent in the inquisitorial criminal procedure employed throughout the entire judicial system. But private plaintiffs may have been discouraged from initiating misdemeanor suits before seigneurial tribunals for other, less obvious reasons. Part of the difficulty of obtaining a fair trial in these tribunals derived from the fact that the officers were often related to the accused. In 1771, for example, a bourgeois innkeeper first took his suit for *excès-réels* before the court of Beynac. But when he learned that the judge, prosecutor, and scribe were all related to the suspect, he appealed directly to the sénéchaussée, explaining in his petition that in Beynac he feared "that matters would not have been conducted with the exactitude necessary in such a case." When Guillaume Maraval came before the sénéchaussée in 1781 to initiate proceedings against several *notables* of Lanquais, who had sounded the tocsin and incited a crowd to attack his house, he stated that he would have been unable to obtain a fair hearing in the jurisdiction of Lanquais because all of the officers there were related to the *notables:* The judge was nephew of one of the accused, the scribe was his close relative, and the lieutenant of the judge was related to the same man by marriage. The acting prosecutor, although unrelated to any of the accused, was beholden to another of them. Maraval therefore recognized that his best chances of success lay with royal justice.[13]

Plaintiffs who initiated criminal proceedings before a local tribunal also ran the risk of personal violence from the family and friends of the accused. Nor were judicial officers immune from violence. In 1773, the jurisdiction of Beynac charged a former soldier and a boatman with *assassinat,* held an inquest, and ordered their arrest. Almost three years later, the two men were captured by the maréchaussée and transferred to Beynac for continuation of the case. But the seigneurial prosecutor was not pleased to see the prisoners arrive. Within ten days, he obtained permission to have them temporarily transferred to Sarlat be-

12. Récolement, September 20, 1777, B 1565, ADD; Présidial: Confrontation, December 13–15, 1782, Confrontation de Jean-Louis Fabre, December 12, 14, 23, 1782, all in B 1671, ADD.

13. Langbein, *Prosecuting Crime,* 246; Plainte, n.d., B 1547, ADD; Plainte, December 27, 1781, B 1575, ADD.

cause of the poor condition of the local prison and because he had been threatened by their relatives. Furthermore, he petitioned the judge of Beynac to have the case definitively transferred to the distant séné-chaussée for continuation.[14] Other officers were physically harmed. In 1787, an angry mason first insulted the seigneurial judge of Monfer-rand and then seriously wounded him with a rock while the judge was performing his police functions.[15]

The sénéchaussée occasionally intervened to discipline seigneurial court officers responsible for procedural irregularities. In the above case at Beynac, the judge heeded the warning of his prosecutor and or-dered the case sent before the sénéchaussée. But when the royal prose-cutor examined the transcript of the inquest held at Beynac, he discov-ered not only that the judge had taken the depositions of the witnesses in the presence of one of the plaintiffs but also that the prosecutor had coached the witnesses in their testimony. The royal court therefore summoned the judge for interrogation. After hearing his responses, the court annulled the inquest held at Beynac and ordered a new inquest by the sénéchaussée at the judge's personal expense. In a similar action, the sénéchaussée annulled an inquest and interrogation conducted by the judge of Carlux because, among other irregularities, he had failed to interrogate the suspect within twenty-four hours of his arrest. The royal prosecutor ordered the entire case reheard by the sénéchaus-sée at the expense of the judge.[16]

Although such measures could prove humiliating and costly for seigneurial judges, they were much less drastic than the action taken against the judge and prosecutor of Montignac, who, in 1770, were formally arraigned by the sénéchaussée for misconduct in office. As noted earlier, the officers were charged with failing to enforce police regulations on weights and measures used in the market and with toler-ating the monopolistic practices of three local merchants, one of whom

14. Plainte du procureur d'office de Beynac au juge de Beynac, January 10, 1776, B 1561, ADD. Also see Tournelle de Sarlat, September 27, 1776, B, ADG.

15. The sénéchaussée subsequently condemned the mason (in absentia) to life in the galleys for attacking a judicial officer. See Récolement, April 15, 1788, B 1594, ADD; Sentence définitive, April 26, 1788, B 1642, ADD.

16. Tournelle de Sarlat, September 27, 1776: Requis du procureur du roy (May 17, 1776), Interrogatoire de Redon (May 22, 1776), and Appointement du lieutenant crimi-nel du Sénéchal (June 8, 1776), B, ADG; Requis du procureur du roy, February 26, 1779, B 1568, ADD.

was the prosecutor's brother-in-law. The royal prosecutor complained that they also neglected their judicial duties.

> It is likewise with criminal justice, which the same officers administer as poorly as they perform their police duties, even to the point where assaults, murders, suicides, young girls killing their offspring, and a number of thefts have been committed within the jurisdiction. These judicial officers were satisfied only to initiate proceedings and then to let the cases go unpursued. Those accused of some of these crimes were arrested and imprisoned, but they are gone now and no one knows quite how or why this happened. In other cases, the same officers were so grossly negligent that they allowed guilty persons the time to flee and then only initiated proceedings after their escape.

The sénéchaussée summoned both officers to answer the charges against them. The judge admitted that a great number of crimes had gone unprosecuted in their jurisdiction during the preceding years, but insisted that the cases they did prosecute were pursued until definitive sentencing. The prosecutor, on the other hand, insisted that since he had been in office only two serious crimes had been committed—one theft by a domestique and one infanticide—both of which were prosecuted.[17]

The risk of procedural abuse was real, but a potentially greater hazard in using seigneurial courts derived from the fact that they were privately owned and staffed by personnel answerable primarily to the seigneurs who employed them. Seigneurial justice was, in effect, predicated upon a hierarchical social structure in which those with power possessed the means to ensure their dominance. Such a court system could prove useful to litigants of equal social status, but a peasant, a sharecropper, or even a local bourgeois could find it frustrating to initiate proceedings against a local seigneur in his own court. Those who chose to avail themselves of seigneurial justice when their opponent was the seigneur did so with the implicit understanding that they recognized and, to a certain degree, submitted to the status quo. The only alternatives were private retaliation and recourse to royal justice.

Intimidation by seigneurs and malfeasance by their judicial officers

---

17. Villepelet, *Inventaire sommaire,* 162; Interrogatoire de Dujarric, July 24, 1770, Interrogatoire de Merilhon, July 25, 1770, both in B 1545, ADD.

were naturally most acute (and visible) in cases where individuals dared to initiate proceedings against either group. Two examples illustrate the risks involved in such a course of action. In 1787, Jean Lalande, a bourgeois from Auriac, attempted to bring suit against the judge of the tribunal of Lafaye-d'Auriac in his own court for insults and menaces. According to the plaintiff's petition, their dispute began four years earlier when Lalande, then in charge of revising the taille rôle, revised the rate of the Sieur Borédon de Labrousse, a bourgeois who leased the château of Lafaye and its lands and served as judge of the tribunal. Soon afterwards, Lalande also challenged Labrousse's right to speak in a community deliberation held in the public square of Auriac. When Labrousse rashly responded by insulting Lalande in public, Lalande forced the judge to submit the affair to informal mediation and succeeded in collecting damages. This "ménagement" further angered and shamed Labrousse because normally only social equals were able to constrain opponents to submit to mediation, whereas inferiors were usually obliged to acquiesce quietly to intimidation. In response, Labrousse brought to bear his considerable influence as seigneurial judge in an effort to redress the balance of power and honor upset by Lalande's challenge.

Their quarrel came to a head in October, 1787, when Labrousse encountered Lalande and his drovers taking wine to market. Labrousse made no attempt to curb his horse when it nearly trampled Lalande, who was on foot. Lalande protested, but Labrousse said he could ride his horse anywhere on the road he pleased and that Lalande "was not fit to order him around." When Lalande continued to object, Labrousse lost his temper and shouted: "F. rascal, f. rogue, f. bugger. I will find you at the right time and place and then f. give you twenty blows with my rod to pay you back for your good intentions in quoting me at a higher rate for farming the estate of Lafaye." Labrousse raised his *baton* to strike Lalande, but realized he had already compromised himself before the drovers, who had heard his threats. He therefore turned to them and, "in a tone of *honnêteté*," attempted to recruit them as witnesses in his favor, claiming that the plaintiff had thrown stones at him. "To persuade them to see things from his point of view," Lalande reported, "he told them he was judge of Auriac and that in this capacity he could be of great service to them." When the drovers refused to accept his story, Labrousse again grew angry and said "he was going to break their master's head within the hour and that if he failed this time, he would blow his brains out the next time he saw him." [18]

Afterwards the judge boasted in public that he would trample Lalande with his horse and do everything in his power "pour lui faire manger son bien." He soon found a pretext to threaten Lalande with an injunction, which the latter countered by attempting to bring criminal charges against the judge for the above incident. He went to the cabaret owned by Labrousse where the tribunal normally held its sessions and tried to file his complaint with the acting prosecutor. But Labrousse and the regular prosecutor arrived and threatened to order Lalande's arrest if he did not leave immediately. Thwarted in his actions, Lalande consequently appealed directly to the sénéchaussée, where he filed his complaint against Labrousse for "insults and ill treatment," as well as abuse of office. [19]

In an example of even more blatant intimidation—this time involving a noble seigneur—a bourgeois from the parish of Saint-Germain brought his suit for *excès-réels* directly to the sénéchaussée. Considering the wealth and influence of his opponent, there can be little doubt why Pierre Boussac avoided the seigneurial court of Saint-Germain: Messire Raymond de Coustin de Caumont, count of Bourzolles and seigneur of Prats, Montagnac, Saint-Germain, Mespoulets, and other places, apparently enjoyed almost absolute control over the parish. His dispute with Boussac was longstanding and essentially economic in origin. Toward the end of December, 1783, Boussac rented his furnished country home to the count for one year only. In the course of that year, he encountered financial difficulties. Wishing to marry and live in the family home, he notified the count midway through the year that the lease would not be renewed. The count had wished for quite some time to live in Boussac's house and therefore objected, telling Boussac that to evict him the bourgeois must take him to court. Boussac had doubted the wisdom of leasing his house to the count in the first place, but through a combination of blandishments and bullying, the count's agent had persuaded him "that it was always advantageous to oblige his seigneur, given the amenities and advantages that could be derived there-

18. Plainte, May 10, 1788, B 1594, ADD.
19. *Ibid.*

from." Now the same agent tried to mediate between the two parties, but Boussac rejected the proposed compromise of allowing the count to stay another year at a higher rent.[20]

The count's motive in refusing to leave was clearly vindictive. One year earlier, Boussac had refused to loan the count his oxen to transport forage, and the count had taken offense and promised to avenge himself. When Boussac asked him to vacate the house after one year, the count saw his opportunity and replied: "Hold on, jean f., you made me wait long enough to get your house. Now I will not leave for nine years. You can take me to court three years at Saint-Germain, three years at Sarlat, and three years at Bordeaux. I know that I will lose at every step of the way, but I am willing to pay the costs." Boussac replied: "I don't give a f. about your justice at Saint-Germain. You have all the officers in your pocket, and they will keep me there for six years. So it won't be at all before them that I will have you summoned but at Sarlat." The count retorted that he would be satisfied to keep Boussac in litigation only three years at Sarlat and another three at Bordeaux, for the entire while he would be living in Boussac's home without paying rent.[21]

From that point onward, their quarrel escalated rapidly. The count boasted in public that he would live in Boussac's house as long as he pleased. "I want to make Boussac 'eat' all of his property, including that of his sisters," he was heard to say. According to the original lease, Boussac reserved the right to use half of the barn and wine store. When the count refused him permission to do so, Boussac was forced to thresh his grain on the public square of Saint-Germain and subsequently lost a large portion of it, as well as much of his wine, through spoilage. Moreover, the count refused to surrender the furniture and family papers in the house or the oxen and forage in the barn. When the lease finally expired, Boussac, "convinced that every citizen can appeal with confidence to the authority of justice despite the authority of individual seigneurs," initiated civil proceedings against the count before the présidial.[22]

On February 24, 1785, Boussac obtained a court order requiring

20. Information, June 16, 1785, B 1602, ADD.
21. *Ibid.*
22. Plainte, February 26, 1785, B 1602, ADD.

the count to vacate the premises. Upon receiving the writ, the count not only menaced the bailiff but also went looking for Boussac. When the bourgeois saw the nobleman approach, he began to lift his hat in salute, but the count slapped him with such force that his hat fell to the ground. When he bent over to retrieve it, the count took Boussac's *baton* from him and broke it over his head with two quick blows. None of the inhabitants of Saint-Germain dared to come to the bourgeois' aid. Boussac stumbled to the home of the curé for the care of his wounds, leaving his hat lying in the mud, but even the town surgeon refused to come examine him. Boussac therefore traveled to Sarlat to obtain a doctor's report on his injuries and, while there, brought criminal charges against the count for assault.[23]

Refusing to submit to intimidation and recognizing the futility of challenging the count in his own seigneurial court, Boussac turned to the only ally available. Royal justice and the rule of objective laws offered an alternative to individuals wishing to extract themselves either from the moral economy of the popular classes or from the bullying of local seigneurs. Just as the person who allowed himself to be the target of a charivari or *azouade* and acquiesced to the crowd's demands effectively recognized the legitimacy of those demands and the right of the crowd to dictate his personal behavior, a commoner who accepted aggression by the rich and powerful effectively acknowledged his own social inferiority and the legitimacy of a hierarchical structure in which wealth and personalized ties of loyalty and protection counted most.

Boussac apparently attempted his own limited campaign of intimidation by resorting to symbolic violence against hats. According to the count, the bourgeois attacked his antagonist's *valet de chambre* in Saint-Germain, took his hat from him, and threw it to the ground. Boussac then challenged anyone to pick it up. He and his allies frightened the count's tenants so much that none of them had the courage to touch the hat. In his petition to the court, the count stated that the hat "undoubtedly would remain on the public square until it rotted" and requested that the sénéchaussée verify this fact as evidence. The court officers acceded to his request and accordingly went to Saint-Germain, where they drew up an official statement confirming that the hat was

23. *Ibid.*

indeed still lying there and ordered that it be confiscated as evidence in the case.[24]

In this case, more was at stake than a question of honor. Boussac and his lawyer seem to have appreciated the historic dimensions of their struggle, for their final petition to the court in 1791 resounded with the spirit of the times.

> The Sieur Boussac has the honor to seek recourse from you and to implore your justice against the unheard of vexations, examples of which would be difficult to find in the times when feudalism reigned with the greatest sway.
>
> Moreover, what did conventions that he did not wish to observe matter to the Sieur Coustin? What did it matter to him once he was in the Sieur Boussac's house that the Sieur Boussac had the right to reclaim it? Did the Sieur Coustin wish to found his rights on justice? Did he know any other right than that of force and violence? Did not his status as Seigneur and his wealth assure him the resources needed to stifle the complaints of an unfortunate?

Given the lawlessness of the count and his ability to obstruct justice, the plaintiff determined to have recourse directly to the sénéchaussée because, as he explained in his petition, he recognized from experience that "this course is the shortest, and your justice assures him of success."[25]

The count also recognized the importance of the contest and brought to bear his considerable power to assure a favorable outcome. When the sénéchaussée held its first inquest early in 1785, only five witnesses came forward to testify, all of whom denied any knowledge of the offense. As a result, Boussac requested the publication of a monitoire, which produced sixty-two witnesses subsequently assigned to testify in a second inquest. As they made their depositions, the full extent of the count's efforts to bribe and intimidate witnesses became apparent. According to a *laboureur,* everyone knew that the count had beaten Boussac and that he had paid six livres to each of the five witnesses called to the first inquest so that they could dine in Sarlat, cautioning them "to be careful not to say too much." The count let it be known in public that anyone who worked for Boussac or testified in his favor would be chased from the parish along with Boussac and the

---

24. Plainte du Seigneur Comte de Bourzolles, April 3, 1785, Procès-verbal, April 4, 1785, both *ibid.*

25. Plainte de Boussac aux M. les juges du tribunal de Belvès séant à Monpazier, February 17, 1791, *ibid.*

curé, who had come to his aid. The count's cook testified that even before the first inquest, the count's agent had reminded her that "servants are sworn to keep secret everything that takes place at their master's." A *laboureur* from the next parish had heard "that a man from Saint-Germain would rather be damned than displease the Sieur de Bourzolles" and that Boussac's own servant had testified against him for fear of the count. Another witness confirmed as much when she testified "that she would prefer to be damned than to tell the truth about all of this business, that she did not wish to attract the hate of the Sieur de Bourzolles for the rest of her life." Her position is understandable considering the extremes to which the count resorted. An employee of the taille from Sarlat testified that while making his rounds in the parish he heard "that the tenants of the said Sieur de Bourzolles did not venture to say anything against him for fear that he would double their rent." [26]

The most revealing testimony came from Bernard Grivet, a schoolmaster originally from Béarn, who apparently first came forward in response to the monitoire. The count learned that he had done so and summoned him to the house the very next day. After sending away the servants, the count asked him if he had indeed responded to the call for information. Grivet replied that he felt obliged to respond to the monitoire and had told the curé what he knew—that the count had beaten Boussac and then bragged about it. "Now the main question," said the nobleman, "is knowing whether you wish to make your retraction. If you do not do so, I will blow your brains out or will have it done by one of my relatives. I will have you run out of the parish. And do not even think about teaching in the vicinity." Grivet feared that the count was serious and therefore promised to retract his statement. On June 5, the count again called him to the house and asked if he was an "honnête homme" and prepared to keep his word. Grivet assented, so the count summoned a notary, who prepared an act of retraction for the schoolteacher to sign. [27]

But the strength of religious conviction that led Grivet and the other witnesses to risk retaliation and reply to the monitoire induced Grivet to go immediately to the rectory and reveal to the curé what had just occurred. The next day his conscience still troubled him, so he

26. Information par addition, June 16–27, 1785, Continuation d'information, July 3, 1785, both *ibid.*

27. Information par addition, June 16, 1785, *ibid.*

went directly to the curé of Sarlat to make another confession, taking care to travel at night to prevent the count from knowing of his mission. When word spread in the parish that Grivet had retracted his testimony, the local innkeeper reproached him for his cowardice. "What would you have had me do?" Grivet asked him. "Would you have let him cut your throat or blow your brains out?" But he added confidentially that he had already gone to Sarlat to deny his retraction, saying "that if he had two souls he would risk one for Monsieur de Bourzolles, but since he had only one, he wished to save it." [28]

The role of parish curés was decisive in persuading witnesses to come forward. By aiding Boussac when he was assaulted, the curé of Saint-Germain exposed himself to the ire of the count, who threatened to have him chased from the parish. But the curé of the nearby parish of Allas took the most public and decisive stance against the nobleman when he read the monitoire from his pulpit on three consecutive Sundays. Without mentioning anyone by name, the curé left no doubt in the minds of his parishioners that he meant the count of Bourzolles. The count therefore brought criminal charges against him for "insulting references in the publication of the monitoire and abuse of office." [29] A joint session of the *officialité* (ecclesiastic tribunal) of the diocese of Sarlat and the sénéchaussée heard the case, with both the canon of the cathedral and the lieutenant particulier assesseur criminel presiding.

The curé of Allas, upon reading the monitoire for the second time, allegedly had warned the listeners of their duty to come forward under pain of excommunication, and then added that they should not let fear of powerful men prevent them from telling the truth. According to the accusation, he was even more explicit on the third Sunday, telling his flock they owed rent to their seigneurs, nothing more, and haranguing them with inflammatory words.

> What is more serious than to see a man who by his status ought to be the protector of the people become their persecutor and oppressor without their consent, maintaining himself in a house by force and seizing furniture and papers? Do you want to know why the earth was given to seigneurs? It is in order to protect the people . . . you must not imagine that it is to vex you. Know your rights. Do not let the seigneurs walk on you. They will succeed in bringing back the old times and will make you work for them if

28. *Ibid.*
29. Information, June 22, 1785, B 1589, ADD.

you let them do it. We are no longer in the old times when seigneurs invaded the houses of individuals to carry off by force whatever they pleased, exercising all sorts of cruelties and vexations. These odious privileges were abolished by our kings. The submission that Saint Paul prescribed toward authorities must not be applied to tyrants and persecutors. You owe nothing to these tyrants that should stop you from coming forward to reveal what you know. Shake off the yoke that they would like to impose on you. Raise yourself up and do not spare them.

The curé denied that his sermon included any such "seditious discourse" and insisted that he never' mentioned anyone by name. The sénéchaussée dropped the charges of insults and sedition against the curé, but evidently found sufficient proof to pronounce him guilty of exceeding the bounds of his ministry and condemned him to pay all expenses incurred by the count in the course of the trial.[30]

With the aid of the curés of Saint-Germain and Allas and the publication of the monitoire, Boussac effectively marshaled sufficient evidence to support his case and to expose the threats and bribes used by the count to suborn the witnesses. As a result, the sénéchaussée issued a warrant for the nobleman's arrest on June 30, 1785. But on July 2, the count exercised his privilege as a noble and appealed directly to the Parlement of Bordeaux. After almost five years, the parlement annulled not only the sénéchaussée ordinance that had authorized the monitoire but also the arrest warrant; it did, however, recognize the remainder of the case as valid. Consequently, in early 1791 Boussac petitioned the newly organized tribunal of Sarlat to reopen the case. Permission was granted, and a new inquest was held on June 2 of that year. The archives do not record the outcome of this protracted struggle, but the count did accomplish what he had boasted in 1784: to embroil Boussac in legal proceedings for at least six years and to cripple him with expenses. Furthermore, in 1791 he was still living in Boussac's paternal home without paying rent and without making any repairs in the intervening years.[31]

Although this case may not be typical, it does graphically illustrate that seigneurs—although surely not the only persons guilty of intimidation—were able to wield this weapon effectively. Persons who found

30. Interrogatoire, February 7, 1786, B 1589, ADD; Sentence définitive, September 18, 1786, B 1641, ADD.
31. Plainte de Boussac au Tribunal de Belvès, February 17, 1791, Plainte au Tribunal de Sarlat, June 1, 1791, both in B 1602, ADD.

themselves the target of their intimidation had three basic choices: Those with sufficient money could appeal to royal justice, whereas those without money were forced to submit or to retaliate. This darker side of seigneurial justice generally did not emerge in police matters or in litigation between parties of roughly equal social status, but rather in affairs involving litigants of unequal rank and especially in cases concerning seigneurial rights and duties. Royal justice did not guarantee equality before the law and was hardly free of bias; nonetheless, in comparison with the highly personalized justice of seigneurial tribunals, it could constitute a decidedly attractive alternative.[32]

The rich and powerful, regardless of whether they held the right to maintain a private court, naturally possessed resources that enabled them to excel at the tactic of intimidation. In contrast, men of modest means could call upon public opinion and bring to bear community pressure for accommodation; in extreme cases, they might attempt to mobilize communally enforced punitive sanctions. But such measures were powerless against persons at both extremes of the social scale—wealthy *notables* and beggars, both of whom stood, in a sense, outside the community and could afford to flout or ignore social pressures. When all else failed, commoners could use the threat of personal violence to intimidate an opponent of superior social status, but they had little other leverage. Nicole Castan contends that the prevalence of intimidation may have grown in Languedoc toward the end of the Old Regime as the mechanism of internal regulation deteriorated and the fear of reprisals increasingly paralyzed judicial action.[33] Intimidation continued to be one of the factors that victims in the Sarladais weighed before seeking legal redress, but it cannot be said to have increased or decreased during this period.

A broad cross section of society still resorted to violence, most frequently to discourage victims of aggression from denouncing them. The wealthy undoubtedly used economic pressure on a quotidian basis to accomplish their purposes without resort to cruder tactics in most cases. But among the region's upper echelons, nobles seem to have been more inclined than bourgeois to threaten and actually employ violence to intimidate their foes. An incident that occurred in Belvès in 1772 clearly illustrates the violence of which young noblemen were capable,

32. De Tocqueville, *The Old Regime and the French Revolution*, 191.
33. N. Castan, *Justice et répression en Languedoc*, 91.

as well as the difficulty of compelling them to abide by informal settlements. The affair began when the Sieurs Bonfils and Sauret went to Jean Brisse's cabaret one evening, ordered wine, and began to harass the serving girl. Brisse's wife intervened, so they grabbed her and tried to kiss her. When she resisted, Bonfils punched her in the face. At that point, Brisse, a former army sergeant, returned to his cabaret. Bonfils, armed with a sword, challenged him to step outside and insulted him in the grossest terms. Brisse, who was unarmed, declined the challenge but the next day, when he met the young noble on the public square of Belvès, reproached him publicly for his conduct. In response, Bonfils, Sauret, and two other young nobles armed with *batons* went to Brisse's cabaret that evening and beat him and his wife senseless. When Brisse's partner and his wife intervened, they, too, were beaten.[34]

All four victims of the assault brought suit before the sénéchaussée. The friends and relatives of the young noblemen—including the Demoiselle Delphine Bontemps—arranged "to assuage this affair." In exchange for the payment of one hundred écus in damages, the plaintiffs agreed to drop their suit and take no further action on the condition that none of the accused or anyone acting on their behalf would repeat the offense. But Bonfils and the Sieur Boyer, another of the accused, resented being forced to settle the affair informally and boasted that they would have their revenge. When the Demoiselle Bontemps reproached Bonfils for the trouble and expense to which she had gone in arranging the settlement, he vowed to make Brisse pay. True to his word, he and Boyer ambushed Brisse outside of town and beat him with their *batons* while holding him on the ground by the hair.[35]

The former sergeant refused to be intimidated and again brought suit against the noblemen for both incidents. His fellow parishioners, however, were not as brave and refused to testify at the inquest. As a result, Brisse requested and obtained a monitoire, which did compel several people to reveal what they knew. One of them, a domestique, explained to the curé that she had not testified at the inquest because "the Demoiselle Boyer, mother of the [Sieur] Boyer, sent for me and forbade me to say anything."[36] The sénéchaussée subsequently assigned the individuals who had come forward to be witnesses in a second in-

34. Plainte, March 17, 1772, B 1552, ADD.
35. Plainte de Jean Brisse, August 1, 1772, Procès-verbal, August 2, 1772, both *ibid.*
36. Révélations devant M. Ducluzeau, curé de Belvès, October 4, 1772, *ibid.*

quest, which resulted in the issuance of an arrest warrant against three of the young men. No record exists of the outcome of the case, which may well have again been settled out of court. The defiant cabaret owner at least gained what must have been the considerable satisfaction of seeing a royal bailiff stand in the public square of Belvès and read a warrant for the arrest of the young nobles.

A similar incident occurred thirteen years later in the town of Molières, when three sieurs assaulted a young locksmith. Antoine Soulier had completed some work for the Sieur Gauliac de Laborie six months earlier and evidently was too insistent on being paid. When Gauliac encountered the locksmith and his father in the street, he attacked them with his *baton*, but the neighbors intervened. So the next evening, Gauliac and his son, aided by the Sieur Chausard de Lafusterie, attacked Soulier in his bed, beating him with their *batons* and warning him that they "would cut him into pieces" if he and his family did not leave town. Soulier and his father nonetheless brought suit against all three assailants, claiming that the motives of the accused were quite clear: "It is very easy to guess the intent of this reckless action. Gauliac was told that the plaintiffs intended to bring suit against him for the assault of which he was guilty the previous day. And to cut short an affair that could only turn to his disadvantage, he imagined that by associating himself with Lafusterie, a very robust and indelicate man, he could force the plaintiffs to flee the area." The sénéchaussée authorized an inquest, but the final outcome of the case is uncertain. Whether it was settled informally or discontinued for lack of funds, the plaintiffs did successfully enlist the aid of royal justice to defy the *notables* of their community.[37]

Aggressors used intimidation to dissuade victims from legal recourse, frighten witnesses into silence, and cow judicial officers into inaction. Even royal judicial officers were subject to intimidation. In 1774, an accused who was the former domestique of a sénéchaussée counselor threw a rock through the magistrate's window and vowed that the officer "would only die by his hands, that he would kill him wherever he found him."[38] But anyone resorting to intimidation also risked driving an opponent into the arms of official justice for protection.

37. Plainte, April 14, 1785, B 1585, ADD.
38. Plainte du Sieur de Pignol, January 20, 1775, B 1558, ADD.

Seigneurial justice constituted a truly viable alternative to royal justice for seigneurs and for commoners involved in petty disputes that did not challenge the status quo. Intimidation was a tool wielded most successfully by those already in possession of economic or political power and social prestige. The balance of the population sought justice through informal communal sanctions and dispute settlement, which proved reliable in disputes between community members of comparable social status. But when involved in highly unequal contests, they could either submit to their superiors or appeal to an external source of justice, the sénéchaussée. The option of last resort was retaliation—the weapon of frustrated or dispossessed persons who looked no further than the act of retaliation itself. Whereas direct action in affairs of honor was essentially "social" in its goal, performed openly, measured, and condoned by public opinion, retaliation was generally an immoderate, antisocial act performed surreptitiously. Most acts of retaliation took place under the cover of darkness, for the culprit could not readily expect social sanctioning of his desperate act. In theory at least, retaliation constituted a distinct alternative to all other forms of justice because it was essentially an individualized form of justice, an act of defiance against the entire social order. But because retaliation offered little beyond an immediate but too-often fleeting sense of satisfaction, it was employed rarely and in last resort.

Retaliation took many different forms, from ambush to violence against property, but most often consisted of actual or threatened personal violence. In a typical example, an ironmonger arrested in 1778 for theft who was reputedly a member of a band of thieves was heard to mutter that the man responsible for denouncing him would repent, because he had five companions who would avenge him. Similarly, the brother of a young *travailleur* imprisoned for theft on the highroad warned one of the many witnesses who came forward to testify that when his brother was released, "the inhabitants of the village would all be sorry that he had spent a year in prison."[39] Threats by persons living on the margins of society—especially vagabonds, itinerant merchants, soldiers, and convicts—were considered particularly serious because such persons not only had little to lose and a reputation for violence

39. Présidial: Continuation d'information, January 21, June 4, July 19–21, 1782, B 1671, ADD.

but also escaped the network of communal sanctions that normally regulated the behavior of the sedentary populace.

Of all retaliatory acts against property, arson was regarded as most serious. In the dispute between the count of Bourzolles and Boussac, the frustrated bourgeois at one point threatened to set fire to his house rather than allow the count to remain there. The count generously replied that if Boussac really wished to do so, "he would surround the house with brushwood to help [Boussac] make a better fire." When two brothers quarreled over their family inheritance in 1789, the younger brother—realizing that he had no legal claim to his father's house— refused a proposed accommodation and threatened to shoot his elder brother and set fire to the house.[40]

As opposed to such threats, the action of a *sabotier* (sabot maker) who attempted to set fire to his landlord's house and barn can truly be characterized as an act of retaliation. On the morning of February 5, 1789, the sabotier learned from the judge of Terrasson that he had no grounds for legal recourse in his dispute with his landlord, Beune. He therefore vowed "that he was going to carry out justice himself." Later that day, after drinking at the local cabaret, he told a peasant "that they did not want to judge his case and that he was resolved to act as judge himself." He added that "Beune was a f. rascal, a f. thief, and that he wanted to take three or four balls of sulphur to set afire and throw onto the four corners of Beune's house." He additionally swore that "he did not give a f. about anything, but that when he would have burned everything down he would be master and would have won his case." That evening, the drunken sabotier climbed onto the gallery of his own house and threw a bucketful of live coals and a burning plank onto the roof of his landlord's house next door. But because the roof was covered in stone tiles, the coals and plank smoldered harmlessly until Beune and his domestiques extinguished them. The would-be arsonist shouted to them: "You are nothing but thieves and rabble. I failed this time, but you cannot always keep watch. I will not fail the next time." Before he could carry out his threat, Beune denounced him to the seigneurial tribunal at Terrasson.[41]

40. Information, June 16, 1785, B 1602, ADD; Plainte, December 5, 1789, B 1596, ADD.
41. Plainte, February 6, 1789, Information à Terrasson, February 7, 1789, B 1598, ADD.

In the above examples, disgruntled individuals threatened to resort to drastic action only when other avenues of recourse had been closed to them. Boussac entertained the idea of arson after he learned that the count had successfully bribed all the witnesses at the first inquest. At that point, even the sénéchaussée seemed incapable of giving him justice. The younger brother who knew he had no legal claim to his father's inheritance swore to gain at least a modicum of satisfaction by depriving his sibling of the patrimony. And the sabotier who actually committed the only act of arson prosecuted by the sénéchaussée during this period did so with the express intention of attaining what the courts would not or could not provide. He vowed to act as his own judge and executioner in order to "carry out justice himself."

Retaliatory violence against property naturally focused on those possessions most coveted in an agricultural society. Besides the house and barn, other common targets were livestock (horses and pigs) and orchards (nut and fruit trees). Because dogs constituted, in a sense, an extension of an individual's persona, they were often the target of retaliatory action. In 1772, the curé of Mouzens shot and killed his neighbor's dog when, he contended, it attempted to bite him as he passed the neighbor's house on the way to the parish church that day (as he did everyday). But the dog's owner, a merchant, claimed that the curé killed the dog expressly to satisfy his animosity and to insult his neighbor; the merchant therefore brought criminal charges against the curé and asked for damages. In a similar case in 1782, a seigneur claimed that a peasant who stoned and seriously injured his dog did so purposely to insult him. He argued in his petition to the sénéchaussée that no one attacked a dog in this way except out of feelings of vengeance, passion, and "evilness" toward the master. The same could surely be said of an unknown assailant who, on the night of October 12, 1787, entered the barn of a miller near Belvès and slashed the ears of two of his horses.[42]

Disputes over property rights could lead men of any station to take the law into their own hands. The scribe of the tribunal of Domme allegedly threatened to poison the livestock of his neighbor, a bourgeois, if the latter continued to claim the right of access across one of his

---

42. Plainte, June 13, 1772, B 1551, ADD; Plainte, January 21, 1782, B 1576, ADD; Procès-verbal redigé par Labat, artiste vétérinaire, October 18, 1787, B 1593, ADD.

fields. Moreover, the scribe's domestique threatened to kill the bourgeois and went so far as to cut down a cherry tree and a plum tree belonging to him. Another bourgeois, Duval, instructed his sharecroppers in the parish of Cénac to sow poisoned grain on their land to kill the trespassing poultry of Jean-Baptiste Sarlat, an avocat en parlement, who owned most of the property surrounding their farms. As can be imagined, the neighbors complained vehemently—especially when Duval's sharecroppers took the even more drastic step of throwing poisoned grain along the roads. Sarlat met with Duval and his sharecroppers to settle the affair informally, but the bourgeois insisted that he would continue to supply his sharecroppers with poison and, in addition, would give them powder, shot, and a gun "to shoot and destroy anything not killed by poison." In response, Sarlat sought protection by initiating criminal proceedings before the sénéchaussée.[43]

The evidence contained in the criminal court archives of procedural abuses and intimidation by seigneurs is essentially anecdotal in nature and does not establish the relative frequency of such abuses. We can only safely state that complaints about such abuses were relatively constant throughout the period under study and therefore cannot alone account for the increased recourse to royal justice in the 1780s. Royal justice was certainly no less expensive and access to it probably no less difficult than previously. We do know, however, that although resentment against seigneurialism was not peculiar to the last years of the Old Regime, small landowners and sharecroppers did feel the relative weight of seigneurialism more acutely during the economic crisis of 1788 and therefore bristled with hostility. As a result, the Aquitaine disturbances of 1789–90 unleashed by the conjuncture of economic crisis and the opening of political debate in the Estates General were essentially antiseigneurial, not antiroyalist. Increased recourse to royal justice derived at least in part from the peasantry's endemic dissatisfaction with the seigneurial regime—including seigneurial justice—and therefore must be understood as a corollary of this wider trend.

In theory at least, members of a peasant community place great emphasis on unity, conformity, and equilibrium. Disputes arise among them from a network of multiple relationships that simultaneously

43. Plainte, January 3, 1770, B 1544, ADD; Plainte, July 7, 1787, B 1592, ADD.

stretch back into the past and far ahead into the future. Popular dispute settlement as practiced in the Sarladais accordingly considered the total history of relations between disputants, concentrated on the ill effects that could arise from continued feuding, and appealed to their mutual interests. In such cases, where the parties shared the same norms and felt the same communal pressure to compromise, reconcilement or mediation followed easily and successfully. On the other hand, when disputants were of unequal status or did not share the same norms, only external authority could impose a judgment. The weaker party could escape the rule of power only through a lawsuit.[44]

Recourse to royal justice was gradually losing the stigma it once had possessed. Litigation had never really constituted a breach of solidarity or a challenge to the social order in single-interest relationships with few or no expectations of harmony, such as those between creditors and debtors. Likewise, in disputes with persons such as vagabonds and beggars, who were clearly outside the community and immune to its sanctions, recourse to outside authority had long been viewed as practical and acceptable. In dealings with all outsiders, members of the community actually welcomed the objective norms of official justice.[45] But in the unequal yet multi-stranded relationship between lord and vassals, traditional expectations of mutual obligation, deference, and service long persisted and effectively stifled recourse to outside authority.

The final years of the Old Regime witnessed the heightening of expectations and a further widening of the gulf that had begun to separate seigneurs, curés, and other collectors of agricultural rent from the shared norms and interests of the village community, turning them into outsiders in their own land and therefore logical initiators and targets of litigation. Hilton Root has observed that in Burgundy on the eve of the Revolution, people who were "no longer dependent on the lord's protection and administration" began to see seigneurial privileges as "vestiges of days when the king was not yet strong enough to protect the village from the violence and oppression of the nobility." In similar fashion, individuals from a widening occupational range and status in the Sarladais apparently began to perceive recourse to royal justice as

44. Kawashima, "Dispute Resolution in Japan," in Aubert (ed.), *Sociology of Law,* 187.

45. Pitt-Rivers, *The People of the Sierra,* 184–85.

socially acceptable, financially manageable, potentially useful, and generally more attractive. Lawsuits also began to contain more aggressive, egalitarian rhetoric, as legal discourse came to anticipate the polemics of the Revolution.[46]

46. Root, "Challenging the Seigneurie," 653, 680–81.

Conclusion

Indeed, history is nothing more than a tableau of crimes and misfortunes.

—Voltaire, *L'Ingénu*

The growing recourse to the sénéchaussée in the 1780s by a clientele expanding to include small proprietors and share-croppers is inextricably linked to the evolution of the alternatives to royal justice. Infrajudicial modes of dispute settlement, direct action in affairs of honor, seigneurial justice, and retaliation all displayed a continued viability throughout the 1770–1790 period. Royal justice nonetheless made inroads among segments of the populace that previously had rarely employed it. Plaintiffs in private suits often combined informal, infrajudicial methods with the legal tactics of official adjudication. In fact, the proportion of private cases for misdemeanors referring to informal settlements increased somewhat over the period. Whereas settlements in public cases involving felonies occurred prior to legal action and were designed to obviate litigation, settlements in private suits generally occurred after legal action had been initiated. Plaintiffs in private suits were not, then, substituting official legal methods for popular modes of dispute settlement, but rather were alternating the two to gain a favorable settlement out of court. The privately initiated criminal lawsuit was the attempt by one party to outflank his opponent in an ongoing contest in which both sides used a variety of tactics. Recourse to royal justice for misdemeanors, particularly verbal violence, therefore constituted an amalgamated form of behavior that combined both traditional and modern strategies.

At the same time there occurred an evolution in the role of the social groups involved in the informal mediation of disputes. Traditional mediators such as seigneurial officers, nobles, and curés were active primarily in the avoidance of litigation. Bourgeois mediators—especially notaries and *praticiens*—who were literate, possessed of capital, and well acquainted with legal proceedings played a prominent role in private suits for which legal action had already been initiated.[1]

Where kinship ties are strong but official justice is still relatively weak, retaliation and dispute settlement reside primarily in the hands of kin. But during this period informal justice enforced by individuals in affairs of honor and by groups in the defense of "territory" came under pressure in the Sarladais both from royal officials and from those in the community anxious to free themselves from the moral economy of the popular classes.[2] Although the great majority of offended parties in affairs of honor undoubtedly still preferred to avenge affronts through direct action, some chose to defend or repair their lost honor through recourse to the sénéchaussée. Some members of the community grew intolerant of youth groups and other self-appointed (or socially designated) agents of popular justice bent on sanctioning offenders of popular morality by means of charivaris. Seigneurial authorities and curés still often advised people unfortunate enough to find themselves targets of ritual chastisement to endure the humiliation and satisfy the demands of the populace—to recognize the primacy of popular justice by a symbolic act of submission. But some individuals rejected popular interference in their private affairs and appealed to royal justice as the only legitimate arbiter in interpersonal relations. In their private suits they singled out for prosecution the leaders of popular actions and accused them of disturbing social order for their own private purposes, arguing that such incidents were not legitimate and spontaneous manifestations of popular justice but the result of the manipulation of the popular tradition of vigilante action by a few cynical ringleaders.[3]

1. Alan Macfarlane and Sarah Harrison found a close relationship between the acceptance of royal justice and the use of informal settlements (*The Justice and the Mare's Ale: Law and Disorder in Seventeenth-Century England* [Cambridge, Eng., 1981], 193–96).
2. Thompson, "The Moral Economy of the English Crowd," 78–79.
3. Whereas longstanding feuds and vendettas were central features of criminality in eighteenth-century France, they were notably absent in England, as were battles be-

In similar fashion, landlords rejected individuals' and groups' claims that they were defending the traditional equilibrium of communal rights and duties that applied to economic relations. They perceived the defense of customary rights of access, grazing, and gathering as well as the rejection of strictly interpreted proprietary rights as obstructions of agricultural progress and violations of their right to dispose of their private property. Anxious to maximize profits at a time of rising grain prices, they shortened leases, raised rents, and, if they were seigneurs, collected seigneurial dues with greater exactitude. Many peasants viewed these activities as usurpations of their customary rights, which they took direct action to defend. In lawsuits stemming from incidents in which traditional usage clearly conflicted with individual rights, the sénéchaussée defended private property when it could do so without jeopardizing public order. Although the sénéchaussée in theory served as repository of the objective norms of official justice, the magistrates who implemented the law were also realists who knew the limitations within which they worked.

Popular justice itself continued to evolve during this period. Unlike the brutal, antistate judicial actions of the seventeenth-century Croquants, the punitive sanctions of the late eighteenth century were relatively tame, symbolic actions directed against noble and non-noble seigneurs and their agents. The lines of fracture were evident in communal solidarity, and the theoretical protection-allegiance bond between nobles and peasants was fast being discredited. As a result, the battle line between official and popular culture had shifted to within the rural world itself. The punitive actions taken collectively by the populace were attracting participants from a narrower range of society, primarily artisans and peasants.

Although the seigneurial tribunals of the Sarladais had by this period undergone some retrenchment (less than half of those existing in 1764 showed signs of activity), the remaining courts maintained their level of activity and even experienced some rejuvenation after the edict of 1772. The enduring characteristics of seigneurial justice continued to discourage victims from seeking redress before local tribunals and explain why some plaintiffs bypassed them to go directly to the séné-

---

tween youth groups (Macfarlane and Harrison, *The Justice and the Mare's Ale*, 180, 188–90).

chaussée. In addition to their inefficiency, corruption, poorly trained personnel, and procedural irregularities, the greatest disadvantage in dealing with seigneurial courts was that they were subject to manipulation by seigneurs eager to protect their own interests.

Dissatisfaction with the alternatives to royal justice evidently prompted an increasing number of individuals to turn to the sénéchaussée for the redress of their grievances. Although in retrospect this modification in behavior can be viewed as a step toward "modernity," we cannot determine whether it actually derived from already altered expectations or in itself constituted a shift in "mentality." Many of the court's new clients undoubtedly employed official judicial methods to accomplish the essentially traditional goals of punishing an offender and of making him "pay," as well as of avenging and restoring lost honor. What we *can* do is measure the extent of this modification, illuminate how it came about, and weigh its consequences. In the final analysis, the retreat of popular justice and the advance of royal justice derived from the evolution of the rural community and its relations with the changing exterior world.

The tenuous equilibrium that popular justice labored to maintain was vanishing, falling victim to royal officialdom and to those individuals who no longer shared the popular vision of the world and instead viewed popular justice and its agents as forces to be neutralized and overcome. In other words, community members no longer concurred that informal mediators, kinship groups, and youth groups were entitled to interpret and enforce popular custom. Some individuals who appealed to the sénéchaussée no longer desired the type of justice that informal tribunals and agents offered: restoration of the status quo. Rather, they preferred rule by official law, which essentially provided the guidelines for a new form of ritualized contest in the judicial arena. Finally, the decline of popular justice and the advance of royal justice are intimately linked to the gradual transfer of political power from the local level to the Crown. The objects of political centralization were uniformity, discipline, reason, and the guarantee of security to facilitate the free play of individualism.

Informal modes of dispute settlement were effective in the Sarladais only among equals. A sharecropper or small peasant proprietor had little hope of constraining his landlord or seigneur to submit to arbitration and less hope of compelling him to abide by the final ruling, especially if it proved unfavorable to him. Anyone who found himself in this predicament and without sufficient funds to appeal to royal justice had no alternative but to submit to economic exploitation and perhaps even physical aggression, thereby tacitly recognizing his own inferiority, or to strike back in desperate retaliation. The Sarladais was still a society of honor predicated upon a hierarchical social structure in which birth was the most significant factor in determining relative degrees of honor. In such a society, members of the community who, for example, wished to base their claim to status on their ability to compete successfully in the marketplace therefore could not assert that claim or avenge insults to their pretensions of honor with the expectation of popular endorsement. Those few who were anxious to subvert the traditional order of honorific precedence and to protest the stifling surveillance of their neighbors necessarily appealed to royal justice—the only external source of authority they could enlist in their cause.

The methods employed by the informal agents of popular justice could be uncertain and volatile. Vengeance in affairs of honor could touch off interminable blood feuds, whereas collective actions such as charivaris were difficult to control owing to the large number of participants. Moreover, predicting their outcome became increasingly difficult as the community fragmented and the targets of such actions denied the popular classes' right to interfere in their lives. In contrast, some individuals found they could use the royal courts with a reasonable degree of confidence in the outcome. These individuals were largely bourgeois accustomed to contractual relations, provided with sufficient capital, and acquainted with the intricacies of legal procedure. Recourse to royal justice appealed to them not only because it was predictable but also because it permitted them to divorce themselves from the common people and identify with the "civilized" world of written, French culture. Inspecteur des Manufactures Latapie praised the rural bourgeoisie during his tour of the Sarladais in 1787 and argued that they should be recognized as the most virtuous, respectable, and productive citizens of the state. By aligning themselves with royal justice, the bourgeois of this area asserted their distinctiveness and their rightful position in society.[4]

For the increasing number of peasant proprietors and sharecrop-

4. Latapie, "L'Industrie et le commerce en Guienne," 431.

pers who appealed to the sénéchaussée in the 1780s, royal justice promised at least some protection and recourse in disputes with their landlords. It offered them the hope of impartiality, if only in criminal affairs of physical and verbal violence. Moreover, the general breakdown of traditional habits of deference and submission may have been affecting the Sarladais, as new ideas of equality and greater geographic and social mobility favored the rise of an egalitarian spirit. A new form of behavior in contrast with the unspoken submission of the past evidenced itself in a few cases, in which persons of lowly status apparently acted on their own initiative against opponents of higher social standing. Bernard Julie, a *travailleur,* leased a small cottage and plot from his landlord, who had unsuccessfully tried several times to reclaim the land. Julie had always refused, so the landlord retaliated by depriving him of another small vineyard he farmed and, on July 3, 1776, attacked him with a *baton.* But Julie refused to be intimidated and petitioned the sénéchaussée for permission to bring charges against his master, explaining that he had no choice but to rely on the royal court for protection because his master had threatened "that most certainly he would die only by his hands." Moreover, Julie argued, the accused was all the more culpable because he was Julie's landlord and ought to have protected, not attacked, him.[5]

In a similar example, a female servant brought suit against her former master, a bourgeois, for "atrocious insults." Marguerite Cabanet evidently had fallen in love with a valet while the two of them were in service in the Sieur Saillot's household. When they both left his service, intending to marry, Saillot grew angry and, in front of a crowd of approximately thirty-five people gathered for a veillée, compromised Cabanet's reputation with his insults. The above examples illustrate the readiness of some of the lowliest members of society to take advantage of the service offered by the royal court to challenge persons of superior social status. Further evidence of egalitarianism can be found in the increasing use of Enlightenment catchwords and phrases in the petitions composed by plaintiffs and their lawyers, who buttressed their arguments with appeals to "natural reason" and "the liberty common to all citizens."[6] In the Sarladais, as in Languedoc, peasants and artisans ap-

5. N. Castan, *Justice et répression en Languedoc,* 88–91; Root, "Challenging the Seigneurie," 668–73; Plainte, July 5, 1776, B 1563, ADD.

6. Plainte, November 6, 1779, Information, November 24, 1779, both in B 1570, ADD; Plainte, April 4, 1778, B 1567, ADD.

parently accorded esteem and respect with somewhat greater parsimony than previously.

Whereas both popular justice in its various forms and seigneurial justice depended on communal solidarity to function effectively, royal justice actually profited from and even accelerated the dissolution of the traditional community. Royal justice at least for serious crimes was basically retributive in nature and fraught with political significance.[7] Because royal justice in this respect contrasted so vividly with popular dispute settlements, the majority of the populace still rejected its intervention in all but the most serious crimes. When the populace first began to replace autoregulation with official legal recourse, it logically did so in the area of privately initiated criminal suits for misdemeanors—in regard to which royal justice was least retributive and therefore most compatible with the goals of popular justice.

The very existence of royal justice served to dissolve the social body by fostering litigation. It did not, of course, create dissent or conflict in society, but nonetheless it did formalize and legitimize disputes by providing opponents with a forum to air their grievances, thereby implicitly encouraging and exacerbating conflicts that traditionally would often have been settled informally.[8] The result was the creation of a clientele that welcomed the official recognition accorded their grievances by royal magistrates who lent a sympathetic ear to them and, in the process, elevated their often-mundane concerns to the status of legal issues. Finally, the desire of many commoners (both bourgeois and increasing numbers of peasants) to free themselves from the domination of the rich and powerful and the meddling of their neighbors coincided with the political need of the Crown to monopolize power.

That the interests of the bourgeoisie and the state coincided is quite understandable. Royal justice did not assure equality before the law but did provide at least a degree of predictability particularly valued in anonymous economic relations. Economic interests were, in general, among the strongest factors influencing the creation and formalization of the law; the objective norms of judicial formalism guaranteed all individuals and groups a relative maximum of freedom and greatly increased the possibility of predicting the legal consequences of their ac-

---

7. Foucault, *Discipline and Punish,* 53–54.

8. Gluckman, "The Judicial Process Among the Barotse," in Aubert (ed.), *Sociology of Law,* 167.

tions. Moreover, it protected them from the arbitrary, personalized justice preferred by traditional elites anxious to preserve the dependency of the individual upon their goodwill and power. Because the development of the market especially required a legal system whose functioning was calculable in accordance with rational rules, the constant expansion of the market favored the consolidation and regulation of coercive power by a single institution, the state.[9] In other words, the driving force behind the advance of legal rationalization under royal auspices was, in the final analysis, the advance of capitalism itself, which, even in a relatively backward area such as the Périgord, had by the end of the eighteenth century begun to transform interpersonal relations and dissolve the solidarity on which popular justice depended.

But the erosion of the economic insularity that choked regions such as the Périgord and the extension of centralized government were part of a long, slow, and complicated process. Although the corrosive effect of state building was often weak and always diluted by the time it reached the local level, it persisted and eventually produced results. As the locus of authority and responsibility gradually shifted from the grassroots level to the central government, the nature of dispute settlement and the control of delinquency also evolved. The transferral of the responsibility for both functions to officially designated agents logically required that private individuals, family, church, and community groups surrender these tasks. Perhaps only in the present are we fully experiencing the consequences of this trend.

The emerging picture of the Sarladais is one of a society in halting yet perceptible transition. Endemic violence persisted but was seldom brutal and far from spontaneous. These who engaged in it were members of a predominantly (but not entirely) self-regulating society who were still preoccupied with pride and privilege and concerned with defending not only their personal and familial honor but also social equilibrium in general. But this society was not static. The increase in private cases before the sénéchaussée involving verbal and physical violence in the 1780s should not be seen as symptomatic of an increase in violence per se but instead viewed as evidence of growing acceptance of royal justice. The expansion in the Sarladais of private litigation for

9. Rheinstein (ed.), *Max Weber on Law in Economy and Society,* 14, 40, 226–31, 267.

crimes of physical and verbal violence is therefore indicative not of retrogression but of the advance of royal justice or, to be more precise, of the more widespread adoption of official legal strategies by individual inhabitants of the Sarladais in the final years of the Old Regime.[10]

10. Violence was often redirected into an astonishing growth of litigation, as the passion that had earlier found expression in direct physical action was transferred to the law courts. See Lawrence Stone, *The Crisis of the Aristocracy, 1558–1641* (abridged ed.; Oxford, 1967), 117. Also see Macfarlane and Harrison, *The Justice and the Mare's Ale,* 15–16.

Bibliography

PRIMARY SOURCES

Manuscripts

Archives Départementales de la Dordogne, Périgueux

Series B: Sénéchaussée et Présidial de Sarlat

B 1544 (1769–70)–B 1604 (1788–92): Plaintes et informations criminelles du Sénéchal, procès-verbaux, et interrogatoires.

B 1636 (1769–73)–B 1642 (1786–91): Sentences criminelles du Sénéchal.

B 1667 (1761–72)–B 1672 (1782–86): Plaintes et informations criminelles du Présidial, procès-verbaux, et interrogatoires.

B 1680 (1771–84): Sentences criminelles du Présidial.

Maréchaussée de Sarlat

B 1684 (1762–77)–B 1689 (1790–91): Informations, procès-verbaux, et interrogatoires de la Maréchaussée de Sarlat.

B 1701 (1775–90): Jugements prévôtaux.

B 1752 (1766–73)–B 1755 (1790–an V): Ecrous des prisons de la ville de Sarlat.

Articles de Supplément

B 3601 (n.d.): Etat des paroisses de la Sénéchaussée de Sarlat.

B 3613 (1676–1783): Sénéchaussée: Requêtes, informations, et sentences.

B 3614 (n.d.): Procédures prévôtales.

Series C: Administration provinciale avant 1790

2 C26: Description de la subdélégation de Sarlat (1756).

2 C31: Prix du grain dans la subdélégation de Sarlat (1756).

2 C31(2): Ordonnance du subdélégué concernant la maladie épidémique des bestiaux (1775).

Subseries 3E: Minutier des notaires

3E 4463–91 (1728–79): Fonds de Laville (notaire royal à Belvès).

3E 4492–4529 (1738–87): Fonds de Jacques de Jean de Fonroque (notaire royal à Belvès).

3E 4553–57 (1781–an VIII): Fonds de Cogniel (notaire royal à Belvès).

3E 4558–61 (1782–93): Fonds de Jean Cosse (notaire royal à Belvès).

3E 4633 (June 15, 1756): Fonds de Doumenjou (notaire royal à Cussac).

Subseries 4E: Communes et municipalités avant 1790

4E 122(3): Déliberations de la communauté de Sarlat (1719–33).

4E 122(4): Déliberations (1757–91).

4E 122(5): Déliberations (1774–83).

4E 124(8): Agrandissement des prisons (1780).

Series M: Personnel et administration générale depuis 1800
    4 M1: Registre de correspondance avec les ministres, ouvert le 6 germinal an VIII.
    6 M10: Recensement général de la population (1806).
    6 M511: Statistique de la République (mois de prairial an VIII).
    6 M525: Statistique générale du département de la Dordogne pendant les années X, XI, et XII.
    6 M528: Divers lettres et rapports sur la situation du département pendant l'an X (addressés au ministre de la police).
    6 M528: Nombre et qualifications des crimes et délits correctionnels commis pendant le trimestre de janvier 1811 (vagabondage et mendicité, brigandage, jeux de hasard, crimes, et délits).

Series V: Cultes depuis 1800
    3 V5 38: Notices sur les paroisses du diocèse (1838), Vols. 1–5.

Collections des manuscrits
    MS 26: Remarques de M. Desmarest (de l'Académie des Sciences) sur la géographie physique, les productions et les manufactures de la généralité de Bordeaux, lors de ses tournées depuis 1761 jusqu'en 1764.

Archives Départementales de la Gironde, Bordeaux

Series B: Parlement
    Tournelle de Sarlat: Unclassified bundles containing 74 cases appealed to the Parlement of Bordeaux from the Sénéchaussée of Sarlat (April 10, 1770–June 20, 1789).

Series C: Administration provinciale avant 1790
    C 467: Correspondance du subdélégué de Sarlat avec l'intendant (1768–69).
    C 473: Correspondance (1760).
    C 475: Correspondance (1770).
    C 476: Correspondance (1771).
    C 478: Correspondance (1773).
    C 479: Correspondance (1774).
    C 481: Correspondance (1775).
    C 482: Correspondance (1776).
    C 485: Correspondance (1778).
    C 488: Correspondance (1780).
    C 489: Correspondance (1781–82).
    C 490: Correspondance (1782–84).
    C 491: Correspondance (1785–86).
    C 1287–88: Dénombrement de la population de l'élection de Sarlat (1770).
    C 1317: Mémoires envoyés à l'intendant sur l'élection de Sarlat (1739–64).
    C 2664: Rapport de Grézin, docteur en médecin, à M. de Jully, subdélégué à Sarlat, de l'intendant de Guyenne (July 19, 1746).
    C 2696: Projet de rôle de la capitation des nobles et privilégiés de l'élection de Sarlat pour l'année 1777.
    C 3650: Subdélégations diverses (1769–76).
    C 3729: Maréchaussée: Tableau des brigades.

Archives Nationales, Paris

Series D, XXXIX(73): Comité des rapports de l'Assemblée Constituante. Dossiers Sarlat et Sarladais. Lettres de 35 curés du Sarladais qui attestent que dans toutes leurs paroisses où avoit planté un mai, en signe de révolte.

Printed Primary Materials

Beaune, Henri. *Journal d'un lieutenant criminel au XVIIIe siècle.* Paris, 1866.

Becquart, Noël. "Le Cahier de doléances de la Roque-Gageac." *Bulletin de la Société Historique et Archéologique du Périgord,* CIII (1976), 207–209.

Boucher d'Argis, André Jean Baptiste. *Observations sur les loix criminelles de France.* Amsterdam, 1781.

Boulainvilliers, H. *Etat de la France, dans lequel on voit tout ci qui regarde le gouvernement ecclésiastique, le militaire, la justice, les finances, le commerce, les manufactures, le nombre des habitants, et en général tout ce qui peut faire connaitre à fond cette monarchie.* 6 vols. London, 1737.

Calendrier historique du Périgord. Limoges, 1789.

De l'administration de la justice dans les campagnes. N.p., n.d.

Delay, M. *Table de comparaison entre les anciennes mésures du département de la Dordogne et celles du nouveau système métrique.* Périgueux, 1809.

Delfau, Guillaume. *Annuaire du département de la Dordogne pour l'année sextile XI, de l'ère français.* Périgueux, 1803.

———. *Annuaire statistique du département de la Dordogne pour l'an XII de la République.* Périgueux, 1804.

Diderot, Denis, ed. *Encyclopédie, ou dictionnaire raisonné des sciences, des arts et des métiers.* 17 vols. Paris, 1751–65.

Duboscq, Guy. "Le Cahier des doléances du Tiers Etat d'Auriac-en-Périgord, 8 mars 1789." *Bulletin de la Société Historique et Archéologique du Périgord,* LXIII (1936), 60–65.

Encyclopédie méthodique, ou par ordre de matières: Géographie moderne. 3 vols. Paris, 1782–88. Vols. XCVI–XCVIII of *Encyclopédie méthodique.* 200 vols. Paris, 1782–1832.

Encyclopédie méthodique, ou par ordre de matières: Jurisprudence. 10 vols. Paris, 1782–91. Vols. CXLIV–CLIII of *Encyclopédie méthodique.* 200 vols. Paris, 1782–1832.

Expilly, Abbé Jean-Joseph. *Dictionnaire des Gaules et de la France.* Paris, 1779.

Fayolle, André de. *Topographie agricole du département de la Dordogne en Fructidor an IX.* Périgueux, 1939.

Guyot, Pierre-Jean-Jacques-Guillaume, *et al. Répertoire universel et raisonné de jurisprudence civile, criminelle, canonique et bénéficiale.* 17 vols. Paris, 1784–85.

Imbert, Jean, ed. *Quelques Procès criminels des XVIIe et XVIIIe siècles.* Paris, 1964.

Isambert, François-André, *et al. Recueil général des anciennes lois françaises, depuis l'an 420 jusqu'à la révolution de 1789.* 29 vols. Paris, 1821–33.

Jousse, Daniel. *Traité de la jurisdiction des présidiaux tant en matière civile que criminelle.* Paris, 1757.

———. *Traité de la justice criminelle de France.* 4 vols. Paris, 1771.

La Mare, Nicolas de. *Traité de la police, où l'on trouvera l'histoire de son établissement, les fonctions et les prérogatives de ses magistrats; toutes les lois et tous les règlements qui la concernent.* 4 vols. Paris, 1713–38.

Latapie, François-de-Paule. "L'Industrie et le commerce en Guienne sous le regne de Louis XVI: Journal de Tournée." *Archives historiques du Département de la Gironde,* XXXVIII (1903), 321–509.

———. "Notices de la Généralité de Bordeaux (1785)." *Archives historiques du Département de la Gironde,* XXXIV (1899), 251–88.

———. "Tournée de 1782." *Archives historiques du Département de la Gironde,* LIV (1921–22), 125–69.

Le Roy, Eugène. *L'Ennemi de la mort.* 1913; rpr. Paris, 1981.

———. *Jacquou le Croquant.* 1900; rpr. Paris, 1976.

Letrosne, Guillaume François. *Vues sur la justice criminelle: Discours prononcé au bailliage d'Orléans.* Paris, 1777.

Loyseau, C. *Discours de l'abus des justices de village.* 2 vols. Paris, 1603–04.

Muyart de Vouglans, P. F. *Instituts au droit criminel, avec un traité particulier des crimes.* Paris, 1757.

———. *Les Lois criminelles de la France dans leur ordre naturel.* Paris, 1780.

Recueil des édits, déclarations, et ordonnances du roi, arrêts du conseil, du parlement de Toulouse, et autres cours, etc. concernant l'ordre judiciaire, et les matières publiques les plus importants. 8 vols. Toulouse, 1782–86.

Serpillon, François. *Code criminel, ou commentaire de l'ordonnance de 1670.* 4 vols. Lyon, 1767.

Young, Arthur. *Travels in France During the Years 1787, 1788, and 1789.* Edited by Constantia Maxwell. Cambridge, Eng., 1929.

SECONDARY SOURCES

Abbiateci, André. "Typologie d'un crime: Les Incendiaires au XVIIIe siècle." *Annales: Economies, sociétés, civilisations,* XXV (1970), 229–48.

Abbiateci, André, et al. *Crimes et criminalité en France sous l'ancien régime, 17e–18e siècles.* Paris, 1971.

Albanese, Ralph, Jr. "Historical and Literary Perceptions on 17th-Century French Criminality." *Stanford French Review,* IV (1980), 417–33.

Antoine, Michel, et al. *Guide des recherches dans les fonds judiciaires de l'Ancien Régime.* Paris, 1958.

Archel, R. *Crimes et châtiments au XVIIIe siècle.* Paris, 1933.

Aubert, Vilhelm, ed. *The Sociology of Law.* Baltimore, 1969.

Aubin, Raoul. *L'Organisation judiciaire d'après les cahiers de 1789.* Paris, 1928.

Aubry, Gérard. *La Jurisprudence criminelle du Châtelet de Paris sous le regne de Louis XVI.* Paris, 1928.

Audebert, Jean-Louis. "La Criminalité des moeurs dans la Sénéchaussée de Périgueux, 1740–1789." *Mémoire* for the D.E.S., Université de Bordeaux, 1971.

Audiganne, Armand. "Le Métayage et la culture dans le Périgord." *Revue des deux mondes,* June 1, 1867, pp. 613–45.

Augustin, Jean-Marie. "Les Capitouls, juges des causes criminelles et de police à la fin de l'Ancien Régime (1780–1790)." *Annales du Midi,* LXXXIV (1972), 183–211.

Aulard, F. V. A. *La Révolution française et le régime féodal.* Paris, 1919.

Baker, Keith Michael, ed. *The Old Regime and the French Revolution.* Chicago, 1987.

Bamford, Paul. *Fighting Ships and Prisons: The Mediterranean Galleys of France in the Age of Louis XIV.* Minneapolis, 1973.

Bayley, David H. "The Police and Political Development in Europe." In *The Formation of National States in Western Europe,* edited by Charles Tilly. Princeton, 1975.

Beattie, J. M. "The Criminality of Women in Eighteenth-Century England." *Journal of Social History,* VIII (1975), 61–79.

———. "The Pattern of Crime in England, 1660–1800." *Past and Present,* LXII (1974), 47–95.

Beaudry, Richard. "Alimentation et population rurale en Périgord au XVIIIe siècle." *Annales de démographie historique* (1976), 41–55.

———. "Subsistances et population en Périgord au XVIIIe siècle, 1740–1789." *Mémoire* for the D.E.S., Université de Bordeaux, 1970.

Becquart, Noël. "Etat d'enseignement en Dordogne en 1789." *Bulletin de la Société Historique et Archéologique du Périgord,* CII (1975), 142–45.

———. *Répertoire numérique des registres paroissiaux et de l'Etat Civil.* Périgueux, 1968.

———. "La Vente des biens nationaux de 1ère origine dans le district de Belvès." *Bulletin de la Société Historique et Archéologique du Périgord,* CIV (1977), 292–315.

Beik, William. *Absolutism and Society in Seventeenth-Century France: State Power and Provincial Aristocracy in Languedoc.* Cambridge, Eng., 1985.

———. "Popular Culture and Elite Repression in Early Modern Europe." *Journal of Interdisciplinary History,* XI (1980), 97–103.

Belmont, Nicole. *Mythes et croyances dans l'ancienne France.* Paris, 1973.

Bercé, Yves-Marie. "Aspects de la criminalité au XVIIe siècle." *Revue Historique,* CCXXXIX (1968), 33–42.

———. "De la criminalité aux troubles sociaux: La Noblesse rurale du Sud-ouest de la France sous Louis XIII." *Annales du Midi* (1964), 41–59.

———. *Fête et révolte: Des mentalités populaires du 16e au 18e siècles.* Paris, 1976.

———. *Histoire des croquants: Etude des soulèvements populaires au XVIIe siècle dans le sud-ouest de la France.* 2 vols. Geneva, 1974.

———. *La Vie quotidienne dans l'Aquitaine du XVIIe siècle.* Paris, 1978.

———, ed. *Croquants et Nu-Pieds: Les Soulèvements paysans en France du XVIe au XIXe siècle.* Paris, 1974.

Berlanstein, Lenard. *The Barristers of Toulouse in the Eighteenth Century (1740–1793).* Baltimore, 1975.

Bernard, R. J. "Peasant Diet in Eighteenth-Century Gévaudan." In *European Diet from Pre-Industrial to Modern Times,* edited by Elborg Forster and Robert Forster. New York, 1975.

Bernaret, Abbé R. "L'Organisation des diocèses de Périgueux et de Sarlat au XVIIIe siècle." *Bulletin de la Société Historique et Archéologique du Périgord,* I (1874), 341–89, III (1876), 226–44.

Billaçois, François. "Pour une enquête sur la criminalité dans la France d'Ancien Régime." *Annales: Economies, sociétés, civilisations,* XXII (1967), 340–49.

Biraben, Jean-Noël. "La Population du département de la Dordogne à la fin du XVIIIe siècle d'après les recensements inédits effectués sous la Révolution." *Bulletin de la Société Historique et Archéologique du Périgord,* LXXXV (1958), 144–52.

Black-Michaud, Jacob. *Cohesive Force: Feud in the Mediterranean and the Middle East.* Oxford, 1975.

Bois, Paul. *Paysans de l'Ouest.* Abridged ed. Paris, 1971.

Bondois, Paul-M. "La Torture dans le ressort du Parlement de Paris au XVIIIe siècle." *Annales historiques de la Révolution française,* V (1928), 322–37.

Bonnichon, Jean-Emmanuel. "Recherches sur l'économie et la société de Périgueux au XVIIIe siècle." *Mémoire* for the D.E.S., Université de Paris, 1957.

Bouchard, Gérard. *Le Village immobile: Sennely-en-Sologne au XVIIIe siècle.* Paris, 1972.

Boucheron, V. "La Montée du flot des errants de 1760 à 1789 dans la généralité d'Alençon." *Annales de Normandie,* XXI (1971), 55–86.

Boutelet, Bernadette. "Etude par sondage de la criminalité du bailliage de Pont-de-l'Arche (XVIIe–XVIIIe siècles): De la violence au vol: En marche vers l'escroquerie." *Annales de Normandie,* XII (1962), 235–62.

Boutier, Jean. "Jacqueries en pays croquant: Les Révoltes paysannes en Aquitaine (décembre 1789–mars 1790)." *Annales: Economies, sociétés, civilisations,* XXXIV (1979), 760–86.

Bouwsma, William J. "Lawyers and Early Modern Culture." *American Historical Review,* LXXVIII (1973), 303–27.

Brennan, Thomas. *Public Drinking and Popular Culture in Eighteenth-Century Paris.* Princeton, 1988.

Brette, Armand. *Atlas des bailliages ou juridictions assimilées ayant formé unité électorale en 1789. . . .* Paris, 1904.

Brown, Keith M. *Bloodfeud in Scotland: Violence, Justice and Politics in an Early Modern Society.* London, 1986.

Brugière, Abbé H. *Le Livre d'Or des diocèses de Périgueux et de Sarlat, ou le clergé du Périgord pendant la période révolutionnaire.* Montreuil-sur-Mer, 1893.

Buffault, P. *Les Bois et forêts du Périgord.* Bordeaux, 1909.

Burke, Peter. *Popular Culture in Early Modern Europe.* New York, 1978.

Bussière, Georges. *Etudes historiques sur la Révolution en Périgord.* 3 vols. Bordeaux, 1877–1903.

Butel, Paul. "Défrichements en Guyenne au XVIIIe siècle." *Annales du Midi,* LXXVII (1965), 179–202.

———. *Les Négociants bordelais: L'Europe et les Iles.* Paris, 1974.

Butel, Paul, and Guy Mandon. "Alphabétisation et scolarisation en Aquitaine au XVIIIe siècle et au début du XIXe siècle." In *Lire et écrire: L'Alphabétisation des français de Calvin à J. Ferry,* edited by François Furet and Jacques Ozouf. Volume II of 2 vols. Paris, 1977.

Butel, Paul, and Jean-Pierre Poussou. *La Vie quotidienne à Bordeaux au XVIIIe siècle.* Paris, 1980.

Butel, Paul, and Philippe Roudié. "La Production et commercialisation des vins du Libournais au début du XIXe siècle." *Annales du Midi,* LXXXI (1969), 379–408.

Calendrier de 1789. Périgueux, 1789.

Cameron, Iain. *Crime and Repression in the Auvergne and the Guyenne, 1720–1790.* Cambridge, Eng., 1981.

———. "The Police in Provincial France: The Maréchaussée of the Auvergne and the Guyenne, 1720–1790." Ph.D. dissertation, University of Reading, 1976.

———. "The Police of Eighteenth-Century France." *European Studies Review,* VII (1977), 47–75.

Carey, John A. *Judicial Reform in France Before the Revolution of 1789.* Cambridge, Mass., 1981.

Carvès, Louis. "Délibération des marchands de Sarlat, 1769–1770." *Bulletin de la Société Historique et Archéologique du Périgord,* XIV (1887), 511–13.

———. "Etat des impositions des paroisses de l'élection de Sarlat en 1701." *Bulletin de la Société Historique et Archéologique du Périgord,* XVIII (1891), 298–311.

———. "Le Froid et la misère en Sarladais au XVIIIe siècle." *Bulletin de la Société Histo-*

rique et Archéologique du Périgord, XII (1886), 504–506.

Castan, Nicole. "La Criminalité à la fin de l'Ancien Régime dans les pays de Languedoc." *Bulletin d'histoire économique et sociale de la Révolution française* (1970), 59–68.

———. "Criminalité et litiges sociaux en Languedoc de 1690 à 1730." Thèse de 3ème cycle, Université de Toulouse-Mirail. Microfiche. Paris, 1973.

———. *Les Criminels de Languedoc: Les Exigences d'ordre et les voies de ressentiment dans une société pré-révolutionnaire.* Toulouse, 1980.

———. *Justice et répression en Languedoc à l'époque des lumières.* Paris, 1980.

———. "La Justice expéditive." *Annales: Economies, sociétés, civilisations,* XXXI (1976), 331–61.

Castan, Yves. *Honnêteté et rélations sociales en Languedoc au XVIIIe siècle.* Paris, 1974.

———. "Les Rapports sociaux dans les procédures criminelles du Parlement de Toulouse au XVIIIe siècle." *Bulletin d'histoire économique et sociale de la Révolution française* (1970), 49–57.

Certeau, Michel de, Dominique Julia, and Jacques Revel. "Une Ethnographie de la langue: L'Enquête de Grégoire sur les patois." *Annales: Economies, sociétés, civilisations,* XXX (1975), 3–42.

Champin, Marie-Madeleine. "Un Cas typique de justice bailliagère: La Criminalité dans le bailliage d'Alençon de 1715 à 1745." *Annales de Normandie,* XXII (1972), 47–84.

Chapgier-Laboissière, Germaine. "Guillaume Gontier de Biran, subdélégué de Bergerac (1743–1766)." *Bulletin de la Société Historique et Archéologique du Périgord,* LIX (1932), 109–17, 146–62, 184–214, 236–65, 283–307.

Chartier, Roger. "Les Elites et les gueux: Quelques Représentations (XVIIe–XVIIIe siècles)." *Revue d'histoire moderne et contemporaine,* XXI (1974), 376–88.

———, ed. *De la Renaissance aux Lumières.* Paris, 1986. Vol. III of Philippe Ariès and Georges Duby (eds.), *Histoire de la vie privée.* 5 vols.

Chartier, Roger, and J. Lecuir. "Pauvreté et assistance dans la France moderne." *Annales: Economies, sociétés, civilisations,* XXVIII (1973), 572–82.

Chaunu, Pierre. "Sur la fin des sorciers au XVIIe siècle." *Annales: Economies, sociétés, civilisations,* XXIV (1969), 895–911.

Church, William F. "The Decline of the French Jurists as Political Theorists, 1660–1789." *French Historical Studies,* V (1967), 1–40.

Claverie, Elisabeth. "L'Honneur: Une Société de défis au XIX siècle." *Annales: Economies, sociétés, civilisations,* XXXIV (1979), 744–59.

Claverie, Elisabeth, and Pierre Lamaison. *L'Impossible Mariage: Violence et parenté en Gévaudan (XVIIe, XVIIIe et XIXe siècles).* Paris, 1982.

Cobb, Richard C. *Death in Paris: The Records of the Basse-Géole de la Seine, October 1795–September 1801.* Oxford, 1978.

———. *Paris and Its Provinces, 1792–1802.* Oxford, 1975.

———. *The Police and the People.* Oxford, 1970.

Cockburn, J. S., ed. *Crime in England, 1550–1800.* Princeton, 1977.

Cocula, Anne-Marie. *Les Gens de la rivière de Dordogne de 1750 à 1850.* Lille, 1979.

———. "Trois Siècles de carnaval à Sarlat." *Annales du Midi,* XCIII (1981), 5–16.

Combier, Amédée. *Les Justices seigneuriales du bailliage de Vermandois sous l'Ancien Régime.* Paris, 1897.

Corbin, Alain. *Archaïsme et modernité en Limousin au XIXe siècle, 1845–1880.* Paris, 1975.

Crépillon, P. "Un 'Gibier des prévôts': Mendiants et vagabonds entre la Vire et la Dives (1720–1789)." *Annales de Normandie*, XVII (1967), 223–52.

Crouzy, Jacques. "La Terre et l'homme en Sarladais." Thèse de 3ème cycle, Université de Bordeaux, 1969.

David, René, and John E. C. Brierly. *Major Legal Systems in the World Today: An Introduction to the Comparative Study of Law*. London, 1968.

Davis, Natalie Zemon. *Society and Culture in Early Modern France*. Stanford, 1975.

Dawson, John P. *A History of Lay Judges*. Cambridge, Mass., 1960.

Dawson, Philip. *Provincial Magistrates and Revolutionary Politics in France, 1789–1795*. Cambridge, Mass., 1972.

Delbreil, Marc. *Le Dialecte sarladais ou patois du Périgord-Noir, ses origines, ses transformations*. Bordeaux, 1938.

Depauw, Jacques. "Illicit Sexual Activity in Eighteenth-Century Nantes." In *Family and Society: Selections from the Annales*, edited by Robert Forster and Orest Ranum. Baltimore, 1976.

———. "Pauvres, Pauvres Mendiants, mendiants valides ou vagabonds? Les Hésitations de la législation royale." *Revue d'histoire moderne et contemporaine*, XXI (1974), 401–18.

Desgraves, Louis. "L'Élection de Sarlat, sa création (1636), ses limites et sa situation dans la première moitié du XVIII siècle." *Bulletin de la Société Historique et Archéologique du Périgord*, LXXVI (1949), 132–43.

———. "La Formation territoriale de la généralité de Guyenne." *Annales du Midi*, LXII (1950), 239–48.

———. "Les Subdélégations et subdélégués de la généralité de Bordeaux au XVIIIe siècle." *Annales du Midi*, LXVI (1954), 143–54.

Dewald, Jonathan. *The Formation of a Provincial Nobility: The Magistrates of the Parlement of Rouen, 1499–1610*. Princeton, 1980.

Deyon, Pierre. *Le Temps des prisons: Essai sur l'histoire de la délinquance et les origines du système pénitentiaire*. Paris, 1975.

Dion, Roger. "L'Ancien Privilège de Bordeaux." *Revue géographique des Pyrénées et du Sud-Ouest*, XXVI (1955), 223–36.

Doyle, William. *The Parlement of Bordeaux and the End of the Old Regime, 1771–1790*. New York, 1974.

———. "The Parlements of France and the Breakdown of the Old Regime." *French Historical Studies*, VI (1970), 415–57.

———. "Was There an Aristocratic Reaction in Pre-Revolutionary France?" *Past and Present*, LVII (1972), 97–122.

Dujarric-Descombes, Léonard Albert. "La Vie privée en Périgord au XVIIIe siècle d'après les livres de raison." *Bulletin de la Société Historique et Archéologique du Périgord*, LI (1924), 147–62, 197–214.

Dupeux, Georges. *La Société française, 1789–1970*. Paris, 1972.

Egret, Jean. *The French Pre-Revolution, 1787–1788*. Chicago, 1977.

Elias, Norbert. *The Development of Manners: Changes in the Code of Conduct and Feeling in Early Modern Times*. New York, 1978. Vol. I of Elias, *The Civilizing Process*. 3 vols.

Escande, Jean-Joseph. *Histoire de Sarlat*. 1903; rpr. Marseilles, 1976.

———. *Histoire du Périgord*. 1934; rpr. Marseilles, 1980.

Esmein, Adhémar. *Histoire de la procédure criminelle en France et spécialement de la procédure inquisitoire depuis le XIIIe siècle jusqu'à nos jours*. Paris, 1882.

Estèbe, J., and B. Vogler. "La Genèse d'une société protestante: Étude comparée de quelques registres consistoires languedociens et palatins vers 1600." *Annales: Economies, sociétés, civilisations,* XXXI (1976), 362–88.

Everat, L. E. *La Sénéchaussée d'Auvergne et le siège présidial de Riom au XVIIIe siècle.* Paris, 1886.

Fairchilds, Cissie C. *Domestic Enemies: Servants and Their Masters in Old Regime France.* Baltimore, 1984.

———. *Poverty and Charity in Aix-en-Provence, 1640–1789.* Baltimore, 1976.

Farge, Arlette. *Délinquance et criminalité: Le Vol d'aliments à Paris au XVIIIe siècle.* Paris, 1974.

———. *La Vie fragile: Violences, pouvoirs et solidarités à Paris au XVIIIe siècle.* Paris, 1986.

———, ed. *Vivre dans la rue à Paris au XVIIIe siècle.* Paris, 1979.

Fayolle, Gérard. *Histoire du Périgord.* Périgueux, 1983.

———. *La Vie quotidienne en Périgord au temps de Jacquou le Croquant.* Paris, 1977.

Fénélon, Paul. *Le Périgord: Étude morphologique.* Paris, 1951.

———. "A travers le Périgord au XVIIIe siècle." *Bulletin de la Société Historique et Archéologique du Périgord,* LXIV (1937), 276–81.

———. *Vocabulaire de géographie agraire.* Gap, 1970.

Ferdinand, Theodore N. "Criminality, the Courts, and the Constabulary in Boston, 1702–1967." *Journal of Research in Crime and Delinquency,* XVII (1980), 190–208.

———. "Criminal Justice: From Colonial Intimacy to Bureaucratic Formality." In *Handbook of Contemporary Urban Life,* edited by David Street. San Francisco, 1978.

———. "The Theft-Violence Ratio in Antebellum Boston." Paper presented at the Tenth World Congress of Sociology, Mexico City, 1982.

Festy, Octave. *Les Délits ruraux et leur repression sous la Révolution et le Consultat.* Paris, 1956.

Fine-Souriac, Agnes. "La Limitation des naissances dans le sud-ouest de la France: Fécondité, allaitement et contraception au Pays de Sault du milieu du XVIIIe siècle à 1914." *Annales du Midi,* XC (1978), 155–88.

Flandrin, Jean-Louis. *Families in Former Times: Kinship, Household and Sexuality in Early Modern France.* Translated by Richard Southern. Cambridge, Eng., 1979.

Florenty, F. "Etude démographique d'une paroisse sarladaise: Domme, 1770–1820." *Mémoire* for the D.E.S., Université de Bordeaux, 1972.

Florenty, Guy. "L'Evolution démographique de Saint-Cyprien et de son canton au XVIIIe siècle." *Mémoire* for the D.E.S., Université de Bordeaux, 1974.

Foucault, Michel. *Discipline and Punish: The Birth of the Prison.* Translated by Alan Sheridan. New York, 1979.

Galet, J. L. *Meurtre à Hautefaye.* Périgueux, 1970.

Gatrell, V. A. C., Bruce Lenman, and Geoffrey Parker, eds. *Crime and the Law: The Social History of Crime in Western Europe Since 1500.* London, 1980.

Gatrell, V. A. C., and T. B. Hadden. "Criminal Statistics and Their Interpretation." In *Nineteenth-Century Society: Essays in the Use of Quantitative Methods for the Study of Social Data,* edited by E. A. Wrigley. Cambridge, Eng., 1972.

Gauvard, Claude, and Altan Gokalp. "Les Conduites de bruit et leur signification à la fin du Moyen Age: Le charivari." *Annales: Economies, sociétés, civilisations,* XXIX (1974), 693–704.

Gégot, Jean-Claude. "Etude par sondage de la criminalité dans le bailliage de Falaise

(XVIIe–XVIIIe siècles): Criminalité diffuse ou société criminelle?" *Annales de Normandie,* XVI (1966), 103–64.

Geremek, Bronislaw. "Criminalité, vagabondage, pauperisme: La Marginalité à l'aube des temps modernes." *Revue d'histoire moderne et contemporaine,* XXI (1974), 337–75.

Gibson, Ralph. "The French Nobility in the Nineteenth Century—Particularly in the Dordogne." In *Elites in France: Origins, Reproduction and Power,* edited by Jolyon Howorth and Philip G. Cerny. London, 1981.

———. "Les Notables et l'Eglise dans le diocèse de Périgueux, 1821–1905." Thèse de 3ème cycle, Université de Lyon, 1979.

———. *A Social History of French Catholicism, 1789–1914.* London, 1989.

Giffard, André. *Les Justices seigneuriales en Bretagne au XVIIe et XVIIIe siècles.* Paris, 1903.

Goubert, Pierre. *Clio parmi les hommes.* Paris, 1976.

———. *The Course of French History.* Translated by Maarten Ultee. New York, 1988.

———. *La Société.* Paris, 1969. *Les Pouvoirs.* Paris, 1973. Vols. I and II of Goubert, *L'Ancien Régime.* 2 vols.

Gourgues, Vicomte de. *Dictionnaire topographique du département de la Dordogne comprenant les noms de lieu anciens et modernes.* Paris, 1873.

Greenburg, Douglas. *Crime and Law Enforcement in the Colony of New York, 1691–1776.* Ithaca, 1976.

Grillon, Louis. "Un Registre des comptes de l'officialité diocésaine de Périgueux (1681–1728)." *Bulletin de la Société Historique et Archéologique du Périgord,* XCIX (1972), 97–106.

Grimmer, Claude. *Vivre à Aurillac au XVIIIe siècle.* Aurillac, 1983.

Gruder, Vivian R. *The Royal Provincial Intendants: A Governing Elite in Eighteenth-Century France.* Ithaca, 1968.

Gurr, Ted Robert. *The Politics of Crime and Conflict: A Comparative History of Four Cities.* Beverly Hills, 1977.

Gutton, Jean-Pierre. *La Sociabilité villageoise dans l'ancienne France: Solidarités et voisinages du XVIe au XVIIIe siècles.* Paris, 1979.

———. *La Société et les pauvres: L'Exemple de la généralité de Lyon (1534–1789).* Paris, 1971.

Hamscher, Albert N. *The Conseil Privé and the Parlements in the Age of Louis XIV: A Study in French Absolutism.* Philadelphia, 1987.

———. *The Parlement of Paris After the Fronde, 1653–1673.* Pittsburgh, 1976.

Hanawalt, Barbara A. *Crime and Conflict in English Communities, 1300–1348.* Cambridge, Mass., 1979.

Hay, Douglas, *et al. Albion's Fatal Tree: Crime and Society in Eighteenth-Century England.* New York, 1975.

Henry, Louis. "La Fécondité des mariages dans le quart Sud-Ouest de la France de 1720 à 1829." *Annales: Economies, sociétés, civilisations,* XXVII (1972), 612–40, 977–1025.

Henry, Philippe. *Crime, justice et société dans la principauté de Neuchâtel au XVIIIe siècle (1707–1806).* Neuchâtel, 1984.

Higounet, Charles, ed. *Documents de l'histoire de l'Aquitaine.* Toulouse, 1973.

Higounet, Charles, *et al. Histoire de l'Aquitaine.* Toulouse, 1971.

Higounet-Nadal, Arlette, ed. *Histoire du Périgord.* Toulouse, 1983.

Hobsbawm, Eric. *Bandits.* New York, 1979.

———. *Primitive Rebels*. New York, 1959.

Hoebel, E. Adamson. *The Law of Primitive Man*. New York, 1974.

Hours, Henri. "Emeutes et émotions populaires dans les campagnes du Lyonnais au XVIIIe siècle." *Cahiers d'histoire* (1964), 137–54.

Howorth, Jolyon, and Philip G. Cerney, eds. *Elites in France: Origins, Reproduction and Power*. London, 1981.

Hufton, Olwen. "Attitudes Towards Authority in Eighteenth-Century Languedoc." *Social History*, III (1978), 281–302.

———. *Bayeux in the Late Eighteenth Century*. Oxford, 1967.

———. "Begging, Vagrancy, Vagabondage and the Law: An Aspect of the Problem of Poverty in Eighteenth-Century France." *Modern European Review*, II (1972), 97–123.

———. *The Poor of Eighteenth-Century France, 1750–1789*. Oxford, 1974.

———. "Women and the Family Economy in Eighteenth-Century France." *French Historical Studies*, IX (1975), 1–22.

———. "Women in the French Revolution, 1789–1796." *Past and Present*, LIII (1971), 90–108.

Inciardi, James A., and Charles E. Faupel, eds. *History and Crime: Implications for Criminal Justice Policy*. Beverly Hills, 1980.

Isherwood, Robert M. *Farce and Fantasy: Popular Entertainment in Eighteenth-Century Paris*. Oxford, 1986.

Jones, Peter M. "Georges Lefebvre and the Peasant Revolution: Fifty Years On." *French Historical Studies*, XVI (1990), 645–63.

———. *The Peasantry in the French Revolution*. Cambridge, Eng., 1988.

———. *Politics and Rural Society in the Southern Massif Central, c. 1750–1800*. Cambridge, Eng., 1985.

———. "The Rural Bourgeoisie of the Southern Massif-Central: A Contribution to the Study of the Social Structure of Ancien Régime France." *Social History*, IV (1979), 65–83.

Kagan, Richard L. "Law Students and Legal Careers in Eighteenth-Century France." *Past and Present*, LXVIII (1975), 38–72.

———. *Lawsuits and Litigants in Castile, 1500–1700*. Chapel Hill, 1981.

Kaiser, Colin. "The Deflation in the Volume of Litigation at Paris in the Eighteenth Century and the Waning of the Old Judicial Order." *European Studies Review*, X (1980), 309–36.

Kaplan, Steven Laurence. *Provisioning Paris: Merchants and Millers in the Grain and Flour Trade During the Eighteenth Century*. Ithaca, 1984.

Kaplow, Jeffry. *The Names of Kings: The Parisian Laboring Poor in the Eighteenth Century*. New York, 1972.

Keohane, Nannerl. *Philosophy and the State in France: The Renaissance to the Enlightenment*. Princeton, 1980.

Labroue, H. *L'Esprit public en Dordogne pendant la Révolution*. Paris, 1911.

Labrousse, Elisabeth, and Alfred Soman. "La Querelle de l'antimoine: Guy Patin sur la sellette." *Histoire, économie et société*, V (1986), 31–45.

Labrousse, Ernest, et al. *Des derniers temps de l'âge seigneurial aux préludes de l'âge industriel (1660–1789)* (Paris, 1970). Vol. II of Fernand Braudel and Ernest Labrousse (eds.), *Histoire économique et sociale de la France*. 4 vols.

Lage, Daniel de. "La Seigneurie de Montpon en Périgord (1344–1789)." *Bulletin de la Société Historique et Archéologique du Périgord*, XLIII (1916), 271–81.

Lane, Roger. "Crime and the Industrial Revolution: British and American Views." *Journal of Social History*, VII (1974), 287–303.

———. *Violent Death in the City: Suicide, Accident and Murder in Nineteenth-Century Philadelphia.* Cambridge, Mass., 1979.

Langbein, John H. *Prosecuting Crime in the Renaissance: England, Germany, France.* Cambridge, Mass., 1974.

———. *Torture and the Law of Proof: Europe and England in the Ancien Régime.* Chicago, 1977.

Laurain, Ernest. *Essai sur les présidiaux.* Paris, 1896.

Lavergne, G. "Les Cabarets du Sarladais au XVIIe siècle." *Bulletin de la Société Historique et Archéologique du Périgord*, XLI (1914), 127–34.

Lebrun, François. *Les Hommes et la mort en Anjou aux 17e et 18e siècles.* Abridged ed. Paris, 1975.

———. "Naissance illégitimes et abandons d'enfants en Anjou au XVIIIe siècle." *Annales: Economies, sociétés, civilisations*, XXVII (1972), 1183–89.

———. *La Vie conjugale sous l'ancien régime.* Paris, 1975.

Lecuir, Jean. "Criminalité et moralité: Montyon, statisticien du Parlement de Paris." *Revue d'histoire moderne et contemporaine*, XXI (1974), 445–93.

Lefebvre, Georges. *The Great Fear of 1789: Rural Panic in Revolutionary France.* Translated by Joan White. New York, 1973.

———. "Urban Society in the Orléanais." *Past and Present*, XIX (1961), 46–75.

Le Goff, Timothy J. A. *Vannes and Its Region: A Study of Town and Country in Eighteenth-Century France.* Oxford, 1981.

Le Goff, Timothy J. A., and D. M. G. Sutherland. "The Revolution and the Rural Community in Eighteenth-Century Brittany." *Past and Present*, LXII (1974), 96–119.

Le Roy Ladurie, Emmanuel. *The Peasants of Languedoc.* Translated by John Day. Urbana, 1974.

———. "Révoltes et contestations rurales en France de 1675 à 1788." *Annales: Economies, sociétés, civilisations*, XXIX (1974), 6–22.

———, ed. *L'Age classique des paysans, 1340–1789.* Paris, 1975. Vol. II of Georges Duby and Armand Wallon, eds. *Histoire de la France rurale.* 4 vols.

Livet, G. "La Vie paysanne avant la Révolution dans la Double du Périgord." *Bulletin de la Société Historique et Archéologique du Périgord*, LXIX (1942), 126–35.

Llewellyn, Karl N., and E. Adamson Hoebel. *The Cheyenne Way: Conflict and Case Law in Primitive Jurisprudence.* Norman, Okla., 1941.

Lodhi, Abdul Qaiyum, and Charles Tilly. "Urbanization, Crime, and Collective Violence in Nineteenth-Century France." *American Journal of Sociology*, LXXIX (1973), 296–318.

Lorédan, Jean. *La Grande Misère et les voleurs au dix-huitième siècle.* Paris, 1910.

Lorgnier, J., and R. Martinage. "L'Activité judiciaire de la maréchaussée de Flandres (1679–1790)." *Revue du Nord*, LXI (1979), 593–608.

Lottin, Alain. *Chavatte, ouvrier Lillois: Un Contemporain de Louis XIV.* Paris, 1979.

———. "Naissances illégitimes et filles mères à Lille au XVIIIe siècle." *Revue d'histoire moderne et contemporaine*, XVII (1970), 278–322.

Macfarlane, Alan, and Sarah Harrison. *The Justice and the Mare's Ale: Law and Disorder in Seventeenth-Century England.* Cambridge, Eng., 1981.

Mackrell, John. *The Attack on "Feudalism" in Eighteenth-Century France.* London, 1973.

———. "Criticism of Seigneurial Justice in Eighteenth-Century France." In *French Gov-*

ernment and Society, 1500–1850: Essays in Memory of Alfred Cobban. Edited by John F. Bosher. London, 1973.

Mandon, Guy. "Les Curés en Périgord au dix-huitième siècle: Contribution à l'étude du clergé paroissial sous l'ancien régime." Thèse de 3ème cycle, Université de Bordeaux, 1979.

———. "Progrès agricoles et défrichements en Périgord au XVIIIe siècle." *Bulletin de la Société Historique et Archéologique du Périgord*, CVII (1980), 159–83.

———. *La Société Périgorde au siècle des Lumières: Le Clergé paroissial*. Périgueux, 1982.

Mandrou, Robert. *Introduction à la France moderne, 1500–1640: Essai de psychologie historique*. Paris, 1974.

Margot, Alain. "La Criminalité dans le bailliage de Mamers (1695–1750)." *Annales de Normandie*, XXII (1972), 185–224.

Marion, Marcel. *Dictionnaire des institutions de la France aux XVIIe et XVIIIe siècles*. 1923; rpr. Paris, 1976.

———. "Etat des classes rurales au XVIIIe siècle dans la généralité de Bordeaux." *Revue des études historiques*, LXVIII (1902), 97–139, 209–35, 335–61, 451–78.

———. *La Garde des Sceaux: Lamoignon et la réforme judiciaire de 1788*. Paris, 1905.

Martin, Gaston. "Les Intendants de Guyenne au XVIIIe siècle et les privilèges des vins bordelais." *Revue historique de Bordeaux et du Département de la Gironde*, I (1908), 461–70.

Maubourguet, Jean. "Le Collège de Sarlat au XVIIIe siècle." *Bulletin de la Société Historique et Archéologique du Périgord*, LXXIX (1952), 205–19.

———. *Sarlat et ses châteaux*. Périgueux, 1960.

Mer, Louis-Bernard. "La Procédure criminelle au XVIIIe siècle: L'Enseignement des archives bretonnes." *Revue historique*, CCLXXIV (1985), 9–42.

Mericskay, Alexandre. "Le Châtelet et la répression de la criminalité à Paris en 1770." Thèse de IIIème cycle, Université de Paris, 1984.

Michel, Léon. *Le Périgord: Le Pays et les hommes*. Périgueux, 1969.

Millon, Patricia. "L'Individu et la famille dans la région de Grasse, d'après les procédures criminelles de la Sénéchaussée (1748–1763)." *Bulletin d'histoire économique et sociale de la Révolution française* (1974), 43–62.

Morineau, Michel. "Y a-t-il eu une révolution agricole en France au XVIIIe siècle?" *Revue historique*, CCXXXIX (1968), 299–326.

Mousnier, Roland. *Les Hierarchies sociales de 1450 à nos jours*. Paris, 1969.

———. *Les Institutions de la France sous la monarchie absolue*. 2 vols. Paris, 1974, 1980.

———. *Peasant Uprisings in Seventeenth-Century France, Russia, and China*. Translated by Brian Pearce. New York, 1970.

Muchembled, Robert. *Culture populaire et culture des élites (XVe–XVIIIe siècles)*. Paris, 1978.

Muller, Dominique. "Les Magistrats français et la peine de mort au 18e siècle." *Dix-huitième siècle*, IV (1972), 79–107.

Nader, Laura, and Harry F. Todd, eds. *Disputing Process in Ten Societies*. New York, 1978.

Ozouf, Mona. *Festivals and the French Revolution*. Translated by Alan Sheridan. Cambridge, Mass., 1988.

Peristiany, J. G., ed. *Honour and Shame: The Values of Mediterranean Society*. London, 1965.

Peter, Jean-Pierre. "Une Enquête de la Société Royale de Médecine (1774–1794): Malades et maladies à la fin du XVIIIe siècle." *Annales: Economies, sociétés, civilisations*, XXII (1967), 711–51.

Pijassou, René. *Regards sur la révolution agricole en Périgord*. Périgueux, 1967.

Pitt-Rivers, Julian. *The Fate of Shechem, or the Politics of Sex: Essays in the Anthropology of the Mediterranean*. Cambridge, Eng., 1977.

———. *The People of the Sierra*. 2nd ed. Chicago, 1971.

———. "Social Class in a French Village." *Anthropological Quarterly*, XXXIII (1960), 1–13.

Poitrineau, Abel. *Remues d'hommes: Les Migrations montagnardes en France, 17e–18e siècles*. Paris, 1983.

———. *La Vie rurale en Basse-Auvergne au XVIIIe siècle*. Paris, 1965.

Pommarède, Pierre. *Sarlat oublié*. Périgueux, 1982.

———. *La Séparation de l'Eglise et de l'Etat en Périgord*. Périgueux, 1976.

Poussou, Jean-Pierre. *Bordeaux et le Sud-Ouest au XVIIIe siècle: Croissance économique et attraction urbaine*. Paris, 1983.

———. "Recherches sur l'alphabétisation de l'Aquitaine au XVIIIe siècle." In *Lire et écrire: L'Alphabétisation des français de Calvin à Jules Ferry*. Edited by François Furet and Jacques Ozouf. Paris, 1977.

———. "Sur le rôle des transports terrestres dans l'économie du Sud-Ouest au XVIIIe siècle." *Annales du Midi*, XC (1978), 389–412.

Raeff, Marc. "The Well-Ordered Police State and the Development of Modernity in Seventeenth and Eighteenth Century Europe: An Attempt at a Comparative Approach." *American Historical Review*, LXXX (1975), 1221–43.

Redfield, Robert. *The Little Community and Peasant Society and Culture*. Chicago, 1960.

Reinhardt, Steven G. "Crime and Royal Justice in Ancien Régime France: Modes of Analysis." *Journal of Interdisciplinary History*, XIII (1983), 437–60.

———. "Ritualized Violence in Eighteenth-Century Périgord." In *The French Revolution in Culture and Society*. Edited by David Troyansky *et al.* Westport, Conn., 1991.

———. "The Selective Prosecution of Crime in Ancien Régime France: Theft in the Sénéchaussée of Sarlat." *European History Quarterly*, XVI (1986), 3–24.

Rheinstein, Max, ed. *Max Weber on Law in Economy and Society*. Translated by Edward Shils and Max Rheinstein. Cambridge, Mass., 1954.

Robert, P. *L'Agriculture en Dordogne*. Bordeaux, 1958.

Roberts, Simon. *Order and Dispute: An Introduction to Legal Anthropology*. New York: 1979.

Rocal, Georges. *Croquants du Périgord*. Périgueux, 1970.

———. *De Brumaire à Waterloo en Périgord*. Paris, 1942.

———. *Les Vieilles Coutumes dévotieuses et magiques du Périgord*. 1922; rpr. Périgueux, 1971.

———. *Le Vieux Périgord*. Périgueux, 1926.

Roche, Daniel. *Le Peuple de Paris: Essai sur la culture populaire au XVIIIe siècle*. Paris, 1981.

———, ed. *Journal de ma vie: Jacques-Louis Ménétra, compagnon vitrier au 18e siècle*. Paris, 1982.

Root, Hilton Lewis. "Challenging the Seigneurie: Community and Contention on the

Eve of the French Revolution." *Journal of Modern History,* LVII (1985), 652–81.

———. "En Bourgogne: L'Etat et la communauté rurale, 1661–1789." *Annales: Economies, sociétés, civilisations,* XXXVII (1982), 288–303.

Roumejoux, Anatole de, Philippe de Bosrédon, and Ferdinand Villepelet. *Bibliographie générale du Périgord.* Périgueux, 1897–99.

Ruff, Julius R. "The Character of Old Regime Justice: The Examples of the Sénéchaussées of Libourne and Bazas." Paper presented at the Twelfth Annual Meeting of the Western Society for French History, October 26, 1984.

———. "Crime, Justice and Public Order in France, 1696–1788: The Sénéchaussée of Libourne." Ph.D. dissertation, University of North Carolina at Chapel Hill, 1979.

———. *Crime, Justice and Public Order in Old Regime France: The Sénéchaussées of Libourne and Bazas, 1696–1789.* London, 1984.

———. "Law and Order in Eighteenth-Century France: The Maréchaussée of Guyenne." *Proceedings of the Western Society for French History,* IV (1976), 174–81.

Ruffray, Patrick de. *L'Affaire d'Hautefaye: Légende, histoire.* Angoulême, 1926.

Saint-Jacob, Pierre de. *Les Paysans de la Bourgogne du nord au dernier siècle de l'ancien régime.* Dijon, 1960.

Saint-Martin, J. "Crimes et délits en Dordogne sous le Consulat et l'Empire (1802–1807)." *Bulletin de la Société Historique et Archéologique du Périgord,* LXXXIV (1957), 127–41.

Saint-Saud, Comte de. *Magistrats des sénéchaussées, présidiaux, et élections.* Bergerac, 1931.

Scargill, Ian. *The Dordogne Region of France.* London, 1974.

Schwartz, Robert M. *Policing the Poor in Eighteenth-Century France.* Chapel Hill, 1988.

Secondat, Marcel. "Evolution économique d'une communauté rurale: Plazac depuis le XVIIIe siècle." *Bulletin de la Société Historique et Archéologique du Périgord,* CII (1975), 177–95, 313–41, CIII (1976), 34–62, 89–100.

Segalen, Martine. "The Family Cycle and Household Structure: Five Generations in a French Village." In *Family and Sexuality in French History.* Edited by Robert Wheaton and Tamara K. Hareven. Philadelphia, 1980.

———. *Historical Anthropology of the Family.* Translated by J. C. Whitehouse and Sarah Matthews. Cambridge, Eng., 1986.

———. *Mari et femme dans la société paysanne.* Paris, 1980.

Seligman, Edmond. *La Justice en France pendant la Révolution.* 2 vols. Paris, 1901.

Sharpe, J. A. *Crime in Early Modern England, 1550–1750.* London, 1984.

Soman, Alfred. "Deviance and Criminal Justice in Western Europe, 1300–1800: An Essay in Structure." *Criminal Justice History,* I (1980), 3–28.

Sonenscher, Michael. *The Hatters of Eighteenth-Century France.* Berkeley, 1987.

Spierenburg, Pieter. *The Spectacle of Suffering: Executions and the Evolution of Repression: From a Preindustrial Metropolis to the European Experience.* Cambridge, Eng., 1984.

———, ed. *The Emergence of Carceral Institutions: Prisons, Galleys and Lunatic Asylums, 1550–1900.* Rotterdam, 1984.

Stone, Bailey. *The Parlement of Paris, 1774–1789.* Chapel Hill, 1981.

Stone, Lawrence. *The Crisis of the Aristocracy, 1558–1641.* Abridged ed. Oxford, 1967.

Sutherland, D. M. G. *France, 1789–1815: Revolution and Counterrevolution.* Oxford, 1985.

Tackett, Timothy. *Priest and Parish in Eighteenth-Century France: A Social and Political*

Study of the Curés in a Diocese of Dauphiné, 1750–1791. Princeton, 1977.

———. *Religion, Revolution, and Regional Culture in Eighteenth-Century France: The Ecclesiastical Oath of 1791.* Princeton, 1986.

Thompson, Edward P. "The Moral Economy of the English Crowd in the Eighteenth Century." *Past and Present,* L (1971), 76–136.

———. " 'Rough Music': Le Charivari anglais." *Annales: Economies, sociétés, civilisations,* XXVII (1972), 285–312.

———. *Whigs and Hunters: The Origins of the Black Act.* New York, 1975.

Tilly, Charles. *The Contentious French: Four Centuries of Popular Struggle.* Cambridge, Mass., 1986.

———. *The Vendée: A Sociological Analysis of the Counterrevolution of 1793.* Cambridge, Mass., 1964.

———, ed. *The Formation of National States in Western Europe.* Princeton, 1975.

Tobias, J. J. *Crime and Industrial Society in the Nineteenth Century.* New York, 1967.

Tocqueville, Alexis de. *The Old Regime and the French Revolution.* Translated by Stuart Gilbert. Garden City, N.Y., 1955.

Traer, James F. "From Reform to Revolution: The Critical Century in the Development of the French Legal System." *Journal of Modern History,* XLIX (1977), 73–88.

Valmary, Pierre. *Familles paysannes au XVIIIe siècle en Bas-Quercy: Étude démographique.* Paris, 1965.

Vidalenc, J. "Quelques Aspects de la délinquance et de la criminalité dans la France d'autrefois." *Revue d'histoire économique et sociale,* XLI (1963), 260–66.

Viguier, J. "Emeutes populaires dans le Quercy en 1789 et 1790." *La Révolution française: Revue d'histoire moderne et contemporaine,* XXI (1891).

Villepelet, Ferdinand. *Inventaire sommaire des archives départementales de la Dordogne: Archives civiles, série B.* 2 vols. Périgueux, 1899.

Villepelet, R. *La Formation du département de la Dordogne.* Périgueux, 1908.

———. "Notes et documents statistiques sur les diocèses de Périgueux et de Sarlat aux XVIIe et XVIIIe siècles." *Bulletin de la Société Historique et Archéologique du Périgord,* XXX (1903), 139–55, 192–213.

———. "Notes et documents sur l'industrie en Périgord." *Bulletin de la Société Historique et Archéologique du Périgord,* XXXIX (1912), 241–62, 309–41.

Weber, Eugen. *Peasants into Frenchmen: The Modernization of Rural France, 1870–1914.* Stanford, 1976.

Weisser, Michael R. *Crime and Punishment in Early Modern Europe.* Atlantic Highlands, N.J., 1979.

Wheaton, Robert, and Tamara K. Hareven, eds. *Family and Sexuality in French History.* Philadelphia, 1980.

Williams, Alan. *The Police of Paris, 1718–1789.* Baton Rouge, 1979.

Wills, Antoinette. *Crime and Punishment in Revolutionary Paris.* Westport, Conn., 1981.

Woloch, Isser. *Eighteenth-Century Europe: Tradition and Progress, 1715–1789.* New York, 1982.

Zehr, Howard. *Crime and the Development of Modern Society: Patterns of Criminality in Nineteenth-Century France and Germany.* London, 1976.

———. "The Modernization of Crime in Germany and France, 1830–1913." *Journal of Social History,* VIII (1975), 117–41.

Zysberg, André. "La Société des galériens au milieu du XVIIIe siècle." *Annales: Economies, sociétés, civilisations,* XXX (1975), 43–65.

Index

COMTÉ DE **PERIGORT**
Par Th. de la Ruë Paris.
A PARIS
Chez Pierre Mariette, Rue St.
Jacques, a l'Enseigne de l'Esperance
Avec priuilege du Roy.